D1710364

CREATING CARMEN MIRANDA

Creating
CARMEN MIRANDA

Race, Camp, and
Transnational
Stardom

Kathryn
Bishop-Sanchez

Vanderbilt University Press | Nashville

Library of Congress Cataloging-in-Publication Data on file
LC control number 2015042857
LC classification number ML420.M53 S26 2016
Dewey class number 782.42164092—dc23

ISBN 978-0-8265-2112-5 (cloth)
ISBN 978-0-8265-2114-9 (ebook)

In memory of my sister Yvette

CONTENTS

ILLUSTRATIONS

ACKNOWLEDGMENTS

When the topic of your research is a flamboyant and well-known star like Carmen Miranda, you inevitably have conversations with a lot of people from all walks of life, many of whom may have interesting ideas they are willing to share, often in the most random circumstances. Over the past ten years—my son's entire life, as he is prompt to remind me—I have been privileged to innumerable impromptu and informal conversations, and I am grateful to everyone who took the time to weigh in on Carmen Miranda's stardom.

The writing of this book has been immensely facilitated by the generosity and assistance of family, friends, colleagues, institutions, and librarian professionals.

I owe a great debt of gratitude to the staff of several archives for their expertise, pertinent advice, and patience. In the Los Angeles area, I was fortunate to spend several months at the fabulous Margaret Herrick Library and benefited from the assistance of its knowledgeable staff, in particular Barbara Hall, Kristine Krueger, Sandra Archer, Stacey Enders, and my dear friend Lea Whittington. At the University of California, Los Angeles, I am grateful to Mark Gens at the Film and Television Archive, Lauren Buisson at the Department of Special Collections, and my dear colleague, Brazilianist, and film expert Randal Johnson. At the library of the University of Southern California, Ned Comstock's assistance was extremely useful. I wholeheartedly thank David Miller at the Twentieth Century-Fox legal department for allowing me to work with the Carmen Miranda files at Fox.

I was fortunate to have access to collections at the New York Public Library in the Performing Arts, the Manuscripts and Archives Division, and the Schomberg Center for Research in Black Culture. Mark Evan Swartz and Maryann Chach made my time at the Shubert Archive both productive and enjoyable, and I thank them for their insights and our many long conversations that greatly enriched my understanding of Miranda's Broadway years.

In Brazil, I am grateful to have worked in the archives of FUNARTE-Rio de Janeiro, the National Library, the National Archives, and the Museum of Images and Sound (MIS). My warmest thanks to Cesar Soares Balbi, the director of the Carmen Miranda Museum, for opening its archive and many hidden treasures; his knowledge of Carmen Miranda is most humbling. At the filmothèque and archives of the Museum of Modern Art, I am especially thankful for the kindness and expertise of Hernani Heffner, who always took time to assist me. I am equally grateful to Alice Gonzaga, Adhemar Gonzaga's daughter, for graciously welcoming me in the Cinédia Studio Archive. Enormous thanks are due Ruy Castro, who has not only written the most superb biography of Carmen Miranda, but is also generous with his knowledge and time, and although our schedules did not correspond and allow us to meet in person, he was gracious to promptly respond to my emails.

This project also received significant institutional support from the University of Wisconsin, Madison. The Graduate School for Research in the Humanities provided much appreciated summer support and research funds over several years. I was awarded time off from teaching to concentrate on writing the manuscript at different points of this project through a sabbatical, a semester leave through a Feminist Scholarship Award from the Center for Research on Gender and Women, and a Race, Ethnicity, and Indigeneity Fellowship at the Institute for Research in the Humanities (IRH). I would like to thank my cohort of fellows at the IRH during the academic year 2010-2011, who greatly enriched my thought process, in particular Jimmy Casas Klausen, Rob Nixon, Mary Lou Roberts, Aliko Songolo, Rachel Brenner, Teju Olaniyan, and (despite being on sabbatical) Susan S. Friedman for her vote of confidence.

Over the years, this project has benefited from the friendly, critical eye of colleagues and mentors at the University of Wisconsin, Madison, whose example and camaraderie I continue to value. I am particularly grateful to my colleagues Alicia Cerezo Paredes, Ellen Sapega, Fernando Tejedo, Glen Close, Ivy Corfis, Juan Egea, Kata Beilin, Ksenija Bilbija, Luís Madureira, Sarli Mercado, Steve Stern, and the late Ray Harris. Infinite thanks to my dearest friend and colleague Severino Albuquerque, whose encouragement, humor, and excellent suggestions over many late dinners proved priceless over the course of these years.

Thanks are due as well to many wonderful colleagues in the dynamic field of Brazilian studies. For their theoretical insights, keen interest, and tolerance in collectively listening to close to two dozen papers on Carmen Miranda, inviting me to give a talk, participating in conferences and panels, and sharing essential bibliographic references, I especially acknowledge my gratitude to Ana López, Ana Paula Ferreira, Anna Klobucka, Anna More, Camilo Gomides, Charles Perrone, Claire Williams, Dário Borim, Darlene Sadlier, David Frier, David Jackson, Emanuelle Oliveira-Monte, Fernando Luiz Lara, Fernando Rocha, Hilary Owen, Inês Dias, Jeremy Lehnen, Jim Green, Leila Lehnen, Luca Bacchini, Lúcia Sá, Luiz Fernando Valente, Marc Herzman, Maria José Barbosa, Paulo de Medeiros, Pedro Meira Monteiro, Peggy Sharpe, Rebecca Atencio, Rex Nielson, Robert Simon, Steven Butterman, and Victor Mendes.

The book has been much improved by the suggestions and corrections made by Bryan McCann and Christopher Dunn. Chris was also very generous with his time while in residence in Madison, and I appreciate our friendship and his willingness to share his vast knowledge of Brazilian music and culture, along with his New Orleans culinary talents. I am grateful to Antônio Carlos Secchin for finding and generously sending to me the absolutely priceless and long-out-of-print Cássio Emmanuel Barsante *Carmen Miranda* book. I am also extremely grateful to Carlos Reis for his kind support of a project that was clearly not "his cup of tea" at first, but for which he generously provided narratological insights and theoretical references, especially during the beginning and completion of this process.

I would like to thank my students at the University of Wisconsin, Madison, who enabled me to rehearse my obsessions in courses on Brazilian culture, race, gender, and film and who frequently contributed brilliant points of view about these topics. Among these students and future colleagues, a special thanks to Djurdja Trajkovic, Israel Pechstein, Jaime Rhemrev, Juan Iso, Robin Peery, and Valerie Klorman. I am also grateful to my undergraduate research assistants, Elizabeth Toussaint, who worked with the Getúlio Vargas diaries, Sarah Kenney, for her work on memorabilia and newspaper film reviews, and Courtney Cottrell, who worked with fashion and magazines.

For their gracious hospitality during research trips and for fabulous cuisine, I remain indebted to Rita Leal and Luiz Eduardo Carvalho in Rio de Janeiro and Fernanda Venancio Filho in New York. A special thanks to my dear friend Regina Figueiredo-Brown, who was great company for unforgettable evenings of camp musical viewing. Thank you also to Leo Burger, my stylist, whose knowledge of popular culture and film made for many enlightening haircuts and whose expectations and encouragement kept me moving the project along.

I am extremely grateful to the staff at Vanderbilt University Press. I cannot thank my wonderful and wise editor Eli Bortz enough for his expert judgment, diligence, patience, and steadfast support throughout the process. My most sincere thanks also to Betsy Phillips, who showed enthusiasm for the project from the beginning, to Joell Smith-Borne, whose flexibility, dedication, and sage guidance helped bring the final product to completion, and to Laura Fry for the excellent copyediting.

My family has shown loving support throughout the writing of this book. My parents have continued to cheer their daughter's success, despite research trips far from home and an erratic work schedule. I thank my husband, Pablo, who lived through this experience and who was crucial for my being able to take the necessary research trips. A special thanks to my two favorite research assistants, Giselle and Tiago, who have grown up with this project and who have humored me by watching innumerable cartoons (some, such as *Futurama*, that we realized too late were not exactly PG), musicals, and "boring black and white films"; they were the best "Carmen Miranda scouts" anyone could hope for. I dedicate *Creating Carmen Miranda* to my late sister Yvette, who accompanied me on my first research trip to Los Angeles at the early stages of this book and would have loved to have seen its completion.

INTRODUCTION

In the early hours of August 5, 1955, Carmen Miranda died in her Beverly Hills home at age forty-six. The day before she had filmed a sequence for the *Jimmy Durante Show* and, as the television program footage clearly shows, at one point she dropped to her knees and muttered she was out of breath. Durante, a quick improviser, told the band to stop the music and helped her up with the reassurance, "I've got your lines." Recovering her breath, Carmen danced on: it would be her last filmed appearance. That evening Miranda, always the gracious hostess, invited friends to her house, and they talked and sang well into the night. When she retired to her room at around half past two, she collapsed again. She was found dead a few hours later that morning, fully dressed lying on the floor. Carmen Miranda had suffered a fatal heart attack.

The shock of Miranda's premature death inundated the Brazilian and US media, which published the details of those last moments and retrospective appreciations of her career and rise to stardom, as her family, friends, and fans attempted to come to terms with the loss of such a beloved and unique "movie comedienne and dancer" at the (erroneously reported) age of 41.[1] The press publicized the events following her death closely: the thousands of mourners who paid their respects as her body rested in state at Cunningham and O'Connor Hollywood Mortuary chapel, the smaller gathering of approximately three hundred close friends and family at the Requiem Mass in the Church of the Good Shepherd in Beverly Hills, and the description of Miranda's burial attire—a simply tailored red suit and a rosary of red beads twined in her left hand—as she was laid to rest in a bronze coffin.[2] Of the hundreds of funeral offerings, film director Walter Lang's floral piece featuring a mixture of fruits on its base drew particular attention.

Brazil anxiously awaited the transfer of Miranda's body to Rio de Janeiro to bring the samba ambassadress back home. Expressing the nation's impatience, the Brazilian newspaper headlines lamented, "Miranda's body is still in Hollywood" and transmitted collective rejoicing when finally there was confirmation the Brazilian government had sent a plane to bring her body home a week after her death on August 12.[3] Returning the body to Brazil was vital for the nation to reclaim ownership of the deceased star and bring her celebrity trajectory full circle, while providing a physical symbol for their collective sorrow. While the United States mourned the passing of a vivacious and much-loved Hollywood star, Brazil had lost Carmen Miranda the national singer, integral part of the cultural patrimony, and greatest ambassadress of their music and nation, despite widespread reservations about her stylized *baiana* and the adulterated image of Brazil and Latin America that she had embodied.[4] She was an extraordinary interpreter of the Brazilian people, and with Carmen Miranda's death a period of her generation's youth—the golden days of 1930s radio and the great Rio casinos—also vanished.[5]

Thousands lined the streets when Miranda's coffin arrived from Rio's Galeão airport and accompanied the fire-engine hearse as it drove slowly from one of Rio's central squares, Praça Mauá, to Cinelândia, where from the evening of August 12 to the morning of the thirteenth hundreds of thousands of mourners paid their last respects to the star.[6] The following day the coffin was closed and taken to its final resting place, the cemetery of São João Batista in Rio, with multitudes accompanying the funeral procession and collectively singing and humming some of Miranda's most well-known Carnival marches and sambas. As her biographer Ruy Castro rightly states, it was Carmen Miranda's greatest carnival with her people (550). The entire nation was in mourning, with newspaper headlines lamenting, "O Brasil perdeu Carmen Miranda" (Brazil has lost Carmen Miranda).[7] Carmen Miranda's death sealed the exceptionality of her stardom: she performed until the very end, and her last screen appearance was as a stylized *baiana*.

In the United States, Carmen Miranda is best remembered nowadays for her Twentieth Century-Fox films in which she stole the show with extravagant bare-midriff dresses, platform shoes, and outrageous fruit-basket headdresses, most filmed in gorgeous Technicolor. This is the signature look of the "Brazilian Bombshell," the performer immediately recognizable for her fruit-laden headdresses and whose distinct appearance, unmistakable accent, dynamic dancing, and explosive, nonsensical singing made her easy to imitate. At the pinnacle of her success in the early 1940s, she was Hollywood's most parodied entertainer as a cultural icon with appeal to a mass audience. The intense visual impact of her exaggerated, glamorous look—matched perfectly by her vivacious demeanor, gracefulness, enormous captivating smile, electrifying rhythm, impeccable accelerated diction, gyrating hips, and elegant hand movements—created an exhibition of stylized effeminacy and excessive female sexuality that for Hollywood would be the Carmen Miranda image. For the Hollywood musical of the wartime period, Miranda was a match made in heaven, with song-and-dance numbers that were always perfectly and elaborately executed, bringing Miranda to dominate at the heart of the show or film, even when she was not at the center of the action. Miranda remains a household name most prominently throughout Brazil, her home country, and the United States, where she performed from 1939 until her death, but Carmen Miranda's widely circulated star image has not yet received thorough, critical analysis.

This is a book about the creation, interpretation, and imitation of Carmen Miranda's image as filtered first through Brazilian society of the 1930s and then through Broadway and Hollywood from the late 1930s to the mid-1950s and the social, political, and cultural importance of this popular Hollywood icon, who has sustained interest to the present day. This study examines Miranda's idiosyncratic celebrity sign and the values it intersects, such as ethnicity, exoticism, comedy, racial difference, and excessive femininity.

When Carmen Miranda came to the United States, the star system, which cannot be dissociated from its industrial setting and institutionalized competitive nature, was in full swing, with impresarios and producers extensively marketing and mythicizing their leading ladies and prime stars as a way to differentiate a company's play or a studio's latest release from all others on the market. The stars were at the core of this "product differentiation" (deCordova 46), even more so than the Broadway companies or the film studios themselves.

Given the screen homogeneity within Miranda's star trajectory—her "immutability and substitutability of the narratives" (López 75)—discussions of her individual films reiterate and deviate little from the core of her image, and plot summaries of her films become negligible as far as a theoretical reading.[8] In reference to her US films, I emphasize her construction as a popular icon whose fixed meaning and visual appeal invited its reproduction, imitation, and instant recognition.[9] The meaning of Miranda's image evolved from its Brazilian origins, yet for the most part in the United States she consistently represented notions of the exotic and otherness, which changed little throughout that part of her career when she corresponded fabulously to Hollywood studios' Latin vogue.

Similar to other enduring icons, Miranda's "renewability" (Curry xvi) stems from her adaptability to the point that she became a performative sign that itself engaged with the impact of her star image. Through camp sensitivity, in particular, I discuss Miranda's own staged engagement with her over-the-top, stylized image, a concept that I refer to as her *performative wink*, which has eluded critics who perceive Miranda as being infantilized and manipulated as part of an institutionalized system of representation. It is my contention that to catch Carmen Miranda's performative wink effectively requires an understanding not only of textual analysis—which is where most readings of Miranda's performativity have found their limitations—but also of production history and conceptualization, including the more general historical, social, and racial context of her image and performance.

It bears emphasizing that, distinct from a biographical or descriptive text couched in historical evidence that aims to divulge the "true story" of the star and readings of Miranda's films, this book focuses on the discussion surrounding the star that creates her depth and, whether contrived or verifiable information, represents and constructs Miranda's stardom and her impact on popular culture and society at large. Several lines of inquiry motivate this approach: the emergence of the *baiana* image, its creation as an entertainment persona, its circulation as a cultural and media sign, and the shift from its initial creation to enhancement and parody, including self-parody.

Miranda as a performer crossed over several performative genres, from radio to stage, theater, film, and television. With the main focus on the visual aspect of Carmen Miranda's performance, I leave the wealth of her radio performances and music recordings for a future study within radio broadcasting history and musicology. Likewise, the reader will notice that prominence is given to Carmen

Miranda's stardom during the Brazilian years and then her tenure with Twentieth Century-Fox, where she received top billing. While mention is made of her subsequent films that carry over her *baiana* image, these films add no further dimension to her stardom as she experienced a progressive fall from the limelight.

Miranda's composite image has risen from innumerous written, visual, and aural representations: the films themselves and their trailers, photographic stills, recorded performances, record albums, and a plethora of promotional and critical texts about these performances, along with commercially produced fan discourse and written reports by contemporary commentators, news reporters, and the studio and theater agents. This study draws upon both contemporary and retrospective sources to discuss articles and illustrations that highlight certain aspects of Miranda's star image at each moment of her career and, through these readings, aims to understand what is Miranda's most enduring and prevailing impact. Through an extensive reading of contemporary articles written about Carmen Miranda during her star years and beyond, patterns can clearly be identified. I have examined a substantial representation of fan magazine, trade, and commercial articles from libraries, archives, individual collections, and online auctions. One archive in particular, the Margaret Herrick Library of the Academy of Motion Picture Arts and Sciences in Beverly Hills, holds a comprehensive collection of publicity stills, film exhibitor pressbooks, promotional posters and lobby cards, studio-produced biographies, and magazine and newspaper articles that provide a greater understanding of Miranda's Hollywood stardom and from which I draw extensively. Many of these narratives in newspapers and fan and mass-market magazines often incorporate quotations from Miranda's own words, contributing to the star's composite image. These ancillary texts, produced by hack writers, gossip columnists, studio-sponsored reviewers, or sensationalist writers, participated in constructing the collective, mediated image of the star.

This multi-layered archival approach is indispensable to defining Miranda's stardom. As John Ellis's basic definition encapsulates, a star is "a performer in a particular medium whose figure enters into subsidiary forms of circulation, and then feeds back into future performances" (91). The challenges inherent to the nature of this work on Miranda's stardom, at the intersections of theory, primary materials, and a vast corpus of secondary materials, drew me to the interrelated lines of race, gender, camp, and performativity. In the case of Carmen Miranda, as with many other stars from the period, there is still little integration of archival research with film and stardom analysis, perhaps due, on the one hand, to the obvious roadblocks to having access to pertinent materials that could never be all-inclusive and, on the other, to the complexities of gender, cultural, and racial politics that beg an interpretation of these materials beyond an anecdotal reading. This book aims to redress this critical oversight by drawing from textual analyses of Carmen Miranda's performances and grounding them in a broader social, political, and racial context.

Although at times gaining access to certain films seemed close to impossible, over the years I was able to view all the films mentioned in this book; some released for commercial usage were borrowed through libraries or personal collections, bought through online auctions, or screened at the UCLA Film and Television Archives. The majority of Carmen Miranda's Hollywood films are now available commercially on DVD with the release of the *Carmen Miranda Collection* (2008) or manufactured on demand.[10] Unfortunately, of her Brazilian films, only *Alô, alô, carnaval!* (Hello, hello, carnival!, 1935) in its entirety and one segment of *Banana da terra* (Banana of the land, 1939) have been preserved.[11]

Transnational Stardom

Stardom contributes to the film narrative beyond the script and transcends the characterization of the players within the individual films. The pioneering work by Christine Gledhill, Edgar Morin, David Marshall, Richard Dyer, and the above-mentioned John Ellis all call for the study of stars as signs that link film to culture, politics, society, and historical contexts. Miranda's star image becomes a site to explore the representation of foreignness, sexualities, gender difference, the spectacle of excess, parody, and the more general concepts of imagining Afro-Brazilianness in Brazil and *Latinidade* in the United States. Carmen Miranda was unique, and numerous were the industries surrounding her performances that chose, similar to Hollywood, to "capitalize on the economic possibilities of difference" (Hershfield xi). The blending of Miranda's on- and offstage and screen personae created a multi-layered matrix. One of my aims in this book is to explore the backwaters of the stage and film businesses surrounding her and her image as portrayed through an array of star publicity and media texts that expand her stardom through meaning "generated in the film text more generally" (Geraghty 183). In doing so, this exploration of Carmen Miranda's stardom promises to be informative far beyond the study of media representation.

Always present at the background of this study is the premise that Miranda became a transnational star once her career took her from Brazil to Broadway and Hollywood. Her career drew its appeal and strength from her interstitial position between both countries: while not belonging here or there, she blended elements from both countries into a unique performative genre, defined across and beyond national lines.[12] I will discuss the construction of her exotic image in the United States and how she transcends the stereotypical image of *Latinidade* by being fiercely unique. Although she was critiqued upon her return to Brazil after only a year abroad for being "too Americanized," this harsh reception on the Carioca stage was a watershed in her development as a singer with North American international success. As a transnational star she was able to reflect upon her position as a samba singer and performer from an international perspective while remaining fervently attached to her Brazilian public. There is camp sensitivity in her transnationalism in that she could poke fun at her unforgiving audience and at her position as a misinterpreted star in Brazil at the beginning of a very promising US-based career.

While there are many definitions of the transnational available for critical co-option, the most prominent points to the persistence of the global in the local. Or, alternatively, we can consider that Miranda's performance went through a process of transculturation, as famously theorized by Fernando Ortiz, which enabled her to attain and maintain her unique star appeal for a North American audience, most prominently during her first seven years in the United States—the years that correspond to her Broadway tenure and Twentieth Century-Fox contract. Transculturation, rather than acculturation, denotes a detachment from European ethnocentrism and is particularly well suited to depict Miranda in the United States through a three-dimensional performative dialogue that spans her entire career at the interstitials of American musical and popular entertainment, her early career and Brazilian background, and the Afro-Brazilianness of her *baiana*. More significantly than ever before, Miranda's success as a transnational star forges a new dimension of Brazilian music and culture abroad, not only to the North American public but also to the rest of the world.

A Brief Biography

Carmen Miranda was born Maria do Carmo Miranda da Cunha on February 9, 1909, in Marco de Canaveses in northern Portugal. Before her first birthday, Miranda's family immigrated to Brazil, a common destination for hundreds of thousands of Portuguese families during the first decades of the twentieth century. Miranda's upbringing was marked by her traditional convent schooling, her employment as a sales clerk at several stores (including a much mythicized apprenticeship as a milliner at the upscale hat store "La Femme Chic" in downtown Rio), and the boarding house that her parents opened in the mid-1920s in the Lapa neighborhood, where boarders and daytime diners often included composers, artists, and musicians. The young Maria do Carmo mingled within this milieu and eventually met the composer and guitar player Josué de Barros in 1928. Soon after she adopted "Carmen Miranda" as her recording and stage name, she recorded her first two songs in 1929, followed the subsequent year by a major hit, Joubert de Carvalho's "Taí," which placed Miranda as the most popular voice of the radio for Carnival 1930.[13] Later that year Miranda negotiated her first recording contract with RCA Victor and went on to record an impressive number of more than 250 songs, many written exclusively for her by composers such as Ari Barroso, Lamartine Babo, Assis Valente, and the above-mentioned Josué de Barros and Joubert de Carvalho—all major names of the time. From this period until her departure to the United States in 1939, Carmen Miranda was one of the main radio and stage voices of Rio and Brazil at large. Hers was a new, refreshing, high-pitched, and extremely rapid yet clear diction, to which she added her unique playfulness and interjected spontaneous Brazilian slang and humorous asides. She invigorated her live audiences with the energy of her highly dynamic performances, along with her contagious feelings of good will, delirious happiness, confidence, and charisma. She created a sense of closeness to her audience through fast-paced gestures and dancing eyes that mesmerized her public. Impish, photogenic, mischievously sensual, exuberant, fun, and funny, Carmen Miranda earned her Brazilian moniker, "a pequena notável" (the remarkable young girl). Her stage persona and style, which were ideally suited for live interactions with her audience, transferred seamlessly to the silver screen. Miranda starred in five Brazilian films, most notably as an up-and-coming radio star in the 1935 film *Estudantes* (Students) and in *Alô, alô, carnaval!* (Hello, hello, carnival!, 1935), in which Carmen and her sister Aurora famously sing the self-referential march "Cantoras do rádio" ([Female] radio singers). Discovered by Lee Shubert in February 1939 as she performed at the Urca Casino in Rio de Janeiro, Miranda secured a contract for the Broadway show *The Streets of Paris* and arrived in New York on May 17, 1939, accompanied by her band, Bando da Lua, thanks to the sponsorship of Brazil's president, Getúlio Vargas.[14] Because Miranda was a performer and entertainer molded under the nationalist umbrella of the Vargas regime, her flight to Broadway and subsequent North American acclimatization produced a hybrid performer whose heart remained loyally Brazilian on a stage far removed from her middle-class radio listeners and the societal elite of the fine Carioca stages. Almost immediately Hollywood scouts courted Miranda, and she made her first film for Twentieth Century-Fox, *Down Argentine Way* (1940), on location in New York because she was unable to leave *The Streets of Paris* long enough to go to Hollywood. She stayed with Twentieth Century-Fox until 1946, filming a total of ten films, all musicals, and then continued independently to star in another four films, none of any real note. She met her husband-to-be, David Sebastian, on the set of *Copacabana* (1947), and they were married after a short courtship on March 17, 1947. Other than an initially unsuccessful (and traumatic) return to Brazil in 1940, where she was accused of having become "too Americanized," Miranda stayed in the United States for the next fourteen years, only returning once again to Rio de Janeiro in early 1955 to receive medical treatment for clinical depression, less than a year before her untimely death on August 5, 1955. In her short life, despite a bumpy ride at times along the way, she achieved transnational stardom in both North and South America and thereby completed what had appeared to be an impossible feat: reconciling the nationalist agenda of Vargas's Brazil and Hollywood's Pan-American Good Neighbor Policy.

From "Remarkable Young Girl" to "Brazilian Bombshell": A Historical Frame

Carmen Miranda's rise to stardom in Brazil as a popular singer, radio and recording artist, and later film actress, from the late 1920s to her departure to the United States in 1939, came at an auspicious period of greater cultural racial integration that ultimately brought samba to reign as Brazil's national rhythm. Miranda's performance style came to embody this felicitous *ménage-à-trois* of more inclusive gender, cultural, and racial politics, and her music became an important bridge across differences of race and class as she participated in the democratization of samba.

In the early 1930s, a vogue of sociology texts, such as Gilberto Freyre's *The Masters and the Slaves* (1933), focused overwhelmingly on the positive contribution of the African diaspora to Brazilian culture, society, traditions, and demography, with a view to celebrating Brazil's racial diversity as a point of national pride. This rise of a new sense of nationhood is indissociable from the repressive government of Getúlio Vargas, who took power after a bloodless military coup against former president-elect Washington Luís in 1930 and remained in power until he was likewise removed by a group of military officers in 1945. He is remembered as a pro-industrialist, nationalist, anti-communist dictator who consolidated his authoritarian rule through the imposition of the *Estado Novo* (New State) from 1937 to 1945. This period, commonly referred to in Brazil as the "Vargas era," spanned the rise of staunch nationalism and national renewal, which symbolically and culturally involved the forefronting of Brazilian images, icons, and music and the democratization of national culture, ushering in a great number of middle-class artists with themes and styles of national appeal. Under Vargas's impetus for national unity and identity, notoriously emblematized by the ceremonial burning of state flags in 1937,[15] Carnival celebrations received state sponsorship as samba schools replaced political satire with national themes focusing on Brazilian traditions, culture, and history, and a more sanitized samba emerged around patriotic themes, with Miranda as one of its most popular interpreters. Under the aegis of Vargas's quest to move the country toward greater modernity, Brazil developed its recording and cinema industries, along with a greater network of radio stations, which Vargas infamously used as a propaganda tool and a symbol of a united country.

In 1930, the film producer and director Adhemar Gonzaga founded Cinédia, which soon became the most important Brazilian film studio of the decade. Working with North American expat Wallace Downey, Gonzaga brought the Brazilian public the first sound movies and revolutionized the Brazilian film industry. Gonzaga's productions bridged radio and cinema by riding the crest of the established radio industry, drawing from the talent of the live radio shows in vogue at the time, and bringing these popular voices to a public eager to see their favorite radio stars on the big screen. As one of the most sought-after popular-music voices of the 1930s, Miranda starred in Cinédia's films along with many of her cohort of radio stars. Brazil's nascent film industry stayed close to the vaudeville format, integrating musical numbers as a means to add cohesion to often loosely constructed plots.

Carmen Miranda arrived on Broadway as the US government was committing to move beyond military and imperialist control of Latin America and resolving to establish cordial relationships with its neighbors to the south under the auspice of Latin-oriented cultural outreach aimed at consolidating diplomatic cooperation and approximation. The launching of the Good Neighbor Policy, first coined by President Herbert Hoover during a goodwill tour following his 1928 election, is mostly associated nowadays with the foreign policy elaborated during Franklin D. Roosevelt's presidency (1933–1945), which grew out of the overlapping geopolitical imperatives of the US government and a pledge of no armed interventions with a will to promoting hemispheric solidarity. Politically, through Roosevelt's Good Neighbor Policy, North and South America's differences could be transcended; culturally, in Hollywood films, this South American craze translated into the international languages of song, music, and dance, as screenplays drew heavily on South American locales, and studios sought to hire authentic or pseudo-authentic Latin players. Vivacious, talented, exotic, and beautiful Carmen Miranda was a godsend to the Good Neighbor Policy, and when Twentieth Century-Fox brought her to Hollywood, "almost singlehandedly Miranda spawned the studio's South American cycle" (Woll, *Hollywood Musical* 115). Carmen Miranda became the muse of the Good Neighbor Policy, one of the most beloved representatives of South America on the US stage and screen, and moving beyond a more specific representation of her native Brazil, she soon came to represent "Latin America" more generically as a token Pan-South American actress.

Carmen Miranda's arrival in Hollywood could not have been more perfectly timed. The late 1930s and the first half of the 1940s corresponded to the golden age of the Hollywood musical, and Miranda, already a seasoned singer, dancer, and performer on the Brazilian silver screen, stepped immediately into her role as the exotic, sensual, and vivacious Latina "other" at the heart of the musicals' large production numbers and often at the center of the films' hallmark moments. The musical is on all accounts a star-driven genre, and Carmen Miranda soon rose to symbolize Twentieth Century-Fox musical productions alongside her blond American costars Betty Grable and Alice Faye. Cinema was the most popular form of entertainment for the emergent middle class, and during wartime the musical became Hollywood's dominant film genre (Woll, *Hollywood Musical* x). Adapting her performance style for a North American public, Miranda sang songs in her native Portuguese but also in English (and often catchy gibberish), and the hybrid performativity that resulted led her to the heights of transnational stardom in her new host country.[16]

Organization of This Book

Carmen Miranda's stardom is uniquely located where representations of race, women on the stage and in film, *Latinidade*, the exotic, otherness, and overt campiness intersect, yet critics have rarely attempted to analyze her star persona theoretically and for the most part have limited themselves to impressionist generalities, close readings of her US films, and biographical anecdotes that echo statements from the pioneering, although at times factually incorrect, Martha Gil-Montero biography *Brazilian Bombshell* (1989) and Helena Solberg's documentary *Bananas Is My Business* (1995), or Ruy Castro's very complete and most timely biography *Carmen. A vida de Carmen Miranda, a brasileira mais famosa do século XX* (Carmen: The life of Carmen Miranda, the most famous Brazilian of the twentieth century, 2005). I am greatly indebted to Ruy Castro's thorough archival work and insights on Miranda's life and work, which are second to none and constitute a biographical subtext to my own study.

Chapter 1, "Brazilian Stardom: From Radio to Casino and the Creation of the *Baiana*," examines the popular figure of the *baiana* in relation to cultural, political, class, and gender politics in the context of early twentieth-century Rio de Janeiro, including the Carnival *baianas*, the transformation of the popular *baiana* dress into a carnivalesque costume, the emergence of the notion of "false *baiana*," and the essential distinction between the authentic *baiana* outfit and the stylized costume. This chapter also discusses the vogue of the stage *baianas* both before and contemporaneous with Carmen Miranda's appropriation of the image, her rise to stardom in Brazil, and her public presence that prepared her for greater international stage stardom.

Chapter 2, "Performing Race: Miranda and Afro-Brazilianness on the Carioca Stage of the 1930s," analyzes the racial implications and ramifications of Carmen Miranda's *baiana* performance and the link between racial politics and cultural expression in order to understand the interracial complexities at play. I engage Miranda's appropriation of the *baiana* with the then still lingering neo-colonialist "whitening ideal" and introduce the notion of *performative race* to access Miranda's embodiment of Afro-Brazilianness through the *baiana*. I examine Miranda's racial crossing-over as a means to both draw from and give back to the Brazilian black community by promoting blackness of sound, manner, and appearance. I relate Miranda's use of blackface to the "tar doll" (*boneca de pixe*) practice in the Carioca imaginary and discuss how her performative race evolves as she creates a new model of Afro-Brazilianness.

Chapter 3, "Staging the Exotic: The Instant Success of the Brazilian Bombshell," examines Carmen Miranda's much-overlooked tenure on Broadway as an immediate exotic sensation that fascinated the media both on and off the stage. In this context I discuss the transculturation of the international *baiana*, which when performed for an American audience no longer bears the distinct mark of Afro-Brazilianness but rapidly becomes a prototypical image of South America. I focus on Miranda's stage performance as a tropical celebrity in *The Streets of Paris* and later in *Sons O' Fun*, her transcultural exoticism through her use of mangled English and other forms of nonverbal communication, and her popularity beyond Broadway as a nightclub entertainer and an official hostess for the Brazilian pavilion at the New York World's Fair, and I accompany her star text as it evolves from that of a foreign singer to an exotic visual sign.

Chapter 4, "Marketing Miranda: Stardom, Fashion, and Gossip in the Media," analyzes the interconnectedness of the screen, consumer culture, and Miranda's star image. I focus on the symbiotic relationship among the films, Miranda as a star, and the extensive discourse around her. I examine the studio's marketing ploys and deliberate construction of Miranda's star persona, with special attention to film posters, trailers, and the promotion of her costumes, as well as the textual commentary surrounding Miranda's star image and the media's discussion of Miranda as an "evolving" comedienne. I discuss Miranda's impact on fashion and her presence in the fan magazines that also contributed to her stardom.

Chapter 5, "Camp Carmen: The Icon on the Screen," focuses on Carmen Miranda's film narrative as a camp aesthetic within the genre of the musical. I discuss in detail the camp interest surrounding Miranda, with an emphasis on her costumes and the large-scale musical numbers of her most emblematic films. I engage Miranda's camp portrayal as a means to critique rather than affirm stereotypical Latin images on film, and I rely on an understanding of Miranda's performative wink in order to grasp her spectacularization. This chapter traces camp throughout her film career at Twentieth Century-Fox, with special attention given to Busby Berkeley's *The Gang's All Here* as a quintessential example of a camp musical.

In Chapter 6, "Imitating Miranda: Playing with Camp, Drag, and Gender Norms," I analyze the impact of Carmen Miranda as an icon that lends itself to appropriations by gay, drag, and carnival cultures. While critics have shied away from a comprehensive analysis of the extensive corpus of Miranda impersonations, this chapter discusses a broad number of both commonly known and lesser-known imitations in a variety of film genres, including musicals, film noirs, family dramas, adventure series, television variety shows, and wartime GI shows. Through an examination of overt drag and same-sex masquerades, I follow the evolution and mediation of Miranda-vogue over the decades, identifying the elements that remain common across most impersonations, as well as the different contexts of these imitations, which are typically done in a spirit of playfulness and gender-role freedom and played strictly for laughs in a farcical, burlesque manner, immune from censorship. The last part of the chapter focuses on the vast number of impersonations housed in the "innocuous" context of animation and children's programming. Here, the critique and subversion of social and gender norms, abstracted from the complexities of real life via camp or make-believe, are portrayed in varying degrees.

A Final Note on Language

I have provided throughout translations of the original Portuguese text, using published translations when available. All other translations are my own. While I indicate the titles of songs, plays, and films in their original, I also include the English translations for clarity. For certain terms when there is no English equivalent, or for which the translation loses part of the meaning or is too cumbersome (such as the oft-repeated *baiana*, for example), I have used the Portuguese word in italics. In the pursuit of readability and consistency, I have modernized the original Portuguese spelling of both common and proper nouns. Because of the vast array of Portuguese terms used to designate African descendants in Brazil, I have often simply opted for "Afro-Brazilians" or "blacks." I use "Carnival" when referring specifically to the Brazilian celebration, and in all other circumstances, "carnival" in lower-case. Throughout, I have preferred the Brazilianized term *Latinidade* (over the Spanish *Latinidad*) in order to emphasize, as Miranda herself would often do, the star's Brazilian musical and performative foundation.

CHAPTER ONE

BRAZILIAN STARDOM

*From Radio to Casino and
the Creation of the* Baiana

When Carmen Miranda takes Broadway by storm in Lee Shubert's 1939 musical *The Streets of Paris*, her performance that lasts a mere six minutes is the first major appearance of the *baiana* on a live North American stage. Carmen Miranda's unique star persona of the Hollywood years, with the extravagant, over-the-top creations, daring in color, texture, and design and superbly enhanced by flashy Technicolor, is far removed from the initial *baiana* Miranda brought to Broadway and has long eclipsed the more humble origins of the "Lady in the Tutti Frutti Hat."

Before her frequently rhapsodized "discovery" by Lee Shubert in Rio's Urca Casino in February 1939, Miranda was a most successful recording artist, a popular celebrity, and a well-liked radio and stage performer throughout Brazil and neighboring Argentina. Miranda has been immortalized by the iconic image of her towering, imaginative turbans, clunky and sparkly jewelry, platform shoes, and daring, bare-midriff, luxurious gowns, but her departure to Broadway was certainly not the beginning of her career. Given the exuberant, camp, stylized Carmen Miranda of the Hollywood films and the greater preservation of images and footage from this period, critics have mostly overlooked Miranda's Brazilian years. In particular, it has become commonplace to trace without contextualization the origins of the "international *baiana*" (as she became known) to the star's last Brazilian film, *Banana da terra* (Banana of the land), a 1938 Sonofilms production in which she is featured performing what became her signature song, "O que é que a baiana tem?" (What does the *baiana* have?) It is also this song and most likely a similar performance that Lee Shubert witnessed on the stage of the Urca Casino, located at the foot of Rio's scenic Sugarloaf Mountain.

In this chapter, I reassess Miranda's Brazilian years of stardom by examining the stylized Miranda *baiana* in its original Carioca context vis-à-vis the cultural, political, class, and gender politics of the time and the artistic license that enabled its creation. To illustrate how Miranda interprets Brazilianness through the *baiana*, it is important to consider how Miranda's *baiana* dialogues with Rio's cultural imaginary of the time, the Carnival *baianas*, Praça Onze (a square at the center of Rio that since the late nineteenth century was known as the "Little Africa" of Rio and the metaphorical cradle of samba), characters such as the famous and influential

Carmen Miranda as a *baiana* in her last Brazilian film, *Banana da terra* (1939).
Courtesy of FUNARTE/Rio de Janeiro

Tia Ciata, and the traditional samba schools. Although *Banana da terra* is a lost film, the scene in which Miranda performs as a *baiana* has been preserved thanks to its inclusion in Helena Solberg's documentary, *Bananas Is My Business* (1995), and constitutes without doubt the closest existing footage of the Miranda-*baiana* before Broadway, thus providing an invaluable visual approximation of her staged Brazilian performance of the *baiana*.[1]

The Origins of the *Baiana*

Generally speaking the *baiana* refers to Afro-Brazilian women from the Northeastern state of Bahia, hence the name. The term originally corresponded to a large contingent of West African women brought to Bahia during the slave trade and their descendants. The Bahian women and their customs, dress, and roles in Brazilian religious societies such as candomblé have been broadly documented and analyzed, mostly by anthropologists, in works such as Donald Pierson's *Negroes in Brazil* (1942), Ruth Landes's *The City of Women* (1947), and Joaquim Ribeiro's *Folclore baiano* (1956), among others. The *baiana* women's visual aspect is the most influential for the creation of the image Miranda used for her performances, as discussed in detail below. The *baiana* costume is unique in that Brazil does not have a great variety of traditional costumes. The *baiana* dress is well defined and original, and as such it is one of the most interesting costumes not only of Brazil but also of Latin America in general (Ribeiro 13). Symbolic of the *baiana*'s importance as synecdoche for Brazilian culture, fourteen *baiana* dolls approximately two feet tall were sent to Portugal for the Exposição

Histórica do Mundo Português (Exhibition of the Portuguese World) in 1940, although the dolls were removed from the Brazilian pavilion because some of the organizers judged it would be "too depressing to present Brazil as a country of blacks and *macumbas*" (Corrêa 178–79).[2] It is a purely urban costume, worn predominantly by black women in Salvador, Bahia, in the south in Rio de Janeiro, and in the north in São Luís and originating from the allegedly "more culturally developed" groups in coastal West Africa, such as the Yoruba and Fon, who were mostly found in cities, rather than from central West African people, such as the Kongo and Mbundu.[3]

There are certain key elements that define the typical *baiana* dress code. Pierson provides a detailed description of the Bahian women, whom he refers to as wearing the *vestimenta baiana*, or typical dress, which includes a wide, hooped skirt of varied colors; a loose-fitting white cotton or silk blouse trimmed with wide lace; a heavy, striped cotton cloth worn over the shoulder or around the waist (*pano da costa*); a cotton or silk turban; strapless, low-heeled sandals; and numerous necklaces and bracelets of coral, cowries, or glass beads (246–47).[4] According to Pierson, an additional ornament, the *balangandan*, has disappeared from the casual *baiana* ensemble and is mostly worn, tied at the waist, on festive occasions; the unusual term ultimately remained fixed in Carioca vocabulary as "balangandás."[5] The item consists of a gold or silver frame on which mystical, mnemonic, whimsical, or religious objects can be hung, and it crossed all class divides, as these objects were used by the upper classes as lucky charms and were more easily accepted in high-class society because of their ornamental quality (Ribeiro 28).[6]

If nowadays the typical *baiana* dress is mostly reserved for candomblé religious ceremonies, Carnival parades, and street vendors or worn near tourist attractions for gratuities, during the late 1930s and early 1940s, the use of authentic clothing was waning but still visible enough to carry the tradition of the *baiana* costume. The *baianas* are frequently mentioned as standing out during festivities because of their spectacular costumes, coming down from Rio's hilltop neighborhoods to celebrate Carnival, singing, dancing, and dominating the religious festivals.[7] Events such as the popular festivals of Bonfim in Salvador, Bahia, were largely taken over by the lower classes, and on these occasions the *baianas* are very visible in their traditional garb (Pierson 366). At religious ceremonies, such as the macumbas or candomblés, the *baianas* dress elaborately to carry out their official roles as *filhas de santo* or, in some cases, *mães de terreiro*.[8] It is in the privacy of these religious ceremonies that the *baiana* regalia are at their most extravagant, often overornamented with amulets and jewelry.

The *baiana* has come to symbolize more generally the female Afro-Brazilian food and fruit vendors throughout Brazil. As is still the case today, in the 1930s the *baiana* vendors were not confined to Bahia and its capital city Salvador or to festive occasions but constituted a strong presence on the streets of Rio and other urban centers. From the last quarter of the nineteenth century, a constant flow of Bahians came to the capital, resulting in a significant lasting presence in Rio as a result of multiple factors, most obviously economic and social changes following abolition but also the hospitable tendency of Rio's already established

Bahian population, who assisted newcomers with basic needs such as food and shelter and facilitated their integration into the new city (Moura 86). Although the Bahians were only a small proportion of Rio de Janeiro's total population, the *baianas* were very visible due to their presence in public spaces and the fact that their traditional dresses were used as a costume during Carnival (Carvalho 140–41).[9] Publicity for carnivalesque films, theater revues, and casino shows invariably pictured a *baiana*, reinforcing the figure as a typical seasonal costume for a national public and a synecdoche for Brazilian folklore for the benefit of foreign tourists. The Portuguese poet João de Barros (1881–1960) corroborates this visibility of the *baianas* in his impressions of a very colorful and animated Praça Onze during Carnival, commenting on the *baianas* in their picturesque dresses alongside women in traditional costumes from the Minho region of his native Portugal and Indians donning feathers (qtd. in Carvalho 150). As João de Barros's account suggests, Praça Onze brought together a mixture of traditions and ethnicities—black, Indian, and white European cultures—symbolized by their diverse dress. The group of black Bahians that inhabited this heterotopic space became the city's social leaders among the mixture of other ethnic groups,[10] such as the Portuguese, Spanish, and Italian immigrants and Brazilians from the Northeast, imposing along with their leadership their customs and traditions.[11] This interaction of cultures at the heart of the city represented Carnival's plurality, at the core of which was the figure of the *baiana*.

The most emblematic *baianas* were the *Tias* ("aunts" or "festive aunties"). During the first two decades of the twentieth century, these matriarchal figures were at the center of the Carioca Afro-Brazilian cultural activities, and they ensured strong black leadership in maintaining traditional festivities in honor of candomblé saints and then in promoting informal gatherings to play music and dance that required special permission from the local authorities. Indelibly linked to Carnival, the earliest *rancho* groups of organized revelers would make an obligatory stop at the *Tias'* homes and receive their blessing before continuing on to participate in the parade (Diniz 21). Without doubt the most influential, prestigious, and well-known *baiana* is Tia Ciata. Because she was hardworking and energetic and had a great spirit of initiative and an enviable knowledge of religious and culinary matters, Tia Ciata became part of the early twentieth-century Carioca tradition of the *baianas quituteiras*, who sold *quitutes* (specialties) and whose activity, grounded in religious meaning, was well received throughout the city.[12] Part of the *baiana* appeal was its marked exoticism, which immediately distinguished these women on the city streets. Tia Ciata was never seen in public without her full *baiana* outfit and is remembered as one of the most emblematic, sought-after, and well-respected *baianas*. Her home on the street Visconde de Itaúna near Praça Onze was the capital of Rio's "Little Africa" and brought together the Afro-Brazilian artists, stevedores, public workers, police, mulatos, and whites of the lower middle class, all intrigued by this vibrant locale of samba, *batuque* groups, festivities, and Carnival (Moura 103; 106). Over time, and even after its demolition for the construction of the multilane President Vargas Avenue in the 1940s, Praça Onze grew in mythic and symbolic status. Praça Onze was the heart of the area known in Rio as Cidade Nova, or New City: its role in the etiology of modern Brazilian identity and its importance for the development of Rio's music, through samba evenings held in the houses of the Bahian matriarchs, cannot be underestimated (Carvalho 137). Tia Ciata's house was the most famous and is historically remembered as the birthplace of the first samba, "Pelo telefone" (On the telephone), allegedly composed there in 1916 and recorded the following year.

Along with her central role as a *quituteira*, Tia Ciata started a small business providing typical *baiana* costumes made by black seamstresses, which were in style for the theater and especially popular for the Carnival groups of the Democráticos, Tenentes, and Fenianos of the lower middle class (Moura 100).[13] One of the most interesting aspects of Tia Ciata's clothing business is that many of her clients were men seeking the *baiana* dress to don during Carnival festivities.[14]

Gay men only began to have an organized presence in Carnival in the early 1930s. In 1930, a drag performer named António Setta formed the Carnival group Caçadores de Veados (literally meaning "deer hunters"), a wonderful play on words with the term *viado* (homosexual). They paraded through the streets of Rio in luxurious sequined gowns, adding a camp element to their apparel, which was very different from previous heterosexual cross-dressers in Carnival, who would dress up in everyday female attire or as pregnant women or prostitutes in a parody of womanhood. Following Carmen Miranda's appearance as a *baiana* in her last Brazilian feature film, *Banana da terra* (1938), the gay presence at Carnival took a more definite form in 1939, as revelers cross-dressed as the *baiana*, taking carnivalesque transgressions to a whole new level through their subversive gender-play.[15] James Green rightly refers to this form of playful parodic cross-dressing as the epitome of Brazilian camp performance during Carnival, given the exaggerated artificiality of the *baiana* imitations (204). Endowed with camp sensitivity, *baianas* embrace the true spirit of the Bakhtinian carnivalesque, which converges with camp through a shared inversion of hierarchy, sexual mockery, deviance, and power reversal.[16] Over time, men in drag would have their own costume contests as part of the Carnival festivities. "What had started in the early 1930s as a homosexual penetration of a clearly heterosexual space became, fifteen years later, part and parcel of carnivalesque celebrations" (J. Green 211).

Alongside these *baianas*, there was also a vogue that became known (and criticized) as the "false *baiana*." In Rio's Carnival festivities the prevalence of *falsa baiana* balls were broadly documented, especially during the decade of the 1950s, when some of the balls became very elaborate events.[17] "Falsa baiana" (False *baiana*) is the title of a song by the Carioca sambista and composer Geraldo Pereira (1918–1955) released in 1944, when Miranda as the official Brazilian *baiana* was at the height of her US stardom. The song lyrics, as the title indicates, point a finger at the fake *baiana*, who dresses up in costume only for Carnival, and mock the claim that all differences can be overcome through this communal reveling. By donning a stylized version of the original *baiana* costume, Miranda was from all regards the most widely known "false *baiana*," yet she certainly could dance the samba beautifully and did not fit the song's description.[18] For the first few years after Miranda's departure to the United States, her stylized *baiana* remained a constant reference of Carnival celebrations and would continue as such in subsequent decades, although not always as prominently.[19] The exception to this trend was the samba school Império Serrano in 1972, which based their annual theme on Carmen Miranda's art and legacy and were that year's winners under the title "Alô, alô, taí: Carmen Miranda" and with the slogan "A nostalgic Carnival for the remarkable girl."[20] The same samba school presented another homage to Carmen Miranda in 2008 that enabled them to improve their ranking and compete the following year in the top bracket of samba schools in Rio de Janeiro, "Grupo Especial" (Special Group).

Before the creation of the samba schools, the *baianas* were already present in the long-standing tradition of the folkloric kings' parades (*ranchos dos reis*), which consisted of a procession commemorating and recreating the three wise men's journey to Bethlehem. Behind the first group of orchestra participants was a group of women referred to as "gypsies" or *baianas* accompanied by male participants carrying allegorical figures; as such, the *ala das baianas* (the *baiana* wing) was an early staple of all Carnival groups.[21] The inclusion of the *baiana* wing in these parades indicates that, from early on, the *baiana* was officially endorsed with a performative quality that reinforced its festive nature. This designation of the *baiana* as a cultural form, transformed through a broad creative license as a stylized carnivalesque figure, removes it from the realities of the native *baiana*, a cultural practice similar to others that have constructed the image of a "frozen Africa, safely distanced from the contemporary realities of blacks in Brazil" (Crook and Johnson 7).

In the 1930s, the samba schools and annual parades were prominently located in Rio, further consolidating this image of the *baiana* with the then capital of the country. The presence of the *baiana* wing may have originated with the processions, but it became mandatory in the early 1930s with the measures put in place to "officialize" Carnival when federal and local government agencies began sponsoring the samba schools as part of a larger plan to attract more tourism to Rio and its Carnival (Hertzman 195–96). The Carnival regulations stipulated the prohibition of wind instruments and the inclusion of an *ala das baianas*, and they required each school to base its performance on a national theme.

The *baiana*'s presence is ubiquitous throughout Rio, and in particular in the Carnival festivities; it was the transformation of the popular *baiana* dress into a carnivalesque costume that enabled the *baiana* outfit to become so popular. Given the current status of the *baiana* as a widespread figure of Brazilian culture both at home and abroad, it is indeed surprising that this costume, which stemmed from a tradition closely associated with Brazil's often marginalized black population, overcame its original stigma through its co-option as a costume for performance. This required a new understanding of the meaning of the *baiana* sign (in the Saussurean sense), from *baiana*-outfit to *baiana*-costume, something that did not happen without resistance, especially in Rio de Janeiro, where for the longest time the *baiana* costume was prohibited in upper-class dances (Ribeiro 25). For some, the disguises of a *baiana* (just as those of a sailor, for example) were banned from the dances of the Municipal Theater in particular because they were considered excessively vulgar.[22] As such, the *baianas* needed to be "dressed up" for the stage, and as a consequence the stylized *baiana* developed a long history in theatrical traditions. In a 1941 interview, by then far removed from Rio and the Carioca carnivalesque tensions, Carmen Miranda reflected on the stigma of the *baiana* costume and commented on the initial resistance she encountered to her wearing the *baiana* on stage. Phonetically transcribing Miranda's words, *Motion Picture* magazine of September 1941 relates: "You can't put theez Baiana dress, they say, because theez dress only Negroes put. Bah! I put, but in gold an' silk an' velvet, an' I seen in Rio. One week before Shubert see me in Casino, I put this Baiana dress" (76). While the chronology of wearing the *baiana* costume for the first time only a week before Shubert arrived at the Urca Casino is highly questionable, this quote transmits the disapproval the *baiana* costume continued to provoke in the Brazilian popular imaginary and the necessity to "dress up" the *baiana*, here in gold, silk, and velvet, to make it acceptable for the stage, a concept that will be taken to creative extremes as Miranda's *baiana* heads north.

The Widespread Stylized *Baiana* in Rio of the 1930s

If Carmen Miranda's performance of the *baiana* had been the original stylized appropriation of this popular figure, we could conclude that she draws from two different types of common vendors: the *baiana* food-vendors, who sold savory dishes and pastries and often transported their wares on trays balanced on their heads, impeccably dressed with necklaces of coral and beads and large gold and silver earrings; and the poorer *baiana*-vendors, who sold mostly fruit. Their dress was simple, and they carried the fruit in large baskets on top of their heads, using a turban to cushion the weight.[23] This has been the consensus among critics who have seen Miranda's adoption of the *baiana* as the first of its kind. However, such an assessment ignores the deep-rooted Carioca tradition of the stylized *baiana* and simplistically bypasses several generations of *baiana* stage and street performances before Miranda's casino days. While naturally Miranda's *baiana* bears resemblance with that of the street vendors, the circulation of its stylized counterpart already held broad currency among the Carioca cultural imaginary, and Miranda's costume was part of the then-current vogue in Rio to dress up as the *baiana*. Curiously, the widespread acceptance of this stylized traditional costume is also present beyond the stage: a case in point is the "cloth witches," stylized doll versions of the *baiana* which children frequently owned and that were also popular among the upper classes, where they were no longer used as toys but as decorations made out of luxurious fabrics (Ribeiro 24).[24]

The distinction between the authentic *baiana* outfit and the stylized costume is beautifully portrayed in a series of thirty-five watercolors and sketches by the renowned contemporary artist, writer, and educator known principally as a poet of Brazilian Modernism: Cecília Meireles (1901–1964). Her paintings, which are almost ethnographic in nature, and the accompanying text make a clear distinction between the authentic or legitimate food-bearing *baiana* or *quituteira* and the mediated, whimsical *baiana* of Carnival. While the *quituteira* wears a skirt of discrete colors such as gray, purple, or dark blue, the Carnival *baiana* dons bright colors (Meireles 22; 36). The authentic *baiana* limits her accessories to a few necklaces of glass beads, colorful seeds, or pieces of wood worn wrapped around her neck several times, a few silver bracelets, and the indispensable amulet, used more as a means of protection fitting with the *baiana*'s mystical beliefs than as a form of embellishment. The Carnival *baiana* takes this element to new heights, with yards and yards of glass beads of different sizes and colors—imitating all the pomp and splendor of precious stones—piled string-upon-string around her neck, arms, and shoulders.

An essential part of Carmen Miranda's outfit is invariably a turban, headpiece, or hat that writers such as Gil-Montero have related back to the trays and baskets the *baiana* women carry on their heads. Whereas the authentic *baiana* wears a white functional scarf tied behind her neck to support the straw basket or tray used to carry her goods from the market, the Carnival *baiana* wears a tightly fitted scarf attached to a miniature lace-covered tray or straw basket that is filled with decorative paper flowers or artificial fruits, serving as a token reminder of a functional basket. This replica of the *balaio*, or round straw basket, is exactly what Carmen Miranda incorporated into her early *baiana* costumes with the sole purpose of likewise emulating those worn by the authentic *baiana*. The overall impression is a diadem-style headpiece that adds a touch of whimsy and playfulness to the *baiana*'s look while reinforcing the reality that this Carnival *baiana* is not the authentic street-vendor *baiana*, just a mimicking nod in her direction as she continues dancing off down the opposite path.

During the time period when the samba groups (the *ranchos*) were transforming into specific samba schools, the pervasiveness of the *baiana* was all the more significant and worn by both men and women. When the Carnival dance lines (*cordões*) left Praça Onze, they would congregate along the Mangue Canal until the early morning hours. There they would form samba and *batuque* circles, sing, and dance, with both "men and women dressed in the same clothing of the *baiana*" (Meireles 48). Children also dressed as miniature *baianos* (*baianinhos*); even the very young ones who could barely walk were dressed in the same manner, their costumes complete with a colorful turban and large numbers of glass-bead necklaces (Meireles 62). Meireles's artwork is a testament to the intricacies of the Carioca *baiana*, which should not be collapsed into a single, homogeneous prototype for Miranda's stage appropriation, and constitutes an important historical document for understanding the characteristics of the different *baianas* in Rio's cultural imaginary at the time. It is this stylized, carnivalesque version of the *baiana* that Carmen Miranda would seek to emulate for an audience already well acquainted with this mediated figure.

The *Baianas* of the Stage

Carmen Miranda was by no means the first to perform the *baiana* on the Carioca stage: she was preceded most immediately by Araci Cortes (1904–1985), the beloved queen of the variety theater (*teatro de revista*), and Elsie Houston (1902–1943), a contemporary singer. Discussing celebrity status in contemporary culture, P. David Marshall indicates that "oppositions, distinctions, and differentiations among various celebrities reveal their functions within the culture" (58). In relation to Miranda, there has been very little discussion of her contemporary stars or those who preceded her through such points of comparison, an approach that is essential to understanding Miranda as part of a systemic conception of celebrities and not, as has been done to date, as an isolated performer of the *baiana* in Rio. The *baiana* performances were common on Rio's stages, and this ubiquitous *baiana*-vogue tradition can be perceived as a Carioca "invented tradition" (Hobsbawm).

There are several different opinions as to who was the very first *baiana* on Rio's stages. Orlando de Barros and José Tinhorão both concur that it is likely that Aurélia Delorme, a Brazilian actress and chorus girl, first took the *baiana* costume to the stage of the Teatro Variedades Dramáticas (a theater for variety shows) in 1889 as part of the revue *O bendegó* by Oscar Pederneiras and Figueiredo Coimbra.[25] A few months later, the Greek-born Ana Monarezzi appeared as the *baiana* in the revue *A república* by the brothers Artur and Aluísio Azevedo, which premièred in the same theater on March 26, 1890, drawing her inspiration from Delorme's version of the *baiana* and enhanced by the Azevedo brothers' ditties. The Spanish-born actress Pepa Ruiz was also among the earliest stars of the revue theater to be associated with the stylized *baiana*, most probably in the Portuguese revue *Tim-tim por tim-tim*, which was staged in Rio in 1892, and also performed as one of the first international *baianas*, in Lisbon in 1906.[26] From this point on, the *baiana* was a stock character of the revue theater, traditionally portrayed as a strong character—a naughty, malicious, seductive exhibitionist and queen of *doubles ententes*—often at the center of the plot. As stylized and stylish *baianas*, they were an impressive feature of the shows, wearing ornate costumes covered in lace trim, necklaces wrapped several times around their necks, often real jewelry (as the above-mentioned Araci Cortes preferred), classical sandals, and turbans (Barros 28).

There were only exceptional appearances of Afro-Brazilians on the stage, and the theatrical casting of the *baiana* is a case in point: those who controlled the Carioca theaters avoided including black actors in prominent roles, and at the turn of the century the *baiana* was typically performed by an actress of white European descent. However, this would change during the 1920s, especially when Araci Cortes began to consistently perform the *baiana* on the stage. In

Araci Cortes dressed to perform as a *baiana* (undated). Courtesy of FUNARTE/Rio de Janeiro

fact, the popularization of the *baiana* as a stage persona of the revue theater is attributed to the work of Cortes, a Brazilian singer best remembered today for being the first artist to record Ari Barroso's patriotic hymn "Aquarela do Brasil" in 1939. She was a mulato singer, dancer, and actress of considerable presence, who exerted great influence on other female singers and performers of her time. Cortes became the most famous *baiana* of the popular revue, beginning her career in 1921, the very same year that the aforementioned Aurélia Delorme, who had initiated this theatrical tradition, passed away. A few years later, Cortes dressed as a *baiana* to interpret composer Sinhô's song "Yaya" in the musical revue *Miss Brasil* (1928). After its success, she played the *baiana* character on many other occasions and became synonymous with the performance. Cortes's appearance in different venues wearing full *baiana* dress bears great resemblance with the stylized models Miranda used later, and Cortes continued to perform as a *baiana* throughout her career.

Alongside Araci Cortes there were other popular performers who impersonated the *baiana* to perfection, such as Margarida Max and Lia Binatti, daughters of European immigrants living in São Paulo and Santa Catarina, respectively, who frequently appeared photographed as *baianas* in the magazine *Para todos* (Barros 31). In the all-black revue company Companhia Negra de Revistas, Rosa Negra, Djanira Flora, and Dalva Spíndola (Araci Cortes's sister) sometimes appeared as *baianas*, most famously Spíndola, who starred as a "comical *baiana*" in one of the troupe's first plays, *Tudo preto* (All black) (Barros 88). For Tiago de Melo Gomes, the stage directions of the play reinforce the *baiana* as an eroticized Afro-Brazilian woman, thus feeding into commonly perceived stereotypes that stemmed from the conflation of the *baiana* and the sensual mulata in the early 1920s, while other parts of the play, fitting with the troupe's militant mission, clearly call for a renegotiation of racial representation beyond these same stereotypes and a valorization of black culture (314–17).[27] Deo Costa, better known by the moniker "Jambo Venus" (*Vênus de Jambo*) from the character she played,[28] also appeared as a *baiana* in the short-lived troupe Ba-Ta-Clan Preta, created by De Chocolat in September 1926 after he left the Companhia Negra de Revistas. The print media of this period illustrates that by the mid-1920s the stylized *baiana* was an established and obligatory figure of the musical revues, played by white and mulato actresses. For example, at the same time that Carmen Miranda was debuting at the Urca Casino in the late 1930s, the Casino Atlântico was staging a musical show that also included, as depicted in the publicity shots, the performance of two *baianas* in traditional costume.[29] What the majority of these stage *baianas* have in common, and as far as available sources confirm, is the impersonation of the *baiana* by white or mulato performers who invariantly sing about the *baiana* way of life and Bahia. A frequent claim in the publicity for these competing shows is that their *baiana* is "the most authentic," an interesting concept given the stylization of this theatrical figure. Only a few of these *baiana*-performing women have remained famous to this day, and only in Brazil, but what is more important for our discussion is this concept of the *baiana* as a symbol on the popular stage, which prepares the way for Miranda and creates the backdrop for her epic *baiana* appropriation.

On the big screen, the *baiana* makes her Hollywood appearance in the film *Flying Down to Rio* (1933). Released by RKO and distributed abroad in 1934, it is best known as the first film to project the dancing duo extraordinaire Fred Astaire and Ginger Rogers, performing their routine on the steps of the Copacabana Palace Hotel. In the long dance number "The Carioca," Etta Motten appears in full *baiana* costume on the stage of a deluxe Brazilian nightclub. It is significant that the director chose an African-American actress to play the *baiana* character who performs this maxixe-based number, which became quite a fad in the United States after the film's release (Seigel 93). It is also interesting to note that her role is listed in the credits as "colored girl," thus set out of context and disassociated from the song she performs so fabulously and at length. This scene, enhanced by improvements in film stock and lighting, stands out as one of the most dazzling musical numbers in the film, complete with exquisite costumes set against an Art Deco backdrop, rich in texture in the improved black-and-white film (T. Sennett 87). On the national screen, Miranda's filmed *baiana* in *Banana da terra* also had a made-in-Brazil predecessor: in *Alô, alô, carnaval!* (1935), Heloísa Helena sings a beautiful samba, "Tempo bom" (Good times), that she allegedly composed with João de Barro (also known as Braguinha), and she appears wearing a *baiana* dress.

With such a precedence of *baiana* performances, Carmen Miranda's appropriation of the *baiana* at the Urca Casino adds another rendition to the repertoire of this well-established figure. However, before Miranda, the *baiana* was mostly performed at low-budget theaters surrounding Tiradentes Square in Rio as part of variety shows that changed their productions frequently and catered to local patrons of the middle to lower-middle classes. Judging by the long tenure of the revue *Boneca de pixe* at the Recreio Theater, Araci Cortes's *baiana* was no doubt also captivating and projected its own unique charm, but being on the ephemeral medium of the stage and without the national projection of film, Cortes remained for the most part a local celebrity of the Carioca nightlife. Miranda gave a poetic, catchy, and beautiful expression to a theme that was already in vogue. While she did not invent the *baiana* for the stage, she gave it irresistible meaning and embodiment, captured by the early Brazilian sound film. Carmen Miranda's *baiana* transferred seamlessly between film and casino venue, en route to international stardom.

Miranda's *Baiana*

Carmen Miranda appropriates the *baiana* at a crucial time in the context of 1930s Brazil during a moment of intense debate surrounding the construction of a new national identity under the Getúlio Vargas government. What Brazil meant as a nation both at home and abroad was high on Vargas's agenda, especially in response to some earlier disparaging statements by leading intellectuals claiming Brazil was a territory but not a nation.[30] Part of the official nationalist agenda of the New State (1937–1945) involved a greater valorization and a redefinition of an authentic Brazilian national culture, an effort constructed around a phrase that became very popular at the time: *coisas nossas* (our things).

Music and performance were at the heart of this new cultural awareness. The 1930s forged the important link between samba and national identity through the lyrics of influential composers (such as Noel Rosa and João de Barro) and the essential medium of the radio, which was instrumental in spreading the sound of Rio's catchy, melodic, but simple tunes all across the nation (McCann 49, 53). Samba would soon reach the level of national song through the initial endorsement by the emergent middle classes, who were seeking a new popular form of recreation and selected samba. This democratization of samba was successful despite the disdain it evoked among certain elites who detected an expression of sensuality not found in the foxtrot or other European or American imports and who required a whitening of samba, a condition *sine qua non* for it to become a national rhythm, by "sanitizing" the music's content and controlling references to *malandros*, a sub-genre of samba popular at the time.[31]

Carmen Miranda's role within this consacration of samba as the national music should not be overlooked. The media, widely considering Miranda the most prominent popular female voice and emphasizing her noted preference for interpreting sambas, claimed her as the quintessential national singer and, by association, contributed to promoting samba to the status of Brazil's national music genre. As early as October 10, 1933, an article in *O cruzeiro* praised Carmen and her sister Aurora for singing national songs, here referring to both the samba and the Carnival *marchinhas*: "Both sisters have the talent to sing our sambas. Our *marchinhas*. These musical genres are the photographs of our soul. . . . They earned the admiration of our country, they know how to sing what is ours" (qtd. in Garcia 38).[32]

Throughout this process of cultural nation building of the 1930s, there are conflicting sentiments between what the public, the performers, and the elite perceive as the hypercivilized, modern, white tendencies and the homegrown Brazilian variety, contemporary to an official discourse of inclusion that attempts to overlook these tensions. This process corresponds to Homi Bhabha's reading of the locality of culture, as developed in his essay "DissemiNation": we witness a "cultural construction of nationness" that can no longer afford to ignore the diverse narratives of the nation and that aims to be hybrid in its articulation of differences and identifications (201). Carmen Miranda's star performance embraces, perhaps more than any other contemporary entertainer's, this hybridity of cultural awareness. Miranda's prominence as a singer, actress, entertainer, and well-loved public figure situated her at an opportune social and cultural intersection at a time when music, race, and gender politics coincided with what she had to offer. Before becoming one of the main attractions at the Urca Casino, Miranda was first and foremost an accomplished interpreter of contemporary Brazilian (and some foreign) songs, a popular voice on the radio, and a successful recording artist.[33] Her vast repertoire of songs included quick, catchy, carnivalesque *marchinhas*, some of the most popular tangos of the day, and—because she was one of the most sought-after interpreters—innumerous sambas that extol Brazil's unique beauty and natural richness. In this she was not exceptional but part of a musical nationalist endeavor that encouraged a glorified Brazilianness, a vogue that would continue well into the 1940s. The most representative song of this period is the aforementioned "Aquarela do Brasil" (Watercolor of Brazil), Ari Barroso's exaltation samba of 1939 that achieved international cinematic visibility by its inclusion in the brilliant Walt Disney film *Saludos Amigos* (1943).[34] The opening lyrics of "Aquarela do Brasil" set the tone for the rest of the samba and summarize its nationalist message, capturing the essence of *brasilidade* like no other phrase: "Brazil, my Brazilian Brazil." As McCann acutely comments, "What adjective could begin to describe the greatness of Brazil? Only, of course,

Brazilian" (70). Among Miranda's repertoire of sambas that sang of the wonders and beauty of Brazil and emphasized Miranda's ardent attachment to her country were songs such as "Terra morena" (Brown earth) and "Minha terra tem palmeiras" (My land has palm trees), both recorded in 1936—the latter title referring to the well-known nineteenth-century poem by Gonçalves Dias. In particular, Bahia was a recurring motif in Carmen's songs, both before and after the recording of Dorival Caymmi's hit "O que é que a baiana tem?" in 1939, which enforced her moniker as the *rainha do samba* (queen of samba).[35] The lyrics of her numerous Bahian-themed songs depict the nostalgia that represented a romanticized Bahia in the mainstream, Carioca-based imaginary: a land of love and happiness, close to the original paradise, where the sensuality of the *baiana* is conflated with the delectable wares of her tray, the aroma of exotic oils, and the sensual movements of her hips.[36]

Local composers wrote many of Miranda's sambas explicitly for her with the hope that the "queen of samba" would record them and increase the chances of their hits attaining national success. Another component of this phenomenon that may have been overlooked is the fact that before Carmen Miranda, popular music typically originated in the revue theater and then descended to the streets and to Carnival. With Miranda's stardom, especially after the release of the Carnival hit of 1930, "Taí" by Joubert de Carvalho, which sold an estimated thirty-five thousand records in the first year alone,[37] the theater lost this privilege: popular theater looked to the streets and to Carnival for its music rather than the reverse. In the wake of the "Miranda phenomenon," composers no longer sought to début their songs on the stages of the city's theaters but preferred to place them with successful recording artists whose hits were widely circulated by the advent of radio.[38]

Dorival Caymmi's song "O que é que a baiana tem?" would become one of Miranda's most popular recordings due to her unique interpretation that would likewise immortalize the composer. The novelty of this trademark song stemmed from Miranda's unusual arm, hand, and hip movements that distinguished her from contemporary stage *baianas* and became a dance/song vogue in its own right. However, as Davis cautions, "co-optation only tells half the story. . . . Miranda's performance and celebration of the Bahiana, like the celebration of myths and icons elsewhere, became important because of the desires and visions of the audience" (*White Face* 149). As demonstrated above, Miranda's *baiana* was a popular enactment of a well-known figure that, through its wide circulation in the public sphere and entertainment halls, was divested of the racially grounded fears that other forms of Afro-Brazilianness might have implied.

The Miranda film enactment of "O que é que a baiana tem?" in *Banana da terra*, partially recovered in the documentary *Bananas Is My Business* (1995), culminates Miranda's appropriation of the *baiana*. Although critics have been quick to comment that she is "wearing" her performance, on close examination, the lyrics do not correspond to the Miranda *baiana* costume that she dons for the occasion. Rather, Miranda's attire is a variation on that described in the lyrics. Whereas the lyrics evoke a typical *baiana*, Miranda's costume already distinguishes itself as a stylized version, common for decades now on the Carioca stage and as a Carnival costume, as detailed above. The song is an exaltation of the *baiana*: the beauty of her dress, her jewelry, and her sensuality adorn the *baiana* as she heads toward the Church of Bonfim in Salvador. The title-question and chorus of "O que é que a baiana tem?" is sung accompanied by Miranda's band, Bando da Lua. The answer contained in the lyrics is that the Bahian woman wears a silk turban, golden earrings, chains, and bracelets, a lace bustier, a shawl made out of cloth (*pano da costa*), an embroidered blouse, a starched skirt, decorated sandals, a gold rosary, and *balangandãs*—and she is graceful like no one else. However, in this segment of *Banana da terra*, Miranda wears a tight, wrap-around satin skirt that emphasizes the movements of her hips, and the blouse she wears is neither silk nor embroidered as the lyrics of the song suggest: it is a satin top made of the same two-tone fabric as the skirt, revealing bare shoulders and arms. Likewise, her earrings, necklaces, and bracelets are not golden, and the shoulder scarf she carries over her arm is not *pano da costa*. Yet the conclusion of this overall image is the production of a stylized *baiana* model. Despite the disparity between lyrics and performance that eventually becomes secondary, it is the marriage of song, dance, and dress that in 1938 marks the creation of the *prototype* Carmen Miranda image.

Far from the over-the-top extravaganzas of future Hollywood films, the headdress Miranda wears as her Brazilian *baiana* is a playful, discrete turban adorned by two small baskets containing berries, small flowers, twigs, leaves, and other shiny elements to complement her attire. With only the resemblance of a functional basket, Miranda's headdress recalls Cecília Meireles's artwork of the carnivalesque *baianas*, whose small baskets adorned their stylized turbans. The high heels, which became indistinguishable from Miranda's look, were originally referred to in Brazil as the "Annabella heels," inspired by the shoes the famous French actress wore at the height of her career, including on a trip to Rio in 1938 during which she courted Tyrone Power.[39] Invariably, Annabella's role in popularizing these shoes was soon forgotten in Brazilian popular culture, overshadowed by Miranda's stage performance. This is the *baiana* that will make Carmen Miranda famous. This is her signature, stylized *baiana*.

Much has been written about Miranda's chance discovery through the *baiana*, yet the actual staging of the musical number on the proscenium scene has been overlooked. The back-and-forth discussion around the theme of "What is it that she has?" plays on the contradistinction between knowledge and mystery, which places the physical appearance of the *baiana* as key to understanding the secrets she holds. Such an emphasis on the *baiana*, with no reference to the male counterpart the *baiano*, reinforces the *baiana*'s status and prominence in the public sphere. In this unusual validation of the woman defined by her gender, apparel, and demeanor, the male is effaced. The *malandros* who sit sprawled out on each side of her, symbolically on a lower level as though subservient to her and the mysterious aura of the *baiana*, echo the title's question as they sway their hats to the rhythm of the music. Although tradition has engendered the gaze that focuses on the female body as male, following in particular Mulvey's work on scopophilia

(60–63), nothing in the song refers to a male voyeuristic gaze, and the *baiana*'s positioning is further problematized by the ambiguity of her dual participation in this fetishizing project: Miranda not only embodies the *baiana* through the donning of her costume and all its accessories but also creates a distance from the *baiana* through the interrogation in the third person. This distancing is an essential part of Miranda's performativity both on and off the stage throughout her career and is perhaps the most misunderstood aspect of her star persona. Here is found, in its embryonic form, what I refer to as the characteristic Miranda *performative wink*: her capacity to be part of the performance but also to distinguish herself from it in order to react, laugh, look, and, in this case, investigate with her audience so as to understand it in the broadest sense. Pointing in a simplistic and repetitive manner to elements of her costume that do not exactly correspond to the lyrics that she sings is part of Miranda's performative game and the complicity that she creates with the knowing public. Likewise, in the reprise the boys come forward rather awkwardly—or at least without great enthusiasm or stage presence—and, with Miranda's nodding approval, touch the same elements of her costume, as though they too are part of this coded performance. As such, Miranda is object, subject, and accomplice of this voyeuristic and fetishistic process. The sexual imbalance that Mulvey attributes to the active/male and passive/female is displaced in this *baiana* mise-en-scène through Miranda's complex positioning and the manner in which she avoids, for most of the duration of the number, staring straight toward the camera as though deflecting the voyeuristic gaze. She looks at the pieces of her costume as she touches them or glances to the side and either up or down, only twice making eye contact obliquely with the public in a coquettish yet seductive manner. She disregards the camera, the live diegetic (internal) audience, and makes only an occasional gesture in the direction of the boys who surround her. After she has sung the verse through twice, the camera cuts to a wide angle as she dances toward the front of the stage and twirls around before coming back to her initial position. Miranda's *baiana*—of whose beauty, mystery, and grace she sings—creates and fuels to-be-looked-at-ness that transcends any specific engendering of desire. Rather, in this scene Miranda and her boys symbolically touch the *baiana*: they own the gaze while inviting others to accompany them. After the first verse, the tempo of the song quickens as Miranda sings an unexpected interlude, "When you sway / Fall on top of me / Fall on top of me / Fall on top of me," briefly evoking in this stanza sexual innuendos that invite the surrounding boys, or whomever her samba addresses, to project their fantasy onto the *baiana*. But the offer to receive the addressee's fall is only momentary, because immediately afterward the samba continues at its previous cadence, and the fleeting opportunity is gone.

It was apparently on the set of *Banana da terra* on the day they were filming "O que é que a baiana tem?" that Dorival Caymmi suggested Miranda emphasize the swinging of her hips and hand movements, which from that moment on would become an integral part of her performance. Whether this story is true or perhaps fabricated to give Caymmi more ownership of the performance,

Miranda's fortuitous full-body enactment of the *baiana* became forever associated with her. However, this first filmed *baiana* performance is far from the exuberant, energetic, and defiantly confident "South American Way" *baiana* of *Down Argentine Way* (1940) filmed just over a year later, in which she looks straight at the camera in an assertive and provocative stance. What is encapsulated in the segment filmed in *Banana da terra* is only the beginning of Miranda's *baiana* screen performance, which in comparison to the subsequent Hollywood versions comes across as a bashful and tentative *baiana* rendition. Although some may attribute Miranda's professional success to a felicitous alignment of her stars that culminated with the ultimate chance encounter with Lee Shubert, in retrospect, and upon close examination of the *baiana* performance in *Banana da terra* that was probably very similar to her Urca Casino number, it becomes evident that more credit for Miranda's rise to international stardom should be attributed to her early professional development and her stage presence beyond the embodiment of the *baiana*.

Early Brazilian Stardom and Public Presence

By considering the Brazilian years as a formative period, previous studies of Miranda's stardom overlook her celebrity status in Brazil and focus almost exclusively on what Marshall refers to as the "elevated individual" (3), aiming to identify the different moments that led her to stardom. Such approaches, as Marshall continues, answer questions "that are looking for the core of the individual and the roots of a causal relationship between the celebrity's actions and the successful consequences of those actions" (3). Easily established and to a certain degree accurate cause-and-effect trajectories have been drawn, for example, between Miranda's days as a milliner's assistant and her creative dexterity applied to hat and costume designs for her later performances, despite the fact that once in Hollywood she would be surrounded by professional costume designers, and her involvement in her own costumes, although perhaps not eliminated altogether, became greatly limited. Several stages of her developing career as a singer have also merited repeat mention by biographers such as Gil-Montero, who sees her "rebellious" singing at the Colégio Santa Teresa nuns' boarding school (where she attended from 1916 to 1923) and her alleged spontaneous outbursts and on-demand singing for clients at different store-floor jobs indicative of her budding talent as a singer soon to become nationally renowned (19–22). Such appreciations tend for the most part to reduce Carmen Miranda's stardom in Brazil to a preparatory phase for her subsequent Hollywood career and bypass the importance of her Brazilian career or, at best, view her Brazilian years as a series of events with pathway markers toward her Hollywood success. While the parallels are interesting and often drawn from reliable sources, to do justice to Miranda's Brazilian years, this period needs to be interpreted as more than a mere springboard to Hollywood fame lest we risk overlooking her role as an interpreter of popular music, a cinema and stage star, and a public personality in Brazil, independent of the international *baiana* of years to come.

Newspapers and magazines were prompt to comment on the qualities and appeal of this unique singing voice and engaging performer, and through this widely proclaimed praise, print media fueled her rise to stardom. The weekly variety magazine *O cruzeiro* of May 3, 1930, presents Miranda as a "new and intelligent artist" whose "singing has soul" and who "animates her songs with the expression of her playful eyes and her attractive smile," all qualities that will remain with her throughout her career (qtd. in Garcia 37). With the greater accessibility of the radio as a means to spread popular music and the importance of Carnival songs as the most competitive forum for contemporary voices, Miranda's interpretation of the above-mentioned Carnival hit "Taí" confirmed her status as a celebrity of the music scene. "In the eyes and ears of the public, she was the first Brazilian woman to create a public personality—and make a living from it" (Castro 92). She became the most legitimate female interpreter of Brazilian popular music, and throughout the 1930s Carmen went from one success to the next as each of her songs was enthusiastically received by an ever-growing, widespread group of fans who owned a radio or a Victrola and who admired not only the quality of her singing but also the energy, gaiety, and soul that Miranda brought to each and every performance regardless of the venue. From this point on, Miranda was one of the most popular touring celebrities throughout Brazil (Bahia, Pernambuco, São Paulo, Rio Grande do Sul, and Minas Gerais) and abroad (Argentina and Uruguay). However, she remained true to her Carioca public and for many became *the* female voice of 1930s Rio de Janeiro.

Miranda's celebrity status benefitted from newly developed technologies, such as the incipient print media industry that documented the lives and careers of these public personae, and other social developments, including gradually improving conditions for women on the stage and in the recording industry. In the predominantly male-controlled entertainment world, Miranda's position of success and prominence was pioneering, as she dominated the radio and the recording industry and established her position with a very personal, charming, and innocently provocative performance style that set her star status on a par with that of Francisco Alves and Mário Reis, the most acclaimed Brazilian white male performers both nationally and internationally. Carmen Miranda was Carioca through and through (*carioquíssima*, as they would say in Portuguese), but she also became a national icon of the Brazilian music scene, crossing all regional boundaries through her interpretation of sambas and *marchinhas* for a far-reaching public. In this pre-television era, singers could only rely on the quality of their voices, their pure singing talent, and Miranda was at the height of her Brazilian singing career, selling records of all her releases in quantities never before reached by a female performing artist.

The consolidation of a radio culture in Brazil cannot be underestimated as instrumental in making Miranda a superstar, because it enabled her to be close to a wide-ranging public, and as a celebrity in Brazil, she was celebrated by the masses.

The versatility and accessibility of Miranda's stardom were key factors to her immediate success as a recording artist first of all, and then as a live performer. On
the one hand, the clever promotion of her recordings was enabled by the record
companies' ingenuous marketing campaigns. On the other, the fact that Miranda's
voice was a sure sell distinguished her from any one specific record label and sent
the message that sambas—most of all Miranda's sambas—sung by a white, female
singer were acceptable for the upper classes. She also held appeal for the masses
of the lower classes and was thus a winning ticket to a national marketing success
story. As a talented interpreter and charismatic performer, she corresponded to an
idealized image of racial, social, and cultural inclusiveness, and in this way Miranda
struck the central, emotional chords of a large, receptive public. From this perspective, we can understand Miranda's enormous popularity as corresponding to the
circumstances of the time: she gathered momentum through a solid following of
the common people of 1930s Brazilian society and was simultaneously promoted
by the elite who controlled the mass media and the performing forums.

Carmen's first published photograph, in 1926, and her name officially in print
as "Carmen Miranda," on March 5, 1929, are benchmarks in the beginning of
a lifelong presence in print media that would accompany her celebrity status in
Brazil and abroad. In 1926 she had begun to sing on the radio, and by 1930 she
signed her first major contract with RCA Victor. Allegedly, her official singing
début was at a National Music Institute (Instituto Nacional de Música) event in
1927, where she sang two tangos in Spanish. From this first public appearance,
Miranda would quickly gain a solid reputation and was soon booked for stage
engagements at a variety of events. Rio was her main performance venue, and there
alone she maintained an active schedule that included Carioca song festivals held in
the city's main theaters and singing competitions such as the official pre-Carnival
competition "Feira de Amostras." She performed innumerous engagements around
town, including live shows at all the main radio stations, local theaters, and casinos,
even promoting her own musical festival, "Festival Carmen Miranda," on one
occasion.[40] This impressive register of live performances is a clear indication that
Miranda was a much-loved celebrity at the peak of her career in Brazil.

Miranda's short-term contract at the Copacabana Casino in January 1936 was
decisive for her career: it was her first repeated stage engagement before a more
elite, upper-class crowd, proving that Miranda and the music she interpreted could
cross class divides and capture a sophisticated audience in a setting beyond the
radio and cinema. She returned to the Copacabana in December 1937 after her
contract with the Urca Casino expired and before renegotiating its renewal, reinforcing the fact that she was in charge of her contracts and their terms.

Innumerable adjectives were used in the Brazilian press to describe the singer
who had taken the samba vogue by storm and made it part of her personal trademark, but *brejeira*, translatable into English as impish, mischievous, coquettish,
wickedly funny, or provocative, was the one most often quoted. Cesar Ladeira, the
radio Mayrink Veiga's main announcer, gave Miranda the nickname "A ditadora
risonha do samba" (The smiling dictator of samba) in 1933—with a wink in the

direction of the country's dictator, Getúlio Vargas—and a year later rechristened her "A pequena notável" (The remarkable young girl).[41] And she remained "A pequena notável" for the rest of her career. Juxtaposing Carmen Miranda and Getúlio Vargas appeared occasionally in the press, although rumors of their having a relationship are unfounded.[42] Circumstantially, however, as Davis rightly intimates, Miranda received the support of the local press (censored after the advent of the New State under Vargas), and her rise to national stardom paralleled Vargas's own trajectory as a populist politician ("Racial Parity" 186–87). As Cesar Ladeira realized on an official assignment as a broadcaster in Argentina in 1935, about which he spoke retrospectively, there were only two "truly Brazilian" (*brasileiríssimo*s) names recognized abroad. The champions of the popularity and sympathy of Argentina toward Brazil were Getúlio Vargas, ambassador of friendship for a brotherly country, and Carmen Miranda, ambassadress of Brazilian popular melodies, both well liked throughout Buenos Aires.[43]

The facts and statistics that corroborate Carmen Miranda's celebrity status aside, what was it about Miranda that made her so "remarkable"? Her younger sister Aurora is said to have had the better singing voice. Miranda commented that she didn't consider herself to have "a great voice," and though she "lacked perfect pitch like that of Judy Garland," she "had projection, and rhythm—something inexplicable" (Brito 33). Indeed, critics have frequently mentioned that Miranda's voice had a seductive quality and a distinguishable high-pitch tone, which she knew how to use to her advantage when paired with her extremely fast yet clear diction, interspersed with spontaneous colloquialisms that added charm and playfulness to her unique performances. The famous composer Vinicius de Moraes once told Miranda she had *verve* (zest), and she was thrilled when she read the corresponding dictionary definition: "warmth of the imagination that animates the artist" (Brito 92). Warmth and animation certainly defined Miranda, paired with her charisma and a freshness of youth and gaiety that fueled her seductive performances as she engaged in a flirtatious complicity with her public. Equally at ease in front of the microphone, the camera, or a live audience, she aimed to please through her charm, her spontaneous interjections, and her coquettish expressions. Even her early photographs capture this love of the spotlight: she poses gaily in front of the camera, often in a forward stance, as she engages with her photographer and, by metonymy, with her public. Radiant, provocative, and seductively impish, with a sensuous smile and dancing eyes, she dominated any stage on which she performed, fully living up to her *brejeira* label. As Ruy Castro pointedly summarizes, "Carmen had the gift of interpretation, the projection of a popular singer—the talent to interject asides in between the phrases, to take liberties with the melodies and surprise the listener with these discoveries . . . she gave the impression of being a fully-accomplished interpreter" (50). Miranda had achieved star status through the uniqueness of a performance that exerted "affective power" on her audience and fans (Marshall xiii). She was, as is characteristic of a celebrity's essential nature, truly unique and enjoyed the support of mass society throughout the country.[44] Miranda's performative individuality distinguished her among her entertainment cohorts. She did more than interpret sambas; she performed them. Whether on a stage or in a recording, there was something about Miranda that transcended the typical function of a singer. After her departure to the United States, there was no substitute for Carmen Miranda, despite her being one of the most imitated performers of that period.[45] For many, she was the most exuberant, lively, entertaining interpreter of Brazilian music of all time.

This public celebration of Miranda as a star during her Brazilian years is also articulated through numerous references, articles, and photographs in the local newspapers. Her constant presence in the media reflects her star status as an object of admiration, as Alberoni theorizes, although some of these newspaper references were more constructed than factual. A case in point is the following example: in the weeks leading up to a beauty competition, the weekly neighborhood newspaper *Beira-mar*, which promoted the happenings of the trendy beach scene and adjacent commercial and residential area of Copacabana, Ipanema, and Leme (CIL), published a photograph of Carmen in her bathing suit on the first page of the November 10, 1929, issue and indicated that "Mlle. Carmen Miranda . . . will be a serious competitor for the 1930 Beauty Contest," a statement that had no founding.[46] During the decade of the 1930s, Miranda certainly had "it" as a celebrity in Rio. The magazine *Cinearte* summarizes her star appeal as follows: "She is a girl who has all the qualities, beyond beauty, that Hollywood has classified for the world as 'it,' 'sex-appeal,' 'zing.'"[47] Ruy Castro, with his characteristic perspicacity and humor, comments on how "it" was indefinable, but Carmen definitely had "it," as was apparent in her first audition with Josué de Barros (Castro 39). Ana Rita Mendonça confirms that "it" was the word most used to describe Miranda, even before she became a film actress in Brazil (33).

Carmen Miranda's constant presence in the Carioca media confirms her popularity as a well-loved radio singer and stage star, often featured in photographs on the beach or at events around town, frequently along with her sister and acting and singing partner Aurora, with the newspaper copy emphasizing its acquaintance with the stars.[48] A reporter for *Beira-mar* published an article on Miranda a few weeks before Carnival and made reference to her ever-growing fame due to her enormous talent and the magic of her interpretation, seeing her as the strongest personality of Brazilian broadcasting and the inspiration behind the numerous imitators, who only added to the prestige of the "greatest singer of the city."[49] The media used this concept to criticize the mediocre Miranda imitations but also to promote lesser-known stars by using Miranda as a cultural reference.[50]

Miranda had a unique relationship with her public and fostered a closeness with her fans by maintaining a very active performing agenda and public visibility around town, and she even fueled her own popularity by sending signed photographs in response to fan requests, thus consolidating her position as a well-loved star, singer, and performer. She performed in a variety of settings for an array of audiences, from the very intimate context of her parents' boarding house to the elite crowd of the upscale casinos, along with a constant production of radio programs and record releases.

The above-mentioned closeness was also something Miranda purposely incorporated into her performances, creating a sense of coparticipation with her audience through direct addresses, the use of slang, the inclusion of Afro-Brazilianness in content and speech, and spontaneous asides. She constructed a social position for her audience through the process that Fiske terms "hailing," which enables the use of language to identify and create a corresponding image for the addressee ("British Cultural Studies" 259). Added interest came from Miranda's ambiguous and playful way of addressing her public. This included using names out of context, such as saying "meu nego" (my black man) to a roomful of white Carioca elites, a verbal masquerade Miranda could pull off beautifully because she herself was white. She was the trendsetter for other radio singers to appear live on stages throughout Brazil singing the music of some of the most prominent songwriters of the time: Pixinguinha, João de Barro, Ari Barroso, Joubert de Carvalho, and Assis Valente, remembered as her favorite composer. Miranda worked her audience both from a distance, up on the stage, and from the proximity of down on the floor, coming off the casino stage to mingle with her audience, creating a sensation of intimacy and familiarity that only added to her star appeal (Castro 145).

Remembered mostly as a performer of the elite casino stage, Miranda also appeared very briefly at the theater, in a show by the well-respected authors Marques Porto and Luiz Peixoto, both geniuses of this art form, who produced *Vai dar o que falar* (Something to talk about) in 1930 at the new João Caetano Theater; and reason for talk it indeed did provide. The rapidly sold-out house was without doubt due to Miranda's presence on the downtown stage in Tiradentes Square, a rare occasion in this part of town. The beginning of the revue went over very well, with the public responding to each presentation with long applauses and requests for encores, and Miranda's performance was one of the most warmly received, as she sang some of her recent hits that were well known on the radio. She was about to return to the stage for her last number when the audience, outraged at a scandalous prostitution scene in the revue, became uncontrollable, leaving Miranda distraught and unable to perform.[51] According to Mário Nunes, the audience interrupted the performance with thunderous foot stomping—as was customary to express audience disapproval—which had not happened in Rio for many years (177). Miranda would never again perform on the local theater stages and instead limited her performances to the more predictable venue of the casino.

The casino was reserved for popular artists who could appeal to middle-class, upper-class, and foreign audiences, and Miranda fit the bill. The casino was a forum more restrictive of class and race than the very numerous revue theaters that dotted the city and sponsored lesser-known artists with a rapid turnover of talent and shows in a constant effort to bring in box office revenue. Furthermore, the shows' genres were very different: the revue theaters drew heavily from local color, *fait divers*, and contemporary social references, whereas at the casino the entertainment was more socially neutral and accessible for out-of-town tourists and international guests alike. Using the appeal of the most popular artists of the day, the casino owners typically cashed in on the easy sell of musical performances to attract local and foreign patrons who would spin away their fortunes at the roulette tables. While Urca was not the largest of venues, it was by far one of the most glamorous of Rio's casinos and was considered the capital city's "social center" (Machado 121). The lavishly built casinos were the centerpieces of Rio's most prestigious neighborhoods of the Southern Zone and brought in the most renowned Brazilian and international stars. They were considered the utmost form of live entertainment and also the most lucrative due to the high-priced entry fee and the gambling revenues. This was the golden age of the Carioca casinos, which lasted until gambling was outlawed by a federal ban in 1946. The Urca Casino at the heart of its namesake residential area competed for the best local and foreign talent against the newly installed casino of the Copacabana Palace Hotel. This is where Miranda felt most at home and soon became the most highly paid casino performer in Rio de Janeiro and throughout Brazil.

From among the already popular radio and stage stars, the film producers of Brazil's developing cinema industry chose its first actors and actresses, capitalizing on their established fame as a means to draw viewers to this new form of entertainment. As in the United States, in Brazil the film industry was in its early stages and still determining its categorical position in the entertainment industry. According to Marshall, in the United States, through its "affiliation with vaudeville, the film industry was part of an already established and successful cultural industry that possessed its own system of fame, prestige, and celebrity" (80). In Brazil, however, although there was some borrowing from the revue theater in terms of musical numbers and a few select actors, it was mostly from the radio and the casino that Brazilian cinema drew its first generation of talented artists.

Miranda was one of these pioneer hybrid performers who made the smooth transition to the silver screen, where she continued to be primarily a singing performer and thus brought many of her popular tunes to an even broader audience. The presentation of her performances did not change drastically as she became a movie star: camera shots at that time were incapable of performing true close-ups and therefore privileged full-stage views and wider angles, similar to the audience's view of a live stage.

Miranda's first film appearance was in *A voz do carnaval* (The voice of carnival) (1933), directed by Adhemar Gonzaga and Humberto Mauro, the first movie of the Carnival genre and also the first of the Brazilian modern films to have the sound recorded by the optical system Movietone.[52] At this time, Brazilian cinema was synonymous with Carioca cinema, since the majority of films were produced and distributed from the capital and concentrated from a few main studios (Ferreira 75–77). These early Brazilian sound films predominantly portrayed the everyday life of Rio de Janeiro, and this created a sense of identity with the Carioca public, guaranteeing a solid cinema-going crowd in the country's capital and other urban centers. Early Brazilian filmmakers drew from samba and comedy to produce what specialists view nowadays as mediocre cinema with the merit, nonetheless, of preserving a slice of quotidian Carioca life in the 1930s (Ferreira 81).

During the 1930s the studio directed by Adhemar Gonzaga, Cinédia, dominated the Brazilian film industry. The popular music scene of the period, with the explosion of samba and *marchinhas* destined for Carnival celebrations and heard year round in festivities and on radios and Victrolas, predated the advent of cinema's delving into this strong Carioca tradition. Popular music and its main interpreters passed over into the new cinema medium that drew heavily from this vibrant musical scene. In *A voz do carnaval*, Miranda appears in two numbers, the Carnival *marcha* "Moleque indigesto" (Unbearable kid) by Lamartine Babo, and "Good Bye!" by Assis Valente, in scenes filmed at the radio studio of Mayrink Veiga. As Tinhorão specifies, *A voz do carnaval* was not a pre-Carnival film, as would later become a cinematic trend, but rather a pseudodocumentary film that used scenes from that year's Carnival interspersed with musical numbers and starred the popular Argentinean comedian Pablo Palitos in the main role as the king of Carnival, "Rei Momo" (253).

Two years later, in 1935, Adhemar Gonzaga in partnership with Wallace Downey launched the first true pre-Carnival film, *Alô, alô, Brasil!* (Hello, hello, Brasil!), starring most of the biggest singers and composers of the time, with the exception of Noel Rosa. Alongside Carmen was her sister Aurora, Almirante, Mário Reis, Francisco Alves, Dircinha Batista, Ari Barroso, Aloísio de Oliveira, and five other boys from the Bando da Lua, among others. The film's plot was straightforward and consisted of successive musical numbers presented by master-of-ceremonies Cesar Ladeira—the most respected radio announcer of the time—playing himself. *Alô, alô, Brasil!* cemented the partnership of radio and national cinema and guaranteed a public for this budding industry from that point forward. A publicity poster for the film drew on this impressive lineup of musical talent, boasting that *Alô, alô, Brasil!* marked the real beginning of an intense production of "filmusicals" in Brazil. The copy on the poster drew from the stardom of the singers: "We are going to hear the greatest repertoire of carnivalesque music sung by the stars of our radio." Indeed, with its practically nonexistent storyline, the movie was supported by twenty-two presentations of the popular Brazilian radio singers. The title indicates the influence of the radio by making reference to the common radio greeting "alô, alô" (hello, hello!) and is also reminiscent of the song "Alô . . . alô?" composed by André Filho, which Miranda recorded with Mário Reis in 1933.[53] The film was an ensemble of carnivalesque and other catchy tunes that enthralled the public, with Miranda's performance of "Primavera no Rio" (Spring in Rio) as the last song of the film, a place of honor intended to showcase the greatest star of the cast. As the magazine *Cena muda* reports, "It was a smart decision to have Carmen Miranda end the film. She brings the theater to their feet, as they vibrate with enthusiasm."[54] Wide publicity was published around the release of the film in Rio, Niterói, São Paulo, and Bahia, where the eight national sound cinemas were located.[55] In particular, critics praised the film's sound quality, especially in the interior scenes, claiming that with *Alô, alô, Brasil!* the national cinema industry was born, capable of rivaling even the best foreign productions.[56] Now consecrated as a big-screen actress, Miranda received vast media coverage for her performance and was noted for the charm of her voice, her photogenic and fascinating figure, and her magnificent interpretation of sambas and *marchas*.[57]

Similar to her performance in *Alô, alô, Brasil!*, Miranda's role in subsequent Brazilian films consisted for the most part of performing musical numbers, as would be the case throughout her Hollywood career. After the success of *Alô, alô, Brasil!*, Miranda was the most popular Brazilian artist of the decade. Adhemar Gonzaga cast Miranda in *Estudantes* (Students, 1935), another vehicle for the era's radio stars, including Aurora Miranda, Mário Reis, and once again the Bando da Lua. The film was scheduled for release in June to coincide with the popular *Festas Juninas* (June festivals) of São João that take place at the beginning of the Brazilian winter.[58] The film transposed the radio stars to a student setting and cast Miranda in the only character role of her Brazilian film career, as a radio vedette with sex appeal ("toda sex-appeal"). In the film, two students, played by Mesquitinha and Barbosa Júnior, fall in love with her music and her charm. Carmen's character is in love with yet another student, played by the popular singer and budding actor Mário Reis, the Brazilian beau of the time, but she humors the others to avoid their heartbreak. While the film received mixed reviews and for many did not surpass the cinematic quality and appeal of *Alô, alô, Brasil!*, the more lenient critics did concur that Brazilian cinema was certainly on the right path toward becoming a competitive and modern industry.[59]

Brazilian film directors drew from the known stars of the radio as a guarantee of success at the box office. Since it was the pretelevision era, and the public at large did not have access to viewing performances at the elite casinos, the radio provided the film industry with the idols they knew the public wanted not only to hear but also to see.[60] This trend was so prevalent that one critic remarked, with irony, how talent followed the technical advances: "with the advent of radio, everyone became a singer. Now with the beginning of the cinematic industry in Brazil, everyone wants to be a star, a supporting cast member, or an extra."[61] From these beginnings of sound cinema, Brazilian Carnival was associated with cinema. The film industry both produced and launched Carnival successes and was able to present for a broad public many artists who, for the most part, were only known through the radio and photographs in the newspapers (Diniz 34).[62] Before Carnival 1936, Downey, in collaboration with Adhemar Gonzaga, launched *Alô, alô, carnaval!* at the Alhambra Cinema in Rio on January 20, 1936, then in São Paulo the following month. The film remained on screen the whole month, a record for the time period, before being distributed throughout the country (Gonzaga, *50 anos* 47).[63] Opening at the Alhambra was also a sign of prestige: the home of Rio's first escalator and elevators that could hold twenty-four people, air conditioning, and comfortable seating, it was considered the jewel of the Carioca movie-palaces, as they had begun to be called with the advent of sound cinema (Gonzaga, *Palácios* 167).

The Miranda sisters were the saving grace of *Alô, alô, carnaval!*, which, despite good directing and technical talent, showed a lack of resources, poor acting, mediocre filming, under-rehearsed scenes, and an incoherent and unrealistic plot. Dennison and Shaw excuse the poor quality of the production as "a legacy of the

Carmen Miranda and Aurora Miranda in *Alô, alô, carnaval!* (1936).
Courtesy of FUNARTE/Rio de Janeiro

radio and the constraints imposed by the equipment available in Brazil" (41). One reviewer writes that Carmen and Aurora were the "queens of the cast" and that Brazilian cinema could not hope for better.[64] Ironically, at the preview of the film the Miranda sisters allegedly were not pleased with their performance of "Cantoras do rádio" ([Female] radio singers), their main musical number that received the most praise by critics and fans during the film's month-long tenure at the Alhambra Theater.[65] They *were* the radio singers: no other singers enjoyed the same level of stardom as the Miranda sisters, both together and apart. At the peak of their careers in Brazil, they dominated the recording industry, the live shows, and now the cinema, which seemed a tailor-made vehicle for their performances. Furthermore, for Carnival 1936, Miranda's rendition of "Querido Adão" (Dear Adam), also included in the movie, was one of the favorite hits of the season.[66] In this scene Miranda is captured on tape with her unique, upbeat performance style that will remain characteristic throughout her career. She engages with the camera as if it were her audience, walking and swaying her hips in a *rebolado* movement from side to side while always facing forward, communicating through the sparkle and movement of her eyes, exaggerated facial expressions, twirling hands, and open arm movements—gestures meant to punctuate her singing or mime the meaning of the lyrics.[67] Her charm is matched with irony and a teasingly provocative attitude expressed throughout.[68] This genre of filmed musical number resembles in every way a live performance through the intimacy Miranda creates with the camera, which will remain Miranda's signature style through the remainder of her Brazilian years and throughout the duration of her US career. Miranda also made a bold fashion statement around town as one of the first women in Brazil to wear bell-bottom pants and a striped sailor's "husler" shirt, proving once again that she was a performing artist with the necessary class, popularity, audacity, and drive to blaze her own unique trail on the stage and in popular culture.

Ever since Miranda recorded "Taí" in 1930, she had been associated with Carnival. Now her film roles consolidated this association. As Coelho writes, "the always-effervescent and vivacious way in which Miranda sang the marchinhas matched the carnivalesque spirit of the genre" (44). Over her career, she recorded over one hundred Carnival *marchas*, some composed specifically for her interpretation. As one reporter summarized a few years later, "Carnival is a beautiful evolution, it is geography studied live, to the sound of a samba by Ary [Barroso] and the voice of Carmen Miranda, within the pagan contagion of the Avenida Rio Branco."[69] *Alô, alô, carnaval!* confirmed and projected for many years to come the felicitous marriage between Carnival, popular music, and national cinema, and it is commonly perceived as the genesis of the *chanchadas*, the popular filmusicals of the 1940s and 1950s.[70]

Carmen Miranda's last full acting and singing role in a Brazilian film was in *Banana da terra*.[71] The tradition of pre-Carnival films had been interrupted for the two previous years and only started up again in 1939 with the pretext of once again launching Carnival music to a greater public through the film media. The film's plot was based on a story by composer and singer João de Barro: an island in the Pacific Ocean, suggestively named "Bananolândia," is faced with the problem of overproduction of bananas. The queen of the island (Linda Batista) is advised by her chief counselor (Oscarito) to go to Brazil to attempt to open a new market for the sale of the surplus bananas.[72] At this stage, no one could have predicted how fitting the banana motif was for Miranda's career; the actress and entertainer would later declare, "I make my business with bananas!" and was forever after associated with the tutti-frutti hat and the banana extravaganza of *The Gang's All Here*.

The release of *Banana da terra* was anticipated with great hype in the media for several weeks before its début, including publicity spots highlighting the star-stacked cast of the film that brought together Carmen Miranda, Dircinha Batista, Oscarito, Almirante, Bando da Lua, Castro Barbosa, artists from the Urca Casino, and Romeu Silva's orchestra. Dircinha Batista (1922–1977) had been elected "Samba Queen" at the Casino Atlântico in January 1939 and is mostly remembered nowadays for the many Carnival songs she made popular. Having previously starred in two of Wallace Downey's films, *Alô, alô, Brasil!* and *Alô, alô, carnaval!*, with her striking looks, pronounced dimples, dark curly hair, and fabulous singing voice, she was a great addition to the cast of *Banana da terra* and justifiably received top billing immediately below Carmen Miranda. While Miranda is constantly featured in publicity shots wearing her *baiana* costume, Dircinha appears dressed in a typical Tyrolese costume, complete with striped knee-high socks, dungaree shorts with bold heart and flower designs, a large neck bow, wide puffy sleeves, and the signature Tyrolean felt hat and feather, which seems to have been in fashion that year given its popularity in newspapers and magazines.[73] Aloísio de Oliveira, making his acting début as a Don Juan, plays opposite Dircinha. Just as Miranda co-opted the *baiana* costume and incorporated it into her repertoire, Dircinha, dressed as a Tyrolean, recorded "Tirolesa" (female from the Tyrol), a *marcha* by Oswald Santiago and Paulo Barbosa that became a great Carnival hit that year. Most importantly, as the publicity slogan indicated, the musical comedy was "gleefully carnivalesque" (*carnavalescamente alegre*), boasting a quick-paced, light-hearted plot with smooth sequence transitions throughout.[74] The film captured the Carnival spirit of the season with the latest musical hits of the moment. A week before the film premiered at the Metro Cinema, the press emphasized the appeal of the songs and the technical perfection of the filming, pointing out that the studio had used the same equipment as that used for the Brazilian version of *Snow White*; in other words, this was a feat of the latest technology. The film's music was praised with superlatives that referred to the "very note-worthy repertoire" (*repertório notabilíssimo*) of the star-stacked musical lineup. Miranda was repeatedly praised for her beautiful number "O que é que a baiana tem?" According to the newspaper reports, this song was one of the film's main attractions and was constantly highlighted in the press with accompanying photographs from the scene. Miranda featured prominently in her *baiana* costume, its appeal romanticized in the media by repeated reference to its similarity with a dress that Miranda had apparently gifted to the popular French actress Annabella when she had visited Rio a few months earlier. The pull of Hollywood stardom cannot be underestimated as Brazilian cinema was slowly getting off its feet. Annabella had just finished filming *Suez* (1938), costarring her soon-to-be husband Tyrone Power, also a popular Hollywood star in Brazil. After touring the country to promote his latest film, Power had given interviews in Hollywood that, according to *Diário carioca*, had increased the popularity of Rio's Carnival.[75]

Regardless of whether there is a direct correlation between Tyrone Power's promotion of Brazil in the United States and the number of visitors arriving during Carnival, North American tourists traveling down to Brazil on the *Normandie* had apparently reserved five hundred places for the great ball at the Urca Casino on the Saturday of Carnival (Lee Shubert would be among these guests).[76] Miranda's performance at the Urca Casino was part of a series of carnivalesque shows put on specifically for tourists coming to Rio during Carnival. The Urca Casino and the Casino Atlântico were vying for these out-of-town guests' patronage, so both venues claimed to be the most authentic carnivalesque spot. Publicity materials for Casino Atlântico, illustrated with images of a *baiana* and a drum-playing Pierrot, claimed, "There is no Carnival outside the Casino Atlântico,"[77] while Urca Casino heavily advertised in several newspapers that their carnivalesque evenings were specifically welcoming to tourists arriving aboard the transatlantic ocean liner *Normandie*.[78]

At the same time as *Banana da terra*'s release, Miranda was appearing nightly at the Urca Casino, and the film's advertising drew on this to strengthen publicity by emphasizing the importance of the "artists from the Urca Casino" in the film. A large announcement that appeared in the *Diário carioca* five days before the film's release reads: "The Casino da Urca Artists are kept very busy in *Banana da terra* . . . and all obey the objective set out by the happy producers: to entertain."[79] The Metro Cinema typically only projected MGM films made in Hollywood, and the publicity made much ado about its screening a Brazilian film, albeit an MGM-Brazil production, "to pay homage to Brazilian cinema, but also to offer to the public in such an appropriate period a spectacle that captures the flavor of the moment."[80] *Banana da terra* opened simultaneously in Rio, São Paulo, Petrópolis, Santos, Recife, Porto Alegre, Bahia, and Belém do Pará, but in Rio the Metro Cinema had exclusive rights to the film for the first sixty days and ran seven shows daily hoping to lure patrons with the added luxury of its air-conditioned theater and comfortable seats.[81]

Concurrently to Miranda's performance in *Banana da terra*, Miranda and Araci Cortes were starring in parallel shows; while Miranda was at the Urca Casino, Cortes was the greatest attraction at the Casino Atlântico, where she appeared on February 8, 1939. On February 10 the *Diário carioca* published a photograph of Araci in a *baiana* costume, and the accompanying copy praises her as "the victorious star of the stage and radio" in whose voice "samba comes alive, with spontaneity, intention and maliciousness" (2). Fitting with the festivities of the season, the article makes reference to Cortes's bringing carnivalesque enthusiasm and vibe to the stage, with the public unable to resist singing along with great gusto. These examples of Carmen Miranda and Araci Cortes are without doubt the most illustrative of the *baiana*'s prominence as a carnivalesque figure in the summer of 1939, but they are not the only ones. The newspapers were packed with *baianas* in a variety of venues to the point that there is barely an issue of a Carioca daily that does not include photographs of a *baiana*. For example, printed photographs of Carnival balls at the Alhambra cinema featured *baianas*, children dressed as *baianas* were photographed in street celebrations, and the Cinédia studios' February 1939 Carnival release, *Está tudo aí*, dressed the actress, singer, and main star of the film, Deo Maia, as a *baiana*.[82] Carmen Miranda's *baiana* of the Urca Casino stage later became the most broadly known and mythicized of them all, but it is important to remember that during Carnival 1939, Miranda's *baiana* was part of a vogue that encompassed stage, screen, and festive gatherings that all adopted the *baiana* costume amidst the celebratory ethos of the season. Given the omnipresence of the *baiana* throughout the city, what Lee Shubert perceived in Miranda's captivating performance was representative of this *baiana* vogue. The *baiana* had already become a most important Carioca cultural symbol, with all its inherent racial, social, and class complexities, and it was soon to be indelibly linked to Carmen Miranda.

Miranda's last appearance in a Brazilian-made film was *Laranja da China* (1940), an oversimplified musical in which the producers seemed to have lost all interest in an appealing plot and no longer even sought the pretense of keeping together a storyline, preferring to merely juxtapose Carnival hits one after the other. *Laranja da China* incorporated archival footage Miranda had filmed for *Banana da terra* the year before, as by then she was already in the United States. The film's newspaper advertisements frequently mention Miranda's success in the United States while still claiming her as the greatest national broadcasting artist.[83] Carmen Miranda's celebrity status continued to grow, as she provided meaning and significance for Brazil's contemporary culture even after her departure. Miranda had derived her first collective fan base from her Brazilian celebrity power, which had consecrated her as a megapopular star and set her at the height of her career, optimally placed to captivate a greater, international audience.

CHAPTER TWO

PERFORMING RACE

*Miranda and Afro-Brazilianness
on the Carioca Stage of the 1930s*

On February 15, 1939, the powerful Broadway impresario and theater owner
Lee Shubert arrived in Rio on the cruise ship the *Normandie* and spent the evening at the Urca Casino, one of the most sought-after venues for tourist groups
wanting to take in the best of Brazilian entertainment during their stay at this
port of call. This particular evening was the scene of the much-romanticized
and celebrated encounter between Lee Shubert and Carmen Miranda: Shubert
watched Miranda perform her *baiana* routine backed by her supporting all-male
band, Bando da Lua, and was immediately sold on the uniqueness of the performance and her charismatic stage persona. Her vivacious facial expressions,
entrancing dance movements, and electrifying singing more than made up for
the Portuguese language barrier: Carmen Miranda was the exotic novelty act that
Shubert needed for his forthcoming Broadway show *The Streets of Paris*, scheduled to open in late spring.

Beyond reconstructing the different developments surrounding this meeting,
critics have focused on this event as Miranda's chance encounter with fame. As
such, and without undermining the significance of this meeting at the Urca
Casino, this springboard to Miranda's North American success has overshadowed
the racial implications and ramifications of Miranda's *baiana* performance on the
Urca stage at this crucial juncture in her career. As a stereotypical embodiment of
Afro-Brazilianness in the Carioca theatrical and carnivalesque tradition, Miranda's
performance of the *baiana* is a racially charged signifier set against the backdrop of
a society in which the notion of race was at the forefront of intellectual discussions,
the concept of a modern nation, and cultural representation. What did it mean
from a racial point of view for Carmen Miranda to interpret the *baiana* in the late
1930s, given in particular its explicit referent of Afro-Brazilianness, along with
its use as a Carnival costume predominantly, but not exclusively, by lower-class,
black, and mixed-race persons? In this chapter I discuss Miranda's white *baiana* as a
performative parallel or analogy of the "whitening ideal," which remained instilled
in the cultural narrative of the Brazilian elite from the late nineteenth century
through the 1940s.

Racial Whitening: Setting the Stage

When Miranda performed her *baiana* on the Urca Casino stage in early 1939, she was one of Brazil's most beloved singers, actors, and entertainers. Enormously popular and widely revered throughout the country, her popularity crossed all racial and social divides. When scholars persistently celebrate Miranda's stylized *baiana* as the starting point for her northbound success without consideration of the racial dynamics of the Carioca stage and society of the time, they quiescently misinterpret the origins of the lady in the tutti-frutti hat. The whitened version of the quintessential icon of female Afro-Brazilianness that Miranda performed for an elite Brazilian and foreign audience was an emblematic performative representation of the sanitized Brazilian racial politics of the 1930s that simultaneously embraced and suppressed racial diversity.

Rather than promoting a greater acknowledgement and acceptance of racial diversity that would represent the will to move the country forward toward racial equality in the aftermath of abolition promulgated in 1888 in Brazil, the leading intellectuals and public figures of the following generations consolidated their position of white racial hegemony. The issue of race, particularly after the First World War and through at least the end of the 1940s (and perhaps even into the mid-1950s), was viewed as a national problem insomuch as Brazil perceived whiteness as its passport to emulate the more "civilized" countries of Western Europe, with whom it had mobilized as a result of its participation in the war, and was prompt to attribute its supposed backwardness to the nation's racial composition.[1] While on the one hand there was an intellectual movement toward coming to terms with Brazil's racial diversity, which brought to the forefront the complex task of no longer ignoring racial difference, on the other hand this awareness ultimately gave way to a widespread tendency to simultaneously acknowledge and contain blackness under the contrived appearance of a white, civilized Brazilian nation of the future.[2] Given these conflicting attitudes toward racial awareness and acceptance, the topic of race was constantly included in public addresses, intellectual debates, and publications with the view of dispelling race-based fears by labeling and minimizing the impact of Afro-Brazilian culture within the national configuration. It was a period of re-evaluation of the "whitening ideal" that evolved from an acceptance of scientific racism (couched in a language of racial superiority and inferiority) to a belief in "ethnic integration" (whereby the hope of a future white nation would come about by a process of assimilation through which Brazil would naturally grow whiter) (Skidmore 207–8). The assimilationist mantra carried over to the most significant black movements of the 1930s, which rallied around the *Frente Negra Brasileira* or FNB (Brazilian Negro Front, 1931–1937) and whose primary focus was black integration into a white society and adherence to its values.[3] These integration ideals became the essence of a political-rights movement through the actions of the FNB and beyond. Even in the state of Bahia, with a higher percentage of mixed-race and black population, the goal of assimilation and acculturation remained widespread and was accompanied by a general tendency toward passive accommodation among the population of color. The conviction that Brazil was entering modernity as a white nation went part and parcel with the endemic social and cultural displacement of blacks in Brazil, masked by declarations to the contrary that claimed positive inclusion of Afro-Brazilians and proffered symbolic forms of racial integration. The whitening process was a paradigm that enabled the social critics and intellectual leaders to distill fears of miscegenation with claims that were often accompanied by statistically proven studies as a racial safety net.

Nonetheless, miscegenation was such a widespread phenomenon in Brazil that it was impossible to deny its reality and impact on Brazilian society as a whole. As the sociologist Donald Pierson concluded from his fieldwork conducted mainly in Bahia in the mid-1930s, "miscegenation has gone on in Brazil in an unobtrusive way over a long period of time. In few places in the world, perhaps, has the interpenetration of peoples of divergent racial stocks proceeded so continuously and on so extensive a scale" (119). It is against a backdrop of tense racial anxieties that the Northeastern sociologist Gilberto Freyre produced his voluminous study *Casa-grande e senzala* in 1933, later translated into English as *The Masters and the Slaves*, a sympathetic historical overview of race relations in Brazil stemming from the harmonious intermingling in close proximity of plantation families and their slaves. Freyre's vision of Brazil corresponded with the new intellectual vogue that accompanied the fundamentals of Vargas's neo-Republic to mold Afro-Brazilianness into an expression of national identity. In his second major work, *The Mansions and the Shanties* (1936), Freyre illustrates his enthusiasm for Brazil as a cultural melting pot—whose ultimate products are enriched by racial, social, and class interactions—through references to samba that channel the raw product of Brazilian blacks, "rounded into something more Bahian than African, danced by Carmen Miranda to the applause of sophisticated international audiences" (qtd. in Vianna 62).

Before Freyre, only a few isolated scholars had worked on the ethnographic presence of Africans and their descendants in Brazil: Sílvio Romero, Nina Rodrigues, João do Rio, and Manoel Querino are among the most prominent researchers from the late nineteenth century through the first decade of the twentieth century to prepare the way for the first period of substantial intellectual debate around the concept of race in 1930s Brazil.[4] Furthermore, Freyre's text did not appear in isolation, despite its undeniable prominence at the time and from then on. Freyre's text eloquently articulates Brazil's racial melting pot, and although the expression "racial democracy" is not explicitly used in Freyre's text, it is from this seminal work that the concept develops to become Brazil's official stance on race relations for years to come.[5] It was in the wake of Freyre's discussion of the nation's ethnic diversity that Brazilian racial dynamics were promoted as harmonious and equitable, "a solved problem," according to sociologist Nelson de Senna in 1938 (qtd. in Degler 6), often set in stark contrast to US race relations.

Although racism *per se* is not a term commonly used by social critics to characterize this period, the underlying reprivileging of the whitening ideal and the conflicting opinions emerging from the nationalist cultural vogue following the Week of Modern Art held in São Paulo in February 1922 accumulated in the need to address the meaning of race in Brazil, which was often synonymous with refuting fears associated with markers of blackness. Despite its apparent celebratory nature and its acknowledgement of the growing recognition that Brazil was a multiracial and multicultural nation, Freyre's text was in essence only a variation on the still widely popular belief in the whitening of the nation. It is not without due cause that the disclaimer "myth" was soon added to this notion of racial democracy, which served to mask the concept's racist undertones that had been conveniently glossed over for several decades. In *The Masters and the Slaves* Freyre emphasizes the hierarchical nature of cultural relations within a hybrid and presumably harmonious society, with maximum profitability from the native cultures for the benefit of the more advanced people (83). Because of the timing of the publication, the widespread racial uncertainties, and the growing awareness of the need for a cultural national identity that would embrace all racial differences, *The Masters and the Slaves* prolonged the longevity of the whitening ideal as the nation's official discourse through the portrayal of an easily acceptable, mythological racial equality. Within clearly defined limits, the book articulated for a wider reading public Brazil's new appreciation of the racial dimensions of its own past while presenting diversity in terms of a white hegemonic future steeped in optimism and national pride, enriched culturally but not dominated by gains from contact with the black or indigenous populations.

Intersections of Race and Culture

By the mid-1930s the importance of Brazil's racial diversity was undeniable. Given the prominence of Afro-Brazilian cultural expressions, the compromise that emerged was a trend that embraced whitened, racially marked practices in order to resolve the representation of blackness on a national scale. Of particular interest is how racial politics of theoretical inclusion yet literal exclusion translates into cultural representations of race.[6] It is as though the "weight" of the African inheritance is eliminated by a movement toward a hybrid cultural representation of Brazil that fits with both the lingering whitening ideal and the recently articulated racial democracy through a rearticulation of a white-dominated hegemonic discourse.[7] However, the hybridity of Brazilian culture was accepted under specific restrictions that promoted whiteness as the main voice of popular music and in the performing arts while embracing Afro-Brazilianness through the themes, techniques, and genres produced within the confines of this hegemonic white dominance.

An outward celebration and inclusion of Afro-Brazilianness is inherent to Brazil's cultural richness, yet blackness, especially during the 1930s, was frequently masked behind the sanitizing white articulation that obliterated the black body proper while drawing from this diversity. The myth of racial democracy, expanded from the social sciences to the performing arts, becomes "a speech act that enunciates itself through white-authored representations of black experience"

(Isfahani-Hammond 5); a speech act that plays with the art of dissimulation, displacement, and erasure; an act of performative racial "cannibalism" that draws its essence from the very richness that it usurps. This is what I refer to as *performative race*. It is the intrinsic value of race in a staged setting, whether formal or informal, theatrical or nontheatrical, intentionally representational (in a mimetic Aristotelian way) or non-representational.

Miranda's performance of race is invested with power as it draws from the appearance of racial hegemony but ultimately reaffirms white supremacy. Miranda's appropriation of Afro-Brazilianness and black racial markers consolidates the performativity of racial identity by framing her co-option as a racialized discourse. Because Miranda is a privileged white performer, she has access to these racial crossings: she concomitantly legitimizes her *baiana* by drawing from this racial identity while reinforcing her own white subjectivity as a performing artist.

As with all forms of representation, even in a postmodern reading it would be difficult to isolate the performance of race from other epistemic notions of power and knowledge, including the racial dynamics that exist in the social life from which it stems and the contemporary racial issues with which it necessarily enters into dialogue and that bear on its interpretation. If, as Crook and Johnson indicate, "notions of race are socially and historically constructed [and] constitute discourses which are relative and subject to conflictive interpretations" (4), the same can be said of the performances of race on the stage: they are located temporally and geopolitically and marked by hyper-performative frames of reference that surpass the stage.

Miranda's *baiana* plays safely within this established matrix of power, without challenging or exposing other boundaries of corporality. Because Miranda appropriates blackness from within these "regimes of regulatory production" (Butler 17), her mise-en-scène of Afro-Brazilianness is acceptable for the white elite producers and audience of the casino stage, with a respectful gesture toward the cultural richness from which it stems. Set against the backdrop of the myth of racial democracy and the covert re-emergence of the whitening ideal, Miranda's *baiana* stage persona conceals and dissimulates—to paraphrase Butler—the conventions of Brazilian popular culture and the performing arts. The symbolic nature of her performance corresponds to Butler's "reiterated practice of racializing interpellations" (18). Reading Miranda's *baiana* from this perspective brings us to question the performative nature of race, which can be co-opted and disguised in a specific sociopolitical, historical, and cultural context. In this we see the interpellation of race performed, similar to how gender, sex, and sexuality contain a performative value.

A racial reading of Miranda's performance is particularly essential during the late years of her Brazilian career, taking precedence over concepts of gender and class, although all are present and interconnected. Once Miranda moves to New York, the very essence of her racialized stage subjectivity is, while not entirely eradicated, substantially modified. As I discuss in subsequent chapters, gender and playing with gender norms become prominent in her newly formed image. Yet during the Brazilian phase of her career as a quintessential racialized figure, it is impossible to deny the theatrically construed projection of race embedded in Miranda's *baiana* alongside other performance strategies of the 1930s Brazilian stage.

Black Performers on the Stage

It is an unfortunate yet undeniable fact that most of the discussion about race in Brazil stems from white intellectual writing and discourses rather than from the general public or minority voices. The reasons for this lopsided view are understandable, since they parallel the dominant voices of academia at large and the racial biases of Brazilian society. Notwithstanding this blind spot, since society's racial dynamics carry over to the performing arts, to approach the situation and circumstances surrounding black performers on the stage it is necessary to understand the racial issues of difference and discrimination Afro-Brazilians have faced in society.

That social discrimination did exist is evidenced by the creation of Negro-rights movements from the beginning of the 1920s into the 1960s, although they were mostly weak and short-lived, lacking in funding, efficient organization, political experience, and leadership. The apparent cordial coexistence, interracial tolerance, and mutual exclusion provided weak grounds for reconfiguring racial relations with a view to greater democratization of the social order. The acceptance of the racial system and the perceived security, dignity, and equality, with the caveat of greater openness, provided little traction to modernizing Brazilian race relations.[8] The better known of these organizations was the above-mentioned self-proclaimed political group Frente Negra Brasileira, founded in 1931, whose motto was "Only we Negroes can feel the color prejudice that exists in Brazil" (qtd. in Fernandes 206) and whose primary goal was to speed up the full integration of the Negro into the social order. In Rio in 1935, prominent intellectuals Arthur Ramos and Edgar Roquette-Pinto sponsored "The Brazilian Movement against Race Prejudice," along with the drafting of documents calling for a greater racial consciousness, such as the "Manifesto against Racial Prejudice." It was only in the following decade with the Constitution of 1946 that an official stance would be adopted that included a statement prohibiting racial discrimination. Likewise, in 1951 the Brazilian congress passed a law, known as the Afonso Arinos Law, officially prohibiting discrimination based on race or color in public places. However, both initiatives were perceived mostly as symbolic gestures with no government enforcement of penalties.[9]

In the aftermath of abolition and throughout the first half of the twentieth century, despite the lack of official discrimination laws, blacks were banned from certain venues, and as a newspaper in São Paulo pointed out, "outlawing color prejudice, as the [1951] bill intended, would not remove the historic barriers to the entrance of Negroes into certain places" (Degler 127).[10] Thales de Azevedo's research, published in French in 1953 under the title *Les élites de couleur*, confirmed the unofficial yet widespread racism against blacks in Bahia, where their entrance and acceptance in social clubs remained a thorny issue dependent on social status. The more elite clubs would accept blacks who were "socially white." As the venues became more modest, the racial barriers became less apparent, and the proportion of mulatos and black associates increased (T. Azevedo, *Les élites* 91).[11] However, if the "socially white" phenomenon opened doors and opportunities in Bahia, this was not the case in Rio or São Paulo, where racial barriers held certain middle- and upper-class venues off limits to the colored population.

Given this situation, in the southern urban centers, such as the cosmopolitan cities of Rio and São Paulo, a parallel form of entertainment known as the *gafieiras* emerged, which functioned as exclusively black nightclubs (Pinto 2). There were also clubs for recreational and literary purposes that attest to the lack of cultural and intellectual integration felt by certain groups of the colored population in Brazil: unable to join mainstream groups, they opted for parallel forms of entertainment and enrichment. As Pinto explains (with debatable optimism), a slim minority of blacks could individually cross the color line and penetrate white society by emulating certain behaviors, since formal discrimination in terms of institutions and laws did not exist (262). This is a form of "social race," a concept Charles Wagley coined to refer to the social hierarchy that dictates a person's situation based on both color and class (qtd. in Degler 105).

Brazilian society has long denied the existence of racism, and this race-blind positioning has delayed the formal inauguration of antidiscriminatory practices. By preferring to represent its social integration as a harmonious, multicultural melting pot, Brazil has diffused the outlets to fight for significant racial equality and justice. The phrase "cordial racism" is appropriate for these circumstances, given the difficulty of confronting racial issues and discrimination in a country where the official discourse denies their very existence. Race was not considered a quantifiable factor on a national scale through the 1930s, as exemplified by the absence of the category "race" on the censuses of 1910, 1920, and 1934 (Fernandes 59).

In general, it has been commonplace to distinguish racial relations in Brazil along a north-south divide, with, as far as these attitudes can be determined, the northern societies demonstrating less proclivity toward racism than those further south. Using late-1930s São Paulo as a case study, Arthur Ramos observed that the further south one went, the more keenly the Negro felt his/her minority condition (174). On the stage, this situation gave rise to two very distinct phenomena. On the one hand, because of greater racial prejudice in the societies of Rio and São Paulo, there were fewer chances for black actors to participate in theatrical shows. On the other hand, because of the existence of this prejudice, it was in these cities that groups challenging the racial status quo emerged and formed the first Negro groups; likewise, it was in these cities that the most prominent Negro leaders came forward to raise their voices in opposition to racial discrimination. These racial dynamics parallel the close proximity in which these populations intermingle differently according to the region, dating back to the slave period when Northeast Brazil was structured around the plantation house as society's economic, institutional, and social core. In stark opposition to Freyre's description of harmonious racial cohabitation, other critics, such as Fernandes, later denounced this appearance of social equality, claiming, to the contrary, "all such contact developed within the most thorough, rigid and unsurmountable racial inequality" (178–79). Since official social segregation was not recognized in Brazil, this likewise sustained an apparent nondiscriminatory and equal society for all, within whose boundaries each group knew how to behave.

During the 1930s, set against the complex racial dynamics as detailed above, it is not surprising that racial discrimination carried over to the performing arts and restricted opportunities for blacks to perform on Rio's stages. Notwithstanding the deep-rooted racism that plagued Brazilian society, blackness was becoming central to defining Brazilianness. Blackness, while not typically expressed by Afro-Brazilians through their performance in mainstream venues, was central to the cultural expression of Brazil. Social practices until the 1950s prohibited blacks from performing on the stage, yet white performers and stage directors often drew from their talent as musicians and composers, progressively validating their importance in the entertainment business and opening new doors and possibilities for the Afro-Brazilian population in this milieu.[12] The whitening ideal that permeated Brazilian cultural representations was reflected in the performing art venues in Rio such as the theaters, the music halls of the very popular revue theater, and the casinos, where the racial dynamics paralleled the divides present in society and provided a collective catharsis for racial tensions to be expressed, suppressed, and dominated. In the performing arts there is a visual representation of racial difference that speaks loudly about the stigma and marginality of blackness on the stage. This widespread prejudice remained inherent to the Brazilian form of inclusion and celebration of blackness in the incipient mass media, which, as in the United States, represented what bell hooks has called "a system of knowledge and power reproducing and maintaining white supremacy" (117). In general, the black participation in Brazilian theater was limited to backstage hands or carpenters rather than actors as part of the spectacle. The darker the skin, the fewer possibilities there were, a situation that from all points of view echoed the racial hegemony of Brazilian society during the first half of the twentieth century. For women, opportunities beyond singing or dancing were scarce, and for the most part the female stars of the theater or recording industry were also white and rarely recognized as composers in these industries that "placed severe limits on women, especially Afro-Brazilians" (Hertzman 125). Among the rare exceptions was black actress and singer Ascendina dos Santos, an acclaimed success at Rio's Carlos Gomes Theater beginning in early 1926.

During the late nineteenth century and in particular from the 1920s on, the heart of Carioca stage entertainment was the *teatro de revista* (revue theater), an authentic genre of Brazilian vaudeville or variety theater that evolved into a "triumphant expression of Brazilian music, dance, stereotype, and cultural pride" (Williams 11). Discussing racial divides on the stage during the first decades of the twentieth century, Brazilian historian Salvyano Cavalcanti de Paiva explains that Afro-Brazilians were rare occurrences on stage since white audiences preferred white women playing the roles of mulatas and at times resorting to blacking up to represent blackness (284). This situation was similar to the *teatro vernáculo* (comic theater) in Cuba during the nineteenth and early twentieth centuries, although to a greater degree of popularity and impact: in Cuba, blackface as a theatrical tradition was far more widespread, with some notable actors crafting their entire career on the genre, and as such it paved the way for the movement commonly referred to as *Afrocubanismo* of the 1920s and 1930s.[13]

Stereotypical roles and limitations of blacks in the Brazilian revue and mainstream theater were maintained throughout the first half of the twentieth century, often resorting to excessive burlesque representations that were "anxiously repeated" (Bhabha 95) to fuel the expectations of a prominently white audience and dispel all racial fears. Among the few exceptions to this general trend was the very prominent mulata Araci Cortes, who earned the moniker of the "reigning mulata queen" of the revue theater.

It is not surprising that given the limited opportunities for black actors and playwrights on the main theatrical stage, the first all-black revue company, the Companhia Negra de Revistas (Black Revue Company), was formed in 1926 and, a few years later, inspired the São Paulo–based troupe Companhia Mulata Brasileira (the Brazilian Mulato Company). The company's success fell short of its expectations as sectors of the Brazilian press drew a marked distinction between the grotesque performances of local companies and the ultra-civilized performances of stars from abroad. As Orlando de Barros explains, for white audiences, black Brazilians on stage did not project the "authenticity" of foreign black theater performers (292). Lisa Shaw discusses this lack of "cosmopolitan allure" of black Brazilian theater performers, concluding that "a token Afro-Brazilian presence on the popular stage could traditionally be tolerated, but not a troupe composed almost entirely of those of African descent" ("What does the *baiana* have?" 96). Only in the 1940s would several theater groups be relatively more successful to make room for black actors in the arts. After several aborted attempts in São Paulo and Bahia, Brazil's first black theatrical group, O Teatro Experimental do Negro, or TEN (the Negro Experimental Theater), was created by the Afro-Brazilian actor, writer, and activist Abdias do Nascimento in Rio in 1944, soon followed by the group Teatro Popular do Negro (the Negro Popular Theater), initiated by Solano Trinidad. Central to the mission of these groups was the need to rectify the paucity of racial diversity on Brazil's theatrical stages and reverse the limited roles and negative stereotypes that were reserved for actors of color. However, although created as a reaction to the lack of Negro actors on Brazilian stages, an important by-product of these initiatives was the impact of TEN beyond the stage, as the group ultimately exceeded its original purposes and became a symbol of ideological pressure.

The above summary is essential to our discussion of race on Rio's stage: whereas the creation of Negro theatrical groups, with some more prominent and longer-lasting than others, began to increase in the 1940s, until this period, and during the time that Carmen Miranda was one of the main stars of Rio's nightlife, actors of color on the stage were few and far between, and even rarer were Afro-Brazilian activists of the caliber and projection of Abdias do Nascimento.

There were a few exceptions to this general tendency, and because a handful of actors were able to cross the color divide, it enabled the media and a predominantly white public to interpret their success as truly exceptional talent, independent of any racial characterizations. These black actors, such as De Chocolat and Grande Otelo, were pigeonholed in comic-relief roles from which they would never escape. The stage names of these two artists are in and of themselves explicitly charged with societal significance folded in with humor, which parallels their roles: the "de" designation of royalty in "De Chocolat" (*of* Chocolate) and the reverse epithet of Grande Otelo (Big Othelo) drawing attention to his short stature.[14] Grande Otelo and De Chocolat's success illustrates the widespread conviction that "failure to rise is a consequence of individual inadequacy and not discrimination" (Degler 199).[15] Whether in a socio-economic context or a cultural setting, and within regional and urban/rural variations, despite empirical data, what is evident through these examples is deep-rooted racial discrimination, which escaped overt codification through the mask of racial democracy but points ultimately to the same conclusion that Brazilian society is upheld by the stilts of discrimination that permeate social relations throughout the country.

The Whitening of Afro-Brazilianness for the Stage

When Carmen Miranda appropriated the Afro-Brazilian *baiana* as her stage persona for the Carioca scene, she participated in a trend coined by Susan Gubar as "racechange," a concept that corresponds to "the traversing of race boundaries, racial imitation or impersonation, cross-racial mimicry or mutability, white passing as black or black passing as white, pan-racial mutuality" (5). In Miranda's case, the assimilation of this Afro-Brazilian image through her white performance was part of an incipient process of modifying cultural traditions for what would become a new national purpose: the whitening of Afro-Brazilianness for inclusion in Brazil's image of modernity. This cross-racial mimicry is charged with a political and social awareness that contains the potential, as phrased by Garber, "to disrupt, expose, and challenge, putting in question the very notion of the 'original' and of stable identity" (16). As discussed in Chapter 1, with its début in the late nineteenth century, by the 1920s the *baiana* was a well-established theatrical type of the revue theater, mostly performed by white actresses until the above-mentioned mulato actress Araci Cortes appropriated the figure and became synonymous with it. Barros mentions how there was something slightly "off" about the white *baianas*, which costumes and makeup attempted to conceal most of the time. However, he explains, "with the arrival of Araci Cortes, the character found the perfect embodiment, since the actress had the ideal physique for the part" (in the original French, "*physique de rôle*") (29).

During the late 1930s, and within the circles that Miranda performed, she knew that she could safely draw from the essence of Afro-Brazilianness: Miranda was a famous, white, beloved singer and performer whose charisma and talent had opened many doors and enabled her to cultivate a following of ardent fans across racial divides. Her mimicry of Afro-Brazilianness enabled her to access a wider public and thus increased her marketability, all within the "safe" zone of performative whiteness.[16] Miranda's *baiana* was part of a whitening movement in vogue at the time, and as an artist living her success in the moment without the perspective that can only come with hindsight, it is possible that neither Miranda nor her producers fully grasped the politics of the whitened *baiana*, all while navigating the established racial norms of the theater.

The whitening of Afro-Brazilianness for mainstream cultural representation points to racial privilege and inequalities, discrimination and segregation, projected in the innocuous medium of the apparently democratic forum of the performing arts and other cultural displays and social venues. This form of appropriation and commodification is a "cannibalistic" act that serves as a cultural illustration for both the whitening ideology and the mythical racial democracy. From the first part of the twentieth century until the 1970s, when the myth of a racial democracy was boldly exposed and a tendency toward re-Africanization ensued, the expressions of Afro-Brazilian culture in Brazil moved "toward the progressive loss of African cultural forms and the 'whitening' of Afro-Brazilian culture through progressive admixture, or 'syncretism' with other traditions" (Brown 213). Miranda's *baiana* was far from an isolated case of racechange, as exemplified in the transformations of such widespread practices as the Umbanda religion, capoeira, and samba. In the case of Umbanda, the whitening came through a synthesis with European (Catholic) rituals. Capoeira as an ambivalent martial art/dance/game evolved by incorporating other forms of sports or martial arts, such as boxing and jiu-jitsu, and integrating white (mostly male) participants, as it increasingly became an expression of cultural hybridity (L. Reis 44–45). Samba followed a similar whitening trend toward achieving the status of national music; ultimately, the type of samba produced prominently in Rio de Janeiro became the country's national symbol.

The "whitening" and appropriation trend of black music by white singers during the 1930s in Brazil is comparable to the major change that came about in the United States at the turn of the twentieth century when, as Sotiropoulos comments, "white audiences coveted black music and black dance—in effect, black style" (238). With the radios, recording companies, live performance halls, theaters, and press monopolized by white directorship and owners, 1930s Brazil was dominated by white voices singing black sounds and black musicians selling their sambas to mainstream performers. This societal imbalance was also the norm in Cuba, as Robin Moore discusses, pointing to a musical labor divide along racial boundaries (17). In the 1930s in particular, during the *Afrocubanismo* movement, African borrowings were perceived as a form of musical blackface (Lane 89). In Brazil, and most particularly in Rio, this commodification of black culture prominently affected samba, both its music and dance form, which progressively became more popular as samba lost its stigma and took prominence over the foreign-bred foxtrot and tango.

Emblematic of this appropriation of black music are the lyrics of Miranda's 1930 samba recording "O nego do samba" (Black man of the samba), which juxtapose the innate talent of the black population to dance the samba against the awkwardness of the white population, reflecting the infiltration of white people into the *terreiro do samba*, an Afro-Brazilian space.[17] The fact that Miranda—a white singer of European descent—recorded the song adds an additional layer of interpretation to the complex racial crossing of her performativity. It is as though she is so readily accepted within the Afro-Brazilian community that she speaks on their behalf and joins them in looking at the white, failed attempts to imitate this Afro-Brazilian form of samba dance, taking on the role of an honorary black performer.

Whereas Brown sees this process of cultural whitening as a form of denigrating African culture and traditions, Letícia Reis interprets the interaction between black and white cultural practices as a dynamic that is not a polarized but a reciprocal interaction (52). Considering Miranda's co-option of Afro-Brazilianness from the perspective of the circularity that Reis describes emphasizes the interchanges between the artist and the Afro-Brazilian community that she embraces. Miranda's fan base was race-blind: her performance held appeal for both the white elite and the black population. As Miranda portrays Afro-Brazilianness through her performance, rather than "denigrating African practices," she draws from this iconic *baiana* figure to project this image to a broader public. Although it could be argued that Miranda is likewise participating in this ongoing "deAfricanization" (Brown 217), the interchanges between her performance as a voice for black Brazilianness and what she gives back to this cultural community in the form of projection and, ultimately, national and international visibility represent more accurately a circularity of exchange. From this perspective, Miranda's performance promoted blackness of sound, manner, and appearance, and, by embodying these aspects of Africaneity, blackness was able to become part of a hegemonic cultural experience.

In a society not yet collectively open to accepting black artists on the stage, it would be inappropriate to view Miranda's performance as displacing or replacing blackness in the arts. Miranda embodies and incorporates blackness through her performance and gives a powerful expression to a voiceless community through her status as a white, privileged artist. Miranda was able to cross all racial boundaries from early on in her career. While she was on tour with her costar Almirante in the state of Recife, a newspaper article emphasized Miranda's closeness to the black race by referring to her as "the charming interpreter of the soul of race through the samba and the songs of the *morro* (hill)."[18] Given that Miranda's performances were a celebration of popular traditions and sounds, she legitimized popular music for all audiences, regardless of color or class, and opened the way for other artists to join in this musical gentrification and promote a new acceptance of this popular music that she also validated.

At the height of her career, Carmen Miranda held several long-term contracts at the Urca Casino and performed intermittently there from 1936 until her departure in mid-1939, over a period of three and a half years. As a white *baiana*, Miranda brought Afro-Brazilianness to the stage with all the outward appearance of racial inclusiveness and without crossing the racial dictates of the casino setting.

Miranda's embodiment of the *baiana* was a "cleansed and sanitized" performance for an upper-class Carioca and foreign audience. The casino space can be perceived as a "space of whiteface," as coined by Gwendolyn Foster, a space where representation "demands class-passing, class othering, giving up ethnic identity to become white" (51). This dual dynamic of embodiment and displacement makes Miranda the site to incorporate blackness through the white body.[19] In Miranda, several racial tendencies are at play: the simultaneous erasure, disavowal, and appreciation of Afro-Brazilian culture, echoing the attitudes of some of Brazil's upper classes, who both fear and are fascinated with Afro-Brazilian culture and its expressions. Miranda's interpretation of Afro-Brazilianness for an exclusive public corresponded to several simultaneous requirements of the time: the inclusion of black diversity without the "object" of otherness itself. This gives the audience the illusion of experiencing inclusion and diversity while remaining safely at a distance from authentic Afro-Brazilianness, considered inferior within their view of a stratified society in which blacks do not mingle socially with the white upper classes.

Miranda perfectly fit the bill for the Urca Casino: as she was a talented, attractive, vivacious, white female performer, the visual quality of her performance sent out a message that already at this stage held appeal for a foreign crowd, as the encounter with Shubert would later illustrate. The casinos in Brazil (and throughout Latin America) were privileged venues for travel encounters, with shows geared to an elite crowd of foreign and national visitors. Since the desired crowd at this exclusive locale was highly selective, the casino entrepreneur and manager Joaquim Rolla knew it was essential to project the image of an ultra-civilized world of Brazilian entertainment. This premise therefore raises the question: what aspects of Afro-Brazilianness were acceptable for a white *baiana* to project at the casino?

Carmen Miranda's stage show embraces the cultural representation of Afro-Brazilianness on many different levels that contribute to the overall performance of race. As Coelho writes in the most thorough reading of Miranda's Africaneity, her performance is a total act that relies on the use of expression, language, song, and the movement of the face, hands, and body. Given the completeness of the image, he likens Miranda's sambista role to an Afro-Brazilian storyteller who transmits the culture and essence of the community she has come to represent through her performance (13). Miranda's performance style resembled those of comic actors who used exaggerated facial expressions while engaging intimately with the audience, as did Miranda with her signature eye rolling and asides (Coelho 76).

As discussed in Chapter 1, one of the most significant components of Miranda's staged Afro-Brazilianness is the donning of the stylized *baiana*. Along with her dress, the lyrics of her songs, the culture she evokes, and the choice of samba itself as a genre, she also performs race by incorporating phonic signifiers of blackness. These phonic signifiers are certain interjections that appear as a form of endearment and that authenticate her song, coupled with phrases and language loaded with slang. As is well known, Miranda grew up mingling daily with black culture. At her parents' boarding house in the district of Lapa—a neighborhood with an important Afro-Brazilian presence—black musicians, composers, and singers were frequent visitors. Miranda's multicultural and multiracial experience and her social and cultural awareness were honed during these formative years as she created her own identity by navigating the different social groups, classes, and races, interiorizing some norms and rejecting others.[20] She greatly admired many of the Bahian composers, and as her career progressed, she was both personally and professionally interlinked with Afro-Brazilian culture. During Miranda's time as a radio star before becoming a live stage performer, her voice was often mistaken for a black voice: her appropriation of blackness through language authentically projected her as possessing the culture expressed by this register of speech. In a postcolonial reversal, the most illustrious Brazilian entertainer, invested with white, European glamor and social status, aimed in all ways to mimic the language of the socially marginalized black community. Her command of this linguistic form of black performance became part of her signature act on the Brazilian stage, and she was able to very naturally incorporate "black talk" in interviews, live programs, and often spontaneously in sound recordings. The incorporation of these linguistic markers of race enabled her to Africanize and to authenticate her Afro-Brazilian song.

The relationship between race and nation is complicated further as these linguistic factors and performative content coalesce in popular musical performances. What do we understand as black cultural practices in the Brazilian context? What is "black music" in the Brazil of the late 1920s and 1930s? Carmen Miranda, along with three other prominent white performers who represented Brazilian music both nationally and internationally, namely Francisco Alves, Mário Reis, and Carmen's sister Aurora Miranda, "quickly became part of a most sought-after circle of performers, although they relied almost exclusively on Afro-Brazilian idioms to help revolutionize Brazil's national music tastes" (Davis, *White Face* xxiii). In Carmen Miranda's performance, we witness the white performer's cannibalization of a black text: her casino repertoire, written almost entirely by Afro-Brazilian composers, most of whom were from Bahia, only reinforces the paradox between what is camouflaged—black authorship and black reality—and its white representation. In Miranda's case, as with the above-mentioned performers, the performance trends of the time promoted what Joseph Roach calls "surrogation" along the routes of the circum-Atlantic triangle: the theatrical principle of substitution of one persona for another, either by standing in for the other or playing more than one role (54–55).[21] Miranda oscillates between both modes of surrogation, standing in for the Afro-Brazilian composer/singer she represents and through which blackness is dispersed into white speech, and doubling as Afro-Brazilian herself through different degrees of black makeup, which adds another layer to ventriloquizing Afro-Brazilianness, another degree to her performative race.

The representation of Afro-Brazilianness on the stage for a predominantly white population was made possible by certain performative strategies. Humor was one of these strategies: Miranda's performance toyed with the subversion of racial, gender, and societal norms in a satirical and humoresque manner as she provocatively sang of black taboo themes and took on the *mulato* or black narrative voice. As she was a white, popular singer, a middle- or upper-class white audience may or may not have known whether to take her at face value, but the intrinsic performative nature of her art, coupling pretense with all levels of seriousness, gave her the license to sing and advocate for popular music at her will. In this I agree with Davis's assertion that Miranda "never begged audiences to value popular music but rather demanded it in humorous ways, or more accurately aggressively claimed authority very often associated with humor" ("Racial Parity" 189). Her open racial and class "passing" added another layer of complexity to her performances and allowed her to revisit stereotypical images of nationhood and blackness through her preferred form of humoristic and satirical sambas.

Blackface (along with its more subdued corollary brownface) was another such performative strategy that enabled Miranda to appropriate Afro-Brazilianness on the stage through its visual materialization. It held international currency for an elitist white audience and, ironically, bore the American trademark of modernity, as did the importation of jazz or the Charleston to Rio's dance floors and music halls. In Miranda's case, the whitening of Afro-Brazilianness is complicated further by this intriguing practice: Miranda's performances in blackface.

Women Blacking Up: Miranda, Blackface, and the Brazilian Stage

In the summer of 1939, the Brazilian press created great anticipation around the release of *Banana da terra*, Miranda's fifth Brazilian film, focusing on Miranda's performance as the *baiana* and her "Pirolito" (Lollipop) dance. The text in *Diário carioca* on January 19, 1939, emphasizes with superlatives the Brazilianness of the film, "*celuloid brasileiríssimo*," and refers to Miranda's "Pirolito" dance as one of the film's most "delightful and mischievous" moments, giving creative credit to Miranda and her dance partner, Almirante (7). A few weeks later, on February 9, 1939, the same newspaper published an advertisement for the film with accompanying photographs that feature both Miranda and Almirante, explicitly marketed as the show's stars, in blackface. The ad makes reference once again to the "Pirolito" dance as one of the film's "most amusing segments." *Banana da terra* proved indeed to be a resounding success at the box office and stayed in theaters across Brazil for several months. In a letter to Almirante, João de Barro mentions that the film beat all the box office records at the Metro Cinema where it was showing, and in the eleven cities where it played it apparently brought in 208 *contos de réis*—almost seven thousand dollars—in only three days (qtd. in Cabral, *No tempo* 141).

The varied accounts of the filming of the Miranda-Almirante segment have focused on the last-minute substitution of Ari Barroso's music with that of an unknown composer at the time: Dorival Caymmi. The many versions of the story concur that Barroso's unreasonable request of five *contos de réis* for each song, the equivalent of $500 for both pieces in today's currency and far more than the usual royalties, forced the producers to replace Ari Barroso's songs (Castro 169). Wallace Downey decided to substitute "Na baixa do sapateiro"

(In the shoemaker's hollow) and "Boneca de pixe" (Tar doll), respectively, with Caymmi's "O que é que a baiana tem?" (What does the *baiana* have?), which would work with the same Bahian backdrop, and a *marchinha*, in vogue at the time, titled "Pirolito" (Lollipop), by none other than João de Barro—the film's director—and Alberto Ribeiro. As a consequence, and thanks to these chance circumstances, Caymmi's song "O que é que a baiana tem?" became a hit overnight, and Miranda embarked on a lifetime career as a *baiana*: after filming the *baiana* segment to this song, Miranda continued to use Caymmi's composition as part of her act at the Urca Casino. There she performed the song accompanied by Aloísio de Oliveira and the boys of the Bando da Lua, who were to be forever associated with Miranda, from Urca to Broadway and on to Hollywood.

Most of the above facts seem undisputed in the different accounts of the film's production, despite the lack of information about Miranda's performances. As Miranda's costar, the singer and composer Almirante, recalls years later in his column "Cantinho das canções" (Little corner of songs) in the newspaper *O dia*, the two main songs that involved Carmen Miranda were Ari Barroso's "Na baixa do sapateiro," for which Carmen dressed as the *baiana* in a church scene, and "Boneca de pixe," also by Ari Barroso, which was originally slated for the Miranda/Almirante duet and for which they were "dressed in character and in blackface, in a simple office" (qtd. in Cabral, *No tempo* 137). Ruy Castro's version differs slightly: he states that the backdrop for "Boneca de pixe" depicted slave quarters, and the setting for the "Na baixa do sapateiro" *baiana* scene recalled a street in Bahia, with a painted moon, houses, and coconut trees. This description seems to correspond with what is visible in the film segment included in Helena Solberg's documentary *Bananas Is My Business*. Both the slave quarters and the Bahian street scene represent settings spatially removed from Rio (and in the case of the slave quarters also historically distant), fitting with the then popular trend of representing a romanticized, stylized Bahia as conducive to projecting "authentic" blackness. Ruy Castro indicates that Carmen was to appear as a "crazy black woman" (*nega maluca*) wearing a checkered dress and scarf, and Almirante was to be dressed in a large white jacket and bowler hat (169). The expression "nega maluca" is used specifically for blackface and was frequent during Carnival. The song "Pirolito" was part of a new dance craze that had taken over Rio at the time, but it had nothing to do with blackness or racial difference.[22] Since the film *Banana da terra* is lost other than Miranda's "O que é que a baiana tem?" segment, we can only speculate whether Almirante and Miranda retained the blackface routine in the movie despite the last-minute song substitution or simply removed it without updating the Associated Press.[23] Nowadays it may appear rather unusual to arrive at such a late point in the production of a film without finalizing the financial details of the music. However, in the 1930s filming resources were few, re-takes were expensive, and the producers had most likely presumed, in good faith, that the composers of the songs would request royalties within the usual price range. As Dorival Caymmi mentions in the oral history he recorded at the Museum of Image and Sound (November 24, 1966), everything happened so quickly that, despite the music change, the producers left the stages and costumes as they had originally planned (qtd. in Cabral, *No tempo* 139). It seems plausible that both of Ari Barroso's songs were cut from *Banana da terra* at the last minute, and the producers had to replace "Boneca de pixe" with "Pirolito" and "Na baixa do sapateiro" with Dorival Caymmi's hit début "O que é que a baiana tem?"

The song "Boneca de pixe" (Tar doll) had quickly become a staple of Miranda and Almirante's repertoire. According to an article in the newspaper *O correio da manhã*, a public of over two hundred thousand people went to the annual Rio trade fair "Feira Internacional de Amostras" on January 4, 1939, designated as the fair's "Popular Music Day," to watch a musical show in which the costars sang "Boneca de pixe" for a very enthusiastic crowd.[24] Miranda and Almirante had recorded the Barroso/Iglésias composition in late August 1938, and it is most probable, as was the custom, that they had already performed "Boneca de pixe" together at other venues around town and on live radio shows to build anticipation for *Banana da terra*'s release. Despite the song's removal from the film, they also performed "Boneca de pixe" among other hits in February 1939 while on tour in Campinas, São Paulo, after the film's completion. A local newspaper refers to their performance of "Boneca de pixe" as "the most popular music of the past few months . . . an electrifying sambinha."[25] After the drama surrounding the last-minute elimination of Ari Barroso's songs from *Banana da terra*, it is rather ironic that both songs would be included in Cinédia's Carnival release *Está tudo aí* (It's all there, 1939), which premiered in Rio only a few months after *Banana da terra*. According to a review in the *Diário carioca* on February 23, 1939, Cinédia studios contracted Ari Barroso for a film score that included some of his great Carnival successes, including "Boneca de pixe" and "Casta Suzana" (Chaste Suzana). Deo Maia, a beloved singer and radio star, took top billing in the cast and also appeared wearing a *baiana* costume at one point of the film, as featured in the publicity materials. It was Deo Maia's first film, and she received highly positive criticism from the media for a role that seemed tailor-made for this budding mulato actress who interpreted this signature song opposite the actor and comedian Apolo Correia.[26] This much-discussed composition also featured in another Cinédia production, *Joujoux e balangandãs* (Trinkets and lucky charms), based on a homonymous musical revue by the playwright Henrique Pongetti and released December 1, 1939.[27]

The motif of "Boneca de pixe" draws from a Brazilian folktale in which a banana-stealing monkey is caught when he is attracted to a dark black doll whom he mistakes for a young girl and of whom he becomes enamored. The *boneca de pixe* (meaning tar doll, also spelled *piche*) is a popular figure that has remained in the Brazilian cultural imaginary as a mystical, presumably female, black doll. Brazil's tar doll is comparable to the standard types that minstrelsy produced in America, such as Jim Crow, the plantation darky Sambo, or the urban dandy Zip Coon, in that the *boneca de pixe* became part of Brazilian popular folklore as an easily recognizable figure, and from there it transitioned into mainstream popular culture through Ari Barroso's composition in 1938.

Carmen Miranda in brownface with her singing and dancing
partner Almirante at the Odeon theater, São Paulo (February
1939). Courtesy of the MIS/Rio de Janeiro

The song "Boneca de pixe" is a playful, catchy, and upbeat tune that points to
the dynamics of the minstrel or blackface shows in which race is characterized as
an amusing, lighthearted element of difference. Although other, mostly female,
artists performed variations of this musical composition, Miranda is remembered
as most closely identifying with this theatrical figure and was the first to record the
song. As is often the case with most performers in blackface, we can only speculate
about Miranda's personal thoughts and feelings about this technique, as she left no
public pronouncement, and biographers have preferred to skim over this aspect
of her performance. However, the blackface technique aside, it is significant that

Miranda not only recorded the song but appropriated so fully the tar-doll persona that she left correspondence signed in this name.[28] She was *the* tar doll ("boneca de pixe"), and as such it is not surprising that, according to *Life* magazine (May 1939), when she sailed away to Broadway, "500 Rio swains reportedly sang a favorite song: 'Boneca de pixe'" (29).

The practice of blackface in Brazil harks back to but distinguishes itself greatly from this practice in the United States. Blackface as a theatrical strategy enjoyed tremendous popularity during the nineteenth century in America and exemplifies Du Bois's reading that the cultural identification of African Americans at that time "restricts their representation to that of a problem in American society" (Fontenot 5). The same can be said of the 1930s in Brazil when, as detailed above, race was at the forefront of political and intellectual discussions. Racial politics of the stage, as articulated through blackface performance, reinstates the theater as a site of representation endowed with power, promoting the "hegemonic unity of an elite, while masking the material exclusion" (Lane 3). The typical consensus on blackface minstrelsy as a postcolonial stage convention is the commodification of an already enslaved, noncitizen people, coupled with a cultural expropriation, which is itself an expression of power (Lott 15). Many scholars read blackface as a form of bigotry that transmits negative stereotypes and reinforces white racism. Pieterse discusses how minstrelsy was a populist and anti-emancipatory theatrical strategy that poked fun at urban blacks just as they were becoming more assimilated into mainstream society in dress, mannerisms, and speech (134). For instance, in Cuba, blackface performance was a means to articulate *mestizaje* as a national ideology, displacing blackness to reinstate a white racial norm (Lane 143).

While most critics condemn blackface because of these reasons, Eric Lott's study has the merit of drawing attention to an antinomy of responses, on the one hand the disdain for blacks and the use of black culture as a racist ploy, and on the other hand a celebration and liberation of this same black culture (17). Given what we know about Miranda's view of the Afro-Brazilian community and culture, there is no doubt that she was conscious of the racial differences embedded in performance politics and was an ardent fan of black cultural expressions, especially music.

By the turn of the century, the demand for large minstrel shows was waning in the United States with the rising popularity of musical comedies and vaudeville, leaving only a few opportunities for black stars and blackface performers such as Bert Williams, Ernest Hogan, and George Walker. In Brazil, the practice of blackface was less common but certainly more complicated than its US counterpart, given the country's complex racial composition. Whereas in the United States there was cultural, political, social, and historical baggage connected and articulated through the use of blackface, in Brazil there was no similar tradition, and blackface could be considered a foreign practice—an urban, modern, Harlem Renaissance tradition copied and imported from the United States, similar to renditions of jazz that were featured as imported products made in the USA. There were very few occurrences in Latin America in general, and in Brazil, blackface was not a typical

Brazilian tradition, with the exception of a new practice in the northern region of Ceará.[29] While blackface was not popular in Brazil, as Roberto Ruiz illustrates, it was a known practice since the 1920s in the revue theater, where jazz numbers were imported along with blacking up in revues such as *Guerra ao mosquito* (War on the mosquito, 1929) and *Diz isso cantando* (Say it with songs, 1929) (156–58). In some cases, Brazilian stage directors and film producers notably travelled abroad and saw some of the lingering blackface shows featured in cities such as Boston, Chicago, and New York. The cowriter of the above-mentioned musical review *Diz isso cantando*, Oduvaldo Vianna, had travelled to the United States a few months before staging the revue and been inspired by the blacking up in Broadway shows that he had seen (Coelho 76). In Vianna's revue, Araci Cortes starred opposite a white actor in blackface, João Martins, to sing "Boneca de pixe" (Ruiz 156).

Beyond these international trips, I would argue that the transnational cultural exchanges were rather fluid in the international entertainment world, especially with the success of cinema. Blackface was common knowledge through the films that were featured throughout the country and was (still is) considered a familiar US stage convention. In *Cinearte*—the prominent Brazilian movie magazine comparable at the time to Hollywood's *Photoplay*, which served as its model—every film that was screened in Rio was reviewed and rated, and among these reviews and photographs are found the occasional references to blackface: some to rather obscure films that have long been forgotten (such as the German silent sports movie, *The Boxer's Bride* of 1926, where Willy Fritsch blackens up) and others to the very memorable films of Al Jolson and the silent-film star Madge Bellamy, who appears in the film *Mother Knows Best* (1928) impersonating Al Jolson singing his signature tune "Mammy" in blackface (Barrios 53), or Fred Astaire in blackface for the first and last time in the amazing dance number "Bojangles of Harlem" in the RKO hit *Swing Time* (1936).

As the above example indicates, women featured occasionally in blackface, in a form that Marjorie Garber views as "cross-cross-dressing," a cinematic representation that "conflated women and blacks as 'boys,' social children, high-spirited but not wholly grown up" (278). In Brazil, there is an added level of "crossing over": the international border-crossing element that brings with it the notion of foreignness, imitation, and mimicry. Similar to the popular-entertainment tradition of "putting-on" racial characteristics as a source of humor in multicultural societies, which William Mahar dates back to the late eighteenth century (331), Miranda's use of blackface, set within Brazil's ethnic melting pot, aligns itself with this humorous appropriation of another's culture through appearance, dialect, and speech patterns. All these layers of understanding are implicit in Miranda's use of blackface when this theatrical strategy is considered a practice imported onto the Brazilian performing landscape.

The engendering of the performance is an important and intriguing aspect. In the deeply gendered domain of the traditionally male-dominated minstrel theater, cross-dressing male actors would perform the female roles, thus emphasizing the parody of the act. Even in a modern film such as Irving Berlin's *This Is the Army* (1942), the female characters in blackface are played by men in feminine costumes.

Women in blackface are rare, and only a few have stood out in performance history—most notably, one of the first female groups, Three Sable Sisters, who performed from 1844 to 1848 at different New York venues, and, in the twentieth century, Sophie Tucker, the most famous vaudevillian to perform in blackface.[30] Although the Brazilian tar doll is labeled female in its designation and is presumed as such in the *boneca de pixe* tradition, there is a gender-neutralizing quality to the black mask. As Mahar indicates, "minstrelsy was generally as ambivalent about gender as it was about race" (343), and this is certainly the case in the tar-doll role: Miranda's checkered dress and headscarf reinforce the femininity of the masquerade and provide the needed female markers to engender the enactment. The Miranda and Almirante duet also worked as a mainstream cinematic and stage segment because both stars were well known and easily recognizable *white* singers and entertainers even in blackface, whether or not they were shown actually in the act of "blacking up," as was so often the case, to assure the film audience that the cast was, against all fears, really white (Stark 76).

The sequence of stills from the above-mentioned article in the *Diário carioca* on February 9, 1939, projects gestures and expressions that portray a feeling of playfulness, perhaps even the childlikeness that Garber referenced above. A correlation between clowning and blackface has always existed, and some writers assume that American blackface developed out of clowning (whose present mask, as Lott writes, is clearly indebted to blackface). For Stark, the use of the parodic clown "to mimic, to mock, to ridicule guided the minstrel show, giving a smiling face to white racism" (16). In the case of the "Boneca de pixe" performance, the clowning/blackface affinity is evident. Most of Miranda's performances are neither carnivalesque, as theorized by Bakhtin, nor subversive, but progressively more camp, as I discuss in Chapter 5. However, an exception to this is the "Boneca de pixe" blackface routine, which is primarily comic, perhaps even burlesque, as can be seen in the images that remain, and projects a tone of playful racial subversion.[31] This segment adds an additional level—the carnivalesque—to Miranda's performative race, so it can appropriately be labeled the "carnivalizing of race" (Lott 21). The overall impression of this performance is a playful toying with race and fantasy represented through the reenactment of the tar-doll trope. This gives us good reason to presume Miranda and Almirante performed this material with their signature vitality, and, as is typical of blackface performances, the material was presented directly through a short, straightforward performance, mimicking the lyrics.[32]

The mise-en-scène of "Boneca de pixe" bears some resemblance to the comic, American antebellum tradition of coquettish flirtation that was often set to the popular song "Miss Lucy Long" (also known as "Lucy Long"), in which male affection is displayed toward a woman who is depicted at times as desirable and at others not, making the singer (the banjo player) the butt of the joke.[33] The Brazilian act was written as a duet with a dynamic to-and-fro between two singers, yet unlike traditional "Lucy Long" numbers, "Boneca de pixe" presents Miranda, rather than a cross-dressing male, in the female role. Davis compares the Miranda/Almirante duo to the 1930s US "blackface" radio show *Amos 'n' Andy*, "except neither of the US actors grew up being so intimately influenced by Afro-diasporic traditions" (*White Face* 79). The comparison is certainly valid to the extent that it emphasizes the staging of a comic pair of entertainers, in either literal (in the case of Miranda and Almirante) or phonic (Amos and Andy) "blackface" performances. Previously, as Stark writes, blackface performances consisted of two men, a banjoist with a dancer or singer, and were featured at the circus or between acts of a play (17). Popular entertainment has given us many similar examples of modern duos, such as Stan Laurel and Oliver Hardy, Chico and Harpo Marx, etc., yet this tradition of the performing duo is the extent of the comparison between Miranda and Almirante and *Amos 'n' Andy*, since the different genres, forums, and content of their messages are more distinct than they are similar. McLeod cautions against the most common tendency among radio critics and social historians to consider *Amos 'n' Andy* as merely a new twist "on the timeworn foundation of blackface minstrelsy," which she views as an extreme oversimplification of the actual content of the radio program that "also overlooks other factors that influenced . . . their work, ranging from popular comic strips to the day-to-day experiences of their own lives" (7). A careful reading of the show reveals an entirely self-reliant black community, devoid of faceless black characters, used to broadly parody the conventions of the white world.

The Miranda/Almirante routine brought together both aspects of the traditional blackface routine: vocal music and comedy. The playful number can be glimpsed through the sequenced snapshots that show Almirante and Miranda gaily dancing around as a pair of carefree, grown-up pickaninnies who have dressed the part. This comic-filled, staged performance nonetheless represents the subordination of blacks and blackness in Brazil and uploads to the Brazilian silver screen the first nationally produced blackface routine. As such, this musical number resonates with the overwhelming whiteness of films produced and exhibited in Brazil's movie theaters: Miranda and Almirante's blackface emphasizes demarcations of racial categories and underlines the racial bias of the cinema. As Butler writes in her discussion of Nella Larsen's novella *Passing*, "what qualifies as a visible marking, is a matter of being able to read a marked body in relation to unmarked bodies, where unmarked bodies constitute the currency of normative whiteness" (170). Miranda and Almirante play off their own "normative whiteness," the common currency on their performance sets, where through their blackface they interpret the over-privileging of whiteness on a stage steeped in racist bias. As was the case with the traditional northern minstrel shows, blackface permits role-reversal and identification, and the Miranda/Almirante duo play with these principles of masquerade by becoming their black alter egos. The blackness provides a blanket of concealment, which "in embracing blackness, . . . interpolates black alterity and utters itself to be a blackless subject" (Conner 65). Miranda's tar doll is a case in point. It is a fun-fueled performance that, albeit at the expense of blackness, fits within the register of make-believe and draws from the well-known Brazilian tar-doll folklore that Ari Barroso's hit song repopularized.

The lyrics of Barroso's "Boneca de pixe" are worth noting, since they emphasize the black-on-white dynamic by drawing from motifs of personal preference and choice. At one point in the song, the *nego* (black man) expresses his love interest in the tar doll, and she returns the sentiment by agreeing "you are black and your taste / no one challenges this / but there are a lot of whites / with painted faces." The song toys with images of blackness with terms such as *azeviche* (jet black or carbon) and *jabuticava*, which is the fruit of the *jabuticabeira*, a tree of the myrtle family, but also another word for black woman. The lyrics emphasize the blacking up through expressions such as *nego de branco* (white negro) and repeated reference to whites in blackface. The fakeness of the blackface creates a level of dissimulation that makes the tar doll appear all the more intriguing.

The blackface component is intrinsic to the *boneca de pixe* image, as was immediately perceived following the release of the hit song that was further popularized by Miranda and Almirante's performances around town despite its being pulled from the film. For the parades of 1939, the Carnival group "Chaleira" from the city of Iguape in São Paulo presented three floats with one designed around the theme of *boneca de pixe*, including a gigantesque blacked-up doll. Dancing and singing duos over the years have recreated this hit song; even comedian Grande Otelo had his own series of *boneca de pixe* performances with actresses such as Josephine Baker (1952), Virginia Lane (1973), Betty Faria (1979), and Xuxa (1991).

The cultural context and the racial implications of this practice by one of the most illustrious performers of the day are intriguing. While Miranda's use of blackface provides an interesting inlet into the racial politics of performance during this period, it also denotes how attached to race was the concept of culture. Carmen Miranda is one of the main voices (on the radio) and artists (in live performances) who expropriates and benefits from this black Brazilian cultural capital.

With a lack of archival sources and sketchy newspaper reviews, it is difficult to know exactly when Miranda used blackface and when she opted to discard it, and even more so to comprehend the public's reactions to the show. In the case of Miranda's *boneca de pixe* routine, the song was an immediate hit, and the musical rendition far outlived the blackface strategy that for most critics has passed unnoticed. It is also essential to read the recorded segment in relation to the film genre and its implied audience against the backdrop of a society striving to embrace the newly articulated concept of racial differences. Despite biographical evidence, critics have skimmed over Miranda's use of blackface, preferring to focus on her white Africaneity without critically engaging with the blacking-up aspect of her performance. However, as the present reading of Miranda's performance emphasizes, the celebratory nature of her donning the *baiana* and her appropriation of blackness, far from discounting Afro-Brazilian subjectivity, brings blackness to the forefront of her creative interpretation, echoing the emergent fascination with Afro-Brazilians and their culture among Brazilian middle and upper classes.

The simultaneous celebration and exploitation of the image shouts loudly about Miranda's whiteness, while at the same time it portrays her (and her producers') understanding and desire to embrace blackness and to try to do so with more than music. However, the use of blackface and the donning of the *baiana* costume operate within two modes of representation and dynamics, and it is important to distinguish between them. The blackface paint, in syntony with Almirante, was used only for their rendition of "Boneca de pixe," as discussed above. It was a short-lived and contained practice that echoed American minstrelsy and the Carioca burlesque revue theater, appearing in Miranda's performances as a refreshing surprise. On the other hand, a subtler skin darkening was used for her appropriation of the *baiana* almost exclusively for "O que é que a baiana tem?" Although critics have been prompt to collapse both uses, they are in fact different, since they are context and content determined. Miranda's facial darkening, which appears in photographs as a shade of light brown, is a sign of Afro-Brazilianness as an extension of her *baiana* costume. Unlike the tar-doll routine, Miranda's *baiana* does not belong to a comic mode of dramatization; it does not aim to caricaturize but to borrow and approximate the already stylized *baiana*, as discussed in the previous chapter.

When Miranda concluded her filming of *Banana da terra*, she was enthralled with her own projection of the *baiana*. Just as she had previously felt the incarnation of the tar doll, she sensed her identification with the *baiana* figure and its imminent success. Even before the film was released, Miranda asked the designer J. Luiz for what would be the beginning of a long tradition: a new creative version of the *baiana* costume. The following details point to her short-lived use of darkened foundation makeup to perform the *baiana*. Dressed in J. Luiz's stylized creation, she performed at the Urca Casino at the end of November and for this act darkened her face. Several months later, during her usual tour of casinos in the State of São Paulo and southern Minas Gerais, she took with her the *baiana* outfit from *Banana da terra* and, for the last time, darkened her face (Castro 175). After she returned from the tour, she discarded this makeup: her natural skin tone would suffice for the remainder of her short Brazilian career.[34] This use of makeup to proximate authenticity is at the origin of some of the most memorable black icons, such as the examples mentioned above. Just as the entertainer Thomas D. Rice had become an "authentic" Negro impersonating Jim Crow in the early 1830s, at least in song and dance if not by true skin color, so does Miranda aim to become the "authentic" *baiana*. The reading of Miranda's *baiana* along the lines of performative race hinges directly on this use and, perhaps more importantly, on the removal of the darkened makeup. Butler defines "realness" as "a standard that is used to judge any given performance within the established categories," and yet, "what determines the effect of realness is the ability to compel belief, to produce the naturalized effect" (129). Miranda's use of makeup to legitimately portray the *baiana* participated in the racialized norms of "realness" connected to this image, that of Afro-Brazilianness. It was an approximation of the *baiana*'s darkened skin that can be read as being "at once a figure, a figure of a body, which is no particular body, but a morphological ideal that remains the standard which regulates the performance, but which no performance fully approximates" (Butler 129). Miranda's stylized *baiana* was this exact embodiment of racialized norms, but it was clear that her interpretation of the *baiana* could never be viewed—or "read," as Butler would say—as authentic: in Miranda's *baiana* the brown facial paint reinforced her whiteness and the performance as an artifice. Her makeup was, as Stark discusses in relation to blackface, "a proclamation of genuine race . . . a 'spotlight' on the issue of race" (18). Miranda could never *pass* for Afro-Brazilian; despite all the components of her performance, her impersonation remained just that, an approximation in which the body performing and the ideal performed appear distinguishable, to paraphrase Butler (129). Since the image embodied would always be a stylized, theatrical *baiana*, the face-paint became unnecessary as Miranda moved further in the direction of presenting her own appropriation of the *baiana*, one that no longer sought authenticity to be validated.

It is significant that the darkened skin color, the most intimate visual representation of race, was the first component of the racialized costume to disappear from Miranda's *baiana*, premonitory of what would become her stage and screen persona in the months to come. Miranda's last season of performances at the Urca Casino (and on occasion at the sister-casino Icaraí across the Guanabara Bay) continued to include Dorival Caymmi's "O que é que a baiana tem?," but there was no mention of darkened makeup. Through this "double" whitening—in relation to the authentic Afro-Brazilian *baiana* and in relation to her own previous performances—she became her own interpretation of the *baiana*, and the blackness that she pointed to did not require the visual aid of theatrical, fake-black skin color. Perhaps more important than her actual (albeit temporary) use of blackface/darkened makeup is this whitening reversal, the removal of the darkened face, a mask that she removed because she could. The racial reversal of the white *baiana* destabilized the black woman as a false site of privilege that needed to be emulated and brought the hegemonic whiteness back to the center of Miranda's performance to seduce an audience whose gaze was filtered through the lens of these same hegemonies. The blackness of the most popular white singer of the day was contrary to the dominant culture, and while blackface can be read as a vehicle to endorse hegemonic norms, the transfiguring effect of the staged blackness had no ontological reality for the white spectators.

Miranda's white staging of blackness was obviously very fitting for the casino forum, but despite the visual "sanitizing" of her image, what she accomplished was a greater blurring of racial boundaries: by removing the most overt marker of difference, Miranda's Africaneity became more fully her own. By using her natural skin color, Miranda collapsed Afro-Brazilianness into her self-same, no longer staging blackness on white subjectivity but, on the contrary, absorbing cultural difference through assimilation. By removing the outward token of blackness, which despite its more reverent appropriation than blatant blackface could still have appeared as leaning too far toward a caricature of the cultural image that Miranda wanted to portray, she positioned herself as an authentic *baiana* in her own right, for which transgressive imitative facial paint was neither appropriate nor necessary. The result was a more sincere representation rather than an attempt to imitate. Her performance would still capture the essence of Afro-Brazilianness through the lyrics, music, and costume, yet by removing the phony skin color, her enactment attained a more real depth, which stood in stark contrast to the hyperblackness of her black-face. In this, her removal of blackening makeup elided the marker of difference. Miranda may also have feared that by appearing in blackface at other venues she was nearing a performance that could be interpreted in the spirit of "grotesque realism," to borrow the expression from Bakhtin's *Rabelais and His World*, which provides the occasion for antibourgeois celebration and whose liberating efforts through degradation would not be appropriate for the Casino audience (18–19).

Regardless of the different interpretations, Miranda and Almirante's performance underlined their whiteness in relation to Afro-Brazilian others. In the case of the blackface routine in particular—a rare example of minstrelsy in Brazilian cinema—Miranda was too personally and intimately a part of the Afro-Brazilian community to even be suspected of poking fun at their racial difference through the mimicking of the facial color. Her songs in Brazil and her personal associations were authentic and real, and blackface contradicted this expression of Afro-Brazilian authenticity. While her performance necessarily resonated with the power dynamics of racial hierarchy and representation in 1930s Brazil, her ventriloquism of African-Brazilian music and culture was a unique aesthetic construction of otherness. Even without the mask of blackface or darkening makeup, Miranda is a perfect example of "a metaphor for one culture's ventriloquial self-expression through the art forms of someone else's" (Lott 95). Miranda's "cannibalization" of blackness can be perceived as a nod in the direction of a racialized performative identity, a subject position that she could exploit as a white entertainer. As Gubar states, whereas whiteness and maleness confer power as well as privilege, "blackness (like femaleness) conveys subordination as well as dependency" (13). The power dynamics remained deeply rooted in Miranda's performance even as she chose her modalities of racial impersonation in such a way as to reinvent the *baiana* figure without breaching performative boundaries dictated by society. Perhaps it was only under these conditions that the subaltern could sing for this particular audience, bringing samba from the margins to the center and placing a masquerade form of otherness at the very heart of Brazilian entertainment. The whitened *baiana* upheld a wider cultural significance that supported the supremacy of whiteness, even more so as her reinvention of whiteness negated Afro-Brazilianness, but this was a formula—white skin, black sound—that made white Brazilian spectators feel comfortable. Through her performances of what would soon become her signature song, "O que é que a baiana tem?," along with innumerous songs that echoed her fascination with Afro-Brazilianness, Miranda represented how much there was to gain from embracing Brazil's cultural diversity, both individually and collectively.

Miranda's casino days coincide with the explosion of black music in Brazil: it was a watershed in Brazilian cultural awareness as exclusion and derision were giving way to the dawning of a new age of proudly multiracial, multicultural Brazil, and even black envy and interracial mutuality. Against this backdrop Miranda's whitened *baiana* reasserted the casino as a white performative space. Yet, on the other hand, we must use caution in our reading of Miranda's Afro-Brazilianness and heed the advice bell hooks offers when she warns against the commodification of black culture by whites, which in no way challenges white supremacy, but rather sees race as "an alternative playground where members of dominating races, genders, sexual practices affirm their power-over in intimate relations with the Other" (23). Is Miranda's *baiana* little more than "the spice that can liven up the dull dish that is mainstream white culture?" (hooks 21), a gratuitous although generous nod toward black culture? It is undeniable that Miranda, already during her Brazilian years as a star, profited commercially from her appropriation of the *baiana*. However, Miranda's transracial crossings, carried out and publicly declared through song, lyrics, gesture, and demeanor, embraced through respect and sincerity the pleasure she found in the performance of racial difference, suggesting that her *baiana* is more than a commodification of otherness. After all, as a radio singer, hidden behind the mask of the airwaves, she was often mistaken as Afro-Brazilian herself. Unlike most of her peers, who would perform on radio shows and in theaters and then perhaps eventually have the opportunity to record their hits, Miranda initially became known through her recordings and only later presented herself in shows and radio programs, which was unusual for this period.

At the same time, when taken out of context, Miranda's signature performance easily detaches itself from the original *baiana*. Miranda's performative race proves that as an artist and entertainer, she was able to assume an alternative racial identity through appropriation and subversion. Despite this essence of Afro-Brazilianness that she embraced, consumed, and "cannibalized" as a form of racialized material, she ultimately also created a new model: her own performative race, one that would thereafter be interpreted no longer as a sign of Afro-Brazilianness but as one of exotic otherness ripe for export. In this we see how race fits into the categories of what Butler perceives as other "regimes of regulatory production [that] contour the materiality of bodies" (17), a category that was superseded by gender and sexual difference as the *baiana* was projected onto North American stages. Indeed, as I discuss in the following chapter, the performative construction of Afro-Brazilianness and blackness so deeply embedded in Miranda's acts disappeared as the *baiana* took to the North American stage, leaving her, from there after, to be remembered as the lady in the tutti-frutti hat, a "Latin" performer rather than an Afro-Brazilian interpreter in any regard, and soon to be representative of all Latin America. As Miranda's signature performance detached itself from the original *baiana*, and Miranda's *baiana* became a distinct entity in its own right, she absorbed, consumed, and adulterated racialized material and created a new model of Afro-Brazilianness ready for export as indicative of national identity.

CHAPTER THREE

STAGING THE EXOTIC

*The Instant Success
of the Brazilian Bombshell*

Staged for Success

When Carmen Miranda stepped off the SS *Uruguay* on May 17, 1939, to join Lee Shubert's cast for his new musical *The Streets of Paris*, she arrived in the midst of a gloomy theater scene with many Broadway shows either closing or suspending their performances each week because of competition with the New York World's Fair, in full swing since late April in Flushing Meadows on the outskirts of the city. For Carmen Miranda the Broadway months were much more than merely a stepping-stone to greater fame in Hollywood; rather, they laid the foundations for her North American star image, which would change very little over her subsequent years as a screen star. The Broadway period framed Miranda's stardom for years to come for a public fascinated equally by her onstage (and later onscreen) performances as with her everyday life. When she arrived in New York, she was a performer at the height of her Brazilian career, and her inclusion in Shubert's musical revue *The Streets of Paris* was sufficient publicity to catapult Miranda to the forefront of the entertainment scene on Broadway.

Several different versions of Miranda's "discovery" variously attribute credit to Lee Shubert; the actress and ice-skater Sonja Henie; the Pan American Airways executive Maxwell Jay Rice and his spouse, former actress Claiborne Foster; or the dramatist Marc Connelly. In reality it was probably a blended effort of all involved.[1] Regardless of the facts of this story, the Shubert contract brought Miranda to the United States, and she remained on his payroll until August 1942.[2]

Building a name for the exotic new Broadway star predated Carmen Miranda's arrival in New York and was mainly facilitated by Jay Rice and Claiborne Foster. It was via Jay Rice that Shubert sent Miranda's contract in late February 1939, and on March 3 Shubert wrote to Rice that he was anxious to have Miranda sign the contract as soon as possible to get publicity started immediately and negotiate the conditions of her band. Miranda signed her contract with Shubert (under Select Theatres Corporation) on March 27, 1939: $500 a week for one engagement, an additional $250 for two simultaneous engagements, with the premise that she could not work for anyone without Shubert's written consent.[3] The role of Jay Rice should not be underestimated. Not only did Rice serve as an intermediary between Shubert and Miranda, but he also spoke in favor of Shubert's contracting Miranda's "boys" to play with her on Broadway. The day Miranda signed her contract, Rice sent a collection of photographs and a few press clippings to Shubert with a note expressing Miranda's concern about the arrangements for her band: "She feels, and *I concur with her*, that it is practically a necessity for her to have them in order to provide the proper background for her type of stuff—at least for an initial period for, considering the unique rhythm and chants peculiar to Brazilian popular music, it would be pretty tough to break in any of our musicians in the States."[4] As this letter indicates, Rice understood the uniqueness of the Brazilian music Miranda would perform in the United States and the importance of being accompanied by her own band to maintain the music's authenticity. From Rice originated the first publicity piece about Miranda, with "facts" that would be repeated countless times in the media, often without further verification, and that established her status as an acclaimed star in Latin America before performing on Broadway. Jay Rice's preliminary material mentioned, among other aspects, that she had been educated in a convent in Rio de Janeiro; was twenty-five years old (when in fact she was already thirty); was the reigning favorite in Rio de Janeiro theaters, night clubs, and radio broadcasting; had made more than three hundred records; and was famous throughout Latin America, particularly in Argentina and Uruguay, having performed nine concert tours which served "to popularize the Brazilian samba and *maxixe* dances in these countries." On a personal note, Rice stated that Miranda "is a good swimmer and goes in for speed-boating and automobiling in a big way. She doesn't diet. Speaks Portuguese and Spanish and three words of English—yes—no—and money."[5] He ended his overview of Carmen Miranda's stardom and biography by mentioning that several Hollywood celebrities had been enthralled with her show, namely Tyrone Power, Sonja Henie, and Annabella. Apparently Miranda, who had previously gifted Annabella with a *baiana*-type dress, also gave Sonja Henie a "typical national costume" with which she took first prize in a Hollywood fancy dress ball: the *baiana* made a splash in Hollywood even before Carmen Miranda's arrival on a Twentieth Century-Fox stage.

This publicity material enabled the US press to build great anticipation around Carmen Miranda's arrival in New York, identifying her as "a Brazilian singer and dancer" under contract to perform in *The Streets of Paris*, arriving in time for rehearsals with "her own troupe of singing instrumentalists."[6] As soon as she arrived, the media established Miranda as a seasoned star in Brazil, "greeted with cheers from critics and audiences ordinarily reserved for long established stars."[7] The press was prompt to emphasize her status as a Brazilian movie star who was eager to go to Hollywood once she learned English.[8] Miranda's immediate success on Broadway leaned on her Brazilian stardom, to reiterate, as stated in a press release by Joe Flynn (the publicity agent for *The Streets of Paris*) that before her inclusion in the Shuberts' show, her "torrid serenades . . . had been known to millions of Latin Americans," where she was "an established entertainer of unmatched fame."[9] As Lisa Shaw rightly states, "the dominant impression given is of a serious artist,

Carmen Miranda on the cover of *CLICK* (November 1939).
Author's collection

with an impressive career in Brazil, whose background is thoroughly respectable"
("Celebritisation" 289).

Carmen Miranda's arrival could not have been more timely: as boldly portrayed with a full-cover, color photograph on the oversized magazine *CLICK* in
November 1939, Carmen Miranda was hailed as "the girl who saved Broadway
from the World's Fair." In the accompanying two-page article, "torrid, infectious,
undulant Carmen Miranda" is represented as the Shuberts' antidote for the drop
in ticket sales, while all other producers despaired (10). To open a new show that
would compete with the World's Fair was viewed as a risky entrepreneurial move,
even on the part of the Shuberts, who were known for their original revues and
were still enjoying the success of *Hellzapoppin'*, which ran for 1404 performances.[10]

Hellzapoppin' was, as Brooks McNamara writes, "an anomaly . . . the madcap comedy, complete with continual pistol shots, hula dancers, fruit tossed into the audience, and men in gorilla suits, was unlike anything that revue audiences of the thirties were used to" (188). *The Streets of Paris* coattailed on the success of this greatest hit show of all time and was likewise produced by Ole Olsen and Chic Johnson, who also performed in the show. Only two other new shows came to Broadway that summer: *Yokel Boy* at the Majestic Theatre, which appears to have been successful, as it ran for 208 performances from July 1939 through January 1940, and the less successful *From Vienna*, which appeared at the Music Box for 79 performances from late June through August. Since the early 1930s, the revue genre—typically a show with a loosely conceived, lighthearted story-line woven around cheerful musical numbers, beautiful girls, brilliant dancing, and colorful costumes and full of witty jokes and repartees—had undergone some drastic changes as elaborate revues and musical comedies were giving way to more socially aware theatrical productions.[11] Despite the general 1930s trend of more sophisticated revues (such as Howard Dietz and Arthur Schwartz's *Three's a Crowd*, *The Band Wagon*, and *Flying Colors* in 1930, 1931, and 1932, respectively), the Shuberts were highly successful with the original revue format, producing zany musical comedies that were all about having a good laugh at gags of the slapstick variety. Musical revues had been the Shubert brothers' specialty for several decades; they were considered easy to produce with few demands on the script and the flexibility to add or remove acts, making them also particularly cheap (McNamara 80).

In its original format, *The Streets of Paris* was a long revue that consisted of twenty-eight scenes divided into two acts, lasting around three hours.[12] This was the first of the new musicals to open in New York in the summer of 1939, making its Boston premiere on May 29 at the Shubert Theatre (as was the Shubert tradition) then coming to Broadway two weeks later. It was conceived in the vein of the highly successful *Hellzapoppin'*, with one reviewer even referring to the show as "'Paris-a-poppen' (sic) with the emphasis on knockabout fooling."[13] However, the producers wanted to take no chances, given the competition with the World's Fair and the usual box office lull during the summer months, so a fundamental difference with *Hellzapoppin'* was *The Streets of Paris'* impressive cast. Herbert Drake, a drama critic for the *New York Herald Tribune*, wrote several reviews of the show, praising its "fine pace and general tone of high geared, smart musical comedy" and defining it as having "all the parts for a musical show in well balanced proportion."[14] For Drake, the slapstick comedians Abbott and Costello were the "big hit of the show," and his summary of their antics gives a wonderful insight into the happenings of the revue, which included pouring water into beds, constant scurrying around, numbers with squashy lemons, grapefruit, and apples, etc.[15] Bobby Clark, a well-known comedian and actor of the Broadway scene, headlined the revue, making his comeback after three years away from the stage, and his shenanigans delighted the critics, who claimed him as "one of America's most beloved comedians."[16] Each scene of the show, in typical revue format, functioned as a humoristic vignette of the laugh-out-loud variety, such as the long, nonsensical dialogue on the importance of mustard for the French, Abbott's accusing Costello of talking like a communist, or Costello's thoughts on women and dating.[17] The show was replete with comedy, stereotypes, a little "off" humor, dancing, and pantomimes, and it brought to the stage several first-time Broadway performers: the above-mentioned comedian "zanies" Abbott and Costello, a trio of dancing sisters from Boston (the "three Boston maids"), and, of course, Carmen Miranda.

The addition of a South American performer such as Carmen Miranda to a French-themed revue may seem odd at first. However, the title of *The Streets of Paris* was fraudulent, and the French connection merely served as a backdrop for a playful extravaganza with a string of burlesque acts, despite the presence of the French actors Jean Sablon and Yvonne Bouvier among the cast to add a touch of authentic flare.[18] The setting of *The Streets of Paris*, as established in the opening number, focused not on Paris but on a "postal card from Gay Paree," warning that parents should keep away the children as the revue might be "a little bit risqué," and nothing is authentic, not even the "phonetic but phoney" French.[19] The French *oh lá lá* factor is woven throughout the show, with references to wild flirtations, bedroom humor, numbers such as the suggestive "History is Made at Night," and the predictable scene in which a respectable American leaves his wife to get her passport photographs taken "Chez Lucien" only to return to find she has modeled with champagne in her hand, a rose in her mouth, and her dress pulled up in a pose that the script refers to as the "Dog's dilemma." In this fast-paced musical revue, characterized by hodge-podge juxtapositions of comedy, song, dance, and pantomime, Shubert was able to bring Miranda into the show by simply adding her number to the end of the first act for a total of six minutes. Aloísio de Oliveira, one of the closest eye-witnesses to Miranda as a dear friend and leader of her band, recalled in his memoirs years later the impression Miranda made on that first North American stage in Boston: "When we walked on stage I realized the magnitude of Carmen's performance. It is not easy to describe what I saw before my eyes. From my position I could observe Carmen and then the audience that progressively became more and more mesmerized by the presence of this young woman, small in stature but she overtook the whole stage before their eyes. . . . There was Carmen as I had never seen her before. The applause was tremendous" (71–72). Even Aloísio de Oliveira lacked the words to adequately convey a description of that opening night.

As the media was prompt to highlight with great enthusiasm, Carmen Miranda was a spectacular stand-alone number to conclude the first part of the show, occupying a place of honor and prominence. As is often the case with musicals, *The Streets of Paris* included a crescendo immediately before the intermission. Initially, the stage director, Eddie Dowling, was not convinced that Miranda should close the first act, having only seen her in rehearsals, where she had scaled back her performance. However, "Lee's stubbornness paid off opening night in Boston, when Miranda, facing a full house, exploded into action" (F. Hirsch 188). Her performance immediately became one of the main draws of the revue, making *The Streets of Paris* the "must-see" show of the season. One critic's appraisal of Miranda's performance sums up the audience's fascination:

Publicity still for *The Streets of Paris*. Carmen Miranda and her band Bando da Lua (Summer 1939). Courtesy of the Shubert Archive

The Streets of Paris opening was a pleasant but not an exciting evening until, at approximately 10 o'clock, six young men carrying various Latin-American musical instruments appeared on the stage and were followed by a vibrant young woman wearing an exotic dress, wrapped with yards and yards of beads, and a turban hat with bananas, peaches, pears and other fruit-stand ware on it. This was the *señorita*, and she proceeded to sing in a soft, throaty mezzo at an astonishing speed. She was of medium height, with red-brown hair and light brown eyes. But the magic of her appeal lay in the degree to which she seemed to be having an enormously good time; that, and in the implication that she loved everybody in general and all men in particular.[20]

Overnight, the unknown Brazilian performer became a singing sensation, as the New York edition of the *Sunday Mirror* recounts the first weekend after the show opened, intrigued by her success: "No one knows why—she doesn't do much; . . . she sings a few Portuguese songs that nobody understands, she rolls her eyes, flutters her hands, wiggles her hips a little—and stops the show!"[21] In contrast to Miranda's subsequent stardom in Hollywood, on Broadway she was recognized and marketed specifically as a Brazilian singer. Her records were sold as the first tie-ins to her Broadway performance, with the Broadhurst playbill advertising three "sensational" records from Miranda's Brazilian repertoire at the inflated cost of seventy-five cents each—the going market value for records was twenty-five to fifty cents.

What was it about Miranda's unusual stage performance that attracted so much media attention and catapulted her to the forefront of Broadway's most popular stars? How did the Shuberts' press agency and the media define her unique and unprecedented performance? Miranda's success drew heavily from the audience's perception of her exoticness. Her stylized *baiana* persona was submitted to a stage acceptance that spectacularized her cultural differences and promoted them as extraordinary, yet beyond the stage it was deconstructed through the merchandising of her signature look to render her foreignness familiar and accessible to all.

The first articles published in the Boston and New York press drew attention to her unique performance, her beauty, and her foreignness, thus feeding the expectations of an exotic performer.[22] While the show was still being staged in Boston, the New York press transmitted news of its success with an emphasis on Miranda's astonishing performance, and the Shuberts, to fuel even greater anticipation, moved the opening date of the show back by a week. The *New York World–Telegram* posted a week before her début on Broadway: "Not yet. But soon. The opening of Shubert's 'Streets of Paris' has been postponed until the evening of Monday the 19. Until then we can only read the out-of-town raves about South America's Carmen Miranda, who wows the roadshow audiences with her *Latin cavorting*."[23] Miranda was already at this stage perceived as a "Latin" star, representative of the general "South American way" of which she sang. Accompanying the *New York World–Telegram* article is an exquisite photograph of Miranda from the waist up in the golden costume that would become her signature Broadway look. The headshot version of this photograph was used as the show's playbill cover in a gorgeous sepia tone and was widely distributed in the media.[24] In contrast to the more vivacious depictions of Miranda during her Hollywood career, this photograph shows her bearing a solemn, downward glance, with eyes half-closed. She is wearing her costume: a harlequin scarf tightly wrapped around her head and adorned with small fruit baskets to the side, necklaces, and large earrings. The overall impression echoes the media's emphasis on her exoticism, beauty, and serious professionalism, an image that would soon be transformed as her fame grew in the United States.

Emblematic of the importance of the new show on Broadway, the famed theater cartoonist Al Hirschfeld at the *New York Herald Tribune* drew a large caricature of the full cast of *The Streets of Paris* that appeared in print on June 18, 1939, the day before the New York opening. This was Miranda's first North American caricature and was typical of the many to follow: she is wearing a spangled skirt, a turban decorated with brims of plants to symbolize the small fruit baskets, large earrings, bracelets, and necklaces, and she is depicted in movement, with a wide, exaggerated smile from ear to ear.[25] The importance of this widely circulated caricature should not be overlooked: Al Hirschfeld's depiction captures the essential details of the Miranda signature look that will remain indelibly linked to her star persona from this point forward.

When finally, after "triumphant weeks in Boston," the revue opened at the air-cooled Broadhurst Theatre on Monday, June 19, 1939, Miranda's success on the North American stage was consecrated.[26] The *Times* featured a photo of Miranda in her dressing room twin-imaged in the mirror and wearing her stage costume—complete with yards of necklaces and bracelets, headdress, shiny bustier, and skirt—with the caption: "A New Star in the White Lights on Broadway." The copy continues below: "Carmen Miranda, who achieved fame overnight in the new musical revue, 'The Streets of Paris.'"[27] Despite the brevity of her performance, the media hailed Miranda as the main reason for the show's success, referring to her as "the rage of Broadway," "the ostensible sensation of the show," and "the biggest theatrical sensation of the year."[28] The *Brooklyn Daily Eagle* colorfully called Miranda the "Inca goddess of good luck to the cast" and the "good luck talisman" in both Boston and New York that would assure the show could not fail.[29] Even several months later, the media continued to discuss the first impressions on Broadway of the previously unknown Brazilian star who "took that opening night audience and wound it around the fingers of her amazingly expressive hands."[30]

Since Miranda was unlike anything Broadway had ever experienced before, her stardom, in part, can be attributed to the novelty of her act, which was closely related to the US audience's perception of her exotic quality. As Marshall explains, "Great works emerge from the break with the horizon of expectation. . . . There is at work in the system of celebrity some conception of innovation and continuous creation of something anew" (68). The *New York Herald Tribune*, like the rest of the press, perceived Miranda as one of the main virtues of *The Streets of Paris*, making reference to her "wriggling personality" and noting that she "does very little but does it so well she is the *outstanding novelty*."[31] This was the Shubert brothers' desired effect. Without knowing exactly what kind of audience-subjectivity Miranda would embody in the United States, they had hoped to capitalize on the exoticism of her performance, so different from the usual North American numbers. Several years later, the *Sunday News* recalled: "Men were dazed and women were disturbed. Everybody came away remembering her staccato and muscular delivery and her bizarre rococo costume. She was different."[32]

It was this difference of their newest and most profitable sensation that the Shuberts' press department attempted to classify and promote most meticulously: they collected newspaper articles that discussed her performance and compiled co-pious lists of quotations under headings such as "her eyes," "her hands," "her hips and torso," "voice" (including her mouth and smile), "language" (and delivery), and a catch-all "miscellaneous" category. This information provided an aesthetic guide to appreciating the qualities of Miranda's unique performance that had made their new star a Latin American sensation on Broadway and had mesmerized audiences nightly at any venue. On many occasions reporters expressed their inadequacy in defining Miranda, as when Russell McLaughlin, writing for the *Detroit News*, states that he "started strong, but finally had to throw in the towel." He writes that there was "enough TNT and night-flares and magnetic mines and armored sledges in those seven minutes to outfit four or five shows. We're a reporter all right, but this is a place where we fall down flat on the job. We can't describe Miss Miranda."[33] The Shuberts' press agency worked the media's perplexity to their advantage in order to amplify Miranda's exoticism and stress the uniqueness of this South American per-former who defied all definite characterization, an aspect that also added a mysterious aura to her star image. Similar to the "list song" format of Miranda's *baiana*, the press attempted to deconstruct Miranda's performance, trying to explain her success by the magic of her eyes, her movements, her dynamic singing. The ongoing challenge to define Carmen Miranda's performance led theater critics to opt for colorful lan-guage and metaphors in an attempt to approximate her performative essence. In the above-mentioned *New York Herald Tribune* article, the drama critic Herbert Drake characterizes Miranda as "quite a sinuous whirlwind in her highly charged way" who is "dark tan and shining with a personality apparently indigenous to Brazil," and he laments she only appeared once in the show to sing "a few monotonously fascinating chants, in Portuguese, perhaps."[34] Reporters tirelessly discussed the brevity and ex-plosiveness of her performances that stopped shows cold, trying to make sense of her meteoric rise to fame.[35]

One of the most comprehensive articles to discuss Miranda's early North American stardom stemmed from an interview conducted in July 1939 by a young Peter Kihss, who would go on to become one of New York's most respected inves-tigative reporters admired for his accuracy, fairness, and detail.[36] Kihss had been a foreign correspondent for the *Times* in Uruguay and Argentina for a year and spoke with Miranda in Spanish. What distinguishes Kihss's column from others covering Miranda's arrival and her first weeks of success on Broadway is the scope of his article, which makes reference to her background, includes a comparative view of her life as an entertainer in Brazil, discusses how she perceives her stardom in the United States, and addresses cultural differences between both countries. Resisting the trend of transcribing Miranda's speech phonetically (a practice that was common among reporters and, while perhaps aiming at faithfully transmitting her speech, ultimately ridiculed and debased the singer), Kihss quotes Miranda's enchantment with the United States and her reception during her first six weeks in the country.[37] From this interview originated the thereafter much-quoted phrase "con movimiento" (or the Portuguese equivalent "com movimento") that Miranda used to describe her singing and dancing.[38]

Along with comments about Miranda's dancing and singing, her costume (with the exposed midriff) was of great interest to the press and added to her much-appreciated exoticism. Herbert Drake refers to her as looking "fabulously like a tropical Tallulah" and makes reference to the overall nudity of the girls' costumes, which "is as much a matter of Irene Sharaff's stunning costumes as anything else."[39] As Gail Brassard writes in her appreciation of Sharaff's work, "The exquisite and unique color sense . . . , the undeniable mastery of the costume in movement, the exactness and delicacy with which she delineated character and supported the actor's craft—all are hallmarks of Sharaff's work" (179). For Miranda's performance "con movimiento," Sharaff's talent to create costumes for dance routines was particularly appropriate. Only a few days after the show's Broadway premiere, *Women's Wear Daily* provided a detailed description of Miranda's fabulous costume that is almost photographic in nature:

> Over an abbreviated bodice that is really a gold lace brassiere with ruffles dropped below the shoulders, are piled innumerable large pearl beads, some in multi-colors, as are the narrow ribbons that draw up the shoulder-ruffles. Wide bracelets, many of them vary between "cuffs" of filigree gold, and colorful beads, and huge gold hoops with a dangle ornament inside the ring, form her earrings. Extremely attractive is her turban draped closely about her head of velvet in multicolor harlequin blocks, terminating at top, in two small baskets filled with the tiny fruits similar to those carried by the fruit vendors of Bahia, of whom she sings in one of her songs. The wide circular skirt is, like the turban, of velvet in harlequin large blocks, suspended from a diamond girdle, posed over a bare diaphragm. Señorita Miranda wears on the stage, as well as off, high pedestal sandals.[40]

The following day, in the *New York Post*, a brief but informative description of Miranda's costume was embedded in an article mostly concerned with Miranda's alleged fascination with American men and New York. Since the vast majority of the existing photographs of Miranda's Broadway performances are in black and white, this description adds an essential element, the fabric colors: the flame-colored bolero jacket of her dress and the red, green, and gold diamond-shaped designs of her long, flaring skirt.[41] One of the few, and perhaps the first, color photographs of Miranda's Broadway performance graced the cover of the *Sunday Mirror*, New York edition, on July 23, 1939. It is a shot of Miranda from the waist up, portraying her fabulous costume, accessories, and open midriff. The color shot shows the gold bustier; green, red, light blue, and golden beads; and a multicolored scarf.

The impact and lasting impression of Miranda's costume is its abundance of colors. One reporter for the *Newark Evening News* succinctly summarized her "look" and demeanor as they met in her dressing room at the Broadhurst as "a brilliant bundle of vivacity in her vari-colored patchwork skirt, her fruit-topped turban and mass of bracelets and beads."[42] This costume made Miranda unconfoundedly recognizable, and she very quickly became a household name throughout the greater New York area. In December 1939, the publication *Where to Go* featured a stunning full-page picture of Miranda in her golden Broadhurst attire laden with yards of beads and bracelets and her signature fruit-turban, with her hands up at neck level, eyes looking upwards, and a wide, glamorous smile. The caption states, "If you don't know at a glance who THIS is, you're obviously so far behind the times."[43] Her hats and turbans in particular had become her signature costume. As implied in a December 30, 1939, *New Yorker* cartoon that pictures two women trying on hats at a milliner's, Miranda was associated with daring hats, quite fitting for end-of-the-year festivities. The caption under the sketch reads, "Come on! Just for fun, be Carmen Miranda!" The date of this cartoon is significant, as it predates Miranda's appearance in the Hollywood films that are generally presumed the source of her widespread hat association. In fact, a few months later, still before the release of her first Twentieth Century-Fox film, Miranda's signature look was so well known that the February 14, 1940, issue of *Variety* referred to it as "the now-familiar Miranda turban headdress."

English and Other "Languages" of Performance

Along with Miranda's trademark appearance, which gave critics much to discuss, the media was quick to focus on her command of the English language, or her lack thereof. On the day of her arrival, and from then on with insistence, the press repeated that barely-off-the-boat Miranda had declared: "I say money, money, money, and I say hot dog! I say yes, no and I say money, money, money, and I say turkey sandwich and I say grape juice."[44] Whether Miranda actually said these exact words or not, this first quote appears intrinsic to the enduring image the press projected of this foreign Latin star thrilled to be arriving in the United States and making a fortune in this land of opportunity. We need to remember that Jay Rice had already conditioned the media to expect Miranda to say "money" as one of the three words she knew in English long before her arrival.[45] This stereotype is reinforced by a presumed follow-up quote reported in the press in reference to this moment of arrival: "Miss Miranda did a few dance steps and turned to an interpreter to pour forth a little Portuguese. The interpreter explained: 'She says everybody who comes to the United States learns to say money.'" Her gaiety upon arriving in the United States is doubled with naive, almost childlike illusions and demeanor: "Nothing could possibly have bothered her this morning. She was convinced she was arriving in a golden land. Fellow passengers said she had been just as vivacious ever since she reached the boat."[46] These "childlike" qualities remained a staple of the media projection of her non-stage appearances, as Joe Flynn writes: "step up and meet La Miranda away from the footlights. The sophistication of her art is nowhere evident. As she rises with flashing smile, to acknowledge introduction, she appears ingenuously enthusiastic, almost naive. The girlishness of her vivacity proclaims her an ebullient, uninhibited child deliciously happy to be the center of so much fuss."[47]

During her time in Boston, one reporter optimistically hoped that she would learn English very quickly and might even "speak American like a Bostonian before the Shubert engagement is over." Apparently Miranda knew only very limited "staple kindergarten vocabulary" with pronunciation flaws such as unnecessary *h*'s in words like "radio-hator."[48] Articles such as the one Michel Mok wrote for the *New York Post* are emblematic of the media's portraying Miranda as a foreigner with broken English and a passion for American men: "When the reporter expressed surprise that she knew English so well, she flashed one of her most engaging smiles and said: 'I know p'raps one hondred werds—prettee good for Sous American gerl, no? Best I know ten Eenglish werds—MEN, MEN, MEN, MEN, MEN and MONNEE, MONNEE, MONNEE, MONNEE, MONNEE!'"[49] As these examples illustrate, "men" and "monnee" were among the few words Miranda apparently repeated for reporters to immortalize, and she was ridiculed for the presumption that these were the "ten" words she knew best. The media never tired of writing mockingly about Miranda's mangling of the English language by transcribing her alleged quotes to reflect her pronunciation, especially her mispronunciation of the dental fricative phoneme *th* and her switching of short for long vowels, and they often further demeaned her as intellectually limited when "learning" new words whose meaning she did not comprehend even when the words were cognates.[50] In particular, the manner in which she pronounced "Souse American Way" had the audience in hysterics, as explained in the *Boston Evening Transcript*: "Three little words of English are about all you'll hear at the Shubert from this vibrant bundle of fireworks. They are 'Souse American Way.' That 'th' is too steep a linguistic hurdle." Once Miranda had been told the meaning of "souse," she allegedly attempted to rectify her pronunciation, but in vain: "I try to say it s-o-u-t-h, but my lips they still say 'souse' and it makes everybody very happy."[51] In retrospect, the *Sunday News* of November 16, 1941, refers to the media's construction of Miranda's early stardom: "The newspapers and magazines blossomed with pictures of Carmen's warm, wide smile and with interviews generously larded with the writers' impressions of her English, which was not only broken but positively pulverized" (72). This degrading use of "pulverized" phonetic transcriptions spanned from the title of the articles to the quotes therein. "Carmen Miranda Loaves America—And Vice Versa" (*Sunday News*, Nov. 9, 1941) and "La Miranda Spikka Da Good Ingliss" (*LA Daily News*, Jan. 20, 1951), published almost a decade apart, show how the media's contemptuous depiction remained a stigma throughout her career, even after she became fluent in the language.

Miranda's projection as an exotic sign through different "languages" of performance was translated by a plethora of colorful, and often inaccurate, assertions in the press. The day after her Broadway premiere, the *New York Times* labeled Miranda the "most magnetic personality" of the cast, who "radiates heat that will tax the Broadhurst air-conditioning plant this summer" and, precipitately, made the assumption she was singing "rapid-rhymed songs in Spanish."[52] This would not be the first reporter to make this mistake of taking all Latin American countries as Spanish-speaking, an error that further emphasized the insignificance of Miranda's lyrics for a North American audience. If this reporter, who presumably saw *The Streets of Paris*, mistook Miranda's singing for Spanish, he or she obviously did not speak the language, and whether it was in Spanish or Portuguese made no difference to the delivery or its reception. For Alberto Sandoval-Sánchez, Miranda had become "such a visual spectacle that the Portuguese lyrics did not interfere with the reception process at all" (38). Miranda's performativity drew from her universal body language, and even when she was singing English lyrics in Hollywood roles, the song choruses often included words devoid of semantic meaning.

Because of this new performance space, and her difficulty with improvising in a foreign language, Miranda's funny snippets were lost on her Broadway public, and she needed to reconfigure the position of the audience due to this breakdown in communication. Since she was no longer able to verbally "hail" her audience, she defaulted to her body language and her facial expressions to convey meaning beyond that of the song lyrics.[53] Unfortunately, there are no recordings of Miranda's performance on Broadway, and to make matters more complex, the songs were either not listed or not listed correctly in the program.[54] The press appeared fascinated by Miranda's movements. The *St. Louis Post* of October 29, 1939, published a series of photographs of Carmen in her *Streets of Paris* dance segment, with different hand gestures in each shot and the corresponding song lyrics under each picture. The article claims that although she sings only four songs in the show, these four numbers "headed by the now familiar 'South American Way,' have sufficed to make her the highest paid singer on Broadway." For this critic, despite the fact that the meanings of her songs are lost on her American audience, the combination of "her movements, expressions and tones leave little doubt as to why New York critics have named her the 'Brazilian Bombshell.'"[55]

Indeed, from all reports, Miranda's six-minute sensational performance gave "summer-jaded Times Square something to rave about."[56] The *Boston Post* printed one of the first reports of Miranda's use (in this case offstage) of gestures and facial expressions to make herself understood on May 29, 1939: "She is trying now to learn English, but it really isn't necessary. Her eyes, shoulders and hands are eloquent enough to make her meaning clear in almost any corner of the globe" (11). Miranda's non-verbal communicability transferred to her stage performances and received immediate commentary in the press even while the show was still in Boston, and this opinion prevailed throughout the media for the extent of her tenure on Broadway.[57]

Compensating for her apparent lack of English, the press stressed Miranda's agility with hand gestures and facial expressions. In an article whose title, "Carmen Gets Unneeded Vocabulary," set the tone from the offset, *Parade* magazine reported that by October 1941 Miranda had learned two thousand English words that "the Miranda way makes . . . go still further. Even in casual conversations she speaks just as she sings, just as she is on the screen—with her eyes flirting, her eyebrows doing hulas, her double-dyed red-fingernailed hands filling in the gaps."[58] The

Sunday News likewise dismissed her songs "as absolutely unintelligible to a North American," whether in Portuguese or "her own special brand of English," claiming, "the effect is substantially the same."[59] Even *Family Circle* joined in this chorus with an article under the suggestive subtitle "Carmen Miranda Sings and Dances in Anatomical Esperanto," which claims: "She does all her explaining with her gestures—and never has that innocent word been used to cover so much innuendo" and that the meaning of the words "would doubtless be a letdown, compared to your imagination."[60] This article emphasizes the sensual quality of Miranda's performance, amplified by a lack of linguistic comprehension that added to her mystical aura. As one reporter for the *Evening Bulletin* writes in February 1940, "Carmen Miranda, the Brazilian bombshell—as theater, radio and phonograph record fans know her—hasn't been handicapped by ignorance of the [English] tongue. She speaks a universal language with hips, arms and eyes and in eight months her income has gone well beyond $100,000."[61]

Most critics have interpreted the avalanche of demeaning quotes in relation to Miranda's poor command of English as the media's reading and projection of the star as a "spectacle of ethnicity" (S. Roberts 3), which began as soon as she reached the United States. Miranda's entrance onto the North American performance scene has been immortalized in its reenactment by the actor Erick Barreto in the Helena Solberg biopic, *Bananas Is My Business*, and rehearsed countless times in critical articles and biographies. As Julian Dibbell writes, "right there on the docks she began projecting the prêt-à-porter persona—a mix of savvy sensualism and effusive naiveté—that would help shape North American perceptions of the Latin South for decades to follow. 'I say money, money, money,' she gushed to the journalists gathered to interview what was then just a curiosity: Brazil's biggest pop star, fresh off the banana boat."[62] Most critics view this scene as a hodge-podge of random statements by a star-stunned celebrity arriving for the first time in a foreign and greatly mythicized mecca of entertainment: New York. Lisa Shaw's reading distinguishes itself from the main trend by suggesting "there is ample evidence that upon arrival in New York she knowingly transformed herself into a caricature, a virtual cartoon character from South of the Border, whose pantomimic excess instantly provoked mimicry, to which she gave her own seal of approval, for comic effect" ("Celebritisation" 290). Without substantial insight that would enable the critic to determine Miranda's actual intentions—Miranda left no autobiography, and even published interviews are subject to third-party editing, selection and, interpretation—and given the epistemological dangers of such an interpretation, it would be more cautious to consider these readings of Miranda's performances, both on stage and off, as media perceptions of her "exoticist spectacle" rather than a self-manufactured and "personally stage-managed" process of celebritization (296). Shaw concludes that "during her first three months in New York, Miranda took the reins of her celebritization, encouraging journalists to speculate on her personal life, more specifically her romantic (and by implication sexual) involvements" (296). This emphasis on Miranda as fueling media gossip and creating a caricatural and comedic star image for herself seems somewhat out of character:

Miranda deliberately kept herself out of the media gossip's limelight throughout her US career, as Ruy Castro carefully develops. This assumption also disavows the very essence of Miranda's self-parody, the performative wink that characterizes her performance and that Miranda knowingly and broadly used as a performative strategy to, on the contrary, distance herself from the caricature of her own image. It is this distanciation, as rightly suggested by Shari Roberts, that enabled Miranda to negotiate her new star image within the North American context of Manhattan, rather than fuel a purposely construed, infantilized, and self-caricatural image. Early proof of this is Miranda's expressed disbelief when she realized the public laughed at her acting parts in *That Night in Rio*. As discussed in detail in Chapter 6, Miranda's participation and wholehearted investment in parodies of her star image are part and parcel of a self-awareness that, when considered through a camp sensibility, gives credit to Miranda's artful and lasting engagement with the complexities of her own iconic celebrity caricature and her conscious distancing from it. Rather than performing her own infantilization and comedic positioning and orienting it, Miranda's characterization—from her Broadway début on—was an intertexual product fabricated by the conflated contributions from the press, the stage, and later the studio.

The manipulation of Miranda's English was evident from her very first character role in the film *That Night in Rio*, as the studio dictated that her screen persona speak in either broken English, colorfully misused idioms, or explosive Portuguese. In her first spoken scene immediately after the opening musical number, Miranda erupts in a rage of jealousy, speaking Portuguese that is here rather cleverly interpreted for an English-speaking audience through the dialogue with Don Ameche, playing her boyfriend and an American entertainer, who repeats her lines in English in his rebuttal of her accusations. Throughout her screen career, her misuse of English remained a staple of her ethnic performance, "an aural metonym for 'Latin' identity" (Shaw, *Carmen* 55). Originally, the scriptwriters included several more of these hotheaded scenes, but early in the script production Darryl Zanuck eliminated most of them.[63] In the conference notes, Zanuck comments on the first-draft continuity: "Your handling of Carmen was good except that she does not need to talk nearly as much as she does in English. You should confine her English to one or two line speeches, and if she has to explode, she should go into Portuguese—ending up with a denunciation of one or two words in English. Also there is a little bit too much of her."[64] The Portuguese explosion ending with an intelligible word or two in English is the exact pattern the writers followed throughout this script and also in her subsequent films. In *That Night in Rio*, one such explosion ends with "dirty pig!" another with "ham!" as an insult for a bad actor. All in all, Zanuck's reworking of Miranda's part eliminated some ten pages of dialogue from the script, both diminishing and adulterating Miranda's onscreen spoken English. Set against the more authentic visual components of the Miranda films, it is without doubt in the aural register that "Hollywood's ethnographic good neighborliness breaks down" (López 77).

Throughout Miranda's tenure at Twentieth Century-Fox, the studio worked along contradictory lines, on the one hand providing a private English instructor and on the other hand making sure, as documented in the studio conference notes, to rework her parts if they felt that her English was too polished for the image they wanted to project.

Unlike the first scene in *That Night in Rio* described above, in subsequent films the studios resorted to leaving Miranda's Portuguese phrases untranslated, letting the language function "as an empty code for ethnicity" (Noriega 61). For Noriega, "there is no need for subtitles [or in this case, onstage diegetic translations] because nothing is said" (61). In Miranda's case, the meaning of what she says is a minor part of Miranda's overall performance. As Shaw indicates, in her slapstick role in *That Night in Rio*, her comic timing is excellent but distinguishes itself from the seriousness with which she performs her highly polished singing and dancing (*Carmen* 45). Or in other words, the incongruity between the two parts of her screen persona, repeated throughout most of her Hollywood career, is itself imbued with camp. As with other aspects of her star image, the media was eager to project Miranda as working on her command of English off the set and thrived on anecdotes of occasions when she allegedly misspoke, such as the time she called her costar John Payne a "sweaty pie" (instead of a "sweetie pie") or announced in a restaurant that the oysters were "simply platonic!"[65] In "candid" snapshots of Miranda around her house, she is shown practicing "her vivid but highly accented English in her studio dressing room."[66] Certain reporters also refer to Miranda's being, to their surprise from an Anglo-centric, hegemonic position, rather intelligent, despite her difficulties with the English language. Along these lines, *Hollywood* magazine writes in an unmistakably patronizing tone: "Somewhat to its astonishment Hollywood has found out that Miranda is not just a new species of Latin-American impetuosity, latest in a long line of passion flowers. Under that basket of fruit and vegetables a well-oiled little brain is ticking away."[67] As these blatant examples depict, while Miranda may have unknowingly projected at the outcome her limited and selective knowledge of the English language (or at least that is what the press picked up on), this sparked the unforeseen consequence that the media would draw relentlessly from this characterization both on and off the screen, and it would forever be associated with her star image.

Tropicalizing Miranda

Carmen Miranda's "incorrect English" was just one aspect of the tropicalized image constructed through the privileged and powerful locations of the Broadway stage and the Hollywood studio and expressed in the printed press. This act of tropicalization in North American entertainment emphasized and reduced Latin American stars to stereotypes that were not only an intrinsic part of their acting roles on the stage and screen, as duly analyzed in many excellent studies, but were also part of the industry's publicity texts, where they were often even more clearly labeled. In synergy with the tropical fruits of Miranda's headdresses and representing the epitome of the good Latin neighbor, press releases, playbills, stage- and studio-designed posters, movie trailers, pressbooks, and fan magazines expanded this characterization of Miranda through a series of epithets and taglines that were frequently repeated. Miranda's most widely used moniker, "Brazilian bombshell," fits within the pattern of reductive, evocative labels that paired geographic or national identities with markers such as *fiery, hot, spitfire, volcano, pepperpot,* and *hurricane* in associations that, as Mary Beltrán laments, are rarely questioned or objected to but became common and accepted forms of nomination, representative of the 1930s and 1940s (10). In the case of Carmen Miranda, a list of very colorful epithets was used to market the Brazilian star: *vivid, exotic, barbaric, torrid-voiced, Brazilian pep girl, South American cyclone, volcanic, tantalizing, sultry, hot-tamale, sensational,* and neologisms such as *mirandemonic.*[68] There is no doubt that the tropicalized slant of Miranda's epithets reduced her to a stereotypical image of Latinidade yet, by the same token, helped translate her unique vivaciousness and dynamic stage and screen presence, which she more elegantly portrayed than her fellow Latin stars Desi Arnaz or Lupe Vélez, for example. In comparison to the many negative characterizations of Latin players, the overwhelmingly positive contemporary reviews of Miranda's much-applauded gaiety, dynamic singing, and talented performance problematized the hegemonic, tropicalizing discursive strategy of her stage and screen presence and spoke mostly to the exuberance of her performative personality rather than the stereotypical reduction of her star image.

Drawing from Carmen Miranda's outstanding reception on the stage, the media was prompt to stress her role in Roosevelt's Good Neighbor Policy, and as early as May 1939, the New York's *Daily Mirror* published an article under the telling title "Love Thy Neighbor," which showcased Miranda, barely one week in the country, as "Brazil's best salesman of the Good Neighbor Policy."[69] From here after, references to Miranda abound, labeling the Brazilian Bombshell as "the most effective South American missionary in the U.S.,"[70] "the greatest event in our relations with South America since the Panama Canal,"[71] and "the best ambassador of good will that's come from those tropical shores,"[72] who "more than justifies the Administration's wish for friendly relations with South America by her contribution to 'The Streets of Paris' at the Broadhurst Theater."[73] Miranda was a godsend to the Good Neighbor initiative as a visual representative of hemispheric unity and diplomacy. Almost overnight, and through a felicitous coincidence of diplomatic events, Carmen Miranda became the most important symbol of the Good Neighbor Policy, with her cultural prominence endowed with diplomatic significance, and the press was keen to promote this image that collided political and cultural status. In July 1939, the *Newark Evening News* reported that, although Miranda could not speak English, "she's done more to rivet the USA-Latin American axis at this end than a dozen diplomatic junkets."[74] According to a US diplomat on a good-will tour, if President Getúlio Vargas had his own way, he "would do away with the entire Brazilian diplomatic corps and start a school for Carmen Mirandas."[75] As exaggerated and unfounded as this statement might be, an undeniable fact is that Miranda's stardom on Broadway, and soon to be in Hollywood, was the point of reference for all Latin performers from that point forward.

Miranda's arrival on Broadway coincided with a Latin rhythm craze in the United States that was initiated in the 1920s with Valentino's sexy and seductive dances, continued through the 1930s with the rhumba vogue, and in the late 1930s and 1940s embraced the samba and the conga alongside these other dance and musical forms. Latin songs were in demand, through the recording industry, dance bands, radio, and cinema, with musicians and bands such as Don Azpiazú's Havana Casino Orchestra, Xavier Cugat, Tito Guizar, and Desi Arnaz, among others. According to a reporter for the *New York Times*, there were more and better Latin musicians, singers, and dancers in Manhattan than in their countries of origin.[76] Hollywood would later capture this Latin dance vogue, and the trade journals fueled its popularity. *Silver Screen* of October 1942 published a double-spread feature titled "Dance Crazy!" that showcased the dance moves of Cesar Romero with Betty Grable and Lupe Vélez with Arnold Kent, twirling to the beat of this Latin-rhythm dance craze (74–75).

On Broadway Miranda performed three Brazilian songs, the quick-paced, tongue-twisting *embolada* "Bambu bambu," the Carnival *marchinha* "Touradas em Madri," and "O que é que a baiana tem?" along with what became the most popular of them all and one of her most imitated songs, the rhumba "South American Way" by the American composers Jimmy McHugh and Al Dubin. Later, however, her Hollywood films, as many critics have noted, seem to pride themselves at confusing national cultures by conflating song styles and Latin American locales to the point of ridicule and presenting a potpourri of music with no regard for national identities, resulting in sambas and rhumbas in Argentina; tangos, rhumbas, and congas in Rio; and so forth. This confusion of nationalities in Carmen Miranda's films began with her very first North American feature film, *Down Argentine Way*. Devoid of any Argentinian music, Betty Grable dances a conga wearing a rhumba-style costume, the native Argentines are depicted as Mexicans, and the "true Argentine" is Charlotte Greenwood's solo performance of "Sing to your Señorita, Sing!" with her characteristic high-kicks, awkward arm flings, and comic turns surrounded by villagers dressed in Spanish-style skirts and flouncy blouses.[77] Miranda does, on all accounts, compensate for the lack of musical complexities and originality with her extravagant visual appearance, yet she is brought to make concessions concerning the "authenticity" of her music. This form of "vulgar exoticism" (Dunn, *Brutality Garden* 35) became more and more pronounced as Carmen Miranda's career developed in the United States, to the point that her strong commitment to the Afro-Brazilian ethos through her samba dancing and singing style is permanently adulterated by the time she performs in her third Hollywood film, *Weekend in Havana* (1941).[78] Incorporating sounds and rhythms from other Latin and Afro-Caribbean cultures, as produced through the lens of US tastes for musical entertainment, Miranda's screen image became more generally representative of "Latin America." She was South American, and it made no difference if she sang in Spanish or Portuguese and danced the conga, the rhumba, the samba, or the salsa. Illustrative of this is the first issue of the entertainment magazine *FRIDAY*, which features Carmen Miranda on the cover and describes her in the accompanying article as "dancing the Conga."[79] However, other reporters were more informed, at least at first, when the original Shubert press releases were still prominently circulated. For the most part, the earlier the article, the more accurate the information tends to have been during her US career. One of the first newspaper articles, in the *Boston Herald*, referred to Miranda as a "singing danseuse from Rio de Janeiro, who arrived in Boston yesterday to introduce the samba, Brazilian native dance, in the 'Streets of Paris.'"[80] Through the mid-1940s, the samba vogue continued to make an imprint on the New York dance scene, catching the eye of the media. A reporter for the *New York Times* dedicated a feature article to the background of the samba dance craze and its origins in Rio, highlighting Miranda as the sponsor of this new dance.[81] As repeated throughout the Brazilian press upon Miranda's departure from Brazil, her main goal in coming to the United States was to introduce samba to the North American public. The May 1939 issue of the magazine *Pranove* published Carmen Miranda's goodbye speech, in which she claimed she was heading to New York to "present the rhythm of Brazilian music" (19). Cesar Ladeira also gave a speech that night, emphasizing that Miranda's contract came about solely through her indisputable talent: "Carmen Miranda will take the music of Brazil in its most charming expression to Broadway—she will give samba an international projection." He ends his speech by conflating Miranda's success metonymically to that of Brazil, claiming national ownership for her international projection: "I am sincerely pleased with Carmen Miranda's success—that will be the success of Brazil."[82]

Musically, as socially and culturally, Miranda had to negotiate the North American stage to make sense and flourish in what James Mandrell has referred to as a state of entrapment, "something of a funhouse mirror that situates her in a cultural no-man's land that is neither Brazilian nor Latin American nor even a Hollywood Technicolor soundstage" (26). This "cultural no-man's land" could also be seen, as proposed by Bianca Freire-Medeiros, as a "contact zone" or a "mediator" centered on Miranda's performance and in particular on her costumes and her body.[83] On Broadway, the *baiana* lost the paradigm of its white blackness only to be perceived widely in the media as a "Latin in Manhattan." With each stage performance, Miranda reinforced her star image, which gave origin to a parodic text of Latino ethnicity and created a new stereotype of Latin Americans for North American popular culture. While Carmen Miranda's *baiana* corresponded to certain previously widespread elements of Latinidade stereotyping (the colorful costumes, exuberant mannerisms, English misusage, comic misunderstandings, and idiom mangling), she also brought to this tradition a new look of outlandish headdresses, the *baiana* costume with all its accessories, and a new form of singing that entailed crystal-sharp diction at an incredibly fast speed. Over time, as theorized by Charles Ramírez Berg, repetition tends to normalize a stereotype, which eventually comes to represent a homogenized group.[84] Miranda's *baiana* would become *the* quintessential, homogenized image of Latin America, despite the fact that Miranda allegedly disliked the expression "Latin American," which she judged as too generalized, and wanted instead to be referred to as "Brazilian" (Brito 61). She embodied an emblematic image that abbreviated the history of the *baiana* and took on a tradition of its own.[85]

At first, Miranda's performances in the United States remained very similar to those at the Urca Casino, yet the interpretation was different once she was removed from the Brazilian cultural imaginary and setting. To a North American audience, the *baiana* had no cultural, regional, racial, social, or historical meaning, so this image became the stereotype for the "Latin" exotic: vivacious, incomprehensible, fruit-laden, colorful, and accompanied by samba or *marchinha* music, whose rhythms were identified as part of the foreign vogue originating from South America.

Beyond Broadway: Miranda Around and About Town

Miranda and her band's performance in its entirety was the epitome of Broadway Latinidade. During its first season on the Boston/New York stage, it was a culturally imported segment that was inscribed with exoticism and otherness for its North American audience as part of a burlesque, musical variety show. The first Broadway season was Miranda's most "Brazilian" season in the United States, and although the stereotype she projected would undergo little transformation, Miranda's own performance would progressively be modified to correspond to North American audiences' expectations. Carmen Miranda's stereotypical image of tropicalism, set within the apparatus of this "contact-zone" discourse, relies on the existence of difference and the superiority of one side, that of the US media. As is apparent in many examples from the print media, Miranda is subjectified and often represented as an imported commodity, which points to the "superiority" of her host society.

Given Miranda's popularity from the Broadway production, the raving reviews in the press, and by word of mouth, she was very soon in high demand at a myriad of different venues around town. Regardless of the event or the medium, Miranda repeated a version of her *Streets of Paris baiana* performance, as that was what the promoters requested. She was in constant demand as a radio guest artist, a nightclub entertainer, and as the Brazilian ambassador's right-hand lady at the World's Fair, with engagements that soon went far beyond the Broadhurst.[86] Carmen Miranda became pigeonholed as the *baiana*, and her repertoire, greatly reduced in comparison to her Brazilian performances, revolved almost entirely around this sole number. In the media, she was always depicted with the signature elements of her costume, namely excessive jewelry, a turban with adornments, a golden bustier and skirt revealing her midriff, and dramatic makeup.

Despite the changes due to the emergence of the motion-picture star system, Broadway producers maximized their proximity to retailers, music-publishing houses, recording companies, radio stations, and television studios as venues for publicizing their shows through product placement, guest stars, and musical promotion. Miranda was frequently invited to guest star on radio programs, a performance medium that she had mastered in Brazil before coming to the United States. She became a regular visitor on the popular Thursday evening show "The Rudy Vallee Hour," where she performed eighteen times during the 1939–1940 season and apparently caused quite the commotion when they prepared and expected her to follow a script.[87] She costarred with some of the most sought-after performers and celebrities of the day, such as Jimmy Durante, Edward Everett Horton, Bela Blau, Walter O'Keefe, Erin O'Brien Moore, Bill Robinson, Lou Holtz, Grover Whalen (the president of the World's Fair), Eleanor Roosevelt, John Charles Thomas, the Merry Macs, and the Ink Spots, among many others, and through these appearances she expanded her ever-growing network of acquaintances. Alongside her appearances on the Rudy Vallee show, Charlie McCarthy and Fred Allen also invited Miranda to their prime airtime slots. Her radio appearances earned her reasonable additional revenue, ranging between $192 and $471, with most earnings in the mid-$400 range.

The Brazilian Pavilion at the New York World's Fair was another prime venue for Carmen Miranda to showcase the music of her home country and continue to fulfill one of her primary roles as ambassadress of Brazil: introduce samba to a North American public. In an incredibly dramatic description of her embarkation on the SS *Uruguay* on May 5, 1939, a reporter from the *Correio da manhã* had asked Miranda in a short interview, "So Carmen are you really ready to introduce the United States to Samba?" to which she allegedly replied, "Samba was born to conquer. Why would it not be successful in the country of the 'blues'?"[88] In November 1936, several years before Carmen Miranda set foot on Broadway, Brazil had been invited to participate in the New York World's Fair and was the first South American country to officially accept this invitation in July 1937.[89] Speculation began soon after concerning which artists would be sent to represent Brazilian music, with Carmen and Aurora Miranda as popular candidates. A few months later, after Carmen Miranda had signed her contract with Shubert, her and her band's participation at the Fair was publicized in the press.[90] According to several sources, the only way to finance Bando da Lua's trip to New York was through their official participation in the Fair, as sponsored by the Brazilian government and facilitated by Getúlio Vargas's daughter, Alzira.[91]

The Fair opened on April 30, 1939, on the occasion of the 150th anniversary of George Washington's inauguration as first president of the United States, and showcased the theme "Building the World of Tomorrow." Carmen Miranda was a natural hostess and in-demand presence for the exotic, modern Brazilian pavilion, with its steel columns, exquisitely designed esplanade, tropical garden of native Brazilian plants, aviary of rare birds, rustling palm-trees near a central pool area, colorfully decorated restaurant, and "Good Neighbor Hall," not to mention the prominence of Brazil's major export, coffee, served at an attractive bar.[92]

In Brazil, under Getúlio Vargas's enthusiastic cultural patriotism, blackness and Afro-Brazilianness played a fundamental role in the construction of the musical forums around Rio, the capital of Brazilian popular music, but at the Fair, the "true Brazilian sounds" showcased at the inauguration of the Brazilian Pavilion on May 7, 1939, were produced by the New York Philharmonic Symphony Orchestra and Schola Cantorum under the direction of Burle Marx, with the participation of Bidu Sayão, a Metropolitan Opera singer.[93] The works of Villa-Lobos, praised as the most famous Brazilian composer, took up most of the program, but other well-known Brazilian composers were also featured, establishing a strong representation of both exotic Brazilian and classic compositions.[94] On July 16, 1939, Miranda also appeared as one of the Queens for a Mardi Gras parade alongside Jane Withers, Lillian Gish, Claire Trevor, Gertrude Niesen, Irene Wicker, Ann Rutherford, Eleanor Holm, and Joan Blondell.[95] Reservations were taken for that evening's Brazilian Carnival Night, titled "Mardi Gras in Rio." Romeu Silva's Samba Orchestra and Bando da Lua provided the music, with Carmen Miranda featured as a guest of honor.[96] Romeu Silva's Samba Orchestra and the Bando da Lua were frequent participants at the Fair and, according to newspaper reports, were enthusiastically received with requests for encores.[97] Another example was the special fair-designated "Coffee Day" on August 31, 1939. Miranda participated in the events, performing several of her musical numbers on the program at the main performance hall, the Court of Peace.[98]

Yet, indisputably, the most symbolic representation of Miranda's status as ambassadress of Brazil and Brazilian music was the "Carmen Miranda Day at the Fair," sponsored by the Brazilian pavilion on October 26, 1939. As part of the planned events, and to reinforce Brazil's Fair presence, Miranda made a speech in English (prepared by a teacher of the Barbizon School of Languages) to her native Brazil via the CBS facilities, a broadcast that lasted half an hour and was delivered in the presence of the Brazilian council-general and Mayor La Guardia. She also performed several songs in Portuguese. Required to be on stage at the Broadhurst Theatre that evening, Miranda was unable to be hailed as Queen of the Fair, which just goes to show Shubert's inflexibility.[99] Carmen Miranda was one, if not *the*, most prominent representative of Brazil to participate at the New York World's Fair, and she was a symbol of Pan-American harmony. In an undated photograph taken at the Fair, Miranda is featured in the presence of key members of Pan-American initiatives: Camille A. Baker, president of the Junior Pan-American League; Mrs. Clark Stearns, international president of the Pan-American League; Montalva Flores of the New York Pan-American Center, and Heloise Brainard, noted authority on Latin American affairs. Miranda is pictured wearing a dark turban with a leafy bow on the front, crisscross sandals with her signature wedge heels, and a short-length mink coat, her arms interlocked with Camille Baker's. The copy accompanying the photograph summarizes

Carmen Miranda drinking coffee with the winner of the coffee making
contest at the New York World's Fair (August 31, 1939). New York
World's Fair 1939–1940 records, Manuscripts and Archives Division,
The New York Public Library, Astor, Lenox and Tilden Foundations

Miranda's importance as a key player in Pan-American unity: "Carmen Miranda,
Brazilian singing star of 'Streets of Paris,' symbolized the accord existing between the United States and the Latin American countries at the meeting of the
Pan-American League at the New York World's Fair stressing the vital importance of hemisphere solidarity in the face of hostilities abroad."[100] Miranda was
brought in for special occasions and was often spotted around the Fair as one
of the Brazilian pavilion's official hosts. *Cena muda* features Miranda, identified
as "the sensational Brazilian artist on Broadway," hosting RKO's Claire Trevor
and Paramount star Susan Hayward in the Brazilian pavilion on the "Brazilian
Press Day."[101] Brazil renewed its participation in the Fair the following year, and
Carmen Miranda's prominence as Brazil's representative continued through the
Fair's second season of 1940, even though for most of the time she was reportedly in Rio de Janeiro, sharing with Elsie Houston the honor as South America's
most popular ambassadors of good will.[102]

Following such a successful summer performance series on Broadway and on the radio, and thanks to her much sought-after presence at the New York World's Fair, the most prestigious New York dining halls were particularly interested in booking Carmen Miranda for their 1939–1940 winter season. In October, after much speculation, Miranda signed a contract with the Waldorf-Astoria to entertain in the Sert Room during supper hours after her *Streets of Paris* performance, every night but Sunday.[103] The reviews in the local newspapers were overwhelmingly positive.[104] Many praised her syntony with the season: "Her costume is a splash of autumnal gold and through lozenge cut-outs at the midriff it reveals a Carmen Miranda in the indubitable flesh, simonized brighter than an October beech leaf," writes one reporter for the *New York Sun*.[105] The Sert Room was one of the most prestigious dining halls in New York and also one of the most expensive of the Waldorf-Astoria Hotel, which had been newly opened on October 1, 1931. The Waldorf-Astoria had achieved international fame not only as an upper-class place for the entertainment of evening patrons but also as the residence of many New Yorkers and hundreds of distinguished guests. Writing in 1939, Lucius Boomer—the creator and mainspring of the modern Waldorf-Astoria and the hotel's president—claimed, "the great number of gatherings of this type in New York soon made the Waldorf-Astoria the social and civic center which it is today" (17). A space of richness, warmth, and the latest in modern equipment, the Sert Room was one of the most beautiful showplaces in the city, "a sparkling jewel" (Towne 94) that had been completely renovated with two floor levels for dancing, making it a coveted venue for events of all types (balls, charity events, banquets, concerts, musical soirées, theatrical performances), and whose decoration reflected its high-class status with its series of exquisite black, silver, and rose panels painted by José Maria Sert, a renowned Catalan painter. It was viewed as a gilded society resort where the high-class guests were entertained by music and dancing while eating dinner or supper, and the names of attendees (and their host) were listed in the *New York Herald Tribune*. The fact that Carmen Miranda was under contract to open the fall season in the Sert Room attests to her enthusiastic reception in New York and places her among the highest class of entertainers of the time. In the week before her first appearance in the Sert Room, the press publicized Miranda's opening evening as an event of grand importance, which only added to the anticipation of the anxious dinner and supper crowds.[106] From the opening night on, some of the most prominent members of society filled the dinner room, and Miranda remained the key attraction for several months with a performance similar to the one that had made her famous on Broadway.[107]

On January 19, 1940, Miranda moved to an after-the-theater engagement at the Club Versailles, a midtown ballroom and supper club that, in its heyday of the late 1930s and 1940s, attracted some of the biggest names in show business. According to the media reports, her show retained its usual staples that continued to delight the evening crowd, and she dressed with her beads, her fabulous turban adorned with its fruit-filled basket, and her bare-midriff skirt. As reported in the

Daily Mirror New York, "it is this combination set off by a gleefully insinuative voice that makes the Brazilian discovery a whole festival by herself."[108]

At the Versailles, Miranda was the top-billed entertainer and was commissioned for special events, such as the fifth-year anniversary of the club, as the main performer.[109] Known as one of the most electrifying singers of the New York scene, she received more invitations than she could possibly fulfill to a wide range of celebrations, commemorations, and charity benefits that attest to her popularity.[110] Many months later, when Miranda was back in New York for her role in another Shubert Broadway show, *Sons O' Fun*, she participated in a charity evening to aid war victims, titled "Fun to be Free," at Madison Square Garden, whose tiered arena sat seventeen thousand spectators. At this event she won "riotous applause" for a rendition of "South American Way," which, amazingly, still held crowd appeal.[111]

The descriptions of Miranda's performances at these diverse events are consistent regardless of the venue. During her tenure at the Versailles, her fame was further immortalized in an oil painting by Paul Meltsner, whose work primarily included portraits of actresses and dancers. Meltsner had a show at the New York Midtown Gallery, where "the exotic Carmen Miranda" figured prominently. As one art critic writes: "Miss Miranda has awakened the most fanciful mood in a picturesque characterization, involving new refinements and subtleties in color and paint quality."[112]

Carmen Miranda's success came with a significant monetary benefit. She quickly became a megastar who earned an incredibly high salary of $1,000 to $1,500 a week for her role in *The Streets of Paris*, taking home, according to her New York State income-tax form for 1939, over $17,500, grossing close to $26,000. Rumor had it that in her engagements at the Waldorf-Astoria and the Club Versailles, she had been the highest-paid cabaret entertainer of the season.[113] As Greneker writes in a press release dated August 20, 1941, before the staging of *Sons O 'Fun*, "it makes no difference to Carmen Miranda whether she entertains behind the footlights, on the air, in an amphitheater, on the screen, or through the smoky haze of a night club—she wows them in any medium."[114] Her success, while for most indefinable, was quantifiable in dollars, and by the beginning of 1940, Miranda was identified as one of four highly successful "foreign gals," alongside Merle Oberon, Ingrid Bergman, and Simone Simon, and her inclusion in this prestigious group is noteworthy as proof of her ever-growing popularity after less than a year in the United States.[115]

The Exotic Carmen Miranda on Broadway Take Two: *Sons O' Fun*

Carmen Miranda was still under contract with Shubert in fall 1941 when the company staged the Broadway show *Sons O' Fun*, yet scholarly criticism has mostly overlooked Miranda's participation in this production, which appears to have been eclipsed by her early Hollywood career. Since her previous Broadway appearance,

Miranda had established her stardom far and wide throughout the US entertainment scene: she had toured with *The Streets of Paris* to Chicago, held long-term engagements at the Waldorf-Astoria's Sert Room, the Club Versailles in New York, and at Chez Paris in Chicago, and appeared on innumerous radio shows. Most significantly, however, for her reputation as a star of national repute, Miranda had starred in three Twentieth Century-Fox films, *Down Argentine Way*, *That Night in Rio*, and *Weekend in Havana*. Carmen Miranda's celebrity status grew most impressively overnight, as acknowledged by her recognition as one of the ten most outstanding women of 1939 in the United States.[116]

As had been the case with *The Streets of Paris*, and as per Shubert tradition, the show *Sons O' Fun* opened first in Boston at the Shubert Theatre, on October 23, 1941, and stayed there for several weeks garnering excellent reviews before moving to the Winter Garden Theatre on December 1, 1941, six days before the bombing of Pearl Harbor. In March, *Sons O' Fun* moved to the 46th Street Theatre, where it remained until Labor Day 1943, reaching a total of 742 performances before embarking on its transcontinental tour.[117] No longer an unknown performer, Carmen Miranda headlined *Sons O' Fun*, forming, alongside the comic duo Ole Olsen and Chic Johnson, the superstar trio of the Shuberts' cast.[118]

Sons O' Fun was an immediate sell-out, and much publicity originated from the return of the Brazilian Bombshell to the Broadway stage for this "new crazy musical of Ole Olsen and Chic Johnson" in the vein of the zanies' first big box office success several years earlier, with the reviewers once again drawing on the longstanding success of *Hellzapoppin'* and indirectly promoting the Shuberts' newest show. The *New York Herald Tribune* considered that "Sons O' Fun is just Hellzapoppin' dressed up a bit and put with a slightly more lavish touch," characterizing it as "noisier, brassier" and "a trifle better looking." *Variety* viewed *Sons O' Fun* as "so superior in production that it is rather a super 'Hellz'" with greater talent.[119] The preshow was apparently more entertaining than the show itself, which was definitely not fit for those reluctant to participate as it knew no boundaries, spilling over the footlights and into the aisles, the lobby, and even the restrooms, requiring a lot of audience hardiness. The advertisements for the show warned first-nighters to be ready to defend themselves, and the warning was by no means to be taken lightly.[120] Critics consistently referred to the accelerated tempo of this show that consisted of thirty scenes, lasted three and a half hours, and for the most part received rave reviews from those able to appreciate this "swift moving, slap-stick, lusty, insane, hilarious frolic."[121]

The Shuberts promoted Miranda as the return of their most exotic star, whose performance maintained its characterizing traits from *The Streets of Paris* but with greater stage presence and a comic English-speaking part. The company's press release set the tone for Miranda's triumphant return to the Broadway stage, emphasizing the "magical effect" of the past two years in America on "the dazzling South American songstress," now with a greater command of English and a solid national presence.[122]

The reviews of *Sons O' Fun* were overwhelmingly positive and hinged heavily on the critics' appreciation of Miranda's performance, with most agreeing that her more involved part was a welcome addition to the show and that her fascination was undiminished.[123] The *New York Herald Tribune* went so far as to claim that Miranda "in her eccentric and highly personalized fashion" is what made the show superior to its predecessor, as "her numbers give the show its one touch of distinction."[124] *Variety* made reference to her different songs and the fact that, being more fluent in English, she no longer sang only in Portuguese but also performed new songs written especially for her by Jack Yellen and Sammy Fain, such as "Thank You, North America" and "Manuelo."[125] Regarding her Portuguese songs, Miranda's repertoire varied slightly over the duration of the show, including a romantic comedy number titled "Ela diz que tem" (She says that she has), "Arca de Noé" (Noah's ark), a fast rhythmic samba titled "Rebola-bola," and at one point the Brazilian folksong "Cangurú" (Kangaroo), a comic description of the kangaroo and his habits, which was later cut from the show.[126] One of the less positive reviews was published in the *New York Journal-American*, which judged her performance to be inferior to the one in *The Streets of Paris*. While she is praised, "as gleaming and mischievous as ever, as provocative and bold," and "her singing captivating, her presence fascinating," this critic deems her material as not quite up to the perfection of her début two years previously and concludes that "she would do better, perhaps, not to dance as much as she does, and her exotic brilliance scarcely fits into the informal colloquy with Olsen and Johnson before the curtain."[127] The interest of this commentary lies in its assessment of Miranda's performance in relation to the rest of the show and in its suggestion that her most widely perceived success was as a specialty act rather than a comedic role. This more critical review of Miranda's part in *Sons O' Fun* appears as the exception to the norm, but it also represents the trend of those who were beginning to tire of the repetitive Miranda performance.

Miranda's performance in *Sons O' Fun* was also a turning point in that, for the first time on either stage or screen, Miranda was such an established entertainer that she could merrily spoof herself and her Hollywood experiences. According to the critics, she did this with great ease. At one point in the show, Miranda remained on stage while being imitated by "Lilliputian" Helen Magna, who came on at the end of Miranda's numbers dressed similarly to the Brazilian Bombshell.[128] Helen Magna's mirroring of Miranda's performance provides an unexpected and different interpretation of the Miranda phenomenon, her miniature stature adding a dollish quality to the impersonation, infantilizing her performance while emphasizing the elements of her signature look.

Similar to her *Streets of Paris* costumes' impact on the media, Miranda's *Sons O' Fun* costumes also received commentary in the press, with praise and credit given to the Broadway designer Raoul Pene du Bois, who is remembered for his "fifty years creating imaginative, colorful costumes and original sets" (Owen 48). C. P. Greneker emphasized the exotic beauty of the star's costumes in the press

Carmen Miranda and her shadow Helen Magna in *Sons O' Fun* at the Winter Garden Theatre (December 1941). Courtesy of the Shubert Archive

release submitted on the company's behalf before the show's opening in Boston, claiming that Raoul Pene du Bois's ingenious work was outdoing "the sensation Miranda's colorful costume created in 'The Streets of Paris,' . . . to design costumes which will bring to full expression her tropical attractiveness."[129] Raoul Pene du Bois had already made a name for himself designing stunning costumes for shows that became box office successes, such as *One for the Money* (1939), *Du Barry was a Lady* (1939), *Hold on to Your Hats* (1940), *Panama Hattie* (1940), and *Two for the Show* (1940), and he had assisted with two Ziegfeld Follies productions (1934 and 1936). Even in critical reviews, the show's costumes were deemed fabulous, and due credit was given to du Bois.[130] Miranda's *Sons O' Fun* costumes, while similar in silhouette and style to the one she wore in *The Streets of Paris*, gained height with a more "Hollywoodized" headdress, stacked high with feathers and other adornments. Her golden skirt was also embellished with golden bobbles and flower motifs, and for each scene she wore a different turban and other headgear yet still appeared with the signature parts of her costume and large, clunky styled bracelets, earrings, and necklaces. *Women's Wear Daily*, which two years earlier had provided the most detailed account of Miranda's costume in *The Streets of Paris*, welcomed Miranda's greater presence on the stage and saw this colorful artist's costumes, footwear, and headgear as sensational.[131] In the *New York Times*, December 21, 1941, Miranda is featured in a fabulous photograph in her *Sons O' Fun* costume, striking a dance pose with her hands up over her left shoulder. The caption refers to Miranda as "the ultimate expression of the Pan-American motif," fitting with one of the main themes of this show built around hemispheric unity.[132] The South American topic was explicitly expressed in two back-to-back songs, "Thank You, South America" (sung by the Scottish singer Ella Logan and indicated in the program as sung "with soldiers"), and "Thank You, North America," performed by Carmen Miranda and her band (credited here as "Caballeros da Lua"). Stereotypes abound in both parts. Fitting with the spirit of the Good Neighbor Policy still in vogue, the United States is depicted as grateful to South America, a "land of life and romance," for music, rhumba, conga, coffee, and seductive women. Carmen Miranda, in turn, thanks North America for its goodwill, measured by the proliferation of rhumba bands and dancers in New York, and its "beautiful banks."[133] Miranda's gratitude toward North America was also captured in a photograph published in the *New York Times* with the legend: "Thank you North America—Carmen Miranda being Pan-American on behalf of 'Sons O' Fun' at the Winter Garden."[134] Miranda's number is the final act before the intermission, similar to her casting in *The Streets of Paris*. The idea of hemispheric cooperation is reiterated in the caption that accompanies a promotional picture of Miranda in her *Sons O' Fun* costume holding a cockerel: "Using every muscle and nerve, together with a couple of indefinable qualities, Carmen Miranda . . . is commonly estimated to have done more for hemispheric solidarity than any hundred diplomats."[135] In this, the media's assessment of Miranda has not varied from her first few months in the country. By the end of 1939, the *New York Journal and American* pointedly summarizes her stardom in the United States in an article bearing the telling title "Miranda IS the South American Way" and including such lines as, "Six months ago Carmen Miranda was just a name. Today she is a vogue. Six months ago 'The South American Way' started out as a song in 'Streets of Paris.' Today it symbolizes a national trend." The critic continues by affirming Miranda's role in bringing South America to the cultural map of the United States: "If the United States is more South American conscious at the present time than ever in the past, considerable credit must go to the impression which this amazing Brazilian singer has made."[136]

Miranda's tenure on Broadway and her first Hollywood years projected a rewriting of the *baiana* for a non-Brazilian public. Drawing from Miranda's performance, popular culture embraced the *baiana*: her significance expanded exponentially, making the Americanized *baiana* an icon of the New York stage and the Hollywood musical. As I discuss in the following chapters, the audiences, fans, fashion gurus, and popular culture in general "made sense" of Miranda by transposing elements of her costume to everyday ready-to-wear items and by using her image as the quintessential representation of Latin America, invested with all its stereotypes and comedic value depending on the context. The impact of

Miranda's star persona stemmed from a combination of auspicious timing for Latin American performers in the United States, an immediate enthusiastic reception from the theater patrons, extensive media coverage and publicity, and the fact that she was a new, different, exotic, charming, and engaging singer and performer. All in all, the power of Miranda's celebrity, to paraphrase Marshall, became activated through the New York entertainment and media scenes' "cultural 'investment' in the construction of [her] celebrity sign" (57). What Miranda represented at this time was the essence of her long-lasting celebrity sign throughout the tenure of her star career. During the Broadway period, however, although her *baiana* became divested of any previous aspect of race or Afro-Brazilianness, it was a sign embedded in the context of the New York stage-musical scene. As her North American career unfolded, Carmen Miranda was considered less frequently as a singer and more consistently as a visual sign that was perceived no longer as specifically from Brazil, but more generally from Latin America: exotic and often outrageous headdresses, excessive jewelry, platform heels, and revealing midriff dresses, as the innumerable Miranda impersonations clearly express. It was the sealing of Miranda's iconic image of the stylized *baiana* for a non-Brazilian audience that catapulted her stardom to the silver screen. Whereas the theatrical stage created an atmosphere of intimacy, the big screen stabilized her image and multiplied her viewing audience, recreating proximity to the theatrical star and her connection to the audience by using film close-up shots that focused on Miranda's costumes and captured the uniqueness of her performances on a proscenium stage. The initial transposition of Miranda's performance from stage to screen was mostly a change in medium. As Sandoval-Sánchez rightly indicates, Miranda's first Fox film, *Down Argentine Way*, incorporated almost in its entirety her original and ephemeral acts from the Broadway stage, fixing on film these lost performances for future audiences (22). What merits emphasizing is the fact that Miranda's star persona is essentially and inherently remembered as being presented in these musical numbers, and her acting parts are dwarfed in the cultural memory by the intensity of her visual image, as I discuss in the following chapters in relation to her reception as a film star and the myriad imitations of her star persona.

CHAPTER FOUR

MARKETING MIRANDA

Stardom, Fashion, and Gossip in the Media

In the opening scene of Carmen Miranda's third Twentieth Century-Fox film, *Weekend in Havana* (1941), the camera zooms in on a snowy New York City storefront window in which life-size cutout figures of Miranda and her band set the ambiance for an agency promoting luxury cruises to the Caribbean. Framing the display, an arrangement of posters aims to lure the passersby with enticing headlines that evoke the sunny tropics, romance, and fun. The camera then cuts to the rhythmic hand movements of one of the percussionists of Miranda's band, who appears to come alive before the spectators' eyes. Dressed in Cuban shirts with frilled sleeves, the band accompanies Miranda in the opening musical number and the film's title-song, "Weekend in Havana."

This cinematic transition ties the promotion of a fun-filled, exotic, gay, and romantic experience to a musical number that reinforces the invitation to escape to a foreign and exciting destination through the lyrics, the music, the performers' costumes, and Miranda's sensual movements—in particular, her trademark "come hither" gesture and enticing fluttering of the eyes. The representation of exotic tourism was a staple of Hollywood films that provided a temporary means of escape and contributed "to the marketing of cultural exoticism as a 'spectacle of difference' available via the travel package or the luxury cruise" (Berry, *Screen Style* 131). Miranda's foreign, exotic, and utterly other aura promoted this associational tropical merchandising (ranging from the film's visual product being packaged for consumption and sold as the illusion of gaiety, to specific items of consumer culture such as her turbans, platform shoes, jewelry, and dresses), as many of her film titles explicitly denote.[1] The spectator vicariously becomes a cultural shopper-tourist who absorbs the images of foreign lands, customs, and people, all mediated through the lens of the studios that have packaged these illusionary destinations for the viewers' consumption.

At the height of the studio system, the interconnectedness between the cinema and consumer culture was at the core of Hollywood's promotion of both its stars and films and fueled the intense commodification surrounding the stars, both on and off the screen. Marketing the stars, especially the top-billed cast, was essential to this profit-maximizing industry governed by best practices, film trends, and audience expectations. The films, doubling as living display windows, showcased the

100

most modern furnishings, accessories, and fashions. As part of the films' extended commercial culture, the industries provided a forum for commodity tie-ins, which were all the rage during this period. The film exhibition windows were seen as publicity opportunities for producers' goods, and stars were widely featured in advertisements, dispersing, as Mary Ann Doane writes, "the fascination of cinema onto a multiplicity of products" (25).[2]

The interconnectedness of film showcasing and manufacturer tie-ups gave rise to the parallel development of business initiatives that employed specialists working both for and outside of the studio. One of the most unique examples of commercial tie-ups connected to a Carmen Miranda feature film was the appropriately named "Copa bras" manufactured by Arrow Brassiere Company. The advertisement, featuring Miranda and some of the cast from *Copacabana* (1947), urged female patrons to watch for the "Copa Girl Contest" at local theaters, promising the most beautiful and shapely contestants elaborate prizes, such as "screen tests, expensive wardrobes, all-expense paid trips to New York and some royal entertainment."[3]

This symbiotic relationship among the films, the stars, and the extensive discourse around them both fueled the industry's "dream factory," which Jane Gaines describes as "the sensorial engulfment of the spectator, a kind of commodity immersion," and consolidated the relation between cinema and consumerism by projecting objects that were enhanced by the magical touch of the silver screen and its stars ("Wanting to Wear" 106; 147). Star adulation is passed on to the products they endorse, creating a unique aura, and unlike any other mutually endorsed media relationship, the cinema/consumption symbiosis is endowed with a particularly strong emotional bond that stems from the stars' projection of success, beauty, and power.[4] This was especially pronounced during the first half of the 1940s, when film attendance reached its all-time apex, averaging around eighty-five million spectators weekly.[5]

This mutual dependence of film viewing and consumption is also ensconced in the physical proximity of exhibition halls and department stores, some of which built theaters inside their stores as early as the 1910s and catered to those skeptical of nighttime showings with matinée projections originally geared, in particular, toward women shoppers (J. Allen 486). At one of these matinée showings of *Weekend in Havana*, women were reportedly overheard claiming they would like to come back and see it all over again.[6]

The exhibition halls were jam-packed with studio-devised marketing ploys that aimed to leave the viewers insatiable and give the film-going public a sense of ownership and a greater connection to the stars. These incentives included games with prizes, audience competitions, give-a-ways, and bond drives, a plethora of ideas that could liven the reception of the feature film and add a participatory level of involvement to the film-going experience.[7] The pairing of Carmen Miranda's distinguishable look with the musical genre provided a goldmine of options, limited only by the studio publicists' imaginations, to assist exhibition halls with promoting her films. Emblematic of this trend is the pressbook for *Greenwich Village*, which suggests an array of options typical of the Miranda films, including rhumba, conga, or samba contests; prizes for the best girl imitation of Miranda;[8] elaborate jewelry showcased in local stores; and blow-ups or mannequins of Miranda wearing the popular Latin American styles.[9]

This tailored marketing of a film through the uniqueness of one of its main female stars was typical of the time period when, more than at any other period in cinematic history, actresses occupied the lion's share of the studio's payrolls.[10] The cast, and primarily the main female stars (with few exceptions), featured prominently in all forms of publicity: they were the subject of trade and commercial newspaper articles, radio interviews, extensive press releases, and pressbooks and were included on movie posters in multiple formats and sizes. The public could not get enough of Hollywood, and its embellished objects of sale—ranging from paper dolls to Dixie Cup lids—fueled the industry's myth-making endeavors, which were essential to film marketing and extended the experience of going to the movies far beyond the film viewing *per se*.[11]

From the 1940s on, celebrity gossip permeated the media, progressively occupying more print space, as journalism in general incorporated more "soft" news such as entertainment and leisure. Stardom, as Richard Dyer has developed, "is the way stars live, this generalized lifestyle that is the assumed backdrop for the specific personality of the star and the details and events of his/her life" (*Only Entertainment* 35). Publicity and advertising focused on and were driven through the stars—their personal lives, loves, tastes, and hobbies—enticing the movie-going public with a projection of the players that extended far beyond the scope of the films themselves, creating an extensive extra-filmic discursive and visual apparatus. Since stars have been defined as actors and actresses whose public interest encompasses their lives beyond their screen performances, consideration of these parafilmic materials is essential to understanding the creation and promotion of Miranda as a star and provides a deeper understanding of her multifaceted stardom. As Gaines has pertinently suggested, fans did not need to see the motion pictures to follow their favorite stars, who were projected just as much through fan magazines, women's fashion, and publicity releases as by their films ("Costume" 198).

Film reviewers provided descriptions and classifications of the films along with their appreciation and judgment, although as John Ellis reminds us, these reviewers often had a limited degree of autonomy in relation to the studio (37). Despite this gap between the industry's official discourses about the films and the press's interpretations on one side, and the empirical experience in the movie theaters themselves on the other, the information contained in the press, as a pseudofictional genre of its own kind, gives the critic an insight to how the films were constructed in the media. What is of interest is not the veracity or validity of the pronouncements but rather a knowledge of what *is* in fact being said, even when in media publications the opinions of a few may become a distorted ruling index of the film's general reception.[12]

Furthermore, the publicity produced by the studio was not always an accurate representation of the film. The film's "narrative image" for a forthcoming release

Carmen Miranda with her lighthouse headdress in a Production Code
photograph for *Doll Face* (1945). Courtesy of the Margaret Herrick Library

does not, as Ellis rightly points out, "summarize the film, it indicates it" (32).[13]
Furthermore, the information included in the publicity material may or may not
be accurate. This was all the more so for musicals, in which scenes with song and
dance numbers that did not further the plot were commonly the first to be cut
if the film length needed to be reduced, often after marketing departments had
already released the film's publicity. A case in point is a widely circulated image of

Miranda with a lighthouse headdress in *Doll Face* for her performance of "True to the Navy," which was cut from the film's final version.[14]

Given Carmen Miranda's charismatic stage and film presence, the media wrote extensive commentary about her stardom, capitalizing on Miranda's unique and flamboyant star-performance and celebrity persona. Careful consideration of these media and publicity texts provides an essential additional level of understanding of Miranda's stardom beyond her filmic portrayal and enables us to analyze the media's construction and interpretation of Miranda. As Gledhill succinctly indicates, "Actors become stars when their off-screen life-styles and personalities equal or surpass acting ability in importance" (xiv). This approach situates Miranda as a foreign-film commodity in relation to the industries' construction of a collective, imagined "Latin-ness" through media products and star publicity, corresponding to a "Hollywood Latinidad," as coined by Mary Beltrán (3). Publicity for Miranda's films highlighted the uniqueness of her physical appearance—in particular, that of her costumes. She figured prominently in promotional materials, as it was an easy transition for the artists to make from film presence to posters, magazine photos, caricatures, and lobby cards.

A Marketing Goldmine: Miranda's Narrative Image

In the late 1930s, nationwide advertising for film releases was orchestrated with the uttermost care by publicity departments, with writers and art staff dedicated to devising aggressive sales campaigns focused on marketing the film's main stars.[15] Some of the challenges inherent to the marketing of Miranda's Twentieth Century-Fox films were common to all the studios: it was essential to ensure interest in the picture before its release to generate expectations and spike the audience's curiosity, and the primary method was to draw on past studio successes while emphasizing the novelty of the new release.[16]

The film posters, in a variety of formats and styles, were the crowning element of the studio publicity effort and were not meant as merely informational but rather as powerful tools to enhance movie sales where it mattered most: at the box office. Similar to the poster cutouts in the aforementioned opening scene of *Weekend in Havana*, the posters were intended to stand out prominently in the exhibition halls, but they also "bombarded the eye from every available vantage point: brilliantly lighted theater lobbies, billboards, brick walls, roofs, fences, buses, even taxicab wheel covers" (Rebello and Allen 13–14). The posters needed to loudly acclaim the film's appeal as the most vital link between the studio and the potential audience by translating into pictorial form, with irresistible draw, the essence of the film, the plot, the stars, and the genre, capturing, as Haralovich writes, "moments of narrative rupture" in posters that were often rim-filled "snapshots" of the film (52). Competing with other forms of entertainment such as the theater, radio, stage shows, fairs, and circuses, the poster's main purpose was to aggressively sell the film. It was not enough to portray an image from the film and provide the essentials about its contents and cast; the poster needed to make the film irresistible for a broad audience, and if necessary that took the form of enhancing its most marketable features. In short, the posters were designed, as Rebello and Allen colorfully summarize, "to sell the sizzle, not the steak. . . . Posters needed to be sensational" (14).

The posters created to promote the Carmen Miranda movies were able to achieve this level of sensationalism by foregrounding her magnificent costumes, using bright, eye-catching colors and artsy compositions that screamed excitement, exoticism, and gaiety and that echoed the copy of the poster. Even for her first film, *Down Argentine Way*, in which she did not have an acting role, the publicists merchandized her foreignness and unique performance with taglines that read: "Introducing tantalizing, torrid voiced Carmen Miranda. She's terrific!" and promised "irresistible rhythms of rhumbas and congas." Miranda was one of the film's "show-stopping new personalities."[17] Several of the artist's drawings used in the posters for *Down Argentine Way* show a slender Miranda at the center of the poster layout, featured with one of her legs exposed, her hands on her hips, and her head to one side, portraying a promise of seduction that is limited in this film, given that Miranda's part is confined to the proscenium stage.[18]

Despite the restrictions of the war period, printing and paper remained relatively cheap, and studios ordered posters with abandon, typically with several posters focusing on the main star and a variety of posters that would appeal to different sensibilities according to the targeted audience.[19] Posters intended for Spanish communities or Spanish-speaking countries, for example, featured Miranda more prominently to emphasize the shared *Latinidad/e*.[20] Ideally, stars' representations had to correspond with their public figure and forefront the traits that the audience expected from the star, toward whom they felt a pull of loyalty, blending continuity effectively with novelty to consistently draw audiences to the box office. In the case of the Twentieth Century-Fox musicals in which Miranda's roles varied very little from film to film, the posters needed to evoke her distinct "look" but also the newness of the film's plot and setting, the music, and her costumes. Typecasting was not peculiar to Miranda; as Alexander Walker discusses, it was a phenomenon of the time period, and the studios manipulated the stars, providing little, if any, margin for change (254). If the studio's marketing strategies were successful, the balance between novelty and coherence was obtained and translated to profit at the box office, as the audience was able to locate the film while being seduced on the expectation of pleasure.[21] Therefore, *That Night in Rio* (1941) was heavily marketed with publicity posters referencing the studio's past success with *Tin Pan Alley* (1940) and Miranda's sensational performance in *Down Argentine Way* (1940).[22] Despite *That Night in Rio*'s being her first full acting role in a US film, Miranda's unique performance style had made a mark on Hollywood: *Photoplay* praised *That Night in Rio* for its "songs in the Carmen Miranda manner," already an established trademark of performativity.[23] As Richard deCordova writes, "the actor's previous film experience worked to establish intertextual connections between films . . . [and] to establish the actor's identity across films. . . . The star system provided not only a means of differentiating films but also a means of grouping them, experiencing their interconnections and even their history" (90, 113). Miranda's films, similar to a film series, are a particularly strong example of how the discourse worked to produce the picture personality across films, since a very similar character with a similar personality appeared repeatedly in film after film.

The positioning of the new film needed to be apparent in the film posters and entice the viewers with a product that would not disappoint. The publicity materials for *The Gang's All Here* promised Miranda's performance would make the audience "shake with laughter," since Carmen Miranda is "delightfully delirious" in this new Twentieth Century-Fox production. In this case, for most audiences the movie probably made good on the splashy promise of the advertising.[24] At this point of her North American career Miranda was at the height of her success, needing little if any introduction. *Screenland* of October 1943 features a full-page, color poster of Miranda in one of the fabulous costumes she wore in *The Gang's All Here*: a green, purple, and white outfit with purple and orange butterflies on a green turban. The artist has depicted Miranda leaning back in her characteristic pose, with her head erect and eyes half-closed, and her signature appears across the top left-hand corner, adding a personable touch to the poster.[25]

The techniques of the Fox artwork, with rich, saturated colors, captured the essence of Miranda's often garish and always strident color scheme. This was true for both the posters and the lobby cards, which were always produced in color, even when the film was in black and white. The Twentieth Century-Fox posters often contained as much information as the lobby cards, typically using every possible inch of white and preferring bright contrasting colors over the pastels or muted primary colors that were the general norm with the art directors and illustrators at MGM, Paramount, and Columbia. Representative of this trend are some of the publicity posters created for *The Gang's All Here*, so packed with copy featuring the top-billed players, supporting actors, director, producer, dance director, screenplay and original story writers, composers, and lyricists, along with the titles of all the feature song hits, that very little space was left to include pictures from the film or of the actors.[26]

The Miranda posters are very typical of the Hollywood musical poster style that Rebello and Allen describe as sporting "cluttered, 'busy' designs, with arcing or rhythmically undulating title treatments. Motifs, including chorus lines, musical bars and notes, fireworks, pinwheels, shooting stars, confetti, and balloons, jollied up the design" (232). Miranda's inclusion in the musicals and depiction on the Twentieth Century-Fox posters was a perfect match for the film's projected image, which promised the audience gaiety and romance, frolicking and dancing, music with an exotic vibe, and a splashing array of costumes, with taglines adding a sense of dynamism to the posters. Although in truth Miranda's visual appeal could forego all narrative necessity, the designers never skimped on the copy that merely emphasized her unique expression of otherness, gaiety, color, and tropical music, all part of the presold premise of each Miranda film. At times, the poster artists' stylized portrayals of Miranda border on caricature, a technique that was often used in posters for comedies and rightly fits with that aspect of Miranda's comedic roles. The use of the caricature also speaks to her popularity and the fact that she was an easily recognizable screen persona.[27] In all cases, as Twentieth Century-Fox illustrators continued to use drawings rather than photographs, they maintained a consistent depiction of Miranda's physical characteristics: emphasizing her "Latin" coloring, eyes, and lips while often portraying a more slender torso and elongated legs than she had in real life; highlighting her in movement and donning fabulous glittering costumes; and always featuring her signature headdress and platform shoes.[28] Most frequently she is depicted smiling rather than singing, which was preferred in the Hollywood poster tradition (Rebello and Allen 243). At times only her head and headdress are featured, in the common cutout technique that designers, especially at Twentieth Century-Fox, utilized as a way to free up more space for the copy.

As often happened, the publicity artists adapted several images from the studio-provided stills, and publicity materials for each film tended to repeat one of Carmen Miranda's most striking costumes that was more clearly distinguishable from all those previously worn. The Carmen Miranda image most widely reproduced for *Greenwich Village* is the striking costume she wears for the nightclub rendition of "O que é que a baiana tem?": a full-length, black and hot-pink, boa-like, feather-adorned skirt bearing a large opening at the front; skimpy black lace flowers covering her breasts; a towering headdress of black plastic flowers; black polka-dot net hose; and long black gloves with pink on the underside. For *Doll Face*, Miranda is portrayed throughout the publicity materials with her lighthouse headdress, which, as mentioned above, ended up on the studio's chopping block. The constant repetition of one costume in particular in a film's publicity images enabled the public to recognize the forthcoming release by providing a visual "trademark" for that specific film.

The posters' composition was symbolic of the importance the marketing executives gave to the different stars, and in Miranda's first seven films, she is pictured prominently in the layouts, even for her first non-acting film, *Down Argentine Way*. For *That Night in Rio*, in several posters she is depicted as one of the three main stars, alongside Alice Faye and Don Ameche, in the same scale and at the forefront of the designs.[29] By the time Miranda starred in *Greenwich Village* (1944), her name was headlining lobby cards and publicity posters, appearing above the "cherry blond" Vivian Blaine's, who was seen as a newcomer. Miranda's poster portrayal was proportional to her outstanding success during the war period, when Latin American themes were heavily marketed.[30] Indeed, there is a noticeable shift in Miranda's prominence starting with the publicity posters for *Something for the Boys* (1944), on which the artists repeatedly draw Miranda in a diminished scale and to the side of the romantically involved couple Michael O'Shea and Vivian Blaine. In hindsight, these images mark the beginning of her popularity decline. In the following release, *Doll Face* (1945), Vivian Blaine takes top billing and appears central in all publicity posters, with Miranda to the side or pictured merely in a headshot. The same occurs in the posters for *If I'm Lucky* (1946), on which Vivian Blaine, Perry Como, and Harry James are pictured as a star trio. The irony of this poster composition is that, according to the reviews of *If I'm Lucky*, Miranda's music, Harry James's trumpet, and Perry Como's songs were the film's saving grace. *Variety* refers to "a generous showing of Carmen Miranda" and concludes that the "jam session in Brazil" with Miss Miranda and the band doing "the Batacuda song is the show's most elaborate number."[31] Miranda would have to wait for her first non-Twentieth Century-Fox role in *Copacabana* to regain the limelight. Paired with Groucho Marx and promoted as the new comedy duo, she once again, but for the last time, shares top billing.

The posters, echoing the narrative from the studio press releases, reflect Miranda's roles as either supporting to the main romantic couple or paired with her own love interest. In this, the Fox posters mirror the typical heterosexual format of Hollywood musicals and Miranda's artistic representation, which often reveals her bare midriff and skirts slit high above the knee, emphasizing Hollywood trends of the late 1930s and early 1940s that "were characterized by the representation of women as objects of male sexual desire and by the display of women's bodies as the focus of sensational heterosexuality" (Haralovich 56). In Carmen Miranda's second feature film, *That Night in Rio*, the publicity translated the studio's heterosexual paradigm through her "heavy romance" with Don Ameche, "which required frequent embraces."[32] A similar suggestion is prominent in Miranda's portrayal in the publicity materials for *Weekend in Havana*, which make broad use the film's grand finale Nango dance number, a tropical riot of colors, textures, and movement. The final camera shot focuses in on the two couples—Carmen Miranda/Cesar Romero and Alice Faye/John Payne—linked arm in arm, and the equal balance of these two couples in this scene is transferred throughout the publicity materials.

This heterosexual dominance of Hollywood musicals was coupled with a white, racial bias, and as a consequence, the posters, like the films they represented, were essentially a white space: if top black performers, such as the Nicholas Brothers, were included on the poster layouts, they were most often featured as "guest performers" who could be eliminated for viewings in the South.[33] Dyer clearly defines the vision of race that the musical constructs as containing blackness in "only entertainment" segments, depriving black characters of any wider screen life beyond their professional entertainer part, making "spontaneous" outbursts of song and dance a white privilege (*Only Entertainment* 39). The posters mirror this marginalization of black entertainers: their artistic depiction is sketchy rather than detailed, with racial markers camouflaged by the common technique of silhouette drawings. Miranda's inclusion as a white "Latin" star was permissible without these artistic limitations, despite her extreme otherness, because of her European origins. She represented the borders of a safety zone of preconceived and widely accepted ideas concerning race and heterosexuality, and the films' narrative image in each poster remains true to these known ideological trends (Ellis 79). It is also not by chance that Miranda would be safely paired with another "Latin" actor, such as Cesar Romero, but never with a US leading star.[34]

The trailers screened at the exhibition theater before the featured films were equally as important as the movie posters and were one of the principal ways the studios hoped movie audiences would become enthused for upcoming releases in the very same venue where the film would be played.[35] Although it is impossible to discern the effectiveness of trailers in general, and unfortunately not all the trailers for Miranda's films have been preserved or made available for viewing, it is telling how the studio showcased Miranda, as the following examples illustrate.[36]

In the trailer for *Down Argentine Way* (1940), Miranda is featured in a ten-second segment with a voice-over introducing her as "the fascinating star of New York's hit *Streets of Paris*, the glamorous, exotic Carmen Miranda, who will teach you to forget . . . in the 'South American Way.'" The trailer encapsulates Miranda's Broadway fame and South American flare and showcases a clip of her singing. She is the only specialty act to be included in the trailer, and her name appears immediately after those of Betty Grable and Don Ameche, an unusual publicity placement for a newcomer.

For Carmen Miranda's next film and first acting role, *That Night in Rio* (1941), the trailer features Miranda immediately after Alice Faye and Don Ameche. She is first presented as "the exotic, fascinating, new screen sensation: Carmen Miranda" with clips from two of her musical scenes, "Chica Chica Boom Chic" and "I, Yi, Yi, Yi, Yi (I like you very much)," and several of her acting scenes. As the announcer boasts, the trailer's desired effect is one of "carefree gaiety, glamor, and enchantment," and Miranda fits right in with "the backdrop of Rio's brilliant boulevards and colorful cafés, all in glorious Technicolor."

In the trailer for Miranda's third film, *Weekend in Havana* (1941), Miranda features more prominently as both a performer and an actress as the studio clearly showcases side by side the two leading ladies, Carmen Miranda and Alice Faye, with their respective beaux, Cesar Romero and John Payne. The audience is invited to join "the lovely Alice Faye in her search for fun and romance" with her soft, contralto songs—the smooth, husky "Romance and Rhumba" and "Tropical Magic" numbers—in contrast to "the sizzling songstress, Carmen Miranda, singing her tantalizing tunes"—the exotic, quick-paced, and colorful numbers and the carnivalesque "Nango" grand finale. The preview shows a segment of a quick-paced scene with Miranda chasing Cesar Romero around a casino floor, punctuated by the tagline "Comedy! A fiesta of fun and frolic," juxtaposed to the next segment with Alice Faye sauntering across the dance floor dressed in a fabulous deep-blue gown and the promise of "Beauty! Scenes of brilliant splendor! Photographed in Technicolor!" As this trailer promotes, Miranda was a top star in Hollywood by the time she filmed *Weekend in Havana*, and the audience was in for a "torrid tropical holiday" with Miranda and Faye at the helm.

For many critics, Miranda's fifth Twentieth Century-Fox film, *The Gang's All Here* (1943), was the peak of her Hollywood career, and the trailer focuses almost entirely on its eight musical numbers. Similar to the trailer for *Weekend in Havana*, the preview alternates between Alice Faye's slow-paced, romantic musical numbers and Carmen Miranda's upbeat performances, along with the big-band numbers of Benny Goodman and his orchestra, all dressed up in vibrant Technicolor. With

complete disregard for the stars in their acting roles, the effect is one of "pure entertainment" (Dyer, *Only Entertainment* 19), bound not to disappoint.

Miranda's last color film at Fox was the 1944 musical *Something for the Boys*.
As the trailer shows, Miranda has top billing, and the studio pitches the film
as "the perfect musical for Carmen Miranda." She is featured performing the
"Samba-Boogie" number with the promise that the audience will experience "more
comedy, more side-splitting laughter, more Technicolor magnificence" than ever
before. After *The Gang's All Here*, any promise the studio could make was sure to
fall flat—none could approximate the tutti-frutti success.

The trailers for *Doll Face* (1945) and *If I'm Lucky* (1946) are a move away from
the effusive and lavish film previews that marketed the previous Miranda musicals and that the audience was accustomed to seeing—as were the films. Both releases, the last for Miranda under Twentieth Century-Fox contract, were printed
in black and white and lacked, along with the by then expected Technicolor, the
excitement and gaiety of the previous Miranda features. Released in the postwar
period, the films flopped at the box office, even though Miranda maintained her
usual spunk in her renditions of "Chico Chico, from Puerto Rico" (in *Doll Face*),
"Follow the Band," and "Bet Your Bottom Dollar" (in *If I'm Lucky*). Throughout
the trailers, Miranda contributes to the films' narrative image as a gleeful, talented,
exotic performer and comedian and adds to each film's preview the dimension of
tropical gaiety, otherness, music, and laughter. Unfortunately, however, this image
had begun to lose its box office appeal, and Miranda's marketing pull was waning.

Dressed to Impress: Miranda's Visual Appeal and the Lure of Costumes

Carmen Miranda's exquisite costumes were an important selling point for her films.
Each presented a variant of the Miranda signature look, enhanced with garish
Technicolor in most of her films and producing an overall striking visual effect
that would become Hollywood's star-image of Carmen Miranda, her "visual shorthand" that remains an easily recognizable iconic symbol to this day.[37] Similar to
Dorothy Lamour and her famed sarong, Miranda's signature "look" was tied to her
costume, which became a deliberate fashion and film statement that could then be
mass marketed in exotic clothing lines, complete with turban, platform shoes, and
bulky jewelry.[38] The mass marketing of fashion appropriated the stars as vehicles
to showcase norms of femininity, and all across the country, women could see the
same actresses and fashion statements, facilitated by the technology of the close-
up and the film's reproducibility.[39] Although at this time the fashion statements
made by actresses such as Miranda were clearly geared toward female imitators and
lines of clothing that would replicate her style at face value, Miranda's popularity
crossed gender divides and held appeal for male viewers also.[40] The exquisiteness
of Miranda's costumes, made out of yards of the best fabrics, ornamented with
sparkling sequins, beads, and jewels, and topped by fascinating headdresses, placed
her at the helm of this category of actress as spectacle and fashion model to be

emulated. Miranda's costumes were all variants of the same style, which would become her "brand-name personality" in fashion.[41] Unlike her English malapropisms, Latin looks, and effervescent and explosive onscreen demeanor—all characteristics she shared to some degree with other Latin stars of the Hollywood golden years—the components of her costumes were her identifying mark and set her in a category apart from all other Latin performers of the time.

Whereas in the case of most actors and actresses, costumes are secondary other than in period films, for Miranda they constituted her screen persona with a heavy emphasis on glamor. In this, Miranda is one of the few cinematic exceptions to the common perception that a successful costume is one that does *not* appear as a costume, for the "troublesome distraction" diverts the viewer's attention from the story itself (Gaines, "Costume" 193). In Miranda's Hollywood films designed around a flimsy plot, her costumes were—quite on the contrary—a welcome distraction. One reviewer sums this up in *Photoplay* in reference to *The Gang's All Here*: "beautiful to look at, lovely to listen to, but so fragile in story is this lavish production."[42]

Moreover, Miranda's costumes accompanied her performance and were often referred to as spectacular in their own right. The publicity director at Twentieth Century-Fox, Harry Brand, summaries the synergy between Miranda's acting and costume in a press release for *Something for the Boys* (1944): "As spectacular as the number and its enactment by the volcanic Miranda is the peacock, cyclamen and royal purple costume designed for the Brazilian Bombshell by 20th Century Fox stylist Yvonne Wood" (3). The "spectacular" quality could be said of any one of Miranda's musical numbers and costumes. As Miranda's US career progressed, the visual presence of her costumes was further enhanced in her films by a new dimension of spoken references: the scriptwriters included commentary about Miranda's costumes in the dialogue, most noticeably in a much-quoted scene in *Springtime in the Rockies* discussed in Chapter 5.

With the fabulously rich possibilities of Miranda's basic costume, especially the infinite variants for the headdress, the studio designers were able to create artistic designs that emphasized her unique appearance but always with a touch of novelty. In this, the Hollywood costume designers, similar to the intellectuals and artists that Bourdieu discusses, "[had] a special predilection for the most risky but also most profitable strategies of distinction, those which [consisted] in asserting the power, which is peculiarly theirs, to constitute insignificant objects as works of art" (282). Miranda's headdresses were built from what might appear to be the most "insignificant" elements, and at times even indistinguishable elements, but the overall effect made the costumes unforgettable.

Miranda was so closely identified with her turbans, jewelry, and platform shoes that her stage and screen persona dominated her life off the set. Miranda was often spotted around town wearing her turban in public, such as to the Academy Awards evening in February 1941 and, most emblematically, at the ceremonial moment when she immortalized her hand and shoe prints at Grauman's Chinese Theatre on March 24, 1941. Miranda was viewed as one of Hollywood's best-dressed stars, both on and off the stage, a characteristic that was formalized by her March

Carmen and Aurora Miranda arrive at the Biltmore Hotel for the 13th Academy Awards ceremony (February 27, 1941). Courtesy of the Margaret Herrick Library

1943 *Photoplay* nomination among Hollywood's best-dressed women, including Claudette Colbert, Loretta Young, and Rosalind Russell, with the justification that her fabulous clothes would turn most women into circus horses but look "superbly right" on her.[43] When articles mentioned Miranda's presence around town, they invariably drew attention to her clothes with reference to the staples of her stage costume. A reporter for *Screenland*, March 1941, writes, "there is no experience more vastly diverting or stimulating than being invited to take luncheon with Carmen Miranda. [She was] dressed in a yellow suede from top to toe, with a sleek fitting turban and accessories in lush, vivid green (her national colors)."[44] Innumerable are the photos of Miranda around town in Hollywood and New York wearing a subdued form of her *baiana* costume.[45] Since Miranda often wore similar accessories off screen as in her films, namely costume jewelry, a turban, and platform shoes, she blurred the distinction between the screen costumes and everyday wear. In social settings, playful comments were also made about her turbans.[46]

Often in Miranda's films, as an intermediary between the proscenium Miranda-actress performing on a stage within the film and her out-of-the-film/ off-the-set appearance, she wears "street clothes" that still hark back to her signature look. In these scenes she does seem rather plain looking, as though something is missing to complete the picture. Following *The Gang's All Here*, the characters she plays continue to have multiple costume changes, but on many occasions she wears a pantsuit and a hat, headscarf, or smaller version of a turban, and always a few key elements are retained, such as platform shoes or bulky jewelry. Even if the look is downplayed, there is a definite reminder of her full-blown, signature costume. In several scenes of *Greenwich Village* and *If I'm Lucky*, she appears with "half-turbans" that reveal her hair in an up-do. In the opening factory scene in *Something for the Boys*, she is wearing a colorful scarf tied in a bow on the top of her head to distinguish her from the costars. These progressive levels of "Mirandization" of her Hollywood costumes, along with the everyday turbans she wore in public, created a sense of consistency between Miranda's onscreen and offscreen personae that collapsed the performative divide. This continuum was further enhanced from film to film by Miranda's being cast as protagonists with interchangeable names (Carmelita, Dorita, Rosita or Conchita) and maintaining her physical appearance and various traits consistently throughout her Twentieth Century-Fox years. In several films, she played "herself" as "Carmen Miranda" (*Down Argentine Way*) or simply "Carmen" (*That Night in Rio*) or "Carmen Novarro" (*Copacabana*), following the practice of naming characters after actors, which "served to diffuse the boundaries between the two and encourage one to take the personality of one for the other" (deCordova 89).

Because of the importance of Carmen Miranda's costumes, for each film the publicity materials boasted that her next release would have the most exquisite and unique costumes to date. Since the late 1920s, an industry-wide emphasis on star costumes had aimed to draw large numbers of women to the theater, and Miranda never moved beyond this "clothes horse" phase of her career, even after she ended her years with Twentieth Century-Fox. The publicity in *Screen Guide*'s March 1944 issue captures this trend: below a large, central photograph of Miranda as she appeared in *Greenwich Village* is the caption: "Preview of fireworks to come is the above picture of Carmen Miranda in a one-of-a-kind costume for a one-of-a-kind Miranda specialty for 20th's gay *Greenwich Village*."[47] As this example illustrates, it is through her costumes that Miranda becomes a spectacle, and for the most part, she is dwarfed and even effaced by their presence.

Since she typically changed costumes for each musical number or scene, with the exception of her first film, *Down Argentine Way*, the studio was able to lure the audience to the exhibition hall with the promise of Miranda's exotic costumes, and publicity releases provided ample discussion about her costumes for each forthcoming film. Both the trade journals and the commercial press drew attention to Miranda's costumes when reviewing the films, and their commentaries were overwhelmingly enthusiastic.[48] *Variety* records that for *Weekend in Havana* Miranda "wears her bizarre costumes with barbaric flair," qualifying Twentieth Century-Fox's chief designer Gwen Wakeling's creation as "striking plumage," an expression that was used several times in the media and that calls forth imagery of tropical birds and the savage customs of an exotic performer.[49] The studio had issued an intentionally enticing statement about the "highly daring nature" of both Alice Faye's and Carmen Miranda's costumes for *Weekend in Havana*, claiming that one of them "barely got by the Hays Office restrictions," and understandably so, given the large open spaces over Miranda's hips, which are only slightly veiled by an almost invisible netting. For this film, Harry Brand played the authenticity card, claiming "the original native costume worn by the native of one of the remote Brazilian provinces is even more daring."[50] This comment leaves ethnographers wondering to what costume Brand could possibly be referring. A commentary in *Screen Guide*, June 1944, about Miranda's forthcoming part in *Greenwich Village* provides another emblematic example of the importance of the costume in the marketing of Miranda's star persona. After a detailed discussion of all her different costumes in the film, which could only be surpassed by the color-splurge of a sunset and would make "rainbows fade away when La Belle Miranda emerges from her dressing room," the article concludes that "the over-all effect gives you an idea of what Miranda means when she says 'I am thee (sic) only one who dresses up for movies!'" (26).

Miranda was so closely associated with her Hollywood turbans that when the producer of *Springtime in the Rockies* opted for her to wear a hat, much ado of this wardrobe change was made in the studio's press releases. They claimed that Miranda never wore hats even as a child because of her personal preference for turbans and that they had battled for weeks to convince Miranda that a hat would not offend her Brazilian fans, creating emotional ties through (fabricated) references to Miranda's childhood and both manipulating and anticipating the audience's reaction.

A new personality for Miranda was also the focus of the publicity for *Greenwich Village*. The pressbook for the film maximized the mystery surrounding Miranda's so-called new personality and look, which were predicted to send "a good portion of the feminine world into a frenzy of anticipation" (16). The publicity department hinted that this new look would be a move away from the "wooden chopping bowls, banana palms, mixed fruit salads, Christmas toys, and fruit compotes on her head" (16) and had to do with the amount of leg she would reveal. If in past musicals she "adamantly refused abbreviated attire," in *Greenwich Village*, "Miss Miranda does an unabashed about-face and dances and sings in a frothy bit of costume which trails about her stilted heels but does not obscure her opera length hose" (17).[51] *Greenwich Village*, after all this hype, remained very close to the usual Miranda performance and costumes, in fact, merely adding new colors to her palette and variants to the headdress. Regardless, the reviews perceived Miranda as the star of the show, claiming it was her picture and she stole every scene.[52] For *Something for the Boys*, Twentieth Century-Fox announced once again that Miranda would have a new personality. The *New York Herald Tribune* wondered with humor if that meant she would "draw less than a Baldwin locomotive for a headpiece by way of change." Apparently she would be wearing "the briefest costume of her career" that "as sparse as a one-piece bathing suit, [would feature] a train lined with ribbon-beaded lace ruffles and opera-length purple stockings." The headdress, allegedly designed by Miranda herself, would consist of "a pair of gold lame open-work baskets filled with multicolored jeweled fruit and leaves, worn over a gold turban."[53] As *Movies* magazine commented, "only Carmen Miranda can get away with a hat like *that*."[54] All in all, this is a more involved, albeit less fruity, version of the same motif, complete with a bejeweled golden turban. In sum, the media did not tire in promoting time after time the same theme of Miranda's acquiring a new personality. Finally, it was in *Doll Face* that Miranda would indeed shed her "fruity headdress." The pressbook makes abundant use of the story, even with humor foreseeing a large drop in the fruit and vegetable markets. The novelty of her costume resides in Miranda's new millinery fashion, as she is quoted saying, "I got to geeve the customers someseeng deeferents." What this "something different" would be was only hinted at in the form of "a large turban with giant snoods and spangles," the mystery of Miranda's next get-up adding to the publicity draw and hoped-for success at the box office.[55]

Despite all the media talk about a new star image for Miranda, her screen persona did not change significantly from the first Fox film to the last, proving that the studio felt the need to maintain continuity with only artistic variations from film to film. Through this intense construction of Miranda's screen personality, the studio built around her an overcoded representation of the Latin performer that reinvents but stays true to itself through variations on her signature style.

Wearing the Show and the Film

By the time Miranda took Broadway by storm and then continued on to Hollywood with never-before-seen costumes in the most lavish combinations, the American sartorial revolution of the late teens and twenties had run its course. Clothing fashion had become democratized with the folding of class distinctions, the production of cheap fashion products, innovations in the ready-to-wear and fashion industries, and the widespread publication of fashion information in newspapers and magazines. With Miranda's image broadly publicized throughout the New York area, and her act on Broadway the hit of the season, very quickly this new star persona translated over into the fashion world, a statement that encompassed a much-desired taste for novelty, exoticism, playfulness, and difference in a world torn by the onset of World War II, which would only be amplified once Miranda became a Hollywood star. Miranda's performance was the epitome of the feminized spectacle and made a mark on the imagination of a predominately female audience seeking novelty and a taste of the exotic.

It is a difficult if not entirely impossible task to ascertain the impact of a fashion trend such as Miranda's turban, jewelry, and platform shoes. One quantifiable measure is the royalties she received: in 1939, the Shubert Company declared that Miranda earned $311.44 in royalties on jewelry and hats, etc., a figure that more than doubled in 1940 to $839.90. The pressbook for her penultimate film, *A Date with Judy* (1948), boasts that Miranda's income from royalties of her millinery designs based on her turbans netted her an annual income of $10,000.[56] However, these figures represent only a slight portion of the Miranda-craze, given that, for the most part, her fashion was imitated without any payment of royalties, causing the

Shubert Company much grief and legal confrontations, with their attorney as early as September 1939 calling the misappropriation of Miranda's name, photograph, and jewelry "unbearable."[57] The branding of Miranda as a trademark continued throughout her tenure on Broadway as Shubert attempted to monopolize the copyright of her signature look, claiming ownership of Miranda's impact on fashion both rhetorically, through press releases mostly written by C. P. Greneker that emphasized her role in trendsetting, and legally, by exerting their right to press charges on inappropriate uses of her trademark and, in particular, the costume jewelry that Miranda had reinvigorated. Despite Greneker's earnest attempts, the popularity of costume jewelry predated Carmen Miranda's Broadway début by over a decade, and Paris had given its stamp of approval at the Art Deco Exposition in 1925 (Whitaker 199). Because of its cheaper cost and the restrictions on fabric for dress designs, costume jewelry was a more important accessory during the Depression and War periods, with popular pieces becoming bigger and bolder, using brightly colored synthetics and incorporating new materials such as cork, shells, copper, and wood into the designs (Whitaker 199). A handful of official documents mention a request for the lawful use of Miranda's trademark style. A December 22, 1941, letter from a retail corporation requests the right to use the title "The Carmen Miranda Turban" in connection with the sale of women's hats.[58] There were also licensing agreements for a line of women's sweaters by Blume Knitwear, a line of blouses by Mitchell and Weber, and the use of Miranda's likeness in a series of Macy's advertisements. In an undated press release, Greneker's imaginative prose aims to emphasize the exotic and unique nature of Miranda's jewelry, "wrought by a silver craftsman in one of Brazil's foremost specialty jewelry shops" and incorporating "many of her own ideas besides exemplifying the bizarre nature of South America." Amusing anecdotes also circulated that relate how Miranda was approached by sales people trying to sell her the newest "Carmen Miranda jewelry" or being overcharged for an item of clothing that she claimed to have invented. Shubert's press agents capitalized on these stories, probably also embellishing them, to emphasize Miranda's uniqueness, creativity, and ownership of the trends that had suddenly become so popular.[59]

The reconstruction of anecdotal evidence in fashion markets, shop windows, magazines, and newspapers of the time are factors with which to approximate Miranda's fashion vogue. As evidence, there are photos of a Macy's "South American Way" display that features a series of mannequins dressed with turbans and heavily adorned with jewelry. Miranda was herself amazed during the 1939 holiday season to see eight mannequins looking just like herself in the window display of Bonwit Teller's flagship store in New York at Fifth Avenue and Fifty-Sixth Street, an upscale department store that specialized in high-end women's apparel.[60] This trend of modeling mannequins after stage and film stars dates from this period, with more women becoming employed in window designs for New York City department and specialty stores, a concept that also took hold elsewhere around the country.[61] The fashion trends she displayed were so flamboyantly unique and recognizable that they almost instantaneously produced a fashion consensus that would find its way into mainstream clothing trends. As early as June 1939, only weeks after her arrival in the United States, an article in *Women's Wear Daily* rightly predicted Miranda's influence on the season's fashions, especially in accessories, headdresses, and millinery, because of her attractiveness as a star, magnetic personality, and stage success.[62] The combination of the radio broadcasts that were so instrumental in promoting Miranda as a star to a broad national audience and the circulation of the visual image of her star persona fueled her star status and led to the popularity of her fashion statement, to the point that, four months after her arrival, the Shubert press department was astounded that "she has seized the imagination of American women to the point where Miranda hats, Miranda jewelry and Miranda dresses are the raging mode."[63] Every mention in the media fueled Miranda's impact on fashion, as reporters tried to define her fashion style. An article in the *New York Times* in July 1939 refers to her necklaces as "big ropes of large gold beads, strands of colored stones, or silver and copper balls, all characteristic of the trend toward a lavish mass of stuff around the neck." The article also notes that because of costume jewelry's flexibility and multiple usages, it has become "the inevitable complement of a plain black dress."[64] Toward the end of the year, when Miranda's fame was far-reaching and undeniable, the *New York Journal and American* states that Miranda is a "godsend to fashion designers" and "has struck at the very lifeblood of the nation—the women's styles!"[65] The *Philadelphia Record* surmised her impact on fashion as the previously unknown performer whose turbans and jewelry had been adopted by American women from coast to coast.[66] New shoe lines were released that drew on Miranda's platform wedges, sometimes explicitly referring to the new Broadway star and other times launching the new product with no mention of the Brazilian Bombshell. An article that appeared after Miranda had barely been in the country a month attributed her with having popularized, if not having invented, the fashion of the wedge heel.[67] This claim endured throughout her Hollywood career: a 1951 article in the *Los Angeles Daily News* takes up this same refrain, adding that Miranda regretted never patenting the item and admitted to having "carelessly tossed away a fortune."[68] Delman's claimed to have made Miranda's Broadway shoes and advertised their "golden tower" product as "fabulous footstools for Carmen Miranda in praise of her flamboyant and opulent fascination. New tapered models to heighten her beauty with six-inch heels, harvests on the toes, intricate appliqué, fantasy jewels."[69] According to *Modern Screen*, several female celebrities, such as Lana Turner, Alice Faye, and Vera Vague, had adopted Miranda's "barbarous, exciting, dramatic" *baiana* costume.[70] The fashion world and, reportedly, her feminine fans especially were wondering what Carmen would do next, or in other words, what they would do next.[71] This image of Miranda remained consistent throughout her Hollywood career.

The film-industry influence on fashion had reached its height; women's magazines continuously entertained the ongoing debate "to wear or not to wear the film," and since the mid-1930s, Hollywood-endorsed fashions had been readily available at all the main department stores.[72] Promotion tie-ins off screen, such as linking a line of clothing to a particular film, created a wider, and more emotionally driven, participatory, cinematic community.[73] The glamorous stars were widely credited with popularizing fads, as women saw the movie costumes as fashion guides that they should adopt/adapt, and onscreen fashion itself was a huge draw at the box office. In particular, while many of Miranda's most outlandish dresses could scarcely be reproduced for mass consumption, the simple turban and costume jewelry were easily accessible, and women could adapt these elements of Miranda-fashion to their personal liking. Miranda's famous turbans were knocked off by countless department stores, yet without the excessive accessories or dramatic paraphernalia. They were scaled down to a more practical style, a process that was common at the time and that transformed the apparent "unwearability" into a fashion starting point (Gaines, "Wanting to Wear" 142). This is explicitly articulated in the pressbook for Miranda's second film, *That Night in Rio*, which suggests: "For everyday purposes the excessive use of jewelry has to be modified, but the effect and the bold color combinations are useful ideas."[74] As this early example illustrates, the studios were fully aware of the impractical nature of Miranda's fashion but aimed to facilitate its integration into women's wardrobes by providing ready-made ideas for its adoption. Macy's featured the turban craze in its "Today's New Macy's Idea" spotlight section with a collection of half body mannequins wearing simple turbans. In the back of the display, they hung a large portrait of Miranda, and in the front they presented biographical information in an "open book" prop that passersby could read.[75] Naturally, turbans pre-existed Miranda's days in New York, but her charismatic performance was enough to give the vogue its most substantial push with an added exotic spin.[76] Despite Miranda's pleasure, and at times astonishment, with her impact on North American fashion, the media made it clear that, although imitable, she remained the real McCoy.[77]

Costume designing was an art at its peak during the heyday of the Hollywood musical, with industry masters leaving their indelible mark on film fashion history. Despite Allen Woll's reference to Miranda's costume as "a combination of native Bahian dress and a designer's nightmare" (*Latin Image* 68), Hollywood designers most likely relished the opportunity to create variations of extravaganza on the Miranda theme, if we are to judge by the results of their unleashed imagination on their fabulous creations. Travis Banton, chief designer at Paramount before moving to Fox in 1938, was known as "the master of shimmer and slink"—which fit Carmen Miranda beautifully. Along with Adrian, Banton was one of the most important designers of the golden years of Hollywood moviemaking, nowadays best remembered for Marlene Dietrich's marvelous beaded dress in *Angel* (1937), dresses for Mae West and Carole Lombard, and Rita Hayworth's strapless gowns. Associating Miranda so early in her career with Travis Banton bestowed a seal of prestige on Miranda's fashionable costumes, with his signature bias-cut styles that accentuated her curves and draped softly.

Sascha Brastoff was another of the designers who left a mark on Miranda's star wardrobe by creating the first screen costume entirely out of plastic for her performance in *If I'm Lucky*. There was much discussion and ink spent on Brastoff's appointment while he was still in the army, since he had never previously worked for the motion-picture industry and was "a professional artist and sculptor maintaining his own studio."[78] The publicity department claimed that Miranda's costume required seventy-five yards of plastic that had been shredded by hand to achieve the required soft effect, a job that took six wardrobe girls two weeks' work. The dress was matched with a white plastic, four-foot-high Miranda headdress, "in the form of an all-white Christmas tree," and plastic bracelets and necklaces.[79] The costume appeared as the focal point of the media attention, given its novelty and being the work of such an innovative young designer, overshadowing the film's divided reception.[80]

Although credit is owed and duly given to the talented costume designers who worked on Miranda's elaborate and always scintillating outfits, the media (the studios included) frequently rehearsed her invention of the headdress as dating back to the first time she wore it in Brazil and promoted Miranda as participating in these extravagant creations, often with a dramatized edge.[81] In *Motion Picture* of December 1944, three months after Miranda's gallstones were removed, Virginia Wood refers to her as "indestructible," "irrepressible," "lying awake until all hours of the night in her usual fashion, planning some new and tricky turban or dreaming up a new dance step," with her characteristic enthusiasm and vitality for the film *Greenwich Village*.[82] Although Miranda was by no means the first actress to participate in designing her own costumes, as this had been the norm in the late teens and twenties,[83] what was unusual, and certainly never the case with her female costars, is that the studio insisted on, and the media echoed, Miranda's personal investment in her costumes, portraying her as participant/producer of her own image rather than what might have been a less flattering alternative: manipulated at the hands of the studio's artistic executives.

The studio knew how to maximize Miranda's unique look by placing her fashion impact within a wider political context of the Good Neighbor Policy and even at times extending this "neighborly costuming" to Miranda's costars. For *Down Argentine Way*, for example, the publicity department claimed that two of the gowns Travis Banton had created for Betty Grable were a nod toward the Good Neighbor Policy because of the organdie fabric, very full skirt, and use of blue and white (the Argentine national colors) for one of them, although this fact would not help the film's reception south of the border, packed as it was with derogatory stereotypes.[84] The pressbook for Miranda's second film, *That Night in Rio*, continued to draw on the goodwill fervor by implying that diplomatic ententes would inevitably lead to fashion exchanges, with Miranda giving the final impetus to this trend by crystallizing a vogue for "fruit-basket" and feather hats.[85]

The success of Miranda's film costumes came to represent the Latin look in the "South American Way" and coincided with the fashion of the late 1930s and early 1940s, which was seeking novel vogues to accompany the exotic feel fostered to counter wartime gloom. *That Night in Rio* was reviewed in *Motion Picture Herald* as "ultra-modern Pan-Americanism," with Miranda ably representing "the Latin influence" along with her orchestra, which also demonstrates "the South American Way."[86] Lisa Shaw develops this idea of fashion ethnicity, which she views as essential for Miranda to become a household name, as "striking the balance between 'strangeness and familiarity' that is central to exoticism" ("Celebritisation" 295).[87]

Placing Miranda's fashion/film look within the larger context of a South American vogue was a natural marketing tool and enabled her to have a greater impact. When screen costumes vibrate with the current fashion trends, they "epitomize that trend and amplify its significance because of its association with a particular star or character" (Berry, *Screen Style* 92). Bourdieu likewise theorizes this need for a broader context for fashions to be popular: a trend "could not function if it could not count on already existing tastes, more or less strong propensities to consume more or less clearly defined goods" (230). There was a widespread appreciation for Latin music during the 1930s on the radio, stage, and dance floor, and Miranda entered the scene at the optimal moment to give this taste a new face and an emblematic silver-screen representation.[88] For the studio, it was a question of marketing Miranda's authenticity, along with that of the film's foreign cultural content.[89]

Defining Miranda the Comedienne

Both the studio and the media provided plenty of commentary on Miranda's acting career, often intermingled with remarks about her English and her comedy, and overall tried to define Miranda's performance on the silver screen. At the release of Miranda's second film (and first North American acting breakthrough), *That Night in Rio*, *The Hollywood Reporter* pointedly writes that Miranda is a "sensational newcomer" who "will soon join [Alice Faye and Don Ameche] as a marquee name of importance."[90] The film received rave reviews with Miranda's part central to the praise. A reporter for the *Miami Herald* writes, "I can't imagine anything more fabulous, more magnificent, more intriguing, more sparkling, more exciting, more comforting and generally delightful than Carmen Miranda . . . in *That Night in Rio*, one of the most dazzling musical pictures ever done in technicolor."[91] An article published in *News* declares that Miranda, who has "no classic beauty" but plenty of "oomph,"[92] has apparently "quietly moved into the 20th-Fox studios and taken them over."[93] As these statements suggest, Miranda was an unexpected all-around success, and her media reception was overwhelming positive.

As Miranda was cast in more complicated character roles, the studio fueled the media with language to define her new film parts. After *That Night in Rio*, the studio claimed that in each subsequent film the public would see Miranda as a true comedienne. Her performance seems to come into its own in the filming of *Weekend in Havana*, her vivaciousness perceived as part of her unique, exotic talent. Second only to the success of *That Night in Rio*, *Weekend in Havana* was highly praised in the print media, with Miranda as one of its main attractions. An article in *Photoplay* includes Miranda as one of the "sights to see" alongside "colorful Cuba," reinforcing the to-be-looked-at-ness of her spectacular performance.[94] *Variety* published a review along the same lines, referring to Miranda as a "whirlwind of tempestuous action" and placing her in the rank of the screen's "top comediennes and most colorful entertainers." Every review that discusses her performance echoes this enthusiastic appraisal of the film and not only agrees that Miranda steals the show, but that with greater acting parts Twentieth Century-Fox's musicals would only get better.[95] It was apparent that by 1941 she was perceived as one of the industry's top-billed actresses, surrounded by praise and excitement, with repeated references to the impact of her "always barbaric and brilliant" costumes, "the flicker of her eyes," and "her singularly expressive hands."[96]

By the time Miranda filmed her forth movie with Twentieth Century-Fox, *Springtime in the Rockies*, she was an established player of the silver screen, although press releases continued to make reference to her "new role" as a comedienne "in addition to her usual sinuous gyrations and songs."[97] Her career to date was summarized by a studio press release as evolving from a specialty act in *Down Argentine Way*, to "a fiery Latin" in *That Night in Rio*, to "a soupçon of comedy" and more "firebrand comedy" in *Weekend in Havana*, to being made into an "out-and-out comedienne" in *Springtime in the Rockies*.[98] As a Latin actress, being a comedian corresponded to one of the reigning stereotypes that Hollywood films deployed to counterbalance the potential of screen seduction, fitting with the necessity of the white, North American beau to not be seriously attracted to and ultimately reject the Latina star. Furthermore, this portrayal undermined Miranda's femininity while confirming the gender bias of the Hollywood musical comedies, which implies that "while a male comedian can have sex appeal—in fact, his humor may contribute to it—a female comedian . . . automatically disqualifies herself as an object of desire" (Haskell 62). Miranda's stylized costumes and comedic parts placed her out of reach as a love interest in the main storylines of her films proportionately to her development, as mentioned above, into a true comedian.

Miranda's becoming a "fully-fledged comedienne" is still lauded in the publicity materials for her seventh film with Twentieth Century-Fox, *Greenwich Village*, where she is said to be "realizing fully the promise of earlier productions in which she was relied upon principally for her inimitable and decorative singing and dancing."[99] After such a play-up, there would seem to be nowhere else to go in promoting Miranda, but for the next film, *Something for the Boys* (1944), the studio promises a new role that veers from "outright slapstick to the most seductive and difficult type of singing-dancing performance she has yet been called upon to do."[100] However, it was following the release of *Something for the Boys* that reviewers started to tire of what they perceived as the same Miranda performance, despite the overall continued positive reviews of the studio's musical productions. As one reviewer writes for the *Los Angeles Examiner* on November 24, 1944, "how customers or the studio either, for that matter, can tell one of these pictures from t'other is beyond us, so uniformly are they cut to pattern," but she reassures the reader that "for those a bit weary of Carmen's indistinguishable lyrics all to the same tune, or at least it's beginning to sound that way, there is fun in her antics as a human radio set."[101]

The success of the Fox films starring Miranda dipped dramatically after *Something for the Boys*, a trend that was felt across the studios as the musical genre reached its popularity threshold. Previously, *Four Jills and a Jeep* had received negative reviews all around, although in all fairness Miranda only made a cameo appearance as a guest-star singer. *Doll Face* (1945) was, in the words of one reviewer, "a heck of a long wait for Carmen Miranda to do a musical number."[102] A critic for the *Commonweal* blatantly writes that the film as a whole is not particularly entertaining: "my interest was kept alive only by the presence of Carmen Miranda in the cast as I knew that sooner or later she would do a number."[103] This critique is not uncommon for the Hollywood film musical. For Ted Sennett, "the musical score and the performances . . . remain the most important components of the musical film. Many a film has been salvaged by its lilting songs, or made more than tolerable by the superior quality of the singing and dancing performances" (13–14). Unfortunately, however, for film viewers of *Doll Face*, there was not a lot of Miranda to keep the interest alive.

Carmen Miranda's meteoric rise to stage and screen fame and her subsequent trajectory that involved more integrated acting parts retained the public's interest for the duration of her Twentieth Century-Fox years and garnered enthusiastic reviews from reporters who continued to marvel at her screen presence, even when her films failed at the box office and she dropped to secondary billing. Despite this disconnect between the studio casting and the media reception, which became all the more pronounced in the case of Miranda's last films at Fox, her vivacious and dynamic performances, with their characteristic gaiety and tropical colorfulness, embodied the essence of the Hollywood musical while the genre was in its heyday.

Miranda in the Media

It is not surprising that Miranda, a successful Hollywood performer with an avid fan following, was the subject of innumerable articles in fan magazines claiming to expose her private life beyond her screen persona. As is well known, the fan magazines were a form of indirect publicity for the studio, an essential marketing tool to circulate the players' behind-the-scenes activities, and many are the critics who write of this magazine and film industry codependence that Slide labels "an incestuous relationship built on trust and mutual necessity" (7). According to Marsha Orgeron, most of the material circulated in the fan magazines, the major purveyors of information about the stars to the public, was generated by the studio's publicity departments and even the stars themselves, enabling the magazines to "fill their pages with 'authorized' and 'exclusive' material" (100–101). The fan magazines explicitly linked the female spectators to the theaters and patterns of consumption, promising attainability and, as Orgeron writes, "if you buy this, you can be like star X" (106). The heyday of the fan magazine accompanied the decades of the studio star system, when going to the movies was the main form of media entertainment in the United States.[104] At any one time, alongside the most popular, widely circulated, and longstanding *Photoplay*, its main competitor, *Modern Screen*, as well as *Motion Picture*, *Movieland*, *Silver Screen*, and *Screenland*, there were dozens of similar, often ephemeral magazines, whose existence varied from several months to several years, frequently merging among themselves as they tried to find a niche in a booming yet volatile industry. The public was hypnotized by Hollywood and its stars, and the articles in the fanzines translated this exhilaration with the movies and players, displaying "an open delight in the glamor and artistic achievements of the industry" (Ohmer 62). The fan magazines were easily accessible, cheap commodities that extended the audience's film viewing experience to encompass the stars' "real" personalities—their lives, loves, tastes, lifestyles, hobbies, homes, beauty and fashion tips—offering the reader a close-up and intimate relationship with their idols.[105] As deCordova rightly argues, "it was very difficult to separate the idea of family life from the idea of home life, so the stars' homes became another area of interest, another aspect of their private existence" (107). These fanzines were popular because readers found them to be simultaneously pleasurable, relevant, informative, and inspiring, and like a modern-day soap opera, they kept the audience coming back for more, month after month, as the insatiable readers wanted to consume Hollywood and the movie images beyond the exhibition hall. Once the fan magazines realized the growing number of middle-class women who went to the movies and devoured any information about the top stars beyond the silver screen, they redesigned their magazines' content to correspond more closely with female consumer desires, including fashion coverage, beauty and health advice, social etiquette, culinary recipes, household refurbishing, home decor, etc., alongside photo spreads of the stars, film reviews, news stories, and gossip columns, a successful formula that varied little from magazine to magazine throughout the years of their existence. In this lies the paradox of the star, "at once ordinary and extraordinary, available for desire and unattainable" (Ellis 91). Columnists such as Hedda Hopper and Louella Parsons, the two reigning divas of the print-gossip world, fueled readers' desire for information, often exposing the stars' private lives and shifting the divide between the public and private, making more intimate aspects of celebrities' lives open to public scrutiny. According to George Eells, "in their heyday Hedda and Louella claimed a combined readership totaling 75,000,000" (14) and were ruthless at obtaining and disseminating gossip before anyone else did. They contributed to the star personas, "a concept that integrated what was known—or what the studios wanted known—about stars both on-screen and off-screen" (Frost 32). Through syndicated gossip columns and fan magazines, the stars' real lives became extensions of their onscreen personas and performances.

In Carmen Miranda's case, gossip in the media focused on emphasizing her *Latinidade*—her signature look and other stereotypical behaviors expected of a Latin star. The gossip discourse around Miranda relayed her uniqueness and difference but was, for the most part, devoid of any truly scandalous stories: Miranda was not known to ever step outside appropriate norms of social behavior, other than a one-time incident on the set of *Weekend in Havana* with a photographer whose low angle revealed Miranda was not wearing any underwear. Both the Shubert press department and the press agents at Twentieth Century-Fox fueled the image of Miranda as a religiously educated foreigner, whose only peccadillo was supposedly having a ravenous appetite.

A sample from a few representative articles about Carmen Miranda is indicative of the most commonly repeated, salient elements of the parafilmic discourse around the Brazilian Bombshell that, as typically happens with stars in the media, privileges certain aspects of their stardom over others. As important research tools, I take heed of Slide's advice to "examine and analyze the articles in part rather than in whole" by focusing on valuable lines or paragraphs (9). As Christopher Finch and Linda Rosenkrantz in *Gone Hollywood* caution, the researcher finds reliable information extremely difficult to come by in the fan magazines, but they remain fascinating documents that "gave the studios a direct line to the hard-core fans and served the important function of giving the stars an existence—however fantasized—separate from the roles they played on screen" (113). It is when these fan-magazine articles have been taken at face value that Miranda's stardom has been distorted in film criticism. The fan magazines contribute to creating affective and emotional ties between the celebrities and the public by providing a behind-the-scenes look at the lives of the stars (Marshall 83). But this behind-the-scenes is often staged and purposely meant to support commonly circulated ideas of the stars. The magazines brought "real-life" snapshots of the stars to their adoring fans, on the set, around town, and at home. However, most often "the fan magazines were as synthetic as the world . . . portrayed by the movies" (Slide 75).

The interest of the discourse surrounding Carmen Miranda, independent of whether said information was factual or "ludicrously unreal,"[106] is important to understanding her impact in popular-media culture and how this image was construed in the magazines at this critical intersection between the stars, the industry, the media, the fans, and the reading and viewing public. Women were able to use fan magazines as a resource to experience creativity, ideals, and fantasies, as transmitted through the lens of the Hollywood studios and stars. As Slide discusses, the relationship between the fan magazine and its reader was mostly articulated around a sense of identification with glamorous stars that the magazines provided to the (mostly female) fans (134). This identification was not a spontaneous or uncalculated by-product of the fanzines: the magazines fostered this process by bringing the stars' lives to the fans and giving the readers the expectation that they, too, could emulate the stars' lives. A 1942 *Photoplay* article articulates this rhetoric in relation to Carmen Miranda. After explaining how Miranda keeps her nails looking spectacular (hand cream, cotton gloves, cuticle care, nail oil treatment, two coats of nail polish, hand exercises), the article concludes with the promising warning: "Better watch out, or before you know it, you'll be just like Miranda!"[107] Orgeron writes that "such feelings of intimacy emerged partly as a result of the familiarizing discourse promoted in the fan magazines, which often situated stars as storytellers, confidants, advisers, and friends to their fans" (107).

Closeness to the stars was also fostered by a process of desacralization that included portraying their private lives while in their home settings, doing mundane activities around town, or on vacation. As Lipovetsky writes, "to be sure, cinema invented more-realistic and less-distant stars, but they were always endowed with exceptional beauty and seductive power" (184). Images of Miranda actively pursuing hobbies or physical activities (such as biking or exercising) fueled the commonly circulated convention of stars living normal, stable, and healthy lives.[108] A glimpse into Miranda's life at home, filtered through the fan-magazine lens, spies a gay and active lifestyle. When she is not filming on the set, she spends her time swimming in her home pool, painting, cooking, entertaining (mostly guests from Brazil), answering fan mail, and even crocheting.[109] As Gamson explains, the presentation of stars in the 1930s had become more and more mortal, promoting "a greater sense of connection and intimacy between the famous and their admirers" (29). Many of these magazine articles on Miranda are composed almost entirely of pictures with one or two captions, rather than any sort of substantial informative narrative, and the photographs function in sequence.[110] The August 1943 issue of *Screenland* illustrates this tendency, consisting of a fabulous double-page layout composed of six photographs featuring Miranda, with the catchy title "Miranda Makes with the Mischief!"[111] One article, appropriately titled "Not all Fun and Frolic," refers to Miranda as a "busy little beaver": making future plans; meeting with her managers, press representative, musical director, and booking agency; taking care of fan mail, interviews, and photographs; and rehearsing new musical numbers.[112] This approach is typical of the hardworking image the media liked to portray of the stars, countering the glamor of the screen with their work ethics behind the scenes, and this is repeated in the press throughout Miranda's career.[113]

Much commentary was provided about Miranda's relaxing by driving around town in her beige Cadillac, reclining on her leopard-skin couch, and ideally getting ten hours of sleep.[114] The motorcar as an indicator of wealth had begun in the 1910s and the beginning of the star system and had carried over as a social-status marker into the 1930s and 1940s, especially during the war period (deCordova 108). Magazine writers commented repeatedly on Miranda's enjoyment of the American way of life and how this feeling was reciprocal.[115] *Modern Screen* of March 1941 discusses Miranda's infatuation with Hollywood with dramatic, euphoric sentences such as "Hollywood, it has treated me so nicely, I am ready to faint." The article claims Miranda spent her days kissing everyone, from her director Irving Cummings to her costar Don Ameche, and had fallen in love with all the beautiful stars of the Hollywood sets.[116] Another reporter writes that she allegedly held his hand during the interview and mentions how "people feel she loves them. Men especially feel she does." Although this physical contact through kissing and handholding is chalked up to being an "old Brazilian custom," Miranda's warmth permeated throughout her media articles both on and off the set.[117] *Silver Screen* of March 1941 tells of her magnetic presence on the set of *That Night in Rio*, which brings her costars Alice Faye and Don Ameche out of their dressing rooms to watch, listen, and lead the applause.[118] *Photoplay* of July 1941 emphasizes how enamored Hollywood was with Miranda, stating that "the place could eat Carmen off a spoon . . . it's that fond of her. . . . There is more warmth in her smile, more friendliness in her hand-clasp, more genuinely 'from the heart' friendliness about her than in any star discovered in ages, with the result that when she is filming a scene the set is packed with everybody in the studio" (6). This "warmth" was naturally present in her live performances, such as her appearances at Grauman's Chinese Theatre, where after her band played an introductory number, "the place lights up with a million watts of human electricity called Miranda—gay skirts swirling, jewels aglitter, headdress like a miniature leaning tower of Pisa. Her radiant smile embraces the audience."[119] With close to nothing in terms of information on concrete love affairs, the media did what it could to create interesting storylines around Miranda's private life, but they were pale in comparison to the loves, divorces, and star scandals of many other players, which had been common since the 1920s.[120]

Food, and especially tropical fruit and exotic dishes, was a frequent topic in press articles dedicated to Miranda, showcasing "candid" images of her in the kitchen demonstrating South American recipes and culinary customs. As deCordova explains, "picture personality" is an effect of the representation of players in a film, or across a number of films, while the illusion and intertextuality is maintained outside the film's frames (87). *Movie Story* of July 1947 features an article by the "Food and Household Editor" Vivian Reade titled "Fruit ees ze Fashion," playing on Miranda's costumes and the summer trend of fruit dishes, including a "blueberry soup" for an "unusual appetizer" and "fruit salad" with strawberries, watercress, peaches, and pineapples.[121] Other articles focus on her "enormous appetite" that was "practically a legend" and the inordinate quantities of food that she presumably was able to eat for lunch on the set.[122] One reporter lists her packing away "a shrimp salad, a meat course, five cups of bouillon, two fancy desserts and a piece of lemon chiffon pie" while her female costars were "sitting around wolfing lettuce sandwiches and shredded carrots . . . tortured by envy."[123] Even Hedda Hopper weighed in on Miranda's appetite in her syndicated *Los Angeles Times* column, stating that Miranda was "one of the few stars who relishes horse sirloin steaks."[124] On the flip side, reporters frequently quoted with humor Miranda's mentioning "being" on a diet. *Screen Life* reports her saying, "Mi mama is here now and she cook what I like in Brazil. Sometimes I eet too much and de meedle geet beeg. Then I go on de diet, maybe for a whole day."[125] And *News* writes, "She loves to eat big meals; always says 'but I will get fat'—after she has eaten the meal. Never before."[126]

The association of Miranda and exotic food was also appropriated to foster good-neighbor topics in the fan magazines, capitalizing on Miranda as the epitome of the good-neighbor cook. The connection between Miranda and exotic dishes was first projected in the pressbook for her second Hollywood film, *That Night in Rio*, where the publicity department suggests in a women's page feature two examples of "'Rio' Recipes" that, apparently, the "glamorous Carmen Miranda," who "is fond of concocting exotic dishes," had shared in between takes on the set: cream of avocado and banana compote.[127] In another such article, Miranda is illustrious of cooking in "The South American Way," with the immediate subtext, "Be a good neighbor and entertain the hospitable way—The South American Way." The article features a posed photograph of Carmen in full turban regalia reading the cookbook *Restaurant La Bahia*, with the caption "Singing and dancing are only two of Carmen Miranda's accomplishments. She is also an excellent cook" (62). In the text body, we read a series of half-truths that make the reader marvel at such an invention: "Carmen Miranda is no 'Latin from Manhattan.' She's the 'real-McCoy'—straight from Bahia, Brazil. . . . Our lovely green-eyed idol from the Amazon not only sings and dances with vivacity; she's an excellent swimmer; and better still, a cook of renown!" (62). Cooking good food in Brazil is considered natural in a "country where 'to eat and be merry' is to live."[128] This article is similar to one found in *Modern Screen* several years later, titled "The Foods of our Allies: Brazil." Under a picture of Miranda tasting her food in the kitchen, wearing an apron and with her hair down around her shoulders, she is portrayed as your everyday cook in the kitchen with a caption that reads: "'I taste eet, then I season eet!' says Carmen Miranda, famous samba specialist of screen and stage. She loves good food and favors dishes prepared at home in the Brazilian manner." The article then promotes a pamphlet of "recipes for Carmen Miranda's Brazilian dishes" that includes picadinho, feijoada, camaroesa bahiana, and crème de abacate (80).[129]

To provide a greater closeness and sense of authenticity to the star, the media and the studio sought to blur the boundaries between Miranda's stage/screen persona and offstage life by underlining the elements that she carried from her performative onstage persona into her regular life. As one reporter writes, "she's not really different off-stage. The face, the voice, the charm, the vitality are unchanged. But the spectacular gives way to simplicity. . . . Shorn of her barbaric splendor, she's still Miranda."[130] This conflation of stars' reel/real life by merging screen roles and offscreen personalities was essential to studio star making and was fueled by the publicity departments, who assured the projection of a celebrity's personal life matched that of the screen character (Gamson 26).

As mentioned above, with the exception of a handful of articles, photographs dominated the fan-magazine pieces on Miranda with very little narrative. On the one hand, her star image included a strong visual component: the bright and often contrasting colors, lush materials, and exotic motifs combined with an original aesthetic of otherness. On the other hand, Miranda led a relatively private life. One fanzine critic reports, "she doesn't go out much. She doesn't drink—except for a glass of champagne to celebrate her birthday. If she has a serious heart interest, gossip hasn't caught up with it. Invited to Ciro's, she'll sometimes accept, but there's always a rider. . . . Indeed, she's been known to appear with her whole entourage, including the band. She never stays long. An hour at most, a couple of rhumbas—her favorite dance—and she's gone."[131] In a *Hollywood magazine* article from September 1941, another critic refers to her as an unapproachable star, "a touch-me-not glamour girl," who always went out with one or a group of chaperones.[132] Over the years of Carmen Miranda's Hollywood stardom, several rumors circulated about her love interests, including a doctor in Rio who apparently telephoned her every weekend (*Time Magazine*, November 9, 1942); Gilberto Souto, who was Don Ameche's Portuguese coach for *That Night in Rio* (*Motion Picture*, November 1942); George Sanders, allegedly one of the hardest-to-get actors in town (*Silver Screen*, July 1941); her costar Cesar Romero (*Photoplay*, November 1942); and the Brazilian composer Ari Barroso (*Photoplay*, July 1944). Even one of the most powerful gossip columnists, Louella Parsons, wrote an article titled "Miranda Will Wed Brazilian," claiming that Carmen had revealed to her privately that she would marry Dr. Roberto Marin, a prominent South American, after the war was over (*Examiner*, May 28, 1945). Ultimately, the media announced Miranda's engagement in early March 1947 to the film producer David Sebastian, followed by their wedding two weeks later in Beverly Hills at the Church of the Good Shepherd. A year and a half later, Hedda Hopper was prompt to announce Miranda's pregnancy: "Carmen Miranda Books Stork—and Celebrates,"[133] while the news of their separation in late September 1949 and reconciliation two months later were also widely advertised.

Yet beyond these rumors, mixed with some facts, the gossip about Miranda's private life was relatively subdued, and as a consequence anecdotes that bordered on ludicrousness were invented to add spice to her stardom. *Motion Picture* of December 1942 reported in the column "The Talkie Town Tattler" that "Carmen Miranda is maaaaaaaaaaaaad because some meanie printed that she had her nose remodeled," a suggestion she fervently denied.[134] *Silver Screen* reported a feud between Miranda and the hot-tempered Mexican spitfire Lupe Vélez over jealousy stemming from a critic's statement that Miranda looked like "an old aunt of Vélez" followed by Miranda's criticism of Vélez for trying to copy her.[135] Perhaps the most outrageous piece of invented gossip surrounding Miranda was *Silver Screen*'s claim in February 1948 that "Carmen Miranda is installing a freezing unit in her swimming pool, so that six hours after a swim, she can whip around on her ice skates," certainly not your usual Brazilian custom.[136]

Despite a few isolated examples of sensationalist articles, for the most part the discourse around Carmen Miranda's stardom created a mediated window into her offstage/offscreen life that reinforced stereotypical aspects of her portrayal as a unique Latin star. With repeated themes that bordered on clichés, the print media enabled her fans to make greater sense of her star image by providing a coherent behind-the-scenes view of her exotic otherness that extended her stage performance, thus blurring the proscenium divide and giving the audience a greater approximation of the Brazilian Bombshell's foreignness.

The media also used Miranda's stardom to promote commercial products, as was customary with Hollywood stars during the 1930s, a period that saw the greatest use of celebrity endorsement. As Fox's publicity director Harry Brand writes in his "Vital Statistics" on *Weekend in Havana*, "although CM has been in pictures less than a year and a half, she now has more commercial tie-ups than any other film star in Hollywood except Disney's famous mouse. Thus far they include furs, cosmetics, radio, coffee, dresses, hats, over a dozen sorts of games, books, phonograph records and a number of other items, including a bathing suit."[137] These tie-ups represented a considerable addition to Miranda's salary and symbolized great prestige for Miranda's career. It is hard to know exactly all the products she endorsed and whether Brand's affirmation is correct or not; what is most

129

evident is that she was in high demand and the studio allowed her to endorse these commercial products to maximize her popularity.

These product endorsements drew on Miranda as an exotic, vivacious, and attractive performer and featured the star in advertisements mostly related to music, beauty, English lessons, and consumable products such as beer—which is definitely odd, as she didn't drink. A telling example is Miranda's endorsement of the then-new General Electric radio, as printed in the February 1945 issue of *Life Magazine*. The caption, drawing from Miranda's colorful attire and gay exoticness, reads, "Conventional radio—lacks color and richness. Something is missing. FM Radio by General Electric—you hear the tones in all their 'natural color' and beauty."[138] As was common practice, the advertisement mentions Miranda by name, her studio, and the film she was currently appearing in, *Something for the Boys*. This design succeeded in capturing the customers' need for a more fulfilling listening experience and correlated Miranda's bright and dynamic Technicolor performances to the tangible object for sale, the new radio set.[139] In this, as in other advertisements, Miranda sets the mood that emanates from her iconic appearance and unique performance as a foreign, attractive, and vivacious actress and singer. Despite the mockery the media made of her supposedly poor command of English, she became the poster gal for the Barbizon English classes, a strategy that Jhally refers to as the technique of "user-centered advertising" (128). If Miranda, with the most widely publicized mangled English, can learn the language, then any foreigner could likewise and thus fulfill the American dream by becoming as successful as she was. The majority of Miranda's advertising drew from her obvious characteristics as a performer, with mentions of her particularly widespread connotations of *Latinidade*, colorfulness, and singing career. It meant that without any equivocal, Miranda was an immediately recognizable star among the greatest of the period. At the same time, her stardom was still used for product endorsement back in Brazil, as in the Eucalol soap and dental paste advertisement that features Miranda in her striking *Streets of Paris* costume alongside a small sketch of the Statue of Liberty and the claim that, although America provides "excellent products," there is nothing comparable to the Eucalol that Carmen Miranda used in her "beloved and distant Brazil." Miranda is pictured as the far-away star in New York who still fondly remembers Brazilian products and, by metonymy, her Brazilian homeland.

Carmen Miranda is perhaps the lone example of a highly successful Latina star during these years able to maintain star billing, if not star roles, and Twentieth Century-Fox fostered this image throughout the production of her ten films with their studio. Yet, the true fascination of her star persona stemmed from the contained frame of her specialty acts—most often disjointed from the plot, behind a distinct and symbolic proscenium stage. And all the while, despite her growing resentment against these pigeonholed parts used for marketing purposes, as chronicled by her biographers, the United States entertainment industry gave the fair-skinned, green-eyed Miss Miranda the best it had to offer: publicity, public appearances, print coverage, and visual images spread widely throughout the media. For several years, Miranda corresponded to a specific, wartime moviegoers' taste, and as a direct consequence, her impact on fashion and music trends was signifi-cant, albeit short lived.[140] As Fiske details, the desire for the new is what fuels the production process (*Reading the Popular* 26) and what launched Miranda's North American career overnight, but this same need for newness caused her downfall, along with the demise of the musical genre as a whole. Yet during her years of popularity, the audience's attraction to Miranda's unique *je ne sais quoi* created a desire to bring components of her star persona closer, allowing them the illusion of approximating her bodily image, a concept that cinematic close-ups enhance and that translated to the popularity of her commercial tie-ups.[141] The promo-tional materials that fueled Miranda's stardom also contributed to bridging the star/fan gap. With several emblematic milestones along the way, such as her im-prints at Grauman's Theatre and her Paul Meltsner portrait, Miranda was one of the most popular celebrities at her prime.[142] Regardless of what certain film re-viewers or movie patrons may have thought, it is undeniable that her broad fan base warranted Twentieth Century-Fox's giving her top billing. *Movie Stars Parade* of September 1946 claimed she was the "highest paid gal in the U.S.," according to Treasury Department statistics.[143] Previously, Miranda had also alluded to her exponential salary: "'In 1944' she explained, 'I was very proud. I was the highest paid woman in the world. I made more than $400,000.'"[144] Furthermore, just as Hollywood did not always choose to promote Latina/o stars, when they did, it showed that they believed he or she was worth the financial investment, and the star, having established an affective relationship with the movie audience, was able to enjoy the benefits of being an economic center of the studio system. The studio's endorsement proved that Miranda was what the public wanted, a wistful collage of exotic, fun, cheery singing and dancing representing an entertaining means of es-capism, all decked in bright colors, inviting the audience to surrender their rational faculties in order to enjoy the fantastic illusions presented in a glorious cornucopia of Technicolor, music, and dance.

With such a unique performance, on film and in live performances, rarely has Franz Liszt's famous remark been truer: Miranda could definitely claim, "the con-cert is—myself."[145]

CHAPTER FIVE

CAMP CARMEN

The Icon on the Screen

Musically Camp

To approach Carmen Miranda through camp theory as an analytical tool enables a reading of her iconic figure in its time and as it is remembered today and provides a gateway to engaging theoretically the imitations that draw from her image. Camp has most often been associated with a homosexual subculture and the idea of potential sexual subversiveness, gender play, and marginality, a meaning that the term acquired during the 1920s in theatrical argot and that, by the mid-1940s, had become more widespread. Though it commonly maintains these connotations, its meaning has been extended to a more mainstream and general usage, and in film lingo, as Paul Roen specifies, "camp has come to mean any brazen triumph of theatrical artifice over dramatic substance" (1: 9). This statement, similar to those by other critics such as Mark Booth or Michael Bronski, harks back to Susan Sontag's 1964 much-rehearsed seminal essay "Notes on Camp," in which she emphasizes the importance of style inherent in camp: "Camp is a vision of the world in terms of style . . . the love of the exaggerated, the 'off,' of things-being-what-they-are-not" (56). Though issue has been taken with Sontag's essay mostly because of its apolitical stance, her text remains the prominent and necessary point of reference in all discussions of camp. Sontag's deliberations are indeed useful to interpreting Carmen Miranda's performance and the importance of camp in general within the Twentieth Century-Fox musicals in which she starred.

Through exaggeration, stylization, transformation, ambivalence, incongruity, and playful deception, camp creates an aesthetic that upturns received norms and realities, changing the natural and the normal into style and phoniness. It is a performance that thrives on glamor and extravagance, a phenomenon that presents itself as serious, although it thwarts, by the same token, its own performativity, knowing that it "cannot be taken altogether seriously because it is 'too much'" (Sontag 59). Yet there must be an element of coherence and consistency for camp· to be convincingly camp.

Camp is essential to understanding how Miranda was part of a masquerade in a way that led her to engage with her star image as an artificial, exaggerated version of the *baiana*, yet without demeaning herself, her gender, or her culture. Through camp we, along with Miranda, can dissociate ourselves from the restrictions of a face-value reading of her *baiana* performance. All is done in the truly playful, make-believe spirit of the Hollywood musical, which likewise enabled Miranda (with full credit given to her awareness) to wholeheartedly participate in imitations and reinterpretations of her image because she was knowingly part of the game. This subtle interstitial distance corresponds to what I refer to as Carmen Miranda's *performative wink* and relies heavily on a camp performativity. It provides a new in-look to this star persona that hopes to remedy, in particular, critical readings that perceive Miranda as naively participating in her caricatural portrayal and fail to consider the distanciation between the image, Miranda's perception of this image, and, most importantly, Miranda's interactions with her public that show she too is "in the know," both at a performative level and behind the scenes.

Engaging Miranda through a camp reading operates along two distinct yet complementary approaches: it acknowledges on the one hand that she was a camp icon both in her films and offscreen, and on the other hand that her characteristics invited the patronage of camp people, or "camping" more generally, because she held a certain appeal by resonating with the camp aesthetic. The focus of this chapter is an analysis of camp in the text of the films themselves and how Miranda exuded camp in a sustained manner in her Twentieth Century-Fox films in particular, through her exaggeratedly feminine figure, humor, and the incongruity of her onscreen persona.[1] If camp remains an area of diverse interpretations, it is my contention that examples will provide the fodder to understanding how the concept applies in Carmen Miranda's films and, in particular, in one of the most camp films of all time, the 1943 Busby Berkeley produced film *The Gang's All Here*.

Miranda musicals were popular in their day and continue to project a captivating aura in part because the viewer understands and enjoys Miranda in a camp way. Despite the studio's cinematic strategies that surpass all naturalist comprehension, the audience that enters into the camp code and captures her performative wink is able to enjoy the artistic camp creation that would otherwise be deemed unrealistic, phony, and cliché. To claim that Miranda is camp is not so much a statement about Miranda as a reflection on our ability to read her as such and understand that we, the viewers, are aware of the playfulness of her star text. Just as Sontag stipulated, "camp sees everything in quotation marks. It's not a lamp, but a 'lamp'; not a woman, but a 'woman'" (56). For example, we know that the "lighthouse" on top of Miranda's head is not a lighthouse but an excuse for an outrageous Mirandesque headdress, and we accept and delight in the different levels of the narrative as ironic mockery of and challenges to normality. Critics have widely and variably discussed this subjective process, which functions both in the films' day and in the present day. For Thomas Hess, an understanding of camp "exists in the smirk of the beholder" (53). The "performative logic of camp" (Farmer 113) makes camp discernable for a select few, the spectators who capture its performative wink. Moreover, the actors or performers can also visibly project themselves as being part of this camp game. This distanciation is essential in Miranda's case: it created a gap for Miranda to view her persona as a stereotype.[2] Miranda's characters all exhibit stylized effeminacy through a camp portrayal that parodies the traditional feminine and, in many cases, also toys with Miranda's over-the-top *Latinidade*.[3] The key to understanding Miranda's image resides in its artifice and exaggeration: its camp qualities. As such, these otherwise condoning stereotypes exist only as surface, and Miranda becomes "sheer spectacle" (S. Roberts 15). Priscilla Peña Ovalle corroborates this reading of Miranda as spectacle from a technical point of view through a careful analysis of the camerawork of her dance sequences, which presented Miranda in wide frames that "made her ever-moving body a figure of entertainment, not identification" (55). While some of Carmen Miranda's musical numbers are filmed with close-ups, the distance established by the camera also plays into this aspect of Miranda as spectacle, allowing the audience to look on from afar, as would the diegetic spectator.

Camp provides a rich discursive space to poke fun at contained sexual/gender identities and to articulate all sorts of "gender trouble" in order to construct new formations of desire and representation. The role gender plays in the articulation of musicals and the camp portrayal in these films is essential to understanding Miranda's screen image, as gender creates a new dimension for the spectator to negotiate the meaning of the film. One of Philip Core's most memorable "rules of camp" is the spirited phrase "camp is gender without genitals" (7). Miranda was often perceived as a drag queen, given her hyperfeminization and the over-the-top artifice of her outfits, concentrated in her lavishly designed hats and turbans but also in the bright, contrasting colors of her dresses and the opulence of her jewelry. She is, to borrow from Sontag, "an aesthetic phenomenon . . . not in terms of beauty, but in terms of the degree of artifice, of stylization" (57). As the performative epitome of artifice and stylization, Miranda's look poked fun at feminine norms through the use of exaggerated heels, hats, jewelry, and glitter-laden outfits and an overabundance of accents (feathers, sparkles, jewels, sequins, baubles), all piled onto her petite frame to instantly create a prime camp icon, one that would be greatly appreciated and appropriated by gender-toying drag queens or imitated in fun-loving, gay impersonations.[4] Miranda was a walking fetish, pure spectacle with little visible existence beyond this spectaculization. Through her camp depiction of what was originally a racial and ethnically charged persona, the *baiana*, Miranda's own persona jettisoned all trace of racial, ethnic, and class difference to become imbued with sexual, engendered, and political meaning, blurring categories of femininity and masculinity, leading to an aesthetics of gender "without genitals." This in-between space opens the door for alternative, nonmainstream social and cultural relationships that camp could represent by toying with heterosexual relations, hyperfemininity, female masculinity, masculine femininity, and androgyny. In the world of straight, predominantly white, upper-class couples of the 1940s Hollywood musicals, in pre-Stonewall fashion, any gender deviance could only be expressed through certain performative strategies such as comic relief or camp sensitivity and give way to a productive queer reading.

Although Miranda has been mentioned in relation to camp in several studies, a thorough analysis has not yet been conducted on Carmen Miranda's star-image as a camp construction and how her camp performativity was integrated into the

A young Mexican-American boy dresses as Carmen Miranda in Los Angeles in the mid-1940s. Courtesy of the Shades of LA collection, Los Angeles Public Library

Hollywood musical. Without necessarily using camp theory, critics unanimously reference Miranda's exaggerated costumes and the overall effect of her stage presence, slightly "off," excessive, and different, through which she is both marginalized and placed center stage—essential camp qualities.[5] As Rocha writes, Miranda's performativity can be viewed as "excessively doing a style of excess" (68). By embedding a major camp icon such as Carmen Miranda within a musical, the most camp of all film genres, this combination creates the ultimate camp experience. Camp permeates the musical; it is the major film genre *par excellence* that relies heavily on artifice, on the trivial, on "'style' over 'content'" (Sontag 62). It is notorious for the lack of convincing plots and is highly stylized and loaded with all forms of literal and metaphorical tinsel and glitter. Ted Sennett views the musical as "a glittering amalgam of music, story, settings, costumes, and performances," and although he does not mention camp *per se*, these combinations of glitter-filled elements are core camp components (13). Indeed, as Roen states in his introduction to a discussion of gay camp and the musical, "the Hollywood musical is a genre which, by definition, exudes camp. Any film in which people intermittently burst into song is obviously theatrical, stylized, and patently unreal. Add to this the fact that musicals tend to be all awash with glitter, tinsel and garish artifice, and you begin to see why people associate camp with this genre more than any other" (1: 11).

In contrast to the melodramas, film noirs, gangster movies, horror films, and screwball comedies that dominated the 1930s and early 1940s, the genre of the musical film stood out as one of the preferred and most lucrative forms of production ever, especially since its early 1930s revival with the Warner Brothers 1933 series of backstage musicals (*42nd Street*, *Footlight Parade*, and *Gold Diggers of 1933*). In particular, the musical brought gaiety, humor, and dreams of luxury, opulence, and evasion to the silver screen and lightened the minds of post-Depression/ pre-World War II movie patrons, and camp strategies were essential to assuring the musical's enduring success. This correlates with some of the aspects Esther Newton defines as essential for understanding the relationship between camp and the musical, namely incongruity as the subject matter, theatricality as its style, and humor as its strategy (106). The incongruity can exist at many different levels of the camp musical, but the producers worked from the premise that no one would mind a disjointedly contrived story when it was pieced together so beautifully with musical intermissions, of which Carmen Miranda's numbers were among the most outstandingly lavish. Audiences delighted in these musical numbers that brought to the big screen the extraordinary talent and precision of Fred Astaire and Ginger Rogers, the artistry and choreographic brilliance of the Nicholas Brothers, the unique voices of Frank Sinatra, Bing Crosby, Judy Garland, Alice Faye, and Betty Grable, and the big bands of Glenn Miller, Benny Goodman, Xavier Cugat, and Harry James, among so many others. What made an exceptional musical film was never the storyline, and the producers knew the importance of loading their musicals with top-quality song-and-dance numbers, many of which were specialty acts, disconnected from the plot and often involving performers who had no acting part. There were two basic types of musical segments, both with potential camp interpretation: staged numbers in which there is an explicit audience in the film that watches the musical presentation—these were the characteristic Carmen Miranda numbers—or the so-called book numbers that originated in the mid-1930s with the release of *Gold Diggers of 1935* (1935) and are integrated as part of the narrative, with at least lip-service toward some connection to the plot, as in the "I-feel-a-song-coming" moods so typical of the Fred Astaire and Ginger Rogers movies (Berry, *Screen Style* 57). While the campiness of book numbers draws from the mere incongruity of the act, the staged numbers have no pretense of being integrated within the plot. As the examples in this chapter illustrate, the sheer excessiveness of these latter segments stages camp through exaggerated theatricality and stylizations, the visual richness of sound and color, sumptuous textures, and dizzying movements as they create an over-the-top, definitely not real, but inevitably appealing fantasy world on the screen.

The musical's garish theatrical qualities, while not reliant on color, were exponentially enhanced by the advent of Technicolor, which became a staple of musicals in the 1940s and part of Twentieth Century-Fox musicals' signature aesthetics. Carmen Miranda was a great match for Hollywood's new color palette: she fitted the "Technicolor type" that Sarah Berry relates to female stars with "vivid features and personalities" ("Hollywood Exoticism" 193). Furthermore, the musical's extravagance of sound, which camp exploits, stems from the abundance of production numbers that ran the full gamut of musical genres, from patriotic big-band swing and jazz to foreign sounds of rhumba, conga, salsa, and samba, often Americanized for a US-based audience and peppered with romantic ballads, since most musicals had some resemblance of a love story. Lastly, grandiose movements achieved through the inclusion of large production numbers with lines of chorus girls dancing, twirling, and gesticulating in all different manners only intensify the overall feeling of abundance. For such extravaganza to be perceived as camp, the spectator must be aware of the film's heightened degree of artifice but willing to play along with this game of make-believe that transcends all norms of reality through an explosion of the senses.

The essential distinction between kitsch and camp merits a brief mention, as both performative aesthetics tend to rely on artificiality and oftentimes imitation. However, while certain scholars have referred to Miranda as kitsch, in this chapter I will demonstrate that her screen persona is undoubtedly far from kitsch, which is synonymous with cheap, overdone themes that are uncreative and often painfully overproduced. As Kjellman-Chapin argues, words used to describe kitsch include "shallow," "superficial," "clichéd," "trivial," and "aesthetically and morally bankrupt" (28). *Impersonations* of Miranda can, and often do, tend toward kitsch aesthetic when reproduced by combining cheap imitation with instant recognition (Linstead 658). In these kitsch interpretations, the imitation artist creates something that is so readily understood that it offers nothing to challenge the viewer and draws on the most stereotypical core aspects of Miranda's image, staying true to the "reiterative character of kitsch, which extracts from an original work only that effect which can be reproduced en mass" (Santos 87). Kitsch objects are taken at face value without pretense or fake aspirations. They are not manufactured to be ironic, unlike the more complex camp aesthetic that plays on the multifaceted nature of its creation. The kitsch nature of many of the Miranda imitations does not necessarily divest them of camp performativity, yet their relative cheapness and clichéd composition, displaced from their original context, remains fundamentally a copy of the original, lavishly artistic Miranda costumes and performances. Kitsch is known to aspire to authenticity through mimicry; unlike kitsch, camp has no such honorable intentions.

From this distinction, my contention that Carmen Miranda's authentic stage persona is essentially and fundamentally camp enables the modern viewer to understand her performance in a way that we can read as deliberate, entertaining, and certainly not altogether serious. Other than in her first film, *Down Argentine Way*, Miranda had a character role to play within the narrative, and there were necessarily different levels to understanding her part. However, as an actress, silenced beneath her extravagant costumes, it is her visual image that drives the scenes where she appears and invariably dominates, rather than any spoken part or even the content of her dialogues.

Although some camp films did feature male actors prominently, as is certainly the case with the Gene Kelly MGM musicals, for most of the Hollywood musicals of the era, women were the center of the narrative and often accompanied by lightweight but very pleasant and nice-looking male actors who, for the most part, remained secondary to the plot with limited time on screen and a lack of close-ups and dialogues.[6] Given this abundance of female camp icons, the question that guides this inquiry is simply, what makes Carmen Miranda so quintessentially camp and distinguishes her from these other women? Among the female film icons, María Montez of Universal Studios is the actress who most closely resembles Miranda's mold of camp representation. Pigeonholed in the role of the foreign princess, always clad in gorgeous costumes, with a ridiculously strong accent and inconsequential dialogues, Montez's screen appeal is primarily visual, featured in exotic settings and alongside young, foreign-looking men or adolescent costars. From the lushly romantic *Arabian Nights* fantasies to the quintessential Montez vehicles of camp and glitz such as *Cobra Woman* (1944), in which she plays twin sisters, or the never-never land of *Gypsy Wildcat* (1944), her roles never change substantially, and some scenes are overloaded with camp perceived through the lush music, Technicolor, gaudy costumes, absurd melodrama, and often second-rate acting, to the point that Roen refers to Montez as "sublimely talentless" (2:11). The similarities between the two actresses appear obvious, yet Miranda's campiness is such an over-the-top spectacularization that she has become an icon in a category all by herself.

Moreover, criticism has tended to dwell on the *baiana* as the inspiration for Miranda's costume yet without being able to make the theoretical leap to Carmen Miranda's trademark vision of excess. Camp performativity is the missing link to critically engaging Miranda's Hollywood screen persona. During her early career, she represented the *baiana* without playing with camp aesthetics: the tensions of incongruence from hyperstylization, explicit gender reversal, mockery, or self-parody were not part of her projected image on the Carioca stage, nor could they be. Miranda's Brazilian *baiana* was too close to original Bahian women, and in particular the Carioca stylized *baiana* that, as discussed in Chapter 1, was ubiquitous throughout Rio. However, during the same period, the cross-dressing male *baiana* impersonators of Rio's Carnival celebrations and parades were much more in line with camp sensitivity as they appropriated the image through a gender-bending, parodic, and fun-loving irreverence that, within the carnavalesque mode of fantasy and lawlessness, exaggerated the femininity of the *baiana*.

Fabulously Camp

While Busby Berkeley's megamusical production *The Gang's All Here* (1943) is discussed later in this chapter in detail, a camp reading of Miranda's other films, with an emphasis on her Twentieth Century-Fox films, is much overdue. Any film starring Carmen Miranda is bound to have camp in abundance, mostly centered on her persona and the grand production numbers of which she was an integral part. The following discussion draws selectively from Miranda's films to illustrate the extent of her camp performance, even though, truth be told, no scene, neither before nor after, could ever outdo Busby Berkeley's "Lady in the Tutti Frutti Hat" in the camp register. Camp performativity is so embedded throughout Miranda's films that, when analyzed, they collectively reveal common aspects. The following examples illustrate how these films portend a camp performativity through the combination of Miranda's eccentric costumes; offstage theatricality, incongruity, and humor; self-referentiality mixed with self-parody; stylized book numbers; and, most memorably, grandly staged musical numbers.

Camp interest in Carmen Miranda's films centers on her costumes; while invariably over-the-top, the majority can only be described as absolutely fabulous. Furthermore, to consistently reinforce the impact of her image, the visual appeal is constantly renewed, as she appears wearing a different designer outfit in each new scene, and each costume presents elite couture in the exclusive Miranda style. Her persona required an excessive use of costume, as her theatricality and screen personality drew from her visual impact, all the more so as her Hollywood film career developed and the audience expected her costumes and scenes to privilege the expressive over the realist effects, with her eccentric styles throwing into disarray all resemblance of a normal star wardrobe.

Miranda's signature look with her fruit-laden headdresses was soon diversified with creative combinations of flowers, feathers, butterflies, lamps, parasols, candy canes, or spikes of wheat, and amazingly nothing seemed out of place. Indeed, so much of Miranda's camp performance draws from her headdresses, and there is a sense of camp playfulness in their creative license. How else could the viewer fully appreciate the striped "Mickey Mouse" turban she wears in *The Gang's All Here* or the candy-cane headdress in *Greenwich Village*? Miranda's headdresses are central to the creation of camp performativity in her films: they transform what would be ordinary hats or turbans into extraordinary ones and mark Miranda's screen presence with their combinations of colors, textures, and materials. While the Miranda look maintains its "formula," the headdress/hat/turban creativity seems to have no boundaries. Simply put, as Babuscio writes, "camp aims to transform the ordinary into something more spectacular" (122). The spectacular quality of Miranda's headdresses was designed for overall impact and drew from the premise that unusual combinations of objects created a sense of whimsy. While items on a headdress may have borne some resemblance of realism, others were fantastical fruits, oddly colored leaves and foliage, or unrecognizable objects that even (or especially) in cinematic close-ups challenged all description. Moreover, the use of unusual color

Carmen Miranda's candy-cane costume in a photo still for *Greenwich Village* (1944). Courtesy of Photofest

combinations or materials enhanced the campiness of her look, such as the stunning, stark-black butterflies created by Sascha Brastoff for a headdress in *If I'm Lucky* or the leopard-print turban in *Doll Face*. Her headdresses complemented the rest of Miranda's outfit, the color scheme, or the set decor, and the overall effect was more striking than the individual parts.

Miranda's most unusual, exquisite, and utterly camp headdresses in plots of little variety were among the few distinguishing elements of the different films.

In *Greenwich Village* (1944) Miranda wears a pink and white outfit reminiscent of a candy cane with a bevy of oversized candy-cane sticks protruding out of her headdress in every direction along with pink lollypops and a large pink ribbon. As though a candy-cane headdress were insufficient in the camp-headdress registry of a single film, in another scene there is a flash shot of Miranda in her dressing room trying on a parrot in a cage for a headdress, combining her tropical, exotic appeal with her iconic, signature headdress in a unique camera fade-in and -out that lasts a blink of an eye.

While some combination of fruit is widely considered to be the more "classic" Miranda headdress, immortalized beyond all proportions in *The Gang's All Here*, it is surprising how few of the headdresses in her films rely on this motif, no doubt also due to the need to add variety and renewed appeal to each subsequent film, as discussed in Chapter 4. The gold-studded butterflies on a lilac cushioned headdress in *The Gang's All Here*, the stunning white pom-poms in *Greenwich Village*'s costume-ball scene, the arrangement of colorful parasols in *Nancy Goes to Rio*, and the assortment of kitchen utensils, complete with forks, knives, an egg-beater, and spaghetti tongs, in *Scared Stiff* are some of the more striking examples of nonfruit Miranda headdresses. These motifs reinforce the concept that the turban, hat, or scarf was literally the platform for the designers' creativity, on which, in a single film, they could juxtapose an array of styles. Yvonne Wood, who designed Miranda's costumes at Twentieth Century-Fox for five of her later films, namely *The Gang's All Here*, *Greenwich Village*, *Four Jills and a Jeep*, *Something for the Boys*, and *Doll Face*, developed her own Miranda-trademark style with a combination of outrageous headdresses interspersed with more discrete but typically unusual and mostly very flamboyant hats or turbans for her offstage scenes. With such a strong identification of Miranda's costume with a headdress, in the scenes where her head garb is played down, something appears rather "off" with her depiction. It is an image that destabilizes her impact because it removes the visual buffer that the headdress portends, yet even "stripped down," she remains an excessively exuberant screen persona. In some scenes, the designers carried the turban motif over into Miranda's offstage appearances in the films, marking her as camp beyond the internal proscenium stage by blurring the onstage/offstage performativity of her character. In *That Night in Rio*, Miranda's character appears at a dinner party hosted by the Baron (a double role played by Don Ameche) in an amazing black outfit covered with sequins and a white turban topped with feathers, one of Travis Banton's most exquisite designs. To perform for the dinner guests, Miranda's character is already wearing one of her fabulously sumptuous turbans and merely removes the upper part of the black outfit to reveal a white long-sleeved top with her signature bare midriff and an abundance of necklaces. In *Weekend in Havana*, there is only a slight distinction between the costumes Miranda's character Rosita Rivas wears as she performs her songs at the Casino Madrileno and those she wears offstage, and all invariably dominate the scenes. At one point on her way to a rehearsal, Rosita shares a scene with the businessman Jay Williams (John Payne), who wears a dull gray suit. In stark contrast, Miranda appears wearing a bright orange and white dress and a white turban, with two large white baskets lined with a sheer orange fabric draped elegantly around her head and framing her face beautifully, and she is excessively accessorized with a large golden pendant, white gloves, thick bracelets, and an oversized white purse. The viewer even catches a glimpse of her platform shoes when the camera pulls back and shows a full-body take as she exits the scene. Later that evening, in another offstage scene at "El Arbolado" fine and private dining, Rosita's outfit is a dazzling white fringe-covered dress, a high-1940s style adapted to Miranda's look, with the addition of two diamond-shaped openings on each side of her midriff. In lieu of a turban, she wears several bright white gardenias in her hair, along with a silver necklace and a large ring for accessories. Both of these costumes clearly hark back to Miranda's signature diegetic stage outfits and are equally as exquisite.

Greenwich Village is the film that most blatantly throughout the plot toys with the blurring of Miranda's character's identity, both on and off the proscenium stage and with a mixture of alleged nationalities. Playing the role of fortune teller and performer Princess Querida O'Toole, Miranda consistently appears in luxurious, colorful costumes, with variants on the headdress and turban that include hair wraps, head scarfs, half-turbans (with her hair rolled up in a front bun or to the side), elaborate hairdos with a scarf for added color, and even a large hair bow when she is depicted sitting in her bed in silk pajamas. While her stage headdresses are quintessentially camp (candy canes, black butterflies, white pom-poms), the dialogues that make specific reference to the differences between her on- and offstage costumes are saturated with irony and point to Miranda's role as first and foremost a spectacle. When Bonnie Watson (Vivian Blaine) bumps into Querida carrying an armful of boas, feathers, accessories, strings of golden beads, and an assortment of small plastic fruits, she wonders what on earth Querida is carrying. "It's my costume!" Querida replies, all the while wearing quite the flamboyant street-clothes outfit, complete with pink and yellow fabric flowers in her bun and a neck full of ruffles.

As these examples illustrate, whether on or off the proscenium stage in her films, Carmen Miranda is always a fashion spectacle. Camp pervades her performativity as she navigates between her on- and offstage theatricality, reinforced by dialogues that either she or her costars articulate and that translate her performative wink through a mixture of good-humored, ironic, and comical commentary on the artificiality of her screen persona. *Springtime in the Rockies* (1942) is the film that most blatantly pries open this gap between Miranda's appearance and its perception through dialogues that revolve around the costumes of her character, Rosita Murphy. Newly hired as a secretary for Dan Christy (John Payne), Rosita wears outfits that are both impractical and comically inappropriate, visually denoting over-the-top artificiality that becomes all the more apparent through the self-referentiality of the dialogues. "Good neighbors!" exclaims Dan as he turns to see Rosita wearing a bright orange skirt; a revealing bodice that exposes her bare midriff; large, frilly, protruding sleeves; and a turban adorned with swinging tassels.

"Is that what a secretary wears in Brazil?" In an infantilized and coquettish voice, Rosita answers, "Why? You don't like my outfits? I think it's a knockdown!" Dan candidly reiterates the carnivalesque aspect of her stylized, out-of-place outfit: "Well what good is it to you if there's not a Mardi Gras in town?" Debra Walters echoes the exact sentiment of this script when she writes that with "Carmen Miranda's small frame and large facial features exaggerated and enhanced by wardrobe and cosmetics, she always seemed prepared for a costume party of the Carnival" (64). The artificiality of the scene is heightened by the unobstructed view of Lake Louise on the backdrop; like so many of these early Technicolor sets, it features a brash use of color that is far from naturalistic but rather a glaring eyesore in a scene already overcharged with color.[7] In a film set at a resort on Lake Louise in the Canadian Rockies, staged against artificial backdrops, with an unrealistic, contrived plot and a motley group of protagonists, Miranda's stylized costumes actually seem to fit right in with the rest of the film's comic absurdity. There are also flash moments of incongruity, which may have been more logical in the plot's first drafts but, after edits, ended up as pointless scenes or unfinished storylines. At one point, there is a glimpse of Miranda running around with an oversized stuffed duck that matches the colors of her outfit. It boggles the mind what the role of such a prop could possibly be, but then again, in a musical where Rosita ends up in the Canadian Rockies, brought there with her six brothers and employed by Dan Christy, who hired her from the tourist counter in the Detroit airport, there certainly are more unanswered questions than realistic situations. After Rosita's first reacquaintance with her boss, she summons her six brothers (Bando da Lua), and what follows is Miranda's only book number in all of her North American films. Rosita asks Dan if he likes Brazilian music, to which he sarcastically and unenthusiastically replies, "I love it!" With this affirmative albeit insincere response, Rosita, accompanied by her brothers, proceeds to perform a Brazilian rendition of "Chattanooga Choo Choo." Miranda moves gracefully around the full space of the lounge, twirling her hands and dancing backward and forward in front of Dan—her audience of one— and even intersperses a few beats of "Chica Chica Boom Chic," rehearsed from her second Twentieth Century-Fox film, *That Night in Rio*, for added "Brazilian" flavor. This scene establishes the nature of the relationship between Dan and Rosita that will have no resemblance of secretarial duties, and when Dan wants to make his ex-girlfriend jealous, he buys Rosita an elegant evening gown that consists of a long white skirt and a bodice exposing her bare midriff, matched with a white synthetic turban topped with a white bow. "All it needs now," Rosita complains to her socially awkward and stiff love interest McTavish (Edward Everett Horton), "is some beads, some flowers, some fruits, baubles, knacks-knicks. Give me ten bucks. I have an idea." Certainly unusual in a Miranda vehicle, Rosita's outfit has a story, and the dialogue highlights the character's role in embellishing the dress. In a subsequent scene, Rosita appears with a much-transformed outfit, now with colors of turquoise and brown, lavishly adorned with jewels, necklaces, exquisite fabric added around the shoulders and turban, and a belt with large jewels, all in all a very tasteful "upgrade" from the plain white dress it originally was made to appear. Later, the Latin beau Victor Prince (Cesar Romero) comments on her dress after dancing a few steps with her, "Miss Murphy, you look ravishing in that gown!" To which she ironically answers, "Oh I feel absolutely undress-ed, like a strip-squeezer!" McTavish also admires the gown as the fruit of his ten-dollar sponsorship. As in many instances throughout Miranda's Hollywood films, her costume's rich textures and luxurious materials evoke a highly tactile sensuality that embellishes the overall camp effect. In this case, the camp performativity is further heightened by the ongoing commentary on her outfit by the film's three main male characters, engendering the gaze directed toward her lavish costume. Moreover, this is one of the most elaborate Miranda costumes worn both on and off the proscenium stage as both a dinner gown and her performance attire when she seamlessly, and with no logical sequencing, takes the floor to perform "Tic-tac do meu coração" (The tick tock of my heart), accompanied by her band.[8] Diffusing the camp effect to one of the other characters, *Springtime in the Rockies* includes an unusual sequence centered on Phoebe Gray (Charlotte Greenwood), the typical unattached "old maid" of the Hollywood storylines. The campiness draws from the tensions present in this scene that juxtapose comedy and awkwardness as Phoebe, in drunken stupor, exhibits herself on an empty dance floor, a sequence that is explicitly narrated through Phoebe's voice-over, and the fact that this marginal character suddenly takes center stage in the film. She degradedly refers to herself as "Phoebe the wallflower" as the camera follows her hunt for an immediate dance partner she hopes will double as a long-term soul mate. In this memorable sequence, Phoebe's voice narrates her situation play by play and reflects back on her lonely condition, with references that are both colorfully humorous and sadly realistic: "It isn't because they can't see me, I'm lit up like a flaming torch!" she says, making reference to her bright orange dress as she heads straight for the dance floor and the spotlight follows her. Stating the obvious, she announces her intentions: "I think I'll buzz about a bit . . . there must be an unattached man around somewhere."[9] The scene loses all sense of decorum as she unexpectedly, and as though even surprising herself, gives a few of her characteristic high leg kicks to the side and then catches herself, chuckling at her own ridicule, "Of course that ain't exactly lady-like . . . are you kidding?" She continues to dance around, making windmills with her arms and side-to-side leg kicks, as other dinner guests are brought into the camera's focus, laughing and applauding her dance "performance." She ends up in the splits and then staggers off the dance floor, doubled over and suddenly horrified that people are watching her, thus ending a brilliantly conducted scene that is both fun and funny for the internal and real audience.[10]

In *Greenwich Village*, the lyrics of the opening song mirror this self-reflective strategy as Miranda's character, Princess Querida, appears dressed in full-body, candy-cane regalia and sings about peppermints and candy. This creates the distanciation that camp requires between the camp object and its perception, as discussed above. "He's sweet like peppermint candy, and just like honey from the tree," proclaim the lyrics, before evolving into a Portuguese verse where Miranda sings of *acarajé* (a traditional dish from Northeastern Brazil) and Praça Mauá (a square in the center of Rio with historical significance as a port of entry to the city) and even translates the lyrics from "he's wild about me" into the Portuguese "anda louquinho por mim." Despite the exactness of the translation—naturally lost on a non-Portuguese speaking audience—these Brazilian cultural references bear no impact on the content of this number that, in true camp fashion, is style devoid of meaning, a spectacle of colors, movement, and sound.

Camp in Grand: Musical Finales

The musical numbers are by their very essence aggregates into the film whose plot was, for the most part, what Ted Sennett referred to as "merely a peg on which to hang the musical score" (13). Throughout her tenure in Hollywood, Miranda's standard role was that of a performer, naturally expected to sing and dance at some point in the film before a proscenium audience with her showstopper costumes and an overall impact of exotic otherness, charisma, and whimsical playfulness, all beautifully camp.

Missing from *Down Argentine Way* but becoming the trend in subsequent Miranda vehicles are the grand, extremely camp, large-scale musical numbers that showcase the star surrounded by chorines or male dancers on stages filled to the brim with color, movement, and texture. Despite the extreme campiness of the finale of *Down Argentine Way*, with its fairytale ending, over-played tunes, unrealistic stage sets, and stylized choreography and singing, complete with a singing horse (at which point one suspends all disbelief), the scene lacks the magnitude and the opulence that emanates from the large-group dance numbers of Miranda's subsequent films, which are possible once Miranda moves to Hollywood, as the following emblematic scenes illustrate.

The opening of *That Night in Rio* presents the standard formula for Miranda's Twentieth Century-Fox musical numbers: a solo number that leads into a spectacular large chorus number, with Miranda returning for the coda. This scene opens on a fantastical backdrop of Rio's Corcovado Mountain flanking a lagoon, with palm trees and a fireworks display, as Miranda enters from the back of the stage, greeted by an archway of sparklers and garbed in one of her most fabulous costumes of all times: a long, shimmering silver skirt, opulent silver jewelry on her neck and wrists, and topped with a silver fruit-laden turban. After Miranda sings her part in Portuguese to "Chica Chica Boom Chic," Don Ameche, dressed as a US Navy admiral, makes his grand entrance in a convertible coupe to sing his salutations in English on behalf of "130 million Americans,"[11] and Miranda joins him for the chorus of "Chica Chica Boom Chic," which "don't make sense" but "it came down the Amazon / From the jungles / Where the natives greet / Everyone they meet / Beatin' on a tom-tom."[12] Continuing the Amazon theme, the camera focuses in on "jungle" drums as the stage is filled with a bevy of mini-Miranda chorines, decked in golden tops and red turbans tied up with orchids. Their skirts resemble tropical birds, with plumage of dark blue, turquoise, green, red, and yellow feathers, outrageously garish and indistinguishably camp as they twirl with their male partners coordinately clad in royal-blue pants and shiny, striped, colorful shirts opened to reveal their hairless bare chests. The colored stage lights add to the dream-sequence effect of the scene and seem to gyrate along with the movement of the dancers. The music accelerates and evolves into a swing jive with a Latin beat, all with an eerie instrumental tone that subsides to welcome Miranda back on the stage for her final chorus. From the stylized Carioca backdrop to the lyrics of the song, the garish costumes, the sparklers, and the fireworks, the scene represents the Hollywood musical at its camp best, purposefully over-the-top, excessively flamboyant, and unrealistically bright, and all of it centered on Carmen Miranda.

The grand finale of *Weekend in Havana* is another of these excessive visual treats that in glorious camp fashion explodes into pure spectacle, fabulously choreographed with the resemblance of a new dance fashion set against a backdrop of a luxurious column-flanked dance floor with a double marble stairway. The original song and dance "The Ñango" features playful, catchy, fun-loving choreography, as was Hermes Pan's signature style, around the theme of "Let's have fun and do the Ñango." Miranda wears one of her most sumptuous costumes: a flamboyant golden skirt, headdress towered high with red, green, and gold feathers and baubles, matching ruffled bodice, and opulent golden necklaces, creating an overall effect of elegance and luxury. As mentioned above, Miranda's costume sets the tone, colors, and textures for the costumes of the chorus girls and male dancers. Miranda's character, Rosita Rivas, introduces the number in a typical solo song and dance that she performers for the internal audience/dinner guests, gliding gracefully from table to table as the camera zooms in on Miranda's fabulous costume. Then Miranda look-a-like chorines wearing beautifully coordinated long yellow, red, and green blocked skirts and turbans adorned with tall, elegant feathers descend the magnificent double stairway and dance to an instrumental movement of "The Ñango," shaking their maracas to mark the beat, soon to be joined by their male partners. The three-toned red, yellow, and green blocks on the male dancers' caps and pants have a jester quality to them. As they dance around pairing off with the chorus girls, there is a gender-neutralizing effect about these men, who appear too feminized in their three-quarter trousers and flouncy sleeves to display any convincing virility. Just when the viewer thinks the spectacle has reached its peak, Miranda breaks out from the dancing and invites the audience to join them on the main dance floor with an emphatic, "Come on, everybody dance!" as all age groups dance around rumbustiously, having instantly learned this new dance craze. There is a sense of wild abandon conveyed in this scene, underscored by unconventional cinematographic techniques such as crane shots, canted angles, and occasional close-ups that add new dimensions to the festivities. The main female star of the film, Nan Spencer (Alice Faye), in a striking, full-length purple gown, stands out among the dancing crowd, where she can be easily spotted, as the love interest Jay Williams (John Payne) enters, they are reunited, and all is forgiven. Likewise, Monte Blanca (Cesar Romero) enters the dance scene, running from a creditor and hoping to "save his life" with a loan from Jay Williams, and ends up securely ensconced in the midst of the dance to complete the tableau next to his fiancée, Rosita. A reprise of the film's theme tune, "Weekend in Havana," brings the musical full circle and re-establishes the prominence of the storyline with the resolution of the two couples dancing gaily with arms linked as the camera fades out. The final camera shot that focuses on the two couples reverts the overwhelming and destabilizing impact of the spectacular number with a nod in the direction of heteronormativity in the midst of such campiness and gender-bending.

Carmen Miranda's next Twentieth Century-Fox film, *Springtime in the Rockies*, ends with an internal staged show featuring a number that is just as impressive as "The Ñango." The scene begins with a song-and-dance duet by Vicky Lane (Betty Grable) and her performing partner Dan Christy (John Payne) in front of a dark proscenium curtain that silhouettes Betty Grable's slender figure emphasized by a long, sleeveless, formfitting white dress with a high slit up its left side. They alternate singing a few phrases of the first part of the "Pan-American Jubilee" that foregrounds hemispheric, good-neighborly unity through its suggestive lyrics: "How would you like to go / To say hello to your neighbors? . . . Come and drink a toast / And get close to your neighbors!" This invitation segues into the grand celebration behind the curtain that is taking place in the spirit of Pan-Americanism, bringing people together through music, singing, and dancing: "You're gonna see the way those Latins / Like to jitter bug / Like to cut a rug / Like a Yankee doodle dandy / Like to do a rhumba / And a samba! / It's goin' down in history as a jumpin' fiesta!" As the curtains open, the tempo of the music accelerates to the rhythm of "voodoo," jungle-sounding drums as the choir takes over the lyrics of the song that has now modulated to a higher pitch, echoing through the change in the music that Pan-Americanism is being taken to another level. The stage is filled with twirling dance partners dressed in colorful "Latin" costumes that match Carmen Miranda's costume as she makes her grand entrance. The overall impression is one of twirling purple, white, pink, and green dresses, sashes, and hats. One of the groups in particular stands out, the men wearing shiny purple pants and the women frilled pink and white skirts, white puffy-sleeved blouses, green scarves tied around their waists revealing bare midriffs, and small brimmed hats on top of discrete, green turbans, all elements that resonate with Miranda's typical colorful costumes. As Miranda enters from the back of the stage, the dancers part to let her through, and her costume steals the show: in contrast to the lightweight fabric of Grable's dress, it consists of a full white skirt adorned with a thick, purple-fur border along the bottom hem and matching fur around a generous off-the-shoulder neckline, and a bare midriff, an outfit that Darlene Sadlier has referred to as a "winterized version of her trademark costume, whose ruffled trim resembles a Sonja Henie skating costume" (180). A headdress topped with towering-high purple flowers that coordinate with the skirt's flower motif complements the outfit. Miranda code-switches as she sings her verses, with the words "samba" and "rhumba" placed at the end of Portuguese phrases, where they are easily discernible. She dances an abbreviated version of a swing routine with Cesar Romero and is then substituted by Betty Grable as the dancers form a circle around them. Grable, now dressed in a short, light-blue dress with long fringes that flair up as she twirls around, dances a quick-paced swing routine with Romero, proving the international unity of the Fiesta Pan-Americana as an American/Latin partnership takes the stage. Even Phoebe Gray (Charlotte Greenwood)—no longer the wallflower, now partnered with the stiff but good-natured McTavish (Edward Everett Horton)—performs a brief dance routine, complete with the signature "Greenwood side kicks." The number ends with the four main characters, joined by Phoebe, linking arms and marching gaily toward the front of the stage and singing with gusto as the camera pulls back. The final shot is an overhead view of this spectacle exploding with color and movement, with the dancers swirling around in unison. It is the apogee of this Pan-Americana fiesta of dancing, singing, textures, languages, and music as the film also comes to an end, merging both the internal show and the film-vehicle, which ends in pure celebratory mode.

Placed centrally in *Greenwich Village*, the costume-ball song-and-dance number is steeped in camp sensitivity through a combination of its carnivalesque qualities, theatricality and incongruity, overall impression of artifice, and self-reflectiveness. The opening song, "Art for Art's Sake," is an original, catchy tune whose repetitive lyrics ("Whatever we do, we only do for art's sake") are a playful spoof of artists' pretensions in general and are all the more pertinent given the context of the musical. *Greenwich Village* is set in the homologous New York City neighborhood in the early 1920s and revolves around the patrons and artists of a speakeasy called "Danny's Den," whose owner, Danny O'Mara (William Bendix), aspires to put on a show, the *Greenwich Village Gaieties*, to outdo the *Ziegfeld Follies* and showcase his star talent and love interest, Bonnie Watson (Vivian Blaine).[13] Camp is present throughout the film, from the decors of the speakeasy (a huge pirate's ship that has no bearing on the plot), to the characters' visible overacting, to the over-the-top musical numbers, to the absurdity of a low-class Manhattan speakeasy owner's aspiring to become the producer of a high-class theatrical production, to all the typical aspects of Carmen Miranda's performance. In the costume-ball scene, the camp performativity is enhanced by the constant blurring of what is considered a stage or an audience as the number develops and leaves the viewer with the uneasy feeling that all the players are both participants and observers, pointing to the truism that "all the world's a stage."

The scene opens with Brophy (B. S. Pully), Danny's right-hand man, singing in his very distinct, raspy, low voice the first few lines of "Art for Art's Sake" and inviting all to join the celebration. Then the gay partygoers take over the chorus as the camera follows through to the main dance hall, where women and men are dancing and singing, some being carried around in a circular motion toward the static camera, with an overall impression of revelry, make-believe, and excess in the neon-bright colors, feathers, tinsel, masks, and boas, not to mention an abundance of bare legs and arms. Danny, dressed as Julio Cesar in a toga, and Bonnie, as a showgirl in a skimpy emerald-green outfit with silver trimmings and a matching, awkwardly tall party hat, are a riot as they make their grand entrance in a chariot, pulled by Brophy in a Renaissance costume and a wig with long, blond ringlets. As though that is not enough camp for the eyes to behold, the trio then takes center stage as they dance together and sing the chorus along with references to the artificiality of disguise, hints at cross-dressing, suggestions of shady street-artistic inspiration, and queer references, such as a character in a "lavender tuxedo."[14] The extravagant scene is replete with visual and spoken cues that translate all levels of camp sensibility and playfully evoke gender-bending and make-believe in a carnivalesque atmosphere that adds to the festivities and general anarchy of a scene where everything is pure spectacle. Then, when the viewer has become accustomed to seeing the revelers as participants and observers of the musical performance, the camera unexpectedly cuts to a balcony and Kenneth Harvey (Don Ameche), an aspiring classical composer from Kansas, smiling and clapping furiously. His dark suit stands out dramatically in contrast to the bright Mardi Gras costumes, and he now appears as part of an audience for whom this song and dance are performed. The camera then zooms back down to the dance floor and picks out Ziegfeld's talent scout dressed in a bright lavender dress, as foretold by the song lyrics. As in all good camp, the transformation is never quite complete in playful "pantomime drag."[15] Very visibly, and comically, the scout's blond wig recedes at the hairline to show his dark hair beneath, the tight-fitting dress constricts his movements, and he takes a few puffs of his cigar (an instant cue of masculinity) before making a beeline for Bonnie, whom he spots off in the distance. He is intercepted by Danny, who through exaggerated gestures expresses his irritation and invites "her highness" to dance, knowing full well that this is Ziegfeld's talent scout. Such "garishly theatrical qualities," as suggested by Roen and found in this scene, as in the film as a whole, "definitely fall under the heading of camp" (1: 10). The conversation underlines the fake femininity of the spy and the natural masculinity that is unmasked. At one point, the scout makes reference to the "gay music" that makes "her" so homesick, and as "she" tickles Danny flirtatiously with "her" feather boa, he responds, "Oh not here, Queen, in front of all these people." The double entendre of this queer-charged exchange with the terms "gay" and "queen" draws attention to the multilevels of reading available to the viewers in a scene where both protagonists are aware of the theatricality of the other. The make-believe code is brutally disrupted by Danny's dragging "her" away from the dance floor and out of the ballroom in perfect sync with the music, which stops as Ziegfeld's talent scout goes down with a loud clatter offscreen.

Just when it appears that the musical number and its spectacle have come to an end, the band picks up the tempo with a clash of the cymbals as the camera now focuses on a curtain in the back of the hall that opens to reveal a stage where Miranda, on a small circular platform trimmed with deep-purple fur, is ready to perform, surrounded by her band and flanked on each side by golden fauns, naked from the waist up, who bear spears in a protective stance, creating yet another level of playful make-believe drawn from these mythological creatures. Fitting with the theme of the costume ball, the members of Miranda's band are garbed with black-and-white striped harem pants, golden sashes at the waist, turbans, and felt jackets over bare torsos, evoking a Moroccan effect that adds to the scheme of the exotic that Miranda's presence inevitably brings forth. These costumes coordinate beautifully with the colors of Miranda's costume: she wears a stunning, narrow, glistening white skirt that drops to the floor, with a daring slit up the front; a skimpy black bodice with large white, frilly sleeves that protrude on each side; opulent white pearl bracelets; a headdress of white pom-poms piled high up on her head; and golden signature platform shoes. She performs in an upbeat yet infantilized style "I Like to be Loved by You," accompanied by her band and the orchestra, to the great applause of the audience on the floor and in the balcony.[16]

The last segment of the costume-ball scene, equally saturated with camp, is a conversation between Bonnie and Kenneth in which Bonnie, still dressed as a showgirl with her excessively high party hat attached to her forehead, congratulates the wannabe composer Kenneth and insists he withdraw his concerto from Danny's show to be played by the great composer Kavosky. The stylization of the whole conversation screams artificiality, culminating with Kenneth's declaring to Bonnie, with the phallic party hat bobbing in front of his eyes, "I don't feel right about this," as Bonnie tries to convince him, in stark contrast to her comically inappropriate outfit, "let's be practical." She then segues into a deep, soulful rendition of "Whispering" that has already been played countless times throughout the musical and that she will repeat once again as a solo at the film's finale, and their mutual entente is sealed by a long embrace, despite the obtrusive party hat.

Kenneth's fascination and idealization with the presumably legendary conductor Kavosky (Emil Rameau) escalates as the film progresses and culminates in the film's grand finale scene, the staging of Danny's *Greenwich Village Gaieties*. Starstruck Kenneth appears giddy with delight as he watches Kavosky conducting his concerto as the opening number of the show with (taking a page out of Busby Berkeley's book) no fewer than three grand pianos played simultaneously on the stage. Set against a fuchsia pink background, the color scheme announces Miranda's costume as the stage slowly rotates and Miranda appears surrounded by her band. Given that the film is set in 1922, Miranda's music and her band are particularly incongruous in all the scenes where they appear, but all the more so when contrasted with the classic "concerto" performed immediately before her final number. Without doubt one of Yvonne Wood's most exquisite designs, Miranda's black and fuchsia dress is trimmed with fur and features a skimpy black bodice designed in the shape of a large-petaled flower, which matches the black headdress made of plastic flowers.[17] The slit at the front of the skirt opens to reveal black fishnet stockings and pink, black, and gold platform shoes. Her long sleeves end with bicolor gloves, and the pink on the palms emphasizes every hand twirl as she dances. It is an absolutely stunning outfit that invariably steals the show. Accompanied by her band, she sings "Give Me a Band and a Bandana," miming the words as she sings, in an infantilized fashion, of her love for dressing up and singing and dancing. The contrast between her outfit and the words of the song adds to the incongruity of the number. As the lyrics declare, she doesn't care for the "hootchy-cootchy" or like "the shimmy." She wants her feet to be treated to "a tropical beat" and her hips "to say hip-hip-hooray." Most importantly, she wants to show Manhattan her "Souse American tricks," and her comical mispronunciation recalls her famous "South

American Way" of her Broadway tenure and first Twentieth Century-Fox film, *Down Argentine Way*. The song segues into an upbeat samba medley, drawing from some of her most well-known songs: a substantial version of "O que é que a baiana tem?" followed by short musical phrases from a series of sambas.[18] While the first part of her performance is high pitched and appears unnatural to Miranda's repertoire, emphasized by her infantilized voice and exaggeratedly pained articulation of the English lyrics, as she moves into the samba interlude the tempo quickens, and she explodes into Portuguese, dancing and singing with great ease and gusto, appearing as always to be having a fabulous time, twirling around and swaying her skirt from side to side as she exposes her legs and dances to the accelerated tempo of the music. Imbued with camp sensitivity, the recall of her signature song is performed in an outfit that has evolved far from the original *baiana* costume. This scene, more than any of Miranda's other segments, marks the disjuncture between the song and its North American mise-en-scène. This variation of "What does the *baiana* have?" is performed by the band asking the signature question and Miranda providing the responses in a role reversal from the song's usual format, transposed to a sharper and more aggressive tone in both the questions and the answers. After Miranda repeats once again the chorus of "Give Me a Band and a Bandana," her band disappears offstage as a bevy of chorus girls, dressed in short orange-frilled, hooped dresses and sombreros, enters and fills the scene, which opens onto a full stage as the orchestra continues to play the tune. The movements of the chorus girls seem unnatural as they dance forward, bending over at the waist with every other step and showing the tops of their sombreros to the audience, a movement later picked up again by the men who join them on the dance floor. A few overhead shots emphasize that the scene is "off" on several levels: the movements are repetitive and awkward, the orange and red colors clash with the bright pink of Miranda's outfit that had established the color palette of the scene, and the geometric formations are neither precise nor spectacular enough to make a major impact. This segment ends with Miranda surrounded by chorines and chorus men repeating that she does not want romance but loves to dance. The final spoken words, "I love to dance!," end the number in a childish register that points once again to "art for art's sake"—very different from the core of the lightweight plot that is about to be resolved through romance. The curtain opens to reveal a platformed staircase flanked by a semicircle of elegant pillars and a balustrade where Bonnie Watson, dressed in a magnificent long, deep-blue gown, sings the last two verses of the film's much-rehearsed theme tune, "Whispering." Although performed on a stage, the song also doubles as a book number: at the song's conclusion, the camera moves in one large, continuous sweep from the empty stage to behind the wings, where either the whole internal audience can see the love interests kissing or the camera suspends all possibility of make-believe to end the film with the plot's romantic resolution. While Blaine does a pleasant enough job of carrying the lead North American female role, despite LeBaron's attempt to establish her in the pantheon of Twentieth Century-Fox girls, she lacks the powerful voice and emotional display of either Alice Faye or Betty Grable. All in all, Seymour Felix's choreography also lags far behind the spectacular nature of Busby Berkeley's productions in *The Gang's All Here*, even though camp is a consistent trait throughout the film.

Two other finale scenes from Carmen Miranda's films merit particular note for their unequivocal camp qualities: "Samba-Boogie" in *Something for the Boys* (1944) and "Batucada" in *If I'm Lucky* (1946)—Miranda's last film for Twentieth Century-Fox. The "Samba-Boogie" number, playing off the title of the well-known hit tune "Rhumboogie" first performed by the Andrews Sisters in *Argentine Nights* (1940) and made popular after that, is peculiar mainly because of Miranda's most unusual costume. Rather than the long, tightfitting skirts the viewer is accustomed to seeing Miranda wear, she appears in tight purple shorts with a train attached at the back and a long-sleeved turquoise top. Her headdress is also unusual in that it bears plastic flowers and other indistinct objects. The characteristic bare midriff and platform shoes complete the look and are the two most distinctively "Miranda" aspects of the costume. Exposing Miranda's bare legs, the shorts are rather unflattering on Miranda's petite frame. Campiness also exudes from the bright combination of colors, and although the costume matches the two-toned pink/lavender color palette of the boys and the chorines who dance with her, the number lacks visual appeal. The pink/lavender combination is overused on the chorines' polka-dot frills at their sleeves, trimmed bodices, and shoes and on the male dancers' pink shirt tops, neckties, and lavender pants, and the scene lacks another, contrasting color for the viewers to rest their eyes. The lyrics of "Samba-Boogie" invite the audience to have fun and enjoy some entertainment by imitating South Americans, as Miranda sings: "If you want your kicks today / Just do it the Souse American Way . . . Do the Samba." At this point, Miranda has definitely overdone the mispronunciation of her trademark saying and here rehearses the clichéd topic of wartime and postwar America's dancing its way through bleak times by emulating its carefree, happy-go-lucky neighbors from the south. Other than Miranda's presence, the spoken reference to the samba, and the drums that open the number and then reintroduce Miranda partway through the act, very little "samba" is present in the "Samba-Boogie," which takes the form of a boogie-woogie swing style that in no way corresponds to the lyrics' call to "take a touch of boogie-woogie out of the samba." The incongruity between Carmen Miranda as the lead performer in this number and the song's rhythm and choreography is striking. It causes Miranda to look awkwardly out of place despite giving it her characteristic dynamism and charisma, winking and smiling at the audience, affectionately touching the faces of the accompanying male dancers (with a constant twinkle in her eyes), twirling her hands as she spins around, and appearing throughout to be having, as always, a fabulous time in front of the camera. This finale number appears all the more uncharacteristic of Miranda's typical performances when compared to her only other musical number in the film, "Batuca, nego," a samba by Ari Barroso that she sings completely in Portuguese (despite a slight infantilization of her voice at the very end, more typical of her English songs) and for which she is dressed in one of her most stunning costumes: a long, shiny white skirt with layered ruffles at the front slit and green accents that match her

Carmen Miranda wearing Yvonne Wood's exquisite creation for her final number of *Greenwich Village* (1944). Courtesy of the Margaret Herrick Library

green sequin-covered slim bodice, off-the-shoulder fluffy sleeves, golden jewelry wrapped around her neck and wrists, a typical fruit-laden headdress, and, draped across her back and over her forearms, a long white shawl with yellow pinstripes that picks up the yellow shirts and pin-striped pants worn by her accompanying band. In comparison to the "Batuca, nego" number, the "Samba-Boogie" has very few of the usual Miranda signature characteristics, and this juxtaposition adds to the incongruity of the film as a whole.

In Carmen Miranda's last film for Twentieth Century-Fox, *If I'm Lucky* (1946), the main musical number is the "Batucada," which despite its Latin theme was written by Josef Myrow and Edgar de Lange. Although the film is in black and white, the print contrast is well defined, and the textures of the scene's elements are sharp and visually appealing. Miranda's all-white costume, designed by Sascha Brastoff, gave the media much to talk about, showcasing shredded plastic on the amazing hairpiece and on the adornments at her wrists and a ruffled, highly revealing skirt with a daring slit up the front, also covered with plastic trimmings. The textured and bejeweled costume, despite its lack of the usual bright colors, creates an impression of masquerade and exquisiteness, as had become expected with Miranda's outfits. Against this white palette, Miranda's dark hair, long polished nails, and expressive facial features stand out in stark contrast. When the number begins, Miranda appears from behind a shimmery curtain and, as she sings, proceeds to introduce each of the native Brazilian instruments, personifying them as she goes: the *cabasa* with its tummy-ache, the poor old *cuíca*, the squared *tamborim* that "lets out a scream," alongside the *regô-regô* and the "pandero-thing." Striking among the costumes on the set are the peculiar, incredibly camp hats that the male instrumentalists and dancers wear, including large squared and curved oversize-brimmed sombreros, tall pointed hats, thick cylinders, and multiple spikes, whereas the girls' black-and-white hats, equally unusual, balance an arrangement of flowers protruding from a large bow on their heads. Camp permeates the set through the costume combinations that draw their inspiration from the black-and-white, curvy sidewalk that flanks Rio's Copacabana beachfront and that is simulated on the stage floor, creating odd, very busy striped effects extending both horizontally across the floor and vertically up through the costumes. In this scene, the limited color palette of the black-and-white contrast "spills over" to embrace differences of textures, forms, and designs and plays with contrasting vertical, horizontal, curved, and straight lines. Harry James joins the number, intermittently performing trumpet solos or singing in response to Miranda's call to do the "Batucada, the new Brazilian jive" as a large group of dancers fills the stage. This is followed by Miranda's reappearing on top of a kettledrum illuminated from beneath and projecting light up Miranda's legs and open skirt, as the shimmering background curtains at the deepest part of the stage appear to go up in flames—one effect sadly lost on the black-and-white print. With both James and Miranda on symmetrically placed kettledrums, the chorines and male chorus dance around them below, forming a sea of black-and-white movement that encircles the stars. The focus is on Miranda, and the male chorines dance around her with their phallic hats, devouring her with their emasculated gaze, their bare midriffs resonating with Miranda's costume, all in all looking effeminate and asexualized, for they could certainly not be taken seriously in those costumes that are simply, in pure camp mode, "too much." Although Miranda introduces the "Batucada" and segues into Portuguese lyrics, the rhythm remains a combination of swing and conga, with only the percussion instruments harking back to any authentic form of *batucada*. When James, from the top of his illuminated kettledrum, repeatedly sings the words "the *batucada*," the Americanization of his pronunciation disavows all aspirations of genuine Brazilianness. The viewer's eye has become saturated with camp, and one wonders where the scene could possibly go from here. Then the music quickens, and the bizarre camera work moves swiftly from overhead shots to knee-high views, creating unusual angles and adding new dimensions to the viewer's perception of the stage. At this point of climax, as typical in the realm of camp, all aesthetic standards are "not only reversed, but also utterly discombobulated," as Roen states. His phrase, "oftentimes, camp is something so bad that it's good," certainly applies here (2: 8). When the stylization could not possibly get any more obvious, James plays his trumpet, and Miranda responds in Portuguese, as though she is interpreting the music through her spoken words as the grand number comes to its end. Although this whole scene is set to the music of a big band, this is typical Carmen Miranda: stealing the show with her fabulous costume, engaging through her gestures and facial expressions with the dancers who accompany her and the internal and viewing public, all while projecting that she is having an absolutely fabulous time. While camp in musicals has often heightened its overall appeal through overripe Technicolor that saturates the color scheme, this atypical black-and-white scene is imbued with the camp effect of textures, unusual designs, unexpected camerawork, incongruous juxtapositions, and the extravagance of shapes and lines.

Among the ten films in which Miranda starred at Twentieth Century-Fox, the 1943 film *The Gang's All Here*, directed by the great Busby Berkeley, the ultimate king of camp creation, is the film in which camp is most excessively portrayed. Miranda's screen persona needs to be perceived in relation to the film as a whole to understand *The Gang's All Here* as a cohesive, fabulously camp musical of its day.

The Gang's All Here: Camp upon Camp

The Gang's All Here (1943) was Carmen Miranda's fourth film with Twentieth Century-Fox, and in it she plays a far more developed character than in any of her previous films. The time Miranda spends on camera equals that of Alice Faye, the film's leading lady and the studio's most prominent musical star, with whom Miranda carries the weight of the film. By the time Miranda starred in *The Gang's All Here*, she was already a major pull at the box office, and the audience knew what to expect from her florid performances and lively acting. In *The Gang's All Here*, she surpasses all expectations as she joins forces with the brilliant camera and stage management of Busby Berkeley.

When Berkeley arrived at Twentieth Century-Fox in 1943, he had already staged or directed over thirty major dance numbers and films at other Hollywood studios, among them some of the most spectacular musical dance numbers in film, such as *Gold Diggers of 1933* (1933), *Dames* (1934), and *Ziegfeld Girl* (1941). *Ziegfeld Girl* staged an abundance of boas, feathers, and luxurious dresses that defy all description, incongruities that bring the audience from fish tanks to headdresses, and two scenes in particular that resonate with *The Gang's All Here*: the anthological "Minnie from Trinidad" that was written explicitly for Judy Garland, in which she sings and dances to a calypso jive against a Caribbean setting, wearing pirate-style hooped earrings and a stuffed parrot on her shoulder while surrounded by chorus boys and girls; and the film's grand finale, "You Stepped out of a Dream," with its hallucinatory quality, in which showgirls parade and gyrate around the set in extravagant costumes created by Adrian and stacked high with feathers, sequins, baubles and pearls.[19] Despite being filmed, regrettably, in black and white rather than the color the film longs for, all elements combine to anchor this Robert Z. Leonard box office hit and Busby Berkeley's choreographies in the camp hall of fame.[20] Yet in all his film experience, Berkeley had not worked with a dancer/performer as readily camp as Carmen Miranda. Judy Garland, while known as a very popular camp icon, is no doubt in the same league, but the difference between Miranda and Garland was that Miranda did not have to speak or act or take on a particular attitude to project camp—her visual aspect was already invested in camp sensitivity.

While all musicals project camp sensibility, the Berkeley musicals are in a category apart as the epitome of extravagant camp productions, and *The Gang's All Here* may be the film most characteristic of his work. The plot involves several groups of professional entertainers, soldiers enlisted in the army, a two-timing boyfriend (played by James Ellison) who is engaged to his childhood sweetheart (Sheila Ryan) and falls in love with a singer (Alice Faye), and is largely inconsequential, yet the costumes, sets, and special effects are definitely best described as camp, foregrounding Carmen Miranda and her signature look. As in the majority of the Miranda musical numbers throughout her career at Twentieth Century-Fox, her performances in *The Gang's All Here* are staged as aggregates to the film. The most iconic number of all, and the one that has received the most critical attention, is the unbelievably camp Berkeley extravaganza "The Lady in the Tutti Frutti Hat." The difference between the "Tutti Frutti Hat" and Miranda's previous numbers resides in the brilliant camera work and design and the magnitude of the dance number that are at the core of this risqué Berkeleyesque production. This segment contains many of Berkeley's signature techniques: kaleidoscopic patterns, chorus girls, implied eroticism, daring camera swoops, bizarre angles, unstageable grandeur, and military formations. This is camera art at the height of Berkeley's career, and the overall impression is both beautiful and uncanny, dizzying and dazzling. Berkeley's photographic dexterity, combined with the electrifying colors of Technicolor and Miranda's eye-popping performance, achieve extravagant effects. Martin Rubin summarizes Berkeley's camera techniques as "spectacularizing the camera" (42). Behind Berkeley's mind-boggling spectacle is the intuition and talent of an artist who creates visual art that the camera commands but that also makes its presence excessively and artificially apparent as it violates all realistic pretense in the name of exhilarating cinematic effects centered on Miranda.

"The Lady in the Tutti Frutti Hat" number opens on an internal audience watching an organ-grinder lead his monkey across the main floor toward the front of the stage, where the grinder coaxes the monkey to climb up a palm tree as the camera pulls back and reveals a row of trees, each with a monkey on top, projecting an uncanny sense of serialization and a preview of the identical chorus girls soon to appear on screen. The monkey's climb draws the viewer's eyes upward, a prelude to the scene's outlandish verticality. Until this point, the transition from the narrative to the performance appears realistic, but a major shift in discourse is about to occur as the spectacle gets underway and the viewer, through an elegant camera sweep, is transported to the opulent setting of a tropical island of palm trees shading a bevy of chorus girls lying under the trees with their naked legs prominently exposed. With no specific geographic location, it is a never-never land, where everything becomes metaphorical. In contrast to their surroundings, and on another level of incongruity, the dehumanized, identically dressed chorus girls are closer to civilized nymphs than savage natives, transported to this idyllic dreamland of sand, sun, and palm trees that conveys an evasive state of mind. The paleness of the girls' skin, in line with the interchangeable young, white, slender, and mostly blond chorines of the *Ziegfeld Follies* series, assures that what is represented are reproducible girls, with no individualized purpose other than to greet Miranda's triumphant, banana-fied entry, play a while, and then return to their starting positions to become once again part of the scenic display.[21] Lucy Fischer provides a pertinent description when she refers to the "zombieism of the Berkeley girls, a quality that they exude beneath the surface of their opaque, dissociative grins" (76).

The initial freeing of the monkey becomes symbolic of the unleashing of the director's imagination, and the passage that follows the monkey's climb between the internal audience and the proscenium stage is essential to Berkeley's ability to spectaculize the number, autonomous from the confines of the narrative and liberated from any constraints of realism. With Darryl F. Zanuck off at the warfront, the producer William LeBaron gave Berkeley free rein for directing the film, and the result is an unleashed, extravagant, opulent, and implicitly erotic feast for the war-weary moviegoers of the 1943 holiday season. Berkeley's sense of the impossible, demonstrated in several of his previous movies, is magnified in the staging of the "Tutti Frutti Hat" number. Here, along with the size of the stage itself, the out-of-proportion camp effect comes from the choice of props used to emphasize the chorus girls' movements: gigantic, "decidedly phallic,"[22] plastic bananas and oversized strawberries that are carried around and lifted up and down in military fashion, forming suspiciously vulvar-shaped patterns, which one critic has pointedly referred to as a "garishly surreal masturbation fantasy" (Roen 1: 74), another "a sensuous slow motion rape" (Woll, *Hollywood Musical* 116). To be more precise, the dizzying effect of the opening and closing of human kaleidoscopic formations, suggestively penetrated by their companions' oversized props, resembles a homoerotic lesbian orgy. In this I echo Alexander Doty, who in his reading of women-dominated musical scenes sees "The Lady in the Tutti Frutti Hat" as "an all-woman group masturbation fantasy involving banana dildos and foot fetishism," triggered by Carmen Miranda (13). What is truly amazing is that this scene passed the Production Code that explicitly prohibited costumes with "indecent or undue exposure" and dances "suggesting or representing sexual actions or indecent

Carmen Miranda in her oxen-driven cart surrounded by her band in *The Gang's All Here* (1943). Courtesy of *www.doctormacro.com*

passion" (Belton 140).[23] This scene defies all heteronormative display, providing a playground for erotica fantasies projected onto an undetermined elsewhere. While certain critics have viewed this scene as an imaginary expression of imperial sexual domination,[24] I suggest that, on the contrary, the coded messages of the chorines' banana-laden performance and the lack of an "exploiter" in this stand-alone scene endow Miranda with the last laugh. After all, similar to the chorus girls who gratify themselves without the presence of potentially seductive men, Miranda, the Latin queen of this make-believe tropical island, reigns supreme as she literally towers over her land and subjects, removed from Western domination, the sexual/sensual self-sufficiency running parallel to its ethnic counterpart.

The music is likewise dwarfed by the overwhelmingly visual aspect of the number and adds to the overall childish effect.[25] The only materializations of male presence are the servants who accompany Miranda as she enters, riding on a cart drawn by two golden-painted oxen. These men are more akin to emasculated eunuchs carrying an empress than to virile men willing to seduce or be seduced by an eager group of chorus girls. After all, by analogy, they enter with a pair of oxen, which are well known as commonly castrated draft animals.

Miranda's costume is in one of her typical eye-catching dresses, with the usual over-the-top jewelry and platform shoes. What distinguishes this fabulous Yvonne

Wood creation from Miranda's previous outfits is the more simple, streamlined, tricolor design: a black sequin-covered dress, with red strawberries and yellow bananas in her headdress. The darkness of her dress contrasts with the light-colored set, a background of light sand and blue skies, and coordinates with the chorus girls' black and yellow costumes consisting of black off-the-shoulder bustier tops with yellow scarves and very short flouncy skorts. The chorines' bare midriffs recall Miranda's signature design, but the long, naked legs infantilize their look in contrast to Miranda's elegant black flowing skirt. Miranda's striking black, red, and yellow costume has a grounding effect, as the long, shaped skirt and headdress emphasize vertical lines and contrast with the short, frilled skorts of the chorus girls.

Berkeley's camera transforms the dance routines and movements into enormous displays of geometric formations and kaleidoscopic shapes through a constantly changing perspective as close-ups, pullbacks, and aerial shots add depth and height to the performance. The chorus girls wave the giant bananas up and down, back and forth to form undulating archways and tunnels and hypnotic waves, reminiscent of Berkeley's signature "writhing snake" effect. The mechanical movements of the chorus girls, momentarily forgotten beneath their gigantic props, lose their humanity, only to regain it seconds later when the camera focuses in on the girls as it moves down the line, contrasting their sameness with unexplored individuality. Toward the end of the number, the camera hovers over the girls lying on the sand, their legs slightly open, in a final sweep that toys with exposure and is suggestive of eroticism.

Drawing extensively from Laura Mulvey's classic text "Visual Pleasure and Narrative Cinema," film critics have noted that as a genre of spectacle, the musical represents sexual difference through clear asymmetry in the production numbers, reinforcing the voyeuristic position of a male spectator. On the one hand, this holds true for "The Lady in the Tutti Frutti Hat," which illustrates, not to say exploits, the blatant display of the female body through Berkeley's trademark overhead camera shots of women arranged to form abstract patterns that epitomize the genre's ability to eroticize the female body, fragmenting and fetishizing it. On the other hand, a camp reading complicates this voyeuristic pleasure that objectifies the female body through a presumed male gaze since, as noted above, a more exact interpretation of the scene is the female's sexual self-sufficiency that elides the male altogether. Central to this understanding is Miranda's position as the lead singer and only vocalist, and also the number's main visual interest. Even before the final shot, Miranda dominates the scene. She is featured as royalty among the maidens: she enters in a position of superiority in the oxcart and remains central to the geometric designs that form around her, culminating with the circular banana-xylophone that she plays with gusto from the center of a circle of chorus girls. López argues that while Miranda is held as both a sexual and an ethnic fetish, she embodies the pleasures of the voyeuristic gaze, but she also "acknowledges and openly participates in her fetishization, staring back at the camera" (77). In comparison to the chorus girls, who look obliquely at the camera or are filmed from the side, Miranda stares straightforward from the center of the frame, and we experience her brilliantly camp performative wink. Miranda engages with the audience, lets them in on her secret that she is an accomplice in the staging of the act (after all, doesn't she sing about her hat being too high?). As she beckons to the viewers with seductive come-hither gestures, she entices them to come closer to the action, to participate in the act while remaining separate from the spectacle. Whereas the lyrics in Miranda's Hollywood-produced songs are mostly devoid of purposeful meaning, "The Lady in the Tutti Frutti Hat" problematizes what has typically been considered the availability of the foreign female and adds a new angle to Miranda's self-parody: if on the one hand she must take off her hat to kiss a guy (something she apparently did once for "Johnny Smith," the allegorical North American, who was "very happy with the lady in the tutti frutti hat"), the hat creates a barrier from prying male seducers; then on the other hand, the glide from gentlemen expecting an acquiescent "Sí, sí" to Miranda's outdoing them through an acculturated "Yes, sir-ee!" portrays Miranda's agency as she renegotiates the terms of their relationship and teasingly warns with an insinuating "ay, ay!" that there could be consequences to removing her hat.[26] In *The Gang's All Here*, Carmen Miranda also participates in "self-othering" by singing about the "Americanos," creating a distinction between her/them. Referring to herself in the third person as "the lady in the tutti frutti hat" plays with Miranda's self-awareness of her star image, which she justifies through her insistence that she dresses gaily. These lyrics also circle back on themselves with a dizzying rhyme: "Some people say I dress too gay / But ev'r'y day I feel so gay / And when I'm gay, I dress this way / Is something wrong with that?" She then immediately answers her own rhetorical question with a screechy, infantilized "no-oh!" This is another song of Miranda's Hollywood repertoire that filters camp sensitivity into the lyrics, not only through the ambiguity of the lady's position as willing/unwilling sexual or sensual prey, but also in the different levels of "gayness" that the staging of costume and lyrics indicate. Mandrell sidesteps an interpretation of the lyrics as beckoning "all queers to dress up and come out to play" (34), yet the reinforced "gayness" of the scene opens the possibility of multilayered readings, including a queer one.

With *The Gang's All Here*, Berkeley directed his first Technicolor musical but brought back to the screen some of the effects and geometric formations that he had used successfully in previous black-and-white films.[27] The addition of color in the case of "The Lady in the Tutti Frutti Hat" softens the psychedelic sensation produced by the black-and-white effects in *Dames* (1934), for example, while at the same time creating intense whirling and dehumanized formations when the chorus girls brandish their oversized strawberries and bananas. These large props are a staple of the musical film and date back to the vaudeville tradition of bringing objects to the stage that could easily be distinguished from the audience. What Berkeley achieves in his numbers is a mass production of these gigantic objects, which amplifies their effect and creates new perspective possibilities through the camera movement. In the above-mentioned scene, the enormous bananas form lines of swaying configurations that the eye becomes accustomed to seeing, Berkeley upturns the viewer's sense of proportion to the point that when the camera cuts to the smaller, wooden, banana-made xylophone, it looks miniature in comparison. The oversized props dwarf the chorus girls, who sidestep along the sand in unison, inching forward on a small scale, typical of Berkeley's choreographies, which usually involve walking, turning, bending, and swaying but very little actual dancing, as the camera does the fancy "footwork." The militarized movements of the chorines' feet is a new twist on the Berkeley classic "parade of faces." While, typically, the camera focuses on a line of chorines marching directly up to the camera, or the camera toward them, here this is replaced by the movement of the naked feet.[28] After the chorines finish swaying their props rhythmically up and down, they break out of their impeccably straight lines as though responding to an inaudible command and abandon the bananas as they scramble back to recline under the palm trees in their initial positions. The shrill cry that they emit seems animalesque in nature, reversing back in time, as though hypnotized by some unseen force that controls their orchestrated movements and sudden departure. The segment comes to its end now that playtime is over and the chorus girls (gratified? or simply exhausted?) have returned to the sandy mound under the palm trees.[29]

In "The Lady in the Tutti Frutti Hat," the girls' whistles, the chattering of the monkeys, and the organ-grinders' kinetic music all resonate within the same register—a screechy, high-pitched acoustical sound that becomes the backdrop for Miranda's vocal performance. Throughout the scene, the staging projects camp performativity with incongruous juxtapositions: beautiful and bizarre, preposterous and enchanting. The scene aspires to leave the audience in a daze of disbelief, wondering where the cinematic journey could possibly go after such a lavish fantasy of imaginative effects. This self-contained, eye-popping extravaganza, the work of Berkeley's choreographic and cinematic brilliance and photographic dexterity, has given the film its longevity as a classic among the 1940s musicals. What one critic writes about the film in general is also applicable to this number: "It's colossal, it's stupendous, and one of the artiest productions ever made. And because of all this and in spite of its extraordinary talent, it's a little tiring."[30]

As the camera returns to the climbing monkey that introduced the segment, the number has come full circle in typical Berkeley style, with the reminder that there is an internal audience, here expressed by the chorus girls and the monkey back in their initial positions.[31] The audience finally relaxes from the visual overstimulation, only to be taken by surprise when the camera returns to the stage that, in a camp-tsunami aftershock, is now completely dominated by a gigantic bunch of bananas, extending ad infinitum from the top of Miranda's head to fill the whole stage and beyond. There could not be a more appropriate conclusion to this phenomenally florid musical: through a visual trick which combines Carmen's turban and a painted backdrop, she stands immobile at the deepest point of the stage flanked by two rows of gigantic strawberries made out of placard cutouts. If "the hallmark of Camp," to draw from Sontag, "is the spirit of extravagance" (59), this ultimate headdress of the "Tutti Frutti Hat" number is the hallmark of all Miranda's headdresses. As Caetano Veloso states, in this image Miranda becomes "the goddess of camp," and "the bananas coming out of the top of her head . . . are confirmation of a deity."[32] This is the Miranda headdress *par excellence*, outdoing all those that came before it and never to be surpassed afterwards. Nor could it ever be equaled: the impossibility of the scale, the repeated motif of the banana, the final unsuccessful trompe l'oeil effect—all combine to create the ultimate camp illustration that is both disturbing and spectacular. The integration of the two-dimensional placards with Miranda and this three-dimensional space is disorienting. After watching gigantic three-dimensional props moved around the stage in hallucinatory formations, there is something unsettling about this forced combination of dimensions, and the reversal to two-dimensional props seems ironically passé in comparison to the oversized bananas and strawberries that the viewer has become accustomed to seeing. The two-dimensional props appear blatantly unreal and disturbingly camp. Indeed, this image, perhaps more than any other associated with Carmen Miranda, is the quintessence of camp. While the viewer attempts to attribute meaning to this visual finale, after the overstimulation of bananaland fantasia, the banana headdress is devoid of any real meaning for an audience whose senses of proportion and reality have been numbed. Just as everything and everyone is back in its place at the end of the number, the narrative has likewise not progressed and is exactly where we left off before this lengthy escape to the fantastic land of Miranda and her chorines, proving that the scene, purposely devoid of narrative relevance, was pure spectacle.

While much has been written about "The Lady in the Tutti Frutti Hat" scene and the final image of Miranda dwarfed by her gargantuan headdress that dominates the frame, it is important to link this epic number to the film's other "impossible" cinematic moments. "There is little modulation in *The Gang's All Here*: it is like a control console on which every dial is turned up to Maximum . . . constituting Berkeley's most sustained achievement of imposing the spectacle style across the entirety of a feature film" (Rubin 161). In the film's opening scene, as the passengers of the SS *Brazil* disembark onto a dock at New York's waterfront, the camera features prize commodity imports such as sugar and coffee and then scans the height of an opulent cargo net bursting with tropical fruits of all kinds, which then becomes none other than Miranda's headdress. The well-established association, both on and off the screen, of Miranda with fruit is immediately projected in this preliminary scene, along with the impossibility of scale, as the camera pulls back to reveal that the SS *Brazil* is in fact part of an enormous stage, and Miranda is a singer in this opening performance. This unexpected change of perspective that Berkeley creates is unsettling and happens so quickly that the viewer barely has time to rethink scale and context before the scene has moved on to introduce Miranda's first number. The lively beat of the opening music accompanies the camera work's accelerated pace and sends a clear message that the show is pushing forward and this disorientation of scale and perspective is just the beginning. The large hamper of mixed tropical fruit descends, and the seamless transition to Miranda's hat rehearses the verticality of her image as a preview to the tutti-frutti hat. Through skillful camera work, the hamper dissolves into a small-brimmed hat with an assortment of a few dainty fruits, completing Miranda's "Minnie-Mouse" look with her black hair coiffed in two small buns over her ears, contrasting with the bright red of her lipstick and headscarf, scintillating gold and silver jewelry on her arms and around her neck, and the signature platform shoes. In this scene, as in the "Tutti Frutti Hat" number, the camera's visual effects and the spectacular color assortment fill the stage, taking prominence over the music and lyrics. The fact that the scene is New York, and a staged scene at that, has no bearing on the plot. As in all Berkeley's great productions, spectacle is the core of the film, with little regard, need, or space for the narrative passages that are "greatly denaturalized" and to a certain extent "de-narrativized" (Rubin 161). The narrative is merely a vehicle to showcase some of Berkeley's finest work, and Miranda enables his "perfectly dreadful and totally fascinating aberration" (T. Sennett 180). In this number, as in "The Lady in the Tutti Frutti Hat," there is a disturbing, almost vertiginous vying between narrative and spectacle. Despite verbal and visual reminders postspectacle (such as the proscenium curtain) that what the viewer has just experienced was intended as a staged production, the fluidity between the performance and the devalued narrative disturbs common points of theatrical reference. Miranda in particular facilitates the flowing together of the different spaces as she continues to wear her stylized, eye-popping costumes in the film's narrative space.

As the film progresses, the typical curtain separating the narrative from the performative space disappears, and in the grand finale it is turned literally upside down by an ascending/descending water fountain that rises at the conclusion of a number and comes down at the beginning, as though the diminished narrative space and the spectacle have changed places.[33] This grand finale is a companion scene to "The Lady in the Tutti Frutti Hat" number, and it constitutes the second mega-Berkeleyesque sequence with a musical trio-combo: "Paducah" / "Polka Dot Polka" / "A Journey to a Star," which features Miranda during the third variation of "Paducah," following the orchestral rendition and Benny Goodman's singing. As the *Hollywood Reporter* enthusiastically summarizes: "The ending is sheer camera magic, a kaleidoscopic creation by Busby Berkeley who stages a startling departure in finales with intricate turntable and mirrored devices."[34] At this point in the film, it has become clear that the spectacular performances have displaced the loosely connected narrative scenes of jovial misunderstandings and bland love interests despite the impressive cast of supporting players who, along with Miranda, include Edward Everett Horton, Eugene Pallette, and Charlotte Greenwood. The "stacking" of musical numbers at the end of the film was characteristic of Berkeley's films at Warner Brothers, although not without exceptions. In *The Gang's All Here*, placing "The Lady in the Tutti Frutti Hat" in the first half of the film creates an early climax, but the grand finale is just as cinematically lavish and reiterates the message, loud and clear, that this film is all about the spectacular.

Dismissing any attempt to resolve the ongoing quid-pro-quo romantic storyline, the last part of the film is engulfed by excessive and purely delightful musical segments blurring one into the next through an explosion of color, movement, and emotions and pushes the limits of technical creativity, leaving behind all sensation of realism, as the hyperspectacularized numbers no longer even refer back to an "excuse" of a narrative. The musical numbers become self-sufficient, and their isolation from the rest of the plot is symbolically suggested by the above-mentioned ascending/descending water fountains that enclose the performers and are brilliantly filmed with a touch of fuchsia, which adds another layer of whimsical magic to the scene's construction. The clear-cut and elegant lines of the bright-white garden statue and the classical violinist trio set the tone for what is to be an upper-class, high-quality musical performance.

The "Paducah" number is a typical 1940s swing affair. It is performed first by Benny Goodman's orchestra, whose musicians Berkeley's camera individualizes as it sweeps along the rows, recalling the close-ups of chorus girls and organ-grinder lines. The next movement is a solo by Benny Goodman, with camera work that showcases the sumptuous gold curtains with their green accents. This creates the backdrop for Miranda's grand entrance: dressed in white but with a fabulous red headdress and elegant flared skirt, with gold necklaces and bracelets that adorn her chest and arms and reverberate off the exquisite gold backdrop. Miranda looks spectacular, as she has throughout the film, always appearing sumptuously dressed and beautifully coordinated. After her solo number, Tony De Marco and Miranda's band, Bando da Lua, join her on the stage and bring the popular sound of Latin music and quickstep dance movements to this cornucopia of sensations, color, and talent that continuously fills the frame.

The swing band's upbeat tempo gives way to a fabulous display of singing and dancing to several variations on a reprise of "A Journey to a Star," with Alice Faye as the main singer. Then, when it would seem that the grand finale has reached its peak, saturated with talent, color, and emotions, the scene leads to a truly bizarre period production in which redheaded, freckled children fill the frame as they dance in couples to the tune of the "Polka Dot Polka." In a production that has revolved consistently around adults, the sudden introduction of children this late in the film appears terribly out of place, camp in and of itself, and harks back to Berkeley's manipulation of the viewers' sense of perspective, so prominently displayed in "The Lady in the Tutti Frutti Hat." The disorienting effect is amplified by the unusual designs of the children's costumes, covered with polka dots and circles. These fabrics recall the circle motif of Miranda's strawberries and the constant circular motions that Berkeley weaves throughout all the musical numbers (the kaleidoscopic designs, the circular wooden xylophone, the organ-grinders, the repetitive lyrics and musical phrases), serving as a prelude to the explosion of circles in the following segment. The lyrics of the song "Polka Dot Polka" emphasize the absurd and contrived correspondence between the polka dance and the polka dot, with the chorus lamenting the end of the dance and the future of the dot. In typical camp free-association style (Core 7), the camera focuses in on one of the dancing children's sleeve. Immediately, the camera cuts to a similar sleeve that now appears, most uncannily, to drape a marble-like white hand. Without pause, the camera drags the viewer from the polka dot of the detached sleeve through a psychedelic tunnel to a neon hoop, all in a mesmerizing whirlwind of visual connections.[35]

The audience is now dismissed, and the viewer, forced to journey to the next segment alone, loses all references to reality, both from within or beyond the musical sequence of numbers that will eventually couch the scene and provide the reassurance that this one-way tunnel is indeed ephemeral theatricality. It is as though the audience, beguiled through the infantilized "Polka Dot Polka," with its deceivingly nonsensical and inconsequential lyrics, is now experiencing the not-so-innocent prediction that the "polka is passé, but the dot is here to stay." The sequence has removed the polka (the children, the dancing, the guiding role of Alice Faye, and all other recognizable actors), and all that remains is abstraction in its purest of forms. This fantasia of Technicolor geometry resembles a science-fiction number *avant la lettre*, as indistinguishable chorus girls in full-length bodysuits pass hoops one to the other with military precision in a scene that is pure spectacle but divested of spectacular grandeur. Far different from the hyperfeminized, chirping maidens of the exotic "Tutti Frutti Hat" segment, these chorines are desexualized through their unisex dress and mechanized by their automated gestures, more akin to an army of programmable Martians, and once again no male dancers appear in this trademark Berkeley feminine space. The scene creates a hypnotizing sensation, bordering on the animalesque, as the nonrepresentational performers, standardized in their cold-hued blue costumes, create patterns of encoded language, with the visual focus on the brightly lit neonized hoops. Whereas the bright, visually pleasant colors of the "Tutti Frutti Hat" sequence focus on warm hues of green, yellow, red, and black with a hint of brown, the hoops/disk scene is designed in the disturbingly cold and dark neon colors of a nightclub, with flashes of fuchsia that hark back to the gentle-toned lighting of the Sheila Ryan/Tony De Marco dance duet but are now rearticulated as brusque, aggressive, and unnatural. Both scenes are imbued with camp dramatic quality, but while the Miranda banana-fantasia leans toward a tropical escapist outlet, the hoop finale is futuristic and anachronistically displaced, resonating with Core's assertion of camp's existence in the future, which doubles back and needs the present so badly (15), even when this present entails no bearings of reality. Only the agents of spectacle remain to produce their art in the absence of explicit viewers. The décor is pure Berkeley technique: an abstract and ambiguous fantasyland, the last stop in a fluid progression of spatial metamorphoses.[36] The camera dominates the scene as hoops transform into disks, turn, and rise through reverse-motion technique, once again destabilizing the viewers' notion of reality through obscure camera angles and perspectives.[37] It is significant that, in particular, the film's main star, Alice Faye, becomes spectacularized as she is literally engulfed by a twirling cape that itself transforms into yet another dizzying, color-filled, and voluptuous kaleidoscopic design. There is no vying for space between narrative and spectacle: even the cast members are now mere bearers of unbelievable visual effects as the borders between both spaces collapse. The actors only reappear for the final curtain-call with the head of each cast member disembodied and set against a disk of a different color and texture as they float toward the camera and sing a line of the by then over-used "A Journey to a Star."[38] As the first line is hoarsely sung, croaked even, by Eugene Pallette, it is clear that the spectacle has become a parody of itself, reusing and adulterating the song out of context in this uncomfortable merging of actors and spectacle, forcibly "off" and indistinguishably camp. The actors have become homogenized as part of the spectacle, further adding to the campiness of the scene by themselves representing "stars" in the sky, all smiling and singing inside of their own brightly colored disks. The finale provides a symbolic resolution to the storyline, by now long forgotten, as Alice Faye's and John Payne's disks gravitate toward each other to be reunited as the number concludes. The film has come full circle: the technique of the disembodied head initiated with Aloísio de Oliveira's singing "Brasil" against the backdrop of a disk in the opening number is now multiplied and extended to embrace all the cast, sending the final message that it is, after all, nothing but a spectacle. Miranda's placement directly below Alice Faye and John Payne in the final scene is a symbolically charged positioning that confirms her importance in the film in general, but most notably, in the spectacle. With the film's ending on a "star"-filled sky, it has evolved into a collage of juxtaposed images of shape and color that have literally overcome gravity, just as the hoops and disks had previously, and have symbolically overruled the narrative—its conditions and its limits—which is, after all, what Miranda's spectacle was all about.

Beyond the two megaspectacular numbers, the "Tutti Frutti Hat" number and the grand finale "Paducah"/ "Polka Dot Polka" / "A Journey to a Star" combo, what makes *The Gang's All Here* one of the most camp films of all time is the sustained hypertheatricality that dominates the film through the audaciously spectacular musical numbers, the centrality of flamboyant Carmen Miranda, and the overabundance of specialty acts by Tony De Marco; Phil Baker (playing himself); Benny Goodman and his orchestra (also in true character); the ever-popular, amusing, and witty Charlotte Greenwood; and the comic, fussbudget, ineffectual character actor Edward Everett Horton. The film is saturated with "incongruous juxtapositions" that oppose, as Newton explains, "high and low status, youth and old age, profane and sacred functions or symbols, cheap and expensive articles . . . frequently used for camp purposes" (107) and frequently projected by the awkward sidekick characters' screen presence. Charlotte Greenwood's character (Mrs. Potter) has several memorable scenes that draw from this camp aesthetic, such as when she dances with a young jitterbug and steals the show with her elongated side and front kicks, or when, as the hostess of the manor, her orange and white striped dress matches the same tones as the house's awning, causing the viewer to do a double-take at this bizarrely "off" coordination. Likewise, Edward Everett Horton's character (Mr. Potter) is found repeatedly and unintentionally in compromising situations with the much younger Dorita, played by Miranda. Part of the camp appeal of Miranda's stage persona stems from her being simultaneously marginalized and ubiquitous, as theorized by Booth (11). She is central to the film's plot, in which she is both mocked and celebrated through her type casting as unique, foreign, and more utterly over-the-top than in any of her other screen roles.

Understandably, as a film artist Miranda did eventually tire of playing the role of the Hollywood *baiana*, which is memorably portrayed in *The Gang's All Here* and repeated throughout her films made under contract with Twentieth Century-Fox. As illustrated throughout this discussion of Miranda's films, these segments provocatively and purposely disrupt the films' narrative flow, couching the film experience in an overwhelming "here and now" of the performed spectacle (Mellencamp 3). A camp reading allows us to make greater sense of Miranda's image: taking as our premise that camp provokes all notions of gender normality through parody and excessive theatricality of style, we can see how Carmen Miranda's stage image, by disrupting the relations of form to content and through elements emphasized and repeated in her films and extrafilmic publicity material, almost immediately became a camp icon. To perceive Carmen Miranda as a producer of camp and as a camp object opens a more positive relationship between the camp spectator and Miranda's images of female excess. This undermines and challenges the presumed naturalness of gender roles, and by this account, Carmen Miranda's playful and flamboyant stylization becomes a powerful tool for critique rather than a mere affirmation of stereotypical *Latinidade* and oppressive images of women. These readings of Miranda's films contribute to a better understanding of her performative wink, an analytical tool necessary to navigating these camp sights of excess, artifice, and theatricality, which decades after her death keep her star text alive.

CHAPTER SIX

IMITATING MIRANDA

Playing with Camp, Drag, and Gender Norms

Carmen Miranda rose to stardom in the United States virtually overnight and became a much sought-after celebrity across the country in a variety of performance venues. She was, to paraphrase Boorstin, a star "well-known for her well-knownness" (97). Miranda's star text was one of exquisite artifice and playful masquerade that provided excessive femininity and extreme theatricality through the very nature of her "stagey" costumes, imbued with notions of her exotic *Latinidade* that projected additional layers of otherness onto the toying with and subversion of gender norms. Her characteristic appearance and gestures were thereafter broadly caricatured and imitated, and these mediated discourses of gender identity and constructs of sexual difference were nuanced by the settings that included—among the most prominent—stage, film, cartoon animation, social events, Carnival, drag shows, and costume parties.

Miranda impersonations typically have mirrored the original format of the proscenium musical number, although there are some, albeit infrequent, examples of Miranda imitations that are fully integrated into the storyline, such as Lucille Ball in "Be a Pal" (1951), Carol Burnett in *Chu Chu and the Philly Flash* (1981), and Bob Hope to a certain degree in *Road to Rio* (1947).

Both women and men have imitated Carmen Miranda, with a prominence of cross-dressing male performances. Whereas not all cross-dressing impersonations of Carmen Miranda are representative of a queer sensibility, her adoption by gays as a cherished iconic figure is significant. Gay sensibility is closely akin to many of the other imitations of Miranda, and the nexus between Miranda impersonations and her projection as a gay icon will set the background for an analysis of the most iconic Miranda imitations on stage, film, and in cartoons.

Miranda as a Gay Icon

In April 2000, the Houston International Festival chose Brazil as the country of honor for the Millennium, with the festival presenting an amalgam of Brazilian culture and arts: capoeira, samba, forró, feijoada, and Carmen Miranda. It is no surprise that Carmen Miranda would be evoked in the context of Brazil, especially at a venue in the United States, yet for the Houston International Festival it was Carmen Miranda as a *gay icon* that was the main appeal. According to Alan Davidson, the official liaison between the festival and Houston's gay community, there could not have been a more appropriate strategy. As he told a writer for Houston's gay and lesbian community magazine, *Outsmart*, "They've been trying to find the right hook . . . something that's respectful of the gay community but is also fun. . . . Carmen Miranda is one of those Hollywood icons that many gay men associate with."[1] To the *Houston Press*, Davidson likewise reiterated, "She was the classic Hollywood icon: she was beautiful, she was foreign, she was funny, she wore great outfits. Gay men just seem to resonate with that."[2] Needless to say, the Carmen Miranda appearances at the festival, which included a band, impersonators, a look-alike contest, and a giant parade float, were an outstanding hit. Charles Treves, the organizer of the festival's Miranda exhibit, summarized it as follows: "there's no other way to put this—she's a real hit with the gays."

This statement demands the following questions: What is it about Carmen Miranda that has made her such a popular "gay icon"? What elements of her star image are prominent in the way homosexual fans have embraced this figure? Harking back to Miranda as a gay icon, Miranda look-alikes frequently participate in Carnival, social events, costume parties, drag-queen shows, and Halloween drag balls, all of which are context specific and often associated with marginality, camp, playfulness, subversion, gender-bending, and overt gay sensitivity, situations that lend themselves wonderfully to the more formal, luxurious, female attire-associated "high drag."[3] In Brazil, the *baiana* had a long-standing status as a motif for gender-bending and cross-dressing, and in the United States the "explosion" of Miranda impersonations was quick to follow suit.[4]

A gay icon—generally considered a popular-culture entertainer and usually a woman—is most typically imbued with a camp sensitivity that fosters queer identification and gender play and requires a significant following among the gay community, particularly among gay men.[5] There is no essential link between camp and gay subjectivities, since both gay and straight identifying subjects may or may not express an affinity with camp tastes and objects; however, as Farmer argues, camp is "constitutively bound to the specific psychosocial contexts inhabited by these [gay] subjects," whom it affects differently than straight men (112).

There is a close resonance between gay camp and female movie stars that stems from the problematic site of the female star-image, specifically those expressed through excessive characterization or who are marginalized and markedly other. Carmen Miranda was both. Who exactly is considered a gay icon will vary depending on the source, but according to one critic writing for *PopMatters*, "the one trait that most all who are listed [as gay icons] have in common is an ability to overcome the odds or fly in the face of conventional wisdom" (Abernethy). This subjective quality of being "too-much" of something (too unattractive, too over-the-top, and too trashy are among Abernethy's examples) carries with it undeniable camp appeal. Gay camp draws from the artifice of the Hollywood film, playing on the stars' instabilities and focusing on their essential "appearing" rather than truly "being." The female stars of the Hollywood musical were particularly fertile sites for camp self-reflectiveness.

Camp was a social, performative, and political response to a period of sexual regulation that coincided with the heyday of the Hollywood musical.[6]

All Miranda's films are musicals, and as such the appeal of these escapist musical spectacles, frequently cited as among the preferred fascinations for gay audiences, extends itself metonymically to Miranda, who became synonymous with this genre. In a society that has traditionally emphasized gender roles and ostracized any deviance from these norms, the lavish scenarios, overripe colors, excess of theatricality, and make-believe combine to open imaginary doors, including alternative sexual identifications, through which, vicariously, gay men could experience fantasies and emotions that they could not act out in real life. This is what Farmer has coined "identificatory performativity," a form of gay spectatorship that "offers a privileged forum in which to define and express their identifications with discourses of gayness" (29).

The greater the perceived theatricality of the female star, the more room there is for gay spectators to express their affinity with forms of feminine identification that they can celebrate as a masquerade of femininity and as a means to destabilize concepts of gender.[7] As Judith Butler argues, nothing succeeds in subverting the straight like excess (147). Miranda's image is a site of gender ambiguity that represents a prime site for gay "camping," which can be read as a form of deviance, non-interpretable "thirdness," or a blurred version of queerness, neither male nor femaleness. The appropriation of Miranda by gay male communities aligns her with a host of female actors, singers, and celebrities with whom gay men have strongly identified, such as Greta Garbo, Marlene Dietrich, and Mae West, who captured the imaginations of gay men, as these women were profane, glamorous, exotic, sexual, and "strikingly androgynous" (Bronski 97).[8]

While Carmen Miranda on stage and screen is the quintessential image of camp as conventionally understood as "style" and "sensibility," the impersonations embody an additional layer of cultural critique, opposing models of bourgeois norms, defying paralyzing labels of compulsory heterosexuality, and gaining a liberty of representation that is only available through this parody.[9] For Moe Meyer, camp as a queer parody is the "only process by which the queer is able to enter representation and to produce social visibility" (11). Generally, Miranda's impersonators opt for a theatrics of Miranda's "too-muchness" that does not disavow the seriousness of the original representation. Rather than a form of mockery, camp permits, as Babuscio rightly defends, "a way of poking fun at the whole cosmology of restrictive sex roles and sexual identifications" (125). In many cases, parodies of stars' performances tend to magnify the original performers' parody of femininity rather than to denigrate those stars. Miranda herself points to this parody of femininity: her self-parodic performances in her first non-Twentieth Century-Fox film, *Copacabana* (1947), and in other screen appearances where she mockingly references her signature "look" emphasize her own long-standing image as a camp performer who understands her star-text as a means to playfully repudiate strictly prescribed gender behaviors.[10] Femininity, homosexuality, and Latinness have privileged positions within camp aesthetics due to their marginalized social status, and they factor into Miranda's appeal among gay men through what Garber refers to

as the "category crisis" that permeates the musical, disrupting by homology formations of sexual queerness and racial otherness (17). These categorical crossings and
displacements along the axis of sexual orientation, gender, and race challenge the
stability of identities and are particularly in tune with queer spectatorial affinities
because they negotiate contradictory binaries of appearance and reality.

From an artistic point of view, Miranda was an immediate success among female impersonators because either skilled or less seasoned performers could use
her figure as the basis of their performances, for she was widely known, had highly
individualistic mannerisms, and was well liked by the gay community, all requirements Newton considers as conducive to making any star more easily imitable
(48). Newton indicates dancing, singing, glamor, and comedy as the four basic
types of female impersonation: Miranda impersonations typically include all four
genres within a single performance, making her one of the most accessible and
flexible drag acts (49).

Emblematic of Carmen Miranda's imitative flexibility and broad cultural impact, as a gay icon she also left her mark on the doll industry. The 1994 Totem
International creation "Billy" was marketed as the world's "first out and proud
gay doll"[11] and, similar to Barbie, relied heavily on his costumes to convey different identities.[12] In 1999, Billy and his Puerto Rican boyfriend, Carlos, donned
drag. Billy dressed in a gingham-checkered pantsuit à la Dolly Parton, and Carlos
wore a Miranda outfit under the slogan "the girl that knows fruits are not the
only fruits."[13] According to one of the dolls' creators, John McKitterick, Billy and
Carlos were meant as more than just "a giggle." They were meant as a political
statement. The launching in the summer of 1999 coincided with the thirtieth
anniversary of New York's Stonewall riots, widely regarded as the beginning of the
gay rights movement.[14] Carlos's outfit consists of an exaggerated series of frills bordering the off-the-shoulder neckline, flounced sleeves, ruffled skirt, and earrings,
with the scarf-wrapped fruit on her head pointing explicitly to Carmen Miranda
and reinventing her image as a gay icon for mass reproduction. The overall image
is awkward due in part to the wide-legged stance, the tight-fitting dress, and the
bulky headdress, which shows, as in all true camp, that the transformation to the
feminine is never complete, even when it's a doll.

Culturally speaking, drag performances as a form of entertainment became
exceedingly more popular during the 1960s, when nonconformity became more
fashionable (Kirk 42). Like several camp icons of her generation, Miranda did not
reach old age, given her untimely death in 1955 at age 46; thus, material for camp
impersonations draws from the prime of her Hollywood career, with a prominence
for Miranda's original films and shows from the 1940s fueling her interpretation
as a gay icon.

Being Carmen Miranda

The first impersonations of Carmen Miranda in the United States were performed
predominantly for comedic value on stages or in settings in close proximity to

Miranda's own performance venues, as they both literally and figuratively dovetailed her success. With time, Miranda impersonations developed a tendency to maximize and privilege the artifice of the performance and its shorthand for Latinness, often at the expense of its elegance and exquisiteness, frequently blending camp sensitivities under a kitsch frame. Miranda interpretations on stage and screen, regardless of the sex of the performer, exploded the gender divide, often playing off one another as they cemented a Miranda drag vogue that continues to this day.

Miranda's image of excessive femininity created a unique model of gender variation that blended *Latinidade*, camp performativity, feminine excess, and marginality, which produced a variety of results of both male femininity and female masculinity in a myriad of performance contexts.[15] The perceived intention of these scenes is that they were (and mostly still are) performed for laughs in a spirit of playfulness and an expression of gender-role freedom, especially during the 1940s and 1950s when the Production Code was more strictly enforced and cross-dressing in films and shows was treated comically, inviting the audience and reviewers to join in on the joke. Many of these actors were well-seasoned and highly talented drag interpreters, which set Carmen Miranda imitations in line with their own personal acting career and genre.

Imogene Coca, a well-liked Broadway actress and fabulous dancer and performer, was possibly *the* first North American Carmen Miranda impersonator whose live performances included Miranda's vocal style and rendition, along with her costume and accessories, while emphasizing the mispronunciation of Miranda's signature song as "Soused American Way." Imogene Coca's imitation of Miranda appears to have been a last-minute addition in the Broadway show *The Straw Hat Revue*. Produced by the Shuberts at the Ambassador Theatre, it opened on September 26, 1939, and ran for seventy-five performances. On the fourth night, "Soused American Way" was added to the playbill at the end of the second act before the full-cast grand finale, with Imogene Coca as the main protagonist whose character name is the wonderful, slightly "off" play on words, "Saramba." It appears to have been a lively, comic, stand-alone musical number with Coca accompanied in the vocals and dancing by other actors. It immediately became almost as popular as Miranda's original performance, and Imogene Coca, who was an experienced mimic with an impressive stage career, was invited to perform the "Soused American Way" at venues around town. One night in early 1940, at the Republican Club's Dance Show held in the grand ballroom of the Waldorf-Astoria, Coca was the star guest performing this number only a few weeks after Miranda had finished her contract at the hotel's Sert Room.[16] Many years later, Imogene Coca recalled how Miranda had coached her with a great sense of humor, dispelling rumors that Miranda had been furious with the parody (F. Hirsch 189). As would also later be the case with Mickey Rooney, Miranda personally taught Coca "the seductive swaying of the hips, the come-hither rolling of eyes that [had made her] something of a Pan-American panic."[17] Miranda's fabulous sense of humor enabled her to distance herself from and facilitate this light-hearted burlesque comedy that she made

Imogene Coca as Carmen Miranda in a publicity still for *The Straw Hat Revue* (circa October 1939). Courtesy of the Shubert Archive

a point of attending on October 22, 1939, "to see herself as Imogene Coca sees her."[18] Carmen Miranda even suggested that Imogene Coca be her understudy over at the Broadhurst in case of emergency, she was so delighted with Coca's imitation of her.[19] The Shuberts, who staged Miranda in *The Streets of Paris* and Coca in *The Straw Hat Revue*, rightly perceived Miranda as a highly individuated product, a star whose imitations would never surpass her fame or status but only harked back to and reinforced her uniqueness, and as such, they were able to maximize the novelty of Miranda's performance through the success of both revues simultaneously.

A few months after Imogene Coca performed at the Waldorf-Astoria, the legendary Harvard Hasty Pudding Club, known for their "boys-will-be-boys transvestite theater" (Garber 65) gave its annual show on April 6, 1940, in the hotel's grand ballroom, an ideal place for musical activities of all kinds (Fenwick 111). The Hasty Pudding Club's show on tour that year was the suggestively titled *Assorted Nuts* and included, as part of the theatrical tomfoolery, "chorus girls" and musical numbers, as well as a cast member in Miranda drag who led the chorus of a Latin-rhythm number titled "Un chico viva" (sic). The press reported that the Hasty Pudding Club's ninety-fourth annual show moved the audience of thirteen hundred alumni, friends, and relatives to loud laughter and was, according to the critics, "the best in years," due in no small part to the contemporaneity of the successful and delightful Miranda performance that had become all the rage.[20]

These examples illustrate how quickly Miranda's image became popular among distinct performance artists, and it was only the beginning. The Carmen Miranda vogue was soon to become a staple of Hollywood film, even before the actress herself appeared on the North American silver screen. The first Miranda-inspired filmed performance is Joan Bennett's "Chula Chihuahua" number in United Artists' crime-drama *The House Across the Bay* (1940). Playing the part of Brenda, a star nightclub singer and future wife of a high-rolling gambler (George Raft, on loan from Warner Brothers), Bennett performs a staged musical number for a nightclub crowd. Her costume consists of a shiny, flowing, silk-flowered skirt; an abbreviated shirred bodice of ivory mousseline de soie; large beaded necklaces, bracelets, and earrings; and a sleek red turban twisted with a jeweled knot and an assortment of small berries—imitating the Miranda look down to the details of her accessories. Joan Bennett looks fabulous in this *baiana*-like outfit, just one of the two-dozen costumes she wears throughout the film that showcase her beauty and sex appeal with a noticeable emphasis on her wardrobe. Bennett dances back and forth with gestures that mimic Miranda's—twisting her wrists, winking at the audience, and rolling her eyes flirtatiously—and ends with her palms raised up near her face and open toward the camera in a signature Miranda pose. Each repetitive ending of the song's phrases consists of a provocative "sí, sí" or "bonito, bonito" to reinforce the number's Latin theme, already evoked by her exotic flair à la Miranda and the presence of the tiny, quirky Chihuahua dog that literally slides up and down the stage dragged on a leash. *The House Across the Bay* was released in March, several months before Miranda's first North American film, *Down Argentine Way*, hit the box office in October, an unequivocal testament to the impact of Miranda's Broadway performance, her costume, dance style, and *Latinidade*.

United Artists was not the only studio to borrow from the newly emerging Miranda craze. Universal and Columbia, with their respective comic trios the Ritz Brothers (Jimmy, Harry, and Al) and the Three Stooges (Larry Fine, Moe Howard, and Jerry "Curly" Howard), known as the slapstick greats of the time period, followed shortly after with their take on the Brazilian Bombshell's unique performance in two of the first drag interpretations filmed in the early 1940s. In Universal's *Argentine Nights* (1940), the Ritz Brothers are paired with another emblematic trio from the period, the close-harmony singing Andrews Sisters (Maxine, Patty, and LaVerne), stars of the swing and boogie-woogie era who were themselves prime material for camp imitations on film and stage shows as their style became "louder, more raucous and more aggressive" (Nimmo 125). Their opening number in *Argentine Nights*, "Rhumboogie," was performed in Carmen Miranda look-alike costumes, setting the sisters up for a drag impersonation by the boisterous Ritz Brothers.[21] Dressed in tightly-wrapped, fruit-laden turbans with beads around their necks and ruffled skirts, the Ritz trio substitute for the Andrews Sisters and lip-synch to their "Rhumboogie" in what is one of the film's most entertaining numbers. "Rhumboogie" became a hit for the Andrews Sisters, although it represents in *Argentine Nights*, as John Storm Roberts notes, one of those token Latin numbers common in a Hollywood musical with no Latin American theme (107). The three brothers dressing and acting identically, as was their signature performance operandi, rather than playing different or contrasting roles, only reinforces the Miranda visual and dynamic effect. Although the campus humor magazine the *Harvard Lampoon* labeled the Andrews Sisters' performance in *Argentine Nights* the "most frightening act in motion pictures in 1940" (qtd. in Nimmo 110), it constituted their film début and that of Miranda drag impersonations on the silver screen.

The following year, Columbia Pictures released *Time Out for Rhythm* (1941), a musical comedy that included, as was fitting with the general Latin dance craze, a rhumba dance number performed by the Three Stooges. *Time Out for Rhythm* featured only one Carmen Miranda look-alike, Curly. Unlike the Ritz Brothers, the Three Stooges always played distinct parts, and Curly was consistently the object of humor and the frustrated patsy of the group. Even though the Andrews Sisters are not explicitly referenced in *Time Out for Rhythm*, the Three Stooges' number points clearly to them, mixing in the Miranda touch for added camp effect. The film received negative reviews all around,[22] yet the two scenes that saved the film from being a complete flop were the Curly à la Miranda dress-up segment that adds comic relief, alongside the now famous "Maharaja: Maha? Aha" routine filmed here for the first time. All things considered, the film was just a longer version of the popular Stooges' shorts, including all the basic elements: knockabout antics, slaps in the face, bops on the head, etc. The Miranda drag scene is similar to the many fun and completely unbelievable cross-dressing segments that the Three Stooges filmed over the years.[23]

Later that same year, Mickey Rooney filmed one of the most emblematic impersonations of Carmen Miranda in MGM's *Babes on Broadway*, released December 1941. For Bell-Metereau, Rooney's performances are among the most competent early film drag acts, played strictly for laughs with "enough discordant male cues to undermine the impression and create a sense of removal rather than identification" (8). *Babes on Broadway* was the third of the Mickey Rooney/Judy Garland releases, and Busby Berkeley directed this delightful tale of stage-struck youth, enhanced by Rooney's inexhaustible zest and Garland's exuberant stage presence and voice. Rooney's Miranda impersonation comes as the pièce de résistance after a series of imitations that take place on the stage of an abandoned theater where legendary actors had once performed, and it constitutes the first number in a fundraiser show staged in the made-over theater. A chorus line spearheaded by Judy Garland promises "a revolution among the ladies at the Ritz" and prepares the audience for "a great big thrill," indeed one of Rooney's greatest moments on film. Rooney enters through the back of the stage and bursts into his Portunhol rendition of "Mamá yo quiero," hobbling on platform shoes, with a very pronounced bare midriff, a shiny silver sequin-covered, skin-tight skirt and top, supercharged with an abundance of necklaces and bracelets, and an exquisite headdress complete with feathers and a wire cone full of fruit leaning to one side;[24] he is ostentatiously the "bombshell that fell over Brazil," as announced by Judy Garland's character. Rooney dances around in the spotlight, gesticulating his arms and hands, which he keeps above his chest to emphasize his breast area, painted nails, and lips, and tilting his head upward as he keeps his eyes flirtatiously half closed. As he dances up and down the stage, he wiggles his rear to the audience, gives abrupt hip-shakes to the side as he walks, and, as he exits through the swinging doors, ends the short parody with an aggressive, salutary "Hey, Ma'!" that gets the audience roaring as the camera zooms in on the character's mother, who has come to see the show. Rooney takes off his headdress as the typical conclusion to a camp drag routine, reiterating that the performance was a masquerade, played beautifully well for laughs within the confines of the theater.

Similar to her excitement over Coca's impersonation a few years before, Miranda was allegedly thrilled when she heard of Rooney's imitating her. In a double-page photo layout in *Silver Screen* of January 1942, posed photos capture the fun both were apparently having as Miranda taught Rooney how to impersonate her, with hints on how to "make the entrance spectacular" and "be more flirtatious." The copy relates Miranda's enthusing about "Carmen Mirooney's" impersonation, and the photos certainly transmit the dynamic chemistry that went into this legendary, private lesson.[25] While the film received mixed reviews, mainly for its trite plot, and was mostly dismissed as one for Rooney and Garland fans, Rooney's impersonations were considered, as a reviewer for the *New Yorker* expresses, the "fresh and stimulating high spots."[26] *Variety* claims, "Rooney is riotous in his travesty of Carmen Miranda doing a what-you-may-call-it,"[27] and *Photoplay* likewise considered Rooney-Miranda one of the picture's high spots.[28]

Segments that stage "spontaneous," nonproscenium Miranda imitations in a youthful, impromptu way can be found in several films of the period, such as *Small Town Deb* (1941) and *Mildred Pierce* (1945)—the first a teenage, domestic comedy, the second a film noir. *Small Town Deb* was a vehicle for Jane Withers that she wrote under her nom de plume, Jerrie Walters. Withers plays the part of fifteen-year-old Patricia, who interferes in the romances and social lives of her older siblings and is caught in the midst of domestic strife between an unsympathetic mother, a snob for a sister, and a brother who is too cool to pay any attention to her. The fabulous Miranda impersonation takes place at a small-town music store, where Patricia asks the storeowner if she can play the "new Carmen Miranda hot

Carmen Miranda gives the camera her mischievous wink with Mickey
Rooney on the set of *Babes on Broadway* (1941). Courtesy of the
Margaret Herrick Library

plate" and then segues into her impersonation, sliding off her sash to tie it around
her head for a turban and reaching over the storekeeper's counter for bracelets to
adorn her arms. To the delight of all the patrons and store clerks, she performs
with great expressivity and energy to Miranda's recording of "I, Yi, Yi, Yi, Yi (I like
you very much)." As the reviews of the film were prompt to highlight, this is the
centerpiece of the film performed by its leading character.[29] Withers and Miranda
were fellow Twentieth Century-Fox stars in 1941, and Withers's impersonation is
a testament to Miranda's popularity, which led the studio to want to "double-dip"

into Miranda's success by reusing this song from the *That Night in Rio* soundtrack, released only a few months earlier.

Another of Carmen Miranda's hit tunes, "South American Way," was emblematic of the era and crossed over film genres and venues, both during the 1940s and beyond. In 1945, the song and a short Miranda impersonation were included in the film noir *Mildred Pierce*, contributing one of the few musical and lively scenes of this family drama. The plot revolves around a single mother, Mildred (Joan Crawford), who is abandoned by her cheating husband and struggles to pay the bills working as a waitress to earn enough money to afford luxuries for her daughters: an expensive singing teacher for Veda, the oldest daughter, who is ungrateful, mean-spirited, and materialistic, and a good dancing school for Kay, the youngest, who is lovable, lively, and somewhat of a tom-boy. When Mildred comes home one afternoon, the upbeat tempo of "South American Way" can be heard coming from the piano room, and she walks in on Veda sitting at the piano, playing and singing beautifully, with Kay behind her, singing, dancing, and twirling her arms to the music, with what resembles curtain fabric draped over a shoulder like a tunic, ribbon bows at her wrists for adornment, and a scarf wrapped up as a turban on her head with a carnation to the side to give the Miranda effect its flowery twist. When later in the film Kay dies of pneumonia, the youthful "South American Way" segment, emblematic of the carefreeness and gaiety portrayed through Latin American scenes in Hollywood musicals of the 1930s and 1940s, stands in stark contrast to the development of the film noir's plot, couched in blackmail, cheating, humiliation, and hatred.

To escape censorship under the Production Code, cross-dressing needed to be portrayed as innocent while hoping to garner as much humor as possible. The Paramount *Road-to* series illustrates this trend through its depiction of Bob Hope cross-dressing in humorous costumes, such as a sarong in *Road to Singapore* (1940), a harem outfit in *Road to Zanzibar* (1941), and his Carmen Miranda get-up in *Road to Rio* (1947). Hope's brief, farcical cross-dressing escapades involve "totally unconvincing, absurdly funny costumes" that present no sexual threat in a comic spirit of anarchy (Bell-Metereau 41). From the beginning of *Road to Rio*, Bob Hope's character, "Hot Lips Barton," has been the scapegoat of the shenanigans while his partner-in-crime, Scat Sweeney (Bing Crosby), makes out unscathed. In the midst of the arranged marriage wedding ceremony, Barton and Sweeney are out to save the fair maiden, Lucia (Dorothy Lamour), whose aunt has hired two ineffective hit men, Trigger (Frank Faylen) and Tony (Joseph Vitale), to stop Barton and Sweeney from thwarting her plans. At one point Trigger, unaware of Barton and Sweeney crawling under the table behind him, nonchalantly eats a banana, blatantly foreshadowing the fruit-laden headdress soon to appear, as the camera follows Barton grabbing a fruit basket and a tablecloth for his slapdash disguise as he escapes. Seconds later, having successfully foiled the goons, Barton returns all dolled up à la Miranda, with Sweeney effeminately garbed in a loose-fitting pirate costume. They are pushed to the center of the dance floor, where they improvise a routine to the fast-paced samba "Batuque no morro" (*Batuque* in the hill) that involves dancing cheek-to-cheek and rear-to-rear, twisting and turning with hands clenched and arms awkwardly entangled.[30] Feigning poise and straining to mimic the Portuguese lyrics, Sweeney sings his own version of the song in English, "Everybody here likes tic-tac-tory," and Barton responds with repetitions of "Ai! Ai! Ai!" and "Ou! Ou! Ou!" that fit with the original music. To postpone leaving the security of the dance floor, for variation Barton removes the fruit basket from his head, and they dance around it on the floor. Barton's headdress is left with nothing but a headscarf boasting two phallic points that resemble bull horns. Symbolically looking like a cuckold, the joke is now on Barton. The dancing duo swing around in circles, quickly losing control as they pick up momentum, and end up landing squarely on the table occupied by the hit squad, who only then recognize Barton under his headscarf. Undermining throughout the femininity of the masquerade, this burlesque-comic scene is a prime example of a cinematic sequence that pokes fun at the female disguise and confirms gender boundaries.[31] At the completion of the dance scene, the lingering indications of their disguises (Sweeney's pirate earrings and Barton's rolled-up pant leg) poke fun at more formal camping by visibly mixing gender-role referents in an unconvincing manner. In true camp fashion, neither protagonist is meant to be convincingly disguised, but both are delightfully comical throughout the brilliantly choreographed dance routine that received rave reviews in the media.[32]

As the plot reaches its apogee, the wedding scene is interspersed with footage of Jerry Colonna as a cavalry captain, exhorting his troops to come to the rescue but never getting there, in a spoof of DeMille adventure epics or the Western's hard-riding horsemen's urgency. The humor dispersed throughout the scene is based on playful gender displacement and thwarted masculinities, centered on the dynamics formed by Sweeney's effeminate pirate portrayal, which has nothing over his "cuckold" partner Barton and his fruit-laden outfit, all set against the backdrop of an impotent cavalry. The gender-crossing and dragging-up process progresses and dismantles itself at such a pace that the power distribution between Barton and Sweeney shifts constantly, and it is not surprising that their dance routine ends up as a symbolic tug-of-war that literally spins them around and ultimately leaves them both defeated. The intimations of homoeroticism or homosocialism (as theorized by Eve Kosofsky Sedgwick) that have often been read in the buddy relationship of the Hope-Crosby *Road-to* series gain another level of gender toying through the comedic framework of the Miranda approximation and the *in situ* Latin references.[33] The film takes Bing Crosby and Bob Hope's capers to new heights with this Latin American dance segment, on all accounts one of the funniest produced on a "Road excursion" to date.

The distinctions between cross-dressing drag and same-sex masquerade are often minimized, since the performative results bear similarities. Simply phrased, drag, defined as cross-gender impersonations, relies on the spectators' knowledge that the performer is really another gender; masquerade, on the other hand, is a same-sex performance. The women who impersonate Carmen Miranda can be understood through a feminist camp reading as displacing drag and cross-dressing:

Bob Hope in his Carmen Miranda "disguise" with Bing Crosby in *Road to Rio* (1947). Courtesy of the Margaret Herrick Library

they create a form of spectacle that disavows the essentiality of gender identity by representing a stereotypical image of the Miranda star-text as though a woman is imitating a man in turn impersonating a female aesthetic. As Halberstam demonstrates in her definition of female masculinity, concepts of female masculinity and masculine femininity meet at a half-way point, though they are not exactly one and the same—female masculinity should be perceived not as "bad imitation of virility but a lively and dramatic staging of hybrid and minority genders."[34] Such Miranda imitations are indeed "lively and dramatic," and this female masculinization of the Miranda star-text—which in its original form was the extreme representation of femininity with the shapeliness of the outfits and emphasis on the midriff and legs—questions the path historically assigned to the feminine: that of mimicry.

Filmed the same year as Bob Hope's Miranda masquerade in *Road to Rio*, Cass Daley's fabulous Miranda impersonation in *Ladies' Man* (1947), a screwball comedy with a few musical numbers and a rags-to-riches storyline, is a fine example of feminine masculinity in the performance of a female icon typically represented by camp cross-dressing men in drag. Daley plays a rough-mannered, energetic single woman, Geraldine Ryan, who wins a radio contest that entitles her to an evening out on the town with a farmer from Oklahoma, Henry Haskell (Eddie Bracken), a simple man who recently became Oklahoma's newest oil-king millionaire and who has come to New York City to try to cure his lovesickness. Daley's character is cast as the typical "always a bridesmaid, never a bride" who ends up playing cupid for the naive country boy. Cass Daley's masculinized Miranda impersonation comes at the very end of the film, performed on the stage of the dinner club where Henry has taken his secret Cinderellas each evening. Geraldine enters through back center-stage, covering her face with her bouffant sleeve for an added surprise effect. She has donned an extravagantly fluffy white Miranda look-alike dress with an exposed midriff, an abundance of necklaces and bracelets, and high-heel shoes. As the music sounds the first few beats of "Mamá yo quiero," Geraldine is unmistakably "Carmen Miranda." This scene showcases Daley's unique comedic talents: grotesque, manic gestures, exaggerated expressions that reveal her signature protruding teeth, and awkward dancing in slapstick comedic style, here accompanied by Daley sending her arms flying into her accompanists, struggling with her toppling headdress, stomping clumsily around the stage in her platform shoes, and even hoisting up her dress to reveal a glimpse of her lanky legs for a little knee-knocking. At the end, she segues into an ungainly mock swing jive as she tries in vain to gracefully make her way off the stage toward Henry, stumbling along and falling into the splits in the process. This is typical Cass Daley style.[35] The casting of Daley in this role is superb, and no actress, before or after, has succeeded in outdoing her "masculinized Miranda" with such natural talent, gusto, and stage presence. With no pretense of elegance or grace, it's feminine camp at its best.

Most of the explicitly Latin Miranda impersonations are chronologically closer to the original films and stage performances. One of the most widely reproduced examples of this trend is the episode "Be a Pal" from the first season of the sitcom *I Love Lucy*, which originally aired October 22, 1951, and catapulted the Lucille Ball/Desi Arnaz duo to confirmed stardom. The storyline of this episode—in what will later come to be considered typical *I Love Lucy* fashion—resolves a marital tiff between Lucy and Ricky. Thinking that Ricky's love for her is growing cold, Lucy attempts to recreate Ricky's childhood in Cuba by turning their apartment into what she and her sidekick neighbor Ethel envision would have been a Cuban hacienda, following the advice found in Dr. Humphrey's guide to marital bliss, *How to Keep the Honeymoon from Ending*. Since Ricky's mother was, according to

Lucy's recollections, a "great singer and dancer," and Dr. Humphrey's publication makes the blatant oedipal claim that "most men marry a woman that reminds them of their mother," Lucy's performance requires she sing and dance in "Cuban style." The blurring of Latin American nationalities without distinction, a common trait in the Miranda films proper, is transposed to this stereotypical staging of the Cuba of Ricky's childhood: chicken coops, palm trees, bananas, *sarapes*, and two "Mexicans" in sombreros—one real (Ethel, disguised with a wig and mustache) and one a decoy—create the setting for Lucy's "Latin" performance. Wearing a playful high-low hemmed dress covered with ruffles on the skirt and sleeves and a headdress adorned with feathers, a bunch of grapes, oranges, and two bananas placed symmetrically like an animal's horns, Lucy dances and lip-synchs to "Mamá yo quiero." She enters the stage with her mouth wide open, denoting full concentration, and then proceeds to sway back and forth, giving out an occasional "olé" to the side as she dances around a stun-shocked Ricky. One of the distinguishing details of this impersonation is Lucy's synchronized lip-synching to the phonograph in the adjacent kitchen: when the record gets stuck, she manically repeats the same gesture over and over until Ethel, her Mexican-drabbed assistant, runs to reset the phonograph's needle. The music's apparent control over Lucy's performance ensures continued variety to the segment and adds another comical dimension as she goes from an accelerated tempo to slow-motion gestures and ends up throwing herself, exhausted, onto the closest chair. The image of Lucille Ball dressed in her Miranda-style outfit has retained its popularity and remained in circulation through the merchandizing of memorabilia immortalizing one of the most memorable *I Love Lucy* segments. The airing of this episode marked the beginning of the trend of televised Miranda impersonations, crossing over from screen and stage to household viewing.

The comic synchronization of performer to phonograph reappears in Jerry Lewis's Carmen Miranda imitation several years later in the film *Scared Stiff* (1953). Both Lucille Ball and Jerry Lewis perform Carmen Miranda as pseudorecord vocalists: although the voice on the soundtrack appears to be theirs, they perform by merely mouthing the words of Miranda's song in performances that use exaggerated comic effects as they gesture and mimic the recorded artist and provide a gesticulated commentary on the words of the song, depending wholly on visual effects.[36] In *Scared Stiff*, both Carmen Miranda's part as the entertainer Carmelita Castinha and Jerry Lewis's impersonation of Miranda have very little to do with the storyline other than the "Latin" setting: two nightclub entertainers, Larry Todd (Dean Martin) and Myron Myron Mertz (Jerry Lewis), have fled from mobsters in New York to Havana, Cuba. Similar to the storyline of *Road to Rio*, the plot revolves around two entertainers escaping the law when unjustly accused of a crime they did not commit and performing together during their travels. En route they get caught up with and come to the aid of Mary Carrol (Lizabeth Scott), the heiress of an island off the coast of Cuba. In scenic foreshadowing, when Myron bumps into Carmelita and her boys, he overtly draws attention to Miranda's signature look: "Miss Castinha! I didn't recognize you without your fruitbowl!" Jerry Lewis's imitation of his costar Miranda is one of the film's comic high moments and is the first in a series of musical numbers presented at the Havana club "El Caribe." When Carmelita finds herself unable to go on stage, Larry, pulling seniority over his younger partner, insists that Myron take her spot. Almost immediately the music strikes up with the first few notes of what resembles conga-line music and then goes into the opening of "Mamá yo quiero," no doubt a very familiar song for a 1953 movie audience, even if somewhat passé by that point. From the far back-right of the stage, the well-known silhouette of Carmen Miranda appears. Then the spotlight reveals Carmelita's substitute appearing rather discombobulated: Myron's demeanor is comically awkward in his tightfitting skirt as he tries to make his way to the front of the stage. He is adorned in shimmering silver fabric, revealing a bare midriff, and is wearing enormous earrings, ostentatious rings, extremely high wedge shoes, and a most outrageous headdress piled high with fruit and ribbons. Although the film is in black and white, the overall effect is one of exuberance and glitter. He twirls his hands, swaying his upper torso back and forth and rolling his eyes as he interacts teasingly with the audience as the camera produces close-ups of his comical facial expressions. He is alone on the stage, but rather than dominating the music, the music dominates him: the irrational phonograph takes charge of the act, as in the *I Love Lucy* "Be a Pal" episode. Lucy's sidekick Ethel is here replaced by Larry to assist with winding up the phonograph and stopping the record from sticking. The changing tempo of the music once again adds variation to the repetitive song, dramatized at times by Myron's accompanying gestures, going cross-eyed as the music slows down and trying to continue the act as the phonograph sticks fittingly at "mamá." In a comic-grotesque gesture, Myron plucks a banana out of his headdress and peels and proceeds to eat it as he continues to sing, his voice dropping to a deep drawl then back to its usual squeaky, high pitch. The banana adds a new dimension to the impersonation, un-camping his costume's aesthetic by showing that the banana is first and foremost just a banana. Before the song reaches its conclusion, the record explodes into one of Miranda's nonsensical lines from a different song, "Chica Chica Boom Chic," as Myron stands with his mouth wide open, face twitching, attempting to lip-synch the sounds. He quickly becomes exasperated and gives up as the music returns to "Mamá yo quiero" with a final "Hey ma'!" cry, reminiscent of Mickey Rooney's years earlier, but Myron misses it, revealing that he was only lip-synching throughout and adding a final touch of comedy to end the performance.

Unlike any other Miranda movie impersonations, *Scared Stiff* is peculiar because Carmen Miranda is a costar, a technique that was mostly popular on televised skits (e.g., with Milton Berle or Jimmy Durante). Although Miranda's part is minor, and apparently Jerry Lewis insisted on her not upstaging him, Carmen Miranda as Carmelita looks on as Myron impersonates her. The camera zooms in on her expression as her jaw drops, denoting astonishment and a hint of mild annoyance, but the show goes on. In typical camp fashion, there must be someone present who reads the situation in all seriousness: in this case that someone is Myron, who does not understand the joke is on him and plays the part in earnest, while those around him perceive his actions as comic.

While the latter two examples are part of a comedy film, as is typical of most Miranda imitations, a most unusual and certainly unexpected impersonation is fabulously performed by Arthur Blake in the Twentieth Century-Fox action drama *Diplomatic Courier* (1952), a Cold War film with Tyrone Power in the title role. Similar to most Carmen Miranda impersonations, the setting is a proscenium stage, but the major difference lies in the genre of the film, a "topnotch spy thriller" set against a European background where the "cloak-and-dagger melodramatics spill out realistically and with suspense."[37] Although the film received varied reactions,[38] the Arthur Blake segments lighten the plot as a whole with his outrageous theatrics on the nightclub stage as he imitates Carmen Miranda and Bette Davis, two of his most acclaimed nitery characters, along with an impersonation of Franklin Delano Roosevelt.[39] From amid an alleged repertoire of some 132 impersonations, his imitations of Miranda and Davis are old hat, but the setting of the film and the fact that Blake's character, Max Ralli (identified in the film as "Maximillian"), is a Soviet agent who has an essential role in the plot bring an additional dramatic level to the acts. Blake was best known as a nightclub impersonator of leading ladies and "arch" men during the late 1940s and early 1950s, and when *Diplomatic Courier* went into production, he was at the height of his career.

In the recent film *Gangster Squad* (2013), Yvette Tucker does a fabulous, credited Carmen Miranda impersonation singing "Chica Chica Boom Chic" with lyrics in both Portuguese and English. She is dressed in a glitter-laden headdress of oversized fabric bananas, feathers, and an assortment of fruit; large, brightly colored beaded necklaces; a generous bare midriff; an off-the-shoulder bodice; and an elegantly draped, flowered, floor-length skirt. The film is set in Los Angeles in 1949, and she performs at the iconic Wilshire nightclub Slapsy Maxie's, a popular 1940s Hollywood hangout used by the celebrity mob king Mickey Cohen for his bookmaking operations. During the Miranda performance, the LAPD "gangster squad" unit attacks the club and violently kills several of Cohen's men. Carmen Miranda not only evokes the musical scene of 1940s Hollywood but is also the epitome of carefree gaiety, exotica, and fun-filled, glamorous entertainment, which creates a sense of incongruity against the violence interposed with the performance.

As the above examples illustrate, three pieces of Miranda's extensive song list became the standard impersonation repertoire: "Mamá yo quiero," "South American Way," and "Chica Chica Boom Chic," attesting to the stylization and reduction of Miranda's talent as filtered through these routines. Yet the variety of filmed Carmen Miranda impersonations, by both men and women, and their inclusion in films of all genres points to the great flexibility of the Miranda image, which held popular currency far beyond the immediate impact of her initial stage and screen appearances and has continued into the twenty-first century without losing any of its original fascination.

In the Army: Miranda at War

The golden age of military female impersonation had begun in World War I and was revived during World War II, as long as army officials endorsed the all-soldiers' performances as a form of morale boosting for the troops. Entertainment for the soldiers provided through USO-Camp Shows Inc. often consisted of plays rather than the soldiers' allegedly preferred genre of vaudeville and light revues. Due to dissatisfaction with these shows, the soldiers resorted to supplying their own forms of diversion with an emphasis on comedy, singing, and dancing.[40] The popularity of female impersonation performances petered off after the end of the war as female roles began to be filled by women, sometimes army nurses or Red Cross workers, and only in isolated places did GIs continue to perform as female impersonators where the military's expanding antihomosexual politics were less felt.[41] The GI shows constitute a particular genre of Carmen Miranda imitations. Miranda had starred in several Hollywood films prior to the United States joining the war effort and had also participated in radio broadcasts and live shows for the troops. As footage from some of these special entertainment shows reveals, Miranda was well known throughout the army camps.[42]

In 1942 Irving Berlin's all-soldier production *This Is the Army* opened on Broadway and, as an overnight success, fast became the prototype for soldier shows nationwide. It was inspired by one of Berlin's former musical revues, *Yip, Yip, Yaphank* (1918), produced during World War I, which included soldiers dressed up as women to perform as Ziegfeld girls. In the film version, *This Is the Army* included several major drag numbers, some even in blackface, at the conclusion of which actors are seen removing their wigs, taking off their feminine dresses, or cleaning off their blackface makeup to reinforce the performative essence of these acts. Miranda was one of the most impersonated female characters by GIs, always bound to get a laugh, immediately recognizable, and relatively easy to carry out, and some of the reviews of these routines have survived and confirm Miranda's popularity among the troops, which eventually led to Miranda overload.[43] Some of the performances were so realistic that, apparently, the audience was disappointed to learn that "Miranda" was actually a GI in drag. To facilitate the Miranda drag routines, in 1944, when the Miranda vogue was at its peak, the Army Service Forces produced a blueprint special for a twenty-four-man GI musical revue titled *Hi, Yank!*, complete with a Miranda costume pattern and detailed choreography.

The footage of one of these typical GI Carmen Miranda drag routines is preserved in the filming of *Winged Victory* (1944), based on Moss Hart's air force play by the same name. Within the traditional format of the backstage storyline, toward the end of the film, the GIs produce a variety show for the troops' Christmas Day celebrations, and Sascha Brastoff, himself a former soldier, stages a burlesque imitation of Miranda. Donning implements for eating and warfare—an army blanket, forks and other utensils, ammunition shells, water cans, mess kits, and frying pans—Brastoff stomps awkwardly around the stage, clashing the pots and pans that hang all over him. Miranda's usual fruit-laden headdress was purposely reinvented using GI implements, as indicated in correspondence surrounding the film's execution.[44] This circumstantial substitution is emblematic of how deeply entrenched Miranda's image was in the American popular imaginary: even without the fruit motifs of her headdress, a soldier in drag adorned with an outrageous headdress harked back to Miranda and was sufficient to pull off the imitation in grand style. After the soldier and his drummer finish their act, they leave the stage to great audience applause. Apparently, Miranda must have been delighted with Brastoff's performance, as she hired him as her costume designer for the film *If I'm Lucky* and was prominently noted attending the Hollywood premiere of *Winged Victory*.[45]

From the Silver Screen to the Home Tube: Miranda on Television

From the late 1940s, the explosion of television broadcasting created a new venue for comedy, and the variety-type shows that were so typical of the theater transferred over to this new medium and enjoyed off-the-chart popularity ratings. Several shows dominated this early television period, among them Milton Berle's show, one of the most popular in the history of television, which ranked number one in the US television ratings for the 1950–1951 season.[46] Milton Berle's style of emceeing and the revival of his vaudeville routines, with slapstick comedy, dragging up in outrageous costumes, and a variety of celebrity guests, were so popular that they earned him the nickname "Mr. Television," and he dominated the Tuesday evening primetime spot from 8:00 p.m. to 9:00 p.m. on NBC for eight years.[47] He invited an array of guests, including dancers, singers, comedians, ventriloquists, acrobats, unicyclists, and singers performing rock 'n' roll, opera, and pop, and viewers were anxious each week to see the guest stars and Berle's opening costume.[48] As a reporter stated in *Newsweek* at the peak of Berle's television stardom, Berle was "never happier than when he [could] put on an outlandish costume and corn up a role."[49]

Because of the nature of Milton Berle's show and his love for dressing up in outrageous costumes and producing situational comedy, skits, and slapstick theatrical gags, Carmen Miranda was one of the Hollywood celebrities frequently associated with Berle, as she provided great material for his comedy act's very visual style. Berle's shows were broadcast live, with no retakes and no cue cards, and only after several seasons at NBC did the network agree to make a kinescope of each episode. One of these preserved episodes of *The Texaco Star Theater* is from January 18, 1949, when Carmen Miranda starred as Milton Berle's guest, the first of four similar visits to the show, which marked Miranda's variety television début. In typical Berle fashion, he welcomes Miranda to the cleverly named "Texacobana" and introduces her as "one of the hottest, grandest young ladies in show business today, star of radio, television, and motion pictures . . . the one and only Carmen Miranda!" Dressed in a rather subdued turban for a hat, with no additional accoutrements, Miranda enters and sings back-to-back "Chica Chica Boom Chic" and "Cuanto le gusta." She is next joined by Tony Martin to sing "Brasil, Brasil" in a mixture of English and Spanish. Then, for the pièce de résistance, Milton Berle re-enters as "Carmen's oldest sister," and the audience explodes with laughter: he is wearing a long, tight-fitted skirt, large, chunky necklaces, and a fruit- and flower-laden headdress. Berle and Martin sing a medley of different songs, dance, and fool around, embracing cheek-to-cheek, with Martin at one point touching "Carmen" up and down. At the show's conclusion, Berle bids his viewers goodnight and takes off his headdress: the fun-filled drag routine is over, and it was all for laughs, as was fitting for a show marketed as family entertainment.

The year 1949 was epic for Milton Berle. His television show was dominating the ratings, the week of May 16 he was featured on the covers of both *Newsweek* (in Miranda-drag, forever associating Berle's propensity to dragging up in outrageous costumes with Miranda) and *Time* magazine, and on November 26, the Saturday after Thanksgiving, Warner Brothers released Berle's musical-comedy movie vehicle *Always Leave Them Laughing.*[50] At almost two hours long, the film is an expansive reprise of many of Berle's gags from his television shows woven around the story-line of Berle's character, Kip Cooper, pilfering other comedians' material, fitting with the film's working title, "The Thief of Broadway." The film was a Berle vehicle that allowed "the Berle style full rein, for better or worse," as *Time* wrote, and garnered mixed reviews with its focus throughout on slapstick comedy—Berle's constant corny jokes, wise-cracks, and overplayed gags and his wearing numerous costumes and clowning around both on and off the proscenium stage.[51] The Carmen Miranda routine is one of several stand-alone staged skits within the film that received positive reviews from the press.[52] The segment is an onstage audition during which a large balloon pops and reveals Berle dressed in Miranda-drag, with exaggerated makeup and extravagant necklaces and bracelets, and he proceeds to sing in complete Spanishfied gibberish as he gesticulates and twirls his wrists with the camera filming from the torso up, his headdress towering high and laden with fruit and opulent jewelry. At the end of this short performance, he asks the judges what they thought and eats a banana out of his headdress, in a typical un-camping gesture, saying he "always comes prepared," as the internal audience goes wild with its applause. The inclusion of this drag routine in the "best of Berle" selection of the film consecrates Carmen Miranda among the most famous and typical Milton Berle impersonations.[53]

Carmen Miranda makes another appearance on *The Texaco Star Theater* in an episode that aired September 23, 1952, in which Berle once again dons his Miranda-drag and plays off Good Neighbor jargon and Latin American stereotypes for a "United Nations debate," with Miranda as the Brazilian delegate sent to "cement Pan-American relations" and Berle with the "pan she would like to cement." The following year, he staged a "South American Way" segment in which one of his chorus girls dresses as Miranda, with a bare-midriff dress, headdress, ruffled sleeves, and accessories; and later in the same season, Berle ends the episode "The Party Date" with a grand coffee-dance number, arriving on stage riding a donkey to the tune of "Mamá yo quiero" and encircled by men carrying sacks of coffee and women wearing Miranda headdresses. Berle seems to have thoroughly enjoyed and explored the many possibilities of the Miranda motif that fit his personality and stage-style fabulously and that he also knew how to perfect.

These comic-burlesque Miranda imitations were frequent episodes in variety shows such as *The Lawrence Welk Show* (1951–1982) and *The Carol Burnett Show* (1967–1978). On *The Lawrence Welk Show*, Mexican-born Anacani, who joined Welk's "Musical Family" from 1973 to 1982, was the token Latin American singer and frequently performed Latin-themed songs, often donning Carmen Miranda-like costumes and imitating her dance moves. The interest of these numbers on *The Lawrence Welk Show* is more collective than individual: they represent the enduring impact Miranda had on popular broadcast entertainment as a homogenized image of South America far beyond the period of her stardom and her untimely death.

Carol Channing, the longtime reigning star of the Broadway hit *Hello, Dolly!*, with her massive smile, red lips, and saucer eyes, was known for her stage imitations, and she mimicked Carmen Miranda beautifully. Teaming up with another Broadway "Dolly" and Tony Award-winning singer and actress, Pearl Bailey, the two gave a memorable evening of song, dance, and comedy at the Winter Garden Theatre in December 1968, "Carol Channing and Pearl Bailey: On Broadway." The Miranda moment comes between another two of Channing's anthological imitations, Marlene Dietrich and Cecilia Sisson, whom Channing introduces with reference to the glitter of the Hollywood musicals in their heyday and Miranda's fabulous headgears—although she regrets she will have to do without one for her performance "as all of the fruit-stands were closed." Dressed in a long, shimmering gold dress, she proceeds to dance and gesticulate around the stage, miming eating a banana with lightning-fast finger and hand movements, twisting her wrists as she emphasizes her breasts and facial features. Channing mostly sings in gibberish, with only a few recognizable Portuguese phrases, and the overall effect is comic relief, foreignness, and unmistakably Carmen Miranda, even *sans* headdress. Channing most likely performed Miranda impersonations on other occasions throughout the late 1960s and 1970s, and she even incorporated a Miranda segment of "I, Yi, Yi, Yi, Yi (I like you very much)" as part of a medley of songs she sang on *The Muppet Show* episode that aired May 10, 1980.

The Carol Burnett Show, a popular comedy television program that maximized the audience's intertextual awareness (such as in the memorable *Gone with the Wind* spoof, the "Went with the Wind" curtain sketch), would pay tribute to bygone eras, classic films, or film studios, with Carol Burnett in the main role alongside her costars, Vicki Lawrence, Harvey Korman, Lyle Waggoner, and Tim Conway. Burnett's impersonation of Carmen Miranda was part of a special tribute to Twentieth Century-Fox that aired on October 25, 1972. Burnett enters the stage in a Miranda-like costume and sings "I, Yi, Yi, Yi, Yi (I like you very much)" surrounded by her supporting cast of three instrumentalists and five chorine girls, who dance around Burnett as she performs. Far from elegant and exuberant, Burnett-Miranda stomps clumsily with ungainly movements around the stage, loses her balance at one point, and ends up flung over one of her boys with inappropriate bodily contact, as the girls, in fruitless, bright-orange Miranda-like costumes, twirl around them. Burnett's costume consists of a pink and silver dress covered in ruffles on the skirt and sleeves, a sparkling silver bikini top, large earrings, and opulent jewelry, with a headdress of feathers and the inevitable fruit. This portrayal could describe one of the original Miranda costumes, but where the imitation clearly distinguishes itself from its original is in the exaggerated details that are purposefully too large, oddly placed, slightly "off," and beautifully camp: the fruit overflows from the headdress, large pieces of fruit are also attached to her dress and to her high-heeled platform shoes, and her skirt is cut high above her knees in the front but flowing floor-length in the back. Bob Mackie, the show's costume designer, was known for his genius designs that would complement perfectly the comedic script and feed into the segment's humor. As Carol Burnett dances around the set, she trips over her shoes—the dangling fruit on her skirt emphasizing the wiggles of her hips—and the segment ends with Burnett thrown on the floor, her legs flung apart, facing the camera with a banana hanging down squarely over the center of her forehead. The overall effect of this musical number is comedy, but comedy with a hint of naughtiness that leans toward an "innocent" camp performance: it leaves the spectator with an uncomfortable feeling that something is slightly "off" and has been done humorously but in bad taste.

Carol Burnett does another fabulously burlesque Carmen Miranda imitation in the 1981 Twentieth Century-Fox film *Chu Chu and the Philly Flash*, in which she stars as a one-woman-band street performer alongside Alan Arkin, who plays a former major-league pitcher known as the "Philly Flash." Set along the streets of San Francisco's Fisherman's Wharf, the offbeat comedy strings together the antics of this zany duo of ragtag misfits who become romantically involved. Chu Chu (or Emily, her civilian name) and Flash come into possession of a leather briefcase containing highly confidential government documents that they attempt to sell back to the original owners through the intermediary of a clueless hotdog vendor while avoiding a band of bumbling bad guys. Snappy dialogues, clichéd stunts, overplayed situations, unconvincing circumstances, and slapstick comedy create a film with a loosely contrived plot that is a spoof of the mystery/adventure genre, with scenes so ridiculous they lose all credibility, such as the suitcase falling off the window ledge directly above Chu Chu's street-crossing in the first place or the runaway hotdog cart going up in smoke. Emily performs as Chu Chu à la Carmen Miranda for spare change: as she admits to Philly Flash, "I do Carmen for money." The overall impersonation is far from the original Miranda glamor and elegance because of the awkwardness of Chu Chu's very forward gestures: blocking the crosswalk for the passersby, stomping around her section of the pavement in her platform shoes, swinging her maracas that hang down past her waist, playing the cymbals as she knocks her knees together, giving out shrill cries, doing hip thrusts, and sticking out her tongue in an attempt to attract attention as she sings a screeching rendition of none other than "I, Yi, Yi, Yi, Yi, (I like you very much)," the same song Burnett had previously performed on *The Carol Burnett Show*. Chu Chu is at best a burlesque rendition of Carmen Miranda, yet not without screen appeal or, as one reporter writes, a "spectacularly untalented performer."[54] Her costume, created by Bob Mackie, amplifies the comic value of her performance with its tight-fitting dress, slit at the waistline, skimpy halter-top,

Carol Burnett in *Chu Chu and the Philly Flash* (1981). Courtesy of
the Margaret Herrick Library

black mesh stockings, platform shoes, and elaborate headdress atop a curly black wig
with plastic mangoes, guavas, limes, and bananas.[55] Emily's Miranda get-up is only
one among several notable costumes that Burnett wears in the course of the film,
including several wigs, sexy black boots with spiked heels, a bright purple vinyl rain-
coat, funky-shaped plastic sunglasses, feather boas, etc. As a reviewer for the *New York
Times* mentions, Burnett's costumes are part of the film's saving grace: "Miss Burnett's
wardrobe . . . is the funniest thing in the movie. . . . Her role is so poorly defined
that she is often upstaged by her costumes."[56] The film blurs the boundaries between
costume and disguise to the point that the spectator is never quite sure what exactly

Emily's normal appearance and natural hair style are until the final scene, when she leaves San Francisco in street clothes to pursue her dreams with Philly Flash. Yet as the camera pulls back on the departing long-distance bus to the tune of "I, Yi, Yi, Yi, Yi," Emily hints that she still has much potential for make-believe: "I've got my costumes, my wigs. I've got my talent."

These examples of Miranda impressions in a broad variety of prime-time television shows and films that imitate the sketch-show format point to the appeal that Miranda's image carries over different media. Miranda has remained immediately recognizable, a fun and flexible "canvas" to creatively play with, and above all, a memorable impact for drag and same-sex comedy in all these contexts that immortalize her as the most emblematic and flamboyant Latin American of the twentieth century.

Emblematic of an Era

As Miranda took Hollywood by storm with her unprecedented success and unique appeal, other studios hoped to emulate Twentieth Century-Fox's Latin vibe by promoting their own version of a Miranda-molded star. Universal Studios promoted María Montez as "the Caribbean Cyclone," and Ann Miller donned ruffled skirts with high slits up the side, exposing her bare midriff à la Miranda as she stomped to Tito Guizar's guitar in Columbia Pictures' *The Thrill of Brazil* (1946).

At Paramount, Olga San Juan, dubbed the "Puerto Rican Pepperpot," was cast in token Latin specialty acts in shorts such as *Caribbean Romance* (1943), *Bombalera* (1945), *Hollywood Victory Caravan* (1945), and television variety shows, famously singing "Babalú" on the *Ed Wynn Show* (January 14, 1950).[57] However, San Juan also carried full-blown character roles, such as second-billed leading lady alongside Ava Gardner in *One Touch of Venus* (Republic, 1948). In the Miranda vein, the stunning Mexican American Lina Romay, with her fabulous diction, outstanding singing in both Spanish and English, and mesmerizing facial expressions, brought beauty and grace with a Latin flavor to MGM. As a specialty act, Romay starred as Xavier Cugat's leading vocalist during the 1940s, most famously in the Fred Astaire and Rita Hayworth vehicle *You Were Never Lovelier* (1942) with the catchy Cuban folksong "Chiu chiu," in which her hand gestures, mischievous winks, and small dance steps closely mirror Miranda's. Similar expressions occur in her onomatopoeic song "Bim, bam, bum" and the popular "Alma llanera" in *Bathing Beauty* (1944), "Guadalajara" in *Weekend at the Waldorf* (1945), and serenades and dances with Mickey Rooney in *Love Laughs at Andy Hardy* (1946), which includes the "Dance a Polka (Jesusita en Chihuahua)" at a country club and the Miranda staple "I, Yi, Yi, Yi, Yi (I like you very much)" at the Hardy home, making the Miranda link all the more evident. As one of the most delightful performers in her genre, Romay is expressive and attractive as she code-switches between English and Spanish, and she mostly typifies Mexican folklore and dress while mixing sounds and rhythms from south of the border. With the homogenization of all things South American in the Hollywood film, the studios attempted to market their leading Latin women while disregarding all approximation of authentic characterization.[58] An essential aspect of Miranda's stardom stemmed from her innate charisma, her unique "oomph" or "it" that was not transferable, too personal and too unique to be imitated as a serious copy through another actress's performance. Because of this uniqueness, it is not surprising in hindsight that Miranda became emblematic of this era while the majority of Miranda-inspired actresses have long since been forgotten.[59]

Woody Allen's outstanding 1987 nostalgia film *Radio Days* captures the essence of Carmen Miranda's popularity not as a Broadway or Hollywood actress, but first and foremost as a singer and a popular voice on the radio during the early 1940s. The film ties together a series of vignettes that have a meaningful connection to the golden era of American radio through the perception and memories of the central character, Little Joe, an eight-year-old boy played by Seth Green but commented on in voice-over narration by Woody Allen. For this period piece, Allen put together a cohesive, calculated musical score from the time of World War II, including "All or Nothing at All," "Remember Pearl Harbor," "September Song," and some of the most representative big-band tracks of the era, performed by Glenn Miller, Xavier Cugat, Benny Goodman, and Tommy Dorsey. The popularity of Latin music during the early 1940s is evoked through featured songs and passing references, namely "Tico tico no fubá," performed by the Brazilian singer Denise Dumont with Tito Puente and his band in a dinner club, and the single Aunt Bea (Dianne Wiest) practicing her conga-line moves as she prepares for an evening with a date she hopes will become her future husband. The centerpiece of this Latin vibe is Carmen Miranda's song "South American Way," which is introduced by the narrator: "Another song we listened to was by Carmen Miranda. I can only think of my cousin Ruthie and how much she loved it." Ruthie is Little Joe's older cousin, a fun-loving adolescent who dreams big and whose most emphasized characteristic is listening in on the neighbors' conversations on the party line. The segment begins with the camera zooming in on cousin Ruthie's backside, legs, and hips as she begins to dance and lip-synch to the radio music. Wearing high-waisted polyester pants, a polyester shirt patterned with palm trees, clunky colorful bracelets, a towel tied tightly around her head simulating a turban, and a banana pendant around her neck, she sings and dances with great gusto and exaggerated facial expressions, gesticulating with her arms up and down, twirling her hands, and spinning as she dances around with the occasional kick to the side, all in a confined space in front of a small, cluttered mirror. The music is portrayed as a household favorite across generations, with Joe's father and his uncle Abe joining in at the chorus, providing the final choruses of "ay yi, ay yi" as they watch their daughter/niece approvingly while twirling their fingers to the song's rhythm. The overall effect of this Miranda segment is contagious gaiety, emblematic of the film's central message and showcasing the importance of the radio in American homes and how it influenced and enhanced their lives by bringing them together around shared favorite songs, radio programs, and news broadcasts. Miranda's hit song "South American Way" is reprised at the end of the film as the credits roll, a reminder of one of the film's most memorable scenes and a welcome repeat of a most beloved song of those radio days.

Along with other of Miranda's popular songs, "South American Way" encapsulated the World War II era with its Latin fever, Good Neighbor Policy, and Hollywood musicals. The period film *Class of '44* (Warner Brothers 1973), a sequel to *Summer of '42*, makes this message clear by repeatedly featuring "South American Way" as part of the soundtrack accompanying the lives of three high school graduates, to the point that one of the main protagonists and graduates, Oscy (Jerry Houser), exclaims to his friend Hermie (Gary Grimes): "This crummy song follows me wherever I go! It's a curse, Hermie—it's a gypsy curse!" Similar to Woody Allen's *Radio Days*, the inclusion of "South American Way" along with cinematic details such as a vintage train, PCC-type streetcars, period costumes, and the radio broadcasting news of the war contribute to reconstructing the bygone period of World War II. However, unlike in *Radio Days*, in *Class of '44* the protagonist repeatedly vocalizes his dislike for the over-played song.

Likewise, in an effort to capitalize on the Latin vogue time period, other songs Miranda performed and recorded have been included in several Hollywood films. A contemporary example is the MGM musical *Easy to Wed* (1946): after plenty of singing and dancing by Van Johnson, swimming by Esther Williams, and clowning by Lucille Ball, the film comes to its grand conclusion with a Williams-Johnson rendition of Ari Barroso's "Boneca de pixe" (Tar doll), although Ethel Smith's brilliant organ playing steals the scene. It is a peculiar choice for a number, as the protagonists are supposedly in Mexico City, but fits within Hollywood's common homogenizing of Latin American ethnicities and draws from Miranda's popularity.[60] The choice of "Boneca de pixe" was also related to Ethel Smith's not-so-distant film soundtrack repertoire, as two years before she had brilliantly performed another Brazilian tune, Carmen Miranda's hit song "Tico tico no fubá," in the film *Bathing Beauty* (1944, also an Ester Williams MGM vehicle), and the song had reached number fourteen on the US pop charts in November of that year.[61]

Two final examples merit mentioning because they point to the conflation of Carmen Miranda and her fruit-laden performances with the golden age of the musicals, along with other connotations. In *Beloved Infidel*, a 1959 biographical drama based on the life of F. Scott Fitzgerald, Fitzgerald (Gregory Peck) and his lover, the radio host Sheilah Graham (Deborah Kerr), go out for the evening to the movies and watch *That Night in Rio*. The film inserts a short segment of the final scene with Don Ameche, Alice Faye, and Carmen Miranda singing the last verses of "Boa noite" with their glasses raised joyously in a celebratory stance toward the audience, in stark contrast to the dark turmoil Fitzgerald is going through, fighting alcoholism after being fired as a Hollywood scriptwriter. The inclusion of this clip from *That Night in Rio* captures the essence of the cinema-going experience of the time in the grand movie theaters, despite the fact that Fitzgerald died several months before *That Night in Rio* was released.[62]

The Carmen Miranda segments of "The Lady in the Tutti Frutti Hat" musical number from *The Gang's All Here* are among the many film clips inserted in the controversial 1970 American comedy *Myra Breckinridge*, also cited as one of the worst films ever made. The film, which depicts the main character's sex-change surgery that transforms Myron into Myra, includes sexual explicitness and off-color humor, and it draws from Miranda's banana-filled musical scenes to punctuate the sexual innuendos of an elaborate musical number performed by the camp queen herself, Mae West, who was long past her prime and came out of retirement for the film, surrounded by camp male dancers. The lyrics of the song overtly state, "You've got to taste all the fruit; you've got to taste all the wine," while one of the core characters, Rusty (Roger Herren), tells Myra (Raquel Welch) that "jail wouldn't be so bad if there wasn't all those faggots . . . There's always some fruit after you! A man should act like a man." Little does Rusty know that he will soon be submitted to Myra's idea of a sexual education in the form of rape by pegging. While the interspersing of Miranda's "Tutti Frutti Hat" segments is not unusual in this film that constantly uses a splicing technique, including a short segment from "Chica Chica Boom Chic," the opening musical number of *That Night in Rio*, which appears earlier in the film, the Mae West scene overworks the banana/fruit/homosexual correlation through not only visual but also spoken and sung cues. Regardless of the contemporary reception of Busby Berkeley's "Tutti Frutti" extravaganza, it is here refurbished for its explicit gender-bending and sexual connotations.

These examples capture Miranda's impact on the musical scene not only during her time but also posthumously and exemplify how, alongside her work as an actress, she was recognized as a singer in performance venues both on and off the silver screen. The subsequent use of her segments has been broad, yet as these films rightly illustrate, Carmen Miranda was without doubt one of the main voices of the 1940s musical era and radio days.

Carmen Miranda Imagined through the World of Cartoons

For many American viewers, the animated cartoons produced by Hollywood studios reinforced the image of Carmen Miranda as a Latin American icon. During the 1940s in the pre-VHS era, over eighty-five million movie tickets were sold on average each week at a time when cartoons accompanied the feature film. For the most part, contemporaneous with Miranda's Hollywood career, the studios produced innumerable cartoons that featured imitations of Miranda, predominantly performed by male cartoon characters in drag. The cartoon medium was ideal for the stylized representation of Miranda look-alikes: the bright colors, the quick tempo of surprise effects and transformations, and the precision of the timing all worked wonderfully to foreground the visual and the body, playing on comedy and camp sensitivity. Cartoon characteristics can be read in the studio portrayal of Miranda's exotic appearance and "inexplicably cartoonish" voice (Mandrell 31), making Carmen Miranda's screen persona prime material for cartoon renditions. Miranda's bright, multitextured outfits and spectacular headdresses are particularly apt for representation in animated cartoons, in which characters are depicted in a wholly created universe through cartoon drawings that, of necessity, simplify reality. The result is unmistakably Carmen Miranda: overtly feminine, the epitome of South Americanness, and pushing gender norms to their limits in the midst of lighthearted comic sequences that are excessive, entertaining, and beautifully camp.

The cartoons of Disney, Max Fleischer, and MGM offer a reading of societal gender "normality" that relies heavily on a heterosexual ideal in which there is little ground for rebellion against the normative gender ideals of masculine dominance and feminine submission or crossover between gender divides. There are only a handful of Carmen Miranda impersonations in the work of these studios, a fact that can be easily understood given that assumptions about gender roles preclude the possibility of toying with gender or positing a camp reading of relationships, which is an intrinsic part of the Miranda text so frequently performed in drag. Warner Brothers, on the other hand, populated almost exclusively by (assumed) male characters, helped "open the possibility of destabilizing gender roles, and thus introducing a critique of them" (Abel 190). In many of these cartoons, the innocuous context of the animated medium, abstracted from the complexities of real life, merrily shatters all types of expected masculine/feminine behavior, often taking the audience by surprise in precise, quick, and highly entertaining twists of roles and relationships that are particularly apt for a camp reading. In most of the cartoon representations of Carmen Miranda, as in all good camp drag, the transition to the feminine is visibly a disguise that reassures the viewer of the farcical nature of the imitation and the provocative gender-bending at play.

While Bugs Bunny is Warner Brothers' star camp artist, he is not alone in the camp arena, and Daffy Duck, as Sam Abel writes, "is the central vehicle for Chuck Jones to camp traditional macho stereotypes" (197). In *Yankee Doodle Daffy* (1943), whose very title bears a whimsical campiness, the camp performance plays out in the toying with make-believe and drag, pushing the boundaries of gender role-play. Porky Pig is a casting director (cue the Academy Award statuette on the wall) and is paired with Daffy Duck, who assails Porky to convince him to take interest in his latest stage discovery, Sleepy LaGoon. As often happens in the topsy-turvy, upside-down world of cartoons, there is very little logic to be found in Daffy's doing Sleepy's routines, and when Sleepy finally puts away his lollipop in a banjo case to take the floor, he chokes up after only a few lines of "In the Garden of My Heart." Among Sleepy's "repertory," Daffy performs a hodgepodge of songs, including the Broadway classic "I'm Just Wild about Harry" later popularized by Al Jolson, Daffy's own lyrics to the popular tune "Cheyenne," and a brief hint of "I'm a Yankee Doodle Dandy" from the Warner Brothers 1942 film starring James Cagney.[63] Daffy's Miranda impersonation is among these clips, and just as he is dressed as a cowboy for the "Cheyenne" number, he appears in full Carmen Miranda garb to interpret "Chica Chica Boom Chic," one of Miranda's most popular songs since her performance of it in *That Night in Rio* (1941). Because he is wearing a long blue, tight-fitting, bare-midriff outfit, gold hoop earrings and gold bracelets, platform shoes, and a fruitbowl of a headdress with bananas, grapes, and apples, Daffy's demeanor is transformed as he sings with a Latin accent and gesticulates his hips, hands, and arms in a flirtatious manner. The lyrics are for the most part indistinguishable, other than the occasional "when she loooooooves him!"—just as Miranda's songs no doubt often appeared to an American public. The number ends with Miranda-Daffy seductively grinning from ear to ear, boasting an exaggeratedly wide mouth full of sparkly white teeth, ending a fabulous segment of an outstandingly zany Looney Tunes cartoon from the vintage early 1940s period at Warner Brothers.[64]

The *Yankee Doodle Daffy* short was Daffy Duck's second Miranda-themed cartoon: in *Daffy's Southern Exposure* (1942), in full war period, Daffy decides to stay north while all his fellow ducks migrate south. His hunger leads him to the cabin of a fox and Abigail the weasel, who, in drag, feed him beans as they get the pot ready to cook their "duck dinner." The storyline has a fairytale feel to it as it bears resemblances to *Little Red Riding Hood* and *Hansel and Gretel* with the famine in the land and the "cannibalistic" twist. In a moment of anagnorisis, Daffy darts out of their cabin and heads south through the snow—so far south that he ends up in Carmen Miranda's headdress in Rio de Janeiro. The film draws on Miranda's popular songs, blending "South American Way" and "Chica Chica Boom Chic" as Daffy emerges from her headdress, now by approximation also wearing his own unmistakable Miranda headdress and earrings, to conclude the act and reinforce the campiness of the scene that stems from the instantaneous drag and opulence of the disguise. As the camera zooms in on his face, he exclaims, "I like the Souse American Way, and I do mean Souse!" Daffy, known for his lisp pronunciation, was ideally chosen to imitate Miranda's mispronounced "souse." The chase sequences in the above cartoons, preeminent by the late 1930s at Warner Brothers, add dynamism and a touch of visual anarchy and are fitting with the speedy Miranda camp transformations.[65]

Warner Brothers' star camp icon of all times, Bugs Bunny, is indelibly tied to Carmen Miranda. In fact, it would not be an overstatement to claim that for many viewers, Miranda was introduced to a wide audience through the Bugs Bunny cartoon short *What's Cookin' Doc?* (1944) and the Bugs-as-Carmen Miranda memorabilia that this cartoon inspired. Directed by Bob Clampett, *What's Cookin' Doc?* is replete with self-awareness and parody as Bugs Bunny attends the Academy Awards, tries to convince the committee that he deserves the Oscar more than the Warner Brothers leading man James Cagney, and runs a clip from *Hiawatha's Rabbit Hunt* to persuade them of a recount, directly addressing the audience and the camera.[66] He desperately tries to fire up the audience's enthusiasm, but as a response he receives a shower of cabbage, apples, carrots, and—symbolically—many tomatoes thrown at his head. This insult does not deter Bugs, who emerges triumphant from beneath the pile of fruit and vegetables looking fabulous in a headdress of bananas, grapes, broccoli, and apples very clearly à la Carmen Miranda, a highly sexualized woman with exaggerated red lipstick and eyelashes. A gold "Booby Prize Oscar" (which greatly resembles Bugs) is hurled at him, breaking the Carmen Miranda spell. Bugs declares his undying love for the statuette, claiming he will cherish him forever and even take him to bed at night. The effeminate statuette, shaped as a foreign gay lover, complete with the all-telling limp wrist, plants a kiss on Bugs and asks in a deep bass, romantic accent, "Do you mean it?," sealing the image of the legendary "gay Bugs."

Immediately after the incongruous, sudden-reversal Miranda drag sequence, Bugs is depicted in a satisfying gay relationship that replaces the public recognition for the Oscar.[67] The Carmen Miranda effect is linked not only to the cartoon's setting (the film industry and Hollywood) but also, more specifically, to the Miranda/fruit association, through which Bugs appropriates a Miranda headdress, reversing and parodying the insult he receives, in true camp style. This leads to the cartoon's conclusion, in which Bugs is able to seduce his statuette, distracting the clip's focus once again from his being the object of insult to the subject of seduction.

Bugs Bunny stars in another delightful short with a Miranda theme when he encounters a cartoon version of Carmen Miranda in *Slick Hare* (1947). At the "Mocrumbo" restaurant, chef Elmer Fudd chases after Bugs to get a "fwied wabbit" for Humphrey Bogart's dinner.[68] Bugs escapes into Miranda's dressing room and tries to delude Fudd by hiding in her headdress of pineapples, apples, bananas, plums, and a new addition to the cocktail: carrots. Bugs's chomping on a carrot, as always, gives him away to Fudd as the camera zooms in on the headdress. In the characteristically safe zone of the proscenium stage, Miranda performs "Sambaiana" while Bugs tranquilly peels a banana from her headdress, eats it, and adds a few asides to Miranda's song. The lyrics, while lost on a non-Portuguese-speaking audience, tell Miranda's story: "Far from the beaches of Copacabana / In the land of the famous Uncle Sam / No one knew what a *baiana* was / As she showed off her *quindins* (coconut cookies) and *balangandás* (lucky charms)." After Miranda leaves the stage area, Bugs is left to dance the samba alone. He grates his carrot to the rubbing sound of a *cuíca* drum and then chomps on his carrot as *ganzás* are added to the percussion accompaniment.[69] The whole cartoon is a brilliantly executed parody of show business and the star power of the late 1940s: Gregory Peck, a terribly thin Frank Sinatra, Ray Milland (in a brief, clever, typewriter-themed parody of *The Lost Weekend*), Leopold Stokowski, Groucho (whom Bugs impersonates), Harpo, and Chico Marx, a stout Sydney Greenstreet, and Lauren Bacall all make an appearance. The Miranda segment draws on her star image on several levels beyond the conveniently comical hideout of the turbanucopia: the cartoon character's darkened skin (much darker than Miranda's actual skin color) projects her *Latinidade*, the song evokes the music of Brazil (its language and instruments), and her inclusion alongside a power house of stars reaffirms her status in Hollywood.

Beyond Warner Brothers, other studios drew inspiration from the Miranda craze, such as Fleischer's 1944 Popeye short *We're on Our Way to Rio*. As is well known, the plots of the Popeye cartoons are for the most part identical: Popeye contends with Bluto for the affection of a physically helpless and typically effaced Olive Oyl; in this fight between good and evil, Popeye triumphs thanks to his magical spinach that gives him the upper hand, and he wins Olive Oyl as his reward. In *We're on Our Way to Rio*, which was clearly a takeoff on the *Road-to* movies starring Bob Hope and Bing Crosby, Popeye and Bluto visit a nightclub in Rio and fall instantly in love with the featured performer, a Hispanic-looking Olive Oyl dressed in a Miranda-like outfit, complete with a fruit-basket headpiece.[70] While both Bluto and Popeye have eyes for Olive, she only has eyes for Popeye, and Bluto's revenge is to humiliate Popeye by telling Olive that Popeye is a champion samba dancer. Of course, Popeye has two left feet until he eats his spinach and dances up an animated storm with Olive, beating up Bluto in the process. The spinach-powered Popeye and Olive Oyl-Miranda finally do such a spin that they end up wearing each other's clothes at the end of the cartoon. There is no gender subversion in this cartoon other than the playful clothes swapping at its conclusion, and for the most part, the cartoon clearly enforces fixed stereotypical and idealized views of "normal" male heterosexual behavior. The characterization of Olive Oyl as Carmen Miranda is superb and becomes the essence of female beauty and exoticism with this *in situ* impersonation performed at the Urca Casino in Rio—a venue of memorable importance for Carmen Miranda's Brazilian career.

In the first half of the 1940s, Disney released two full-length cartoons with a Latin American theme, *Saludos Amigos* (1943) and *The Three Caballeros* (1945). As several critics have commented, José (Zé) Carioca, the pugnacious Brazilian parrot who appears in both of these full-length cartoons, features as "Walt Disney's birdlike version of Carmen Miranda" (Woll, *Latin Image* 65).[71] In the last segment of *Saludos Amigos*, an overjoyed Zé Carioca gives Donald Duck a warm Carioca welcome and sweeps him off to experience "the land of the samba," which he introduces by marking the beat with his umbrella on the brim of his hat. After a drink of *cachaça*, Donald Duck's hiccups enable him to feel the samba rhythm, and the film ends with the dancing silhouettes of Donald Duck and a *baiana* projected onto a backdrop of Rio's most popular nightspots, the Copacabana, Atlântico, and Urca Casinos, to the reprise of the film's opening exaltation samba, "Brasil," sung by Aloísio de Oliveira. *Saludos Amigos* premiered in Rio under the auspices of the first lady, Darcy Vargas, the night after Brazil's declaration of war on the Axis powers, and according to some news reports, the Brazilian public gave the Disney picture "the greatest reception ever accorded an American film."[72] Not surprisingly Zé Carioca was so popular that he became a comic-strip character in the first Brazilian edition of *Donald Duck* on the newsstands in July 1950 (R. Reis 89). Apparently, the Rockefeller Committee desired a representative Miss Pan-Americana, but they received the playful, gender-toying, Brazilian "jitterbird" Zé Carioca in her stead.[73]

In the sequel *The Three Caballeros*, Zé Carioca is featured alongside Donald Duck and the Mexican rooster Panchito Pistoles as the headliners. Zé appears out of a pop-up book titled *Brasil*, given to Donald Duck as one of his birthday presents, and takes him to Bahia, "the land of romance, moonlight." As he sings a bilingual version of Dorival Caymmi's "Você já foi a Bahia?" (Have you ever been to Bahia?), Zé first transforms into a quartet of four identical Zé Cariocas; then, to illustrate his next question, "Do you like the samba?," he multiplies into four "Mirandas" dancing in unison before a mesmerized Donald Duck. His simple garb of bananas and flowers on his headdress, platform shoes, skirt, and necklace is enough to recall Miranda as he twirls and sways for the few seconds of this quick-paced sequence to the sound of the verse sung in Portuguese: "Nas sacadas dos sobrados / Da velha São Salvador / Há lembranças de donzelas / Do tempo do Imperador" (On the balconies of the houses / Of the old city São Salvador / There are reminders of the maidens / From the time of the Emperor). As he sambas back and forth, he maintains a touch of masculinity by holding on to his cigar, a masculine cue that makes clear, as Bell-Metereau indicates, "that the man who dresses as a woman is really quite manly" (40). Then, in a last transformative sequence, Zé becomes multiple *malandros*, foreshadowing Donald's greatest competition in Bahia.

Through a photographic process that took Disney five years to perfect and that enables cartooned and actual live characters to interact on the same screen,[74] Aurora Miranda impersonates the white *baiana* made so famous by her sister. Aurora Miranda plays Iaiá—"a baiana, a baianinha tão bonita," as Zé announces in Portuguese ("the *baiana*, the young and so beautiful *baiana*")—the street cookie vendor who dances and sings with her tray of *quindins* (coconut) cookies. *The Three Caballeros* depicts a romanticized, exotic, and sanitized version of Bahia, "nearly devoid of African culture, sung and danced by musicians with light complexions" (Galm 275). Donald Duck, smitten at first sight with Iaiá, chases after her and is outdone by the singing *malandros* of Bando da Lua, who leave him literally green with envy. He pairs up with Zé Carioca in a moment of homosocial dancing, as they have both been pushed out of the *baiana's* spotlight. Donald Duck is upstaged not only by the *malandros*, but also by his feathered counterparts, Zé Carioca and Panchito, who carry phallic objects such as cigars, umbrellas, and guns to symbolize their masculine superiority over Donald (Burton 34). Only for a brief instant when Iaiá lags behind the *malandros* and Donald offers her a bouquet of flowers does he have his one moment of *baiana* ecstasy, which leads him later to fondly remember Bahia and momentarily transform into a female version of himself as he flusters with the delight of the memory. After all, hadn't Zé Carioca predicted that Bahia "is like a song in my heart, a song with love and beautiful memories"?

Since Miranda's appearance was so immediately recognizable, several very quick impersonations by cartoon characters capture the essence of her performance. *Hollywood Canine Canteen* (1946) is a great illustration of Miranda's cartoon adaptability: in the familiar Hollywood USO club, cartoon dogs spoof stars and famous musicians, including Abbott and Costello, Bing Crosby, Jimmy Durante, Dorothy Lamour, Frank Sinatra, and Leopold Stokowski, among many others.[75] Under a fruit hat of the usual grapes, bananas, pineapple, and oranges, while sporting the colors of the Brazilian flag with green doggy bows at the ankles and a yellow bikini top and skirt, the Miranda dog boasts an exaggerated smile of sparkling white teeth while performing a few steps to "South American Way." A similar example, also of the canine anthropomorphic variety, is the quick-paced Tex Avery cartoon *Magical Maestro* (1952), in which Spike the bulldog plays Poochini, a famous baritone opera star performing the ever cartoon-popular *Barber of Seville*. Poochini scornfully rejects a magician, who takes his revenge by transforming him into a series of recognizable characters: a ballet dancer, a football player, Shirley Temple, a Hawaiian singer, and Carmen Miranda, among others. The Miranda act is a quick drag number as part of this serialization of flash imitations, initiated from a disgruntled audience member, who from the balcony throws a bowl of fruit that lands in a pile on Poochini's head to form a headdress. The transformation becomes complete with Poochini in a skimpy bikini top and skirt, high heels, bracelets and necklaces, exaggerated eyebrows, and red-painted lips as he sings the first lines of "Mamá yo quiero," with sidekick rabbits in miniature Miranda drag playing their banjos and providing the characteristic response phrases. The curse of the Miranda segment ends with Poochini lifting his skirt up, facing the audience, and revealing his male undies and platform shoes in an additional moment of slightly "off" humor mixed with humiliation that, in typical camp fashion, reinforces the artificiality of the feminine transformation. "Mamá yo quiero" was used repeatedly in cartoon representations. Another example is *Juke Box Jamboree* (1942), which transposes this music to a most unusual Spanish version sung by a lobster in Carmen Miranda drag. An empty café comes to life after hours to the tunes of a magical jukebox, and among the dancing spirits, bottles, turtles, cacti, mice, and peanuts, a lobster rises up on its plate with olives and a white cloth napkin for a turban, a lettuce scarf draped around its neck for added adornment, and gesticulates its pincer claws while turning on its tail, swaying from side to side as it sings. The impersonation draws from Miranda's signature song and elements of her look that here add gaiety to a fantastical scene, echoing Miranda's extreme contemporaneous popularity during the early 1940s. "Mamá yo quiero" likewise appears in the *Tom and Jerry* short *Baby Puss* (Dec. 25, 1943) when Tom is treated and dressed as a baby by the young girl of the house, Nancy, and is mocked by Jerry and his alley-cat friends. With a subtext of street culture, this short is rather similar to Bob Clampett's *Tin Pan Alley Cats* (June 26, 1943), which incorporated a vision of African American urban culture and comic absurdity that is present in *Baby Puss* but with a more violent twist. The alley cats slap Baby Puss, toss him around, violently rock his crib, and snap his pacifier on his face, among other kinds of abuse. As a final gesture, they throw a fish into his diaper, and as the fish begins to flip around, the diaper simulates a hip thrust from side to side, and this leads into "Mamá yo quiero." The alley cats use Tom as an instrument, pulling his whiskers taut and striking them with a coat hanger, snapping his diaper and stomping on his head to create the bass beat, while the youngest alley cat twirls around with baby rattles for maracas. To the words "dar chupeta" (to give a pacifier), they squirt Tom with milk, reinforcing the theme of the lyrics. The youngest cat is fantastically transformed into a Carmen Miranda caricature, complete with lipstick, bulky necklace, exaggerated eyelashes, and the signature fruit bowl on its head, with bananas centrally protruding. The lyrics are slightly modified as "South American Way" and "Mamá yo quiero" merge into one with the final verse whimsically rendered as "*dar chupeta* the South American way." The whole cartoon revolves around Tom's babyfication; he becomes powerless, at the mercy of the ruthless alley cats instigated by Jerry, but he also represents slightly "off" entertainment, here so ironically and cruelly portrayed with a touch of scatological humor.

Further removed chronologically from this prominent Miranda phase of 1940s cartoons is the episode "The Ticklefeather Machine" (1964) of the animated cartoon series *Underdog* (1964–1967), in which the main female character, canine reporter Sweet Polly Purebred, performs to a Miranda jive *in situ* against a Rio de Janeiro backdrop. The plot is similar to most *Underdog* episodes, with the anthropomorphic superhero coming to the rescue of Sweet Polly Purebred, Underdog's love interest. In this episode, Underdog's nemesis, Simon Bar Sinister, uses his laugh-inducing ticklefeather machine to take control of the nation and orders Polly Purebred to put on a "spectacular TV show for his entertainment." What could be more entertaining than a Carmen Miranda impersonation? Polly Purebred exchanges her signature black skirt, white shirt, and red sweater for a pineapple-colored outfit and Miranda turban of exotic fruit, and her reporter's microphone for shakers. She dances side to side in front of the camera, performing a live broadcast of a "Bongo Congo" solo chant, and Underdog, "being a true hero, instantly sprang into action" to save the helpless damsel in distress and the nation.

Daytime television has broadcast countless Carmen Miranda segments over the years (many probably lost, unidentified in television archives) to a young audience who, without the original Miranda context, could still enjoy the playfulness of the image. Scooby-Doo, Minnie Mouse, Kermit the Frog, Miss Piggy, Bear in the Big Blue House, Lilo and Stitch, and no doubt countless other children's television icons have at some point donned the Miranda headdress.[76] The format of *Sesame Street* (1969–present), the *Muppet Show* (1976–1981), and other Jim Henson Company productions with comedy sketches, humorous parodies, ease of costume changes, and make-believe settings was optimal for the inclusion of playful Miranda segments and featured innumerable puppets and guest stars wearing fruit-laden headdresses and singing either one of Miranda's famed songs or a banana-related one as they danced, swayed, joked, or laughed around the stage.[77] One of the most memorable segments is the cleverly conceived Mad Hatter's party in the *Sesame Street* direct-to-DVD film *Abby in Wonderland* (2008), in which the usual characters are transformed: Abby Cadabby as Alice, Elmo as the Red Rabbit, Grover as the Mad Hatter, Cookie Monster as the Cheshire Cookie Cat, etc. When Abby-Alice encounters Grover-Mad Hatter, he presents in song a series of his hats, his favorite one being laden with bananas and an assortment of colorful fruit. This clip is typical of the usage that has been made of the Miranda motif when different hats are needed to add fun, color, and variety to a segment. In the one-hour special *The Muppets Go Hollywood* (1979), a fabulous spoof on the Hollywood highlife with Muppets and celebrities mingling at a party thrown by Kermit the Frog, Rita Moreno performs "I, Yi, Yi, Yi, Yi (I like you very much)" to "represent the Coconut Grove in the 1930s," as the emcee of the party, Dick van Dyke, speculates in a conversation with Peter Falk of *Columbo* fame. Adorned in a flashy, bright orange and pink frilled dress and matching headdress with the characteristic fruits and feathers, Moreno sings an infantilized, screechy version of the song, accompanied by gawky movements as she dances around the stage, stumbling over the purple full-bodied dancing trio of monsters, the Mutations, who act as her backups. Other than the characteristic Miranda aspect, the anachronistic reference to Miranda as a Hollywood star of the 1930s shows how she has been remembered more generally, and in this case incorrectly, as iconic of an era.

Drawing from both the Miranda image and the popular Chiquita Banana logo, *Sesame Street* aired two segments of an animated version of Carmen Miranda they called Fruta Manzana. In both episodes, Fruta Manzana appears with an oversized brimmed hat piled high with fruit and sings and dances about being happy and healthy (episode 2040; March 1, 1985) and conscientious about throwing fruit waste in the trashcan (episode 2358; November 18, 1987). What stands out in these short segments is the choppiness of the animation as Fruta Manzana spins around, juggles, and sits on and hides behind oversized pieces of fruit, creating unsettling perspective angles. She also wields a hand-held mirror that adds an eerie, fantastical dimension to the segments, at times distorting and objectifying her image by reducing her reflection to two large red lips that occupy the full width of the mirror. At one point, she is standing between rows of oversized bananas, oranges, grapes, and pears that dwarf her on each side, and the visual inevitably recalls Busby Berkeley's signature "Lady in the Tutti Frutti Hat" moment from *The Gang's All Here*. The originality of this Miranda reinterpretation for a cartoon segment lies in its didactic component, which uses the staged performance, fruit motif, and catchy remake of the Chiquita song to teach children the simple importance of eating fruit to be "healthy and happy" and keeping one's surroundings clean.[78]

Although *muppet.wikia* credits the music of Fruta Manzana as an "original fruit song," the tune is the well-known "Chiquita Banana" jingle, used in publicity for the United Fruit Company in 1944 as one of the very first examples of a new twentieth-century art form: the singing commercial. There has been much discussion about how United Fruit executives drew on Miranda's "popular Latinized female image" to create the Chiquita Banana logo (Enloe 2) and that she refused to be the model for the design. Shaw makes an interesting connection between this commercial mascot and Miranda's role in *Something for the Boys* (1944) as Chiquita Hart (*Carmen* 94). However, it is more likely that Dik Browne drew his inspiration from the general Miranda vogue following *The Gang's All Here* (1943), and the namesake worked in the opposite direction, as his Chiquita cartoon had been commissioned in 1943 and was released several months before *Something for the Boys* (Meyler 68). The calypso-style music and cartoon character that resembles a Mirandaesque banana-woman with a fruit hat, along with the sticker branding from the early 1960s, aimed to "create in housewives a brand-name loyalty for a generic fruit" (Enloe 129).[79] In 1950, the United Fruit Company even produced a *Chiquita Banana's Recipe Book* with instructions on how to best choose, preserve, cook, and serve bananas, and the "Chiquita Banana" song has remained ingrained in popular culture, even appearing in the occasional feature film.[80]

Into the twenty-first century, Miranda impersonations have continued to en-thrall young spectators now several generations removed, with new twists to the tried-and-true theme. *The Cat in the Hat* (2003), a feature-length adaptation of the Dr. Seuss book, stars Mike Myers as the anthropomorphic, wise-cracking, mul-tipersonality Cat with a Brooklyn accent who does an uncanny Miranda imper-sonation as one of his specialty acts, one of the highlights of a film that received overwhelmingly negative reviews. Among the film's constant criticisms feature the adult content, innuendos, and potty humor, and the Miranda sequence has all these. With half melons and a watermelon emphasizing his breasts and behind, respectively, the customary fruit headdress topped with tall feathers, endless beads strung around his neck and wrists, and gold shimmery bands as an indication of sleeves and a skirt, the Cat, after throwing up a hair ball, snaps his castanets and begins to sing "Fun, Fun, Fun" while twirling his wrists and grabbing his behind and breasts. Spotlights and confetti add to the segment's festive ambiance. The lyrics are mildly scatological with references to defecating ("never used the litter box, he made a mess in the hall") and castration ("they sent him to a vet to cut off both his boo-boo-boo"). One reviewer refers to the Cat's "morbidly obese ver-sion of Carmen Miranda" in a "misbegotten mess" of a film.[81] The children's look of shock and disgust at the Miranda-Cat performance sums up the tone of the number, which is luckily brief.

A more genuinely PG Miranda-inspired segment is included in Pixar's *Cars Toons: Mater's Tall Tales* (2008), a series of computer-animated short films starring Mater, Lightning McQueen, and the rest of the gang from Radiator Springs. In each episode, Mater tells a far-fetched, action-packed story from his past that also involves the heroics of Lightning McQueen. The short *Mater Private Eye* (2008), inspired by film noir and filmed in black and white, relates Mater's past as a private detective trying to solve a case involving a counterfeit tire ring. His ex-flame, Tia, persuades Mater to find her missing sister, Mia, who was last seen working for "Big D" at the Carbacabana, a fabulous pun on the well-known Copacabana club. The film cuts to the inside of the Carbacabana, where a female car named Carmen performs with a Miranda headdress of bananas, plums, and a large pineapple. She sings to a car-themed cha-cha-cha tune accompanied by her band of sombrero-wearing mariachi pitties on guitar, drums, and maracas, which fits with the Latin theme resonating throughout the club's decor. After the crime is solved, the short reverts back to the present Radiator Springs, now filmed in color. McQueen laughs at Mater's tall tale just as Carmen (now with a bright and colorful headdress) and her band speed by, and she yells out for everyone to "join the conga." In an inter-view, *Cars Toons* director Rob Gibbs mentions the limitations of working with the animation of cars and the need to push the characters' expressions to give them the action that is needed. In the Miranda car portrayal, the expressive eye and lip movements, the car's swaying from side to side, and her foreign accent compensate for the lack of hand movements while creating a seductive act that is unmistakably Carmen Miranda.[82] In this same interview, Gibbs admits that Bugs Bunny is his favorite cartoon character; perhaps it was Bugs, rather than Carmen Miranda, who inspired this short.

As featured in *Cars Toons: Mater's Tall Tales*, in the cartoon world the headdress alone is sufficient to indicate the Carmen Miranda look, with all its connotations. Similarly, in the DreamWorks Animation feature film *Madagascar: Escape 2 Africa* (2008), set in the African savanna, the main protagonist, Alex the Lion, is forced to wear a fruity headdress as the "hat of shame" when he fails to fight his opponent, Teetsi, in a set-up against him and his family orchestrated by his evil uncle, Makunga. Alex is banished from the reserve and leaves wearing his headdress of pineapple, grapes, watermelon, strawberries, bananas, oranges, plums, and peaches, which appears all the more opulent in contrast to his naked lion body and creates a magical silhouette as he walks away, acquiescing to the shame that he has brought upon his family by not knowing how to fight. As the film progresses Alex continues to wear the headdress until the climactic moment: during a fight with humans, they hurl a spear through his headdress, and he loses it. Symbolically, Alex has proven his lion-hood as a son worthy of his royal lineage. Likely without knowing it, the producers of *Madagascar 2* encapsulated in their portrayal of the tutti-frutti hat the contradictory essence of the Miranda headdress, a combination of comedy and shame that the Tropicalists embraced as representative of the Pride/Shame conundrum.

While the above examples are connected through theme, locale, or musical genre to Carmen Miranda, a handful of film moments include one of Miranda's signature tunes in the most unexpected segments. The adult animated science-fiction comedy film *Futurama: The Beast with a Billion Backs* (2008) is a case in point: it includes Miranda's "I, Yi, Yi, Yi, Yi (I like you very much)" as the soundtrack for the moment when three of the main characters, in escalating degrees of repugnance for the viewer, are shown shaving their face, legs, and back as they prepare for dates with the monster Yivo of a thousand tentacles/genitals. This Miranda best-selling hit has certainly been widely used.

In the Blue Sky Studios feature-length *Rio: The Movie* (2011), a Carmen Miranda moment is to be expected in a film bursting with the colors and sounds of Rio de Janeiro during Carnival as it chronicles a trip to save a species of blue macaws from extinction that goes drastically wrong. In pursuit of lost birds, the protagonists find themselves in the heart of the Carnival festivities in the Sambadrome, where the twirling and swaying of exaggeratedly large *baiana* skirts create a canopy overflowing with the richness of its colors, sounds, and movement. It is in this setting that Luiz, the bulldog, ends up with a towering headdress of fruit piled high on his head, an ultra-quick drag element that is used purely for laughs. Although the scene lasts no more than a few minutes, the iconic image of Luiz with the tutti-frutti headdress captures the essence of the locale and the humor of the film, and it was the image adopted to represent Luiz in the film's publicity and commercial tie-ins.[83]

The wide appeal of Carmen Miranda's star-text, composed by moments of spectacle from the very beginning of her US career through to the present day, far transcends her film roles, as her "text" has been broadly appropriated, transformed, reinterpreted, and performed. Dissecting aspects of the Miranda "look," these imitations have drawn predominantly on the image of fruit and excess femininity, with the inevitable headdress, bare-midriff dress style, opulent jewelry, wedged heels, and bright makeup. Taking as a premise that camp provokes all notions of gender normality through parody and excessive theatricality of style, we can comprehend how Carmen Miranda's star image provided impersonators and cartoon directors with a fertile site of raw material to project a counter-hegemonic perspective of gender norms: over-the-top, beautifully artificial, and overtly feminine. The wealth of Carmen Miranda impersonations during the 1940s and beyond reinforces her image as an optimal potential for marginalized minorities, predominantly gay viewers, to use her parodic spectacle as an allowable expression of their subjectivity. Following one of camp's characteristics, "being" Carmen Miranda was and still is predominantly great fun—and funny, with the audience's laughter as its aim.[84] These innumerable Carmen Miranda imitations and reinterpretations maintain common currency decades beyond her last screen appearance, reaffirming the versatility and timelessness of her star image and contributing to her legacy as a unique and universal icon.

CONCLUSION

The Legacy of an Icon

Carmen Miranda's last filmed appearance was on the *Jimmy Durante Show*, and the final program was a combination of all that Miranda enjoyed as a performer and was known for on the screen: laughter, dancing, singing, joking around, speaking in her signature lightning-quick Portuguese and her heavily accented English, and accompanied by a group of her "boys." The last picture of Carmen Miranda alive was taken with Durante on the set, complementing the taped show later that week that aired, with the family's permission, after her death.[1] Durante added a moving prologue to the show's opening: "One of the greatest performers I've ever known was the little lady from Brazil, Carmen Miranda. Her last appearance was here on this show with me, and she was never better." The *Jimmy Durante Show* episode was the first filmed tribute to the memory of the deceased star, with the peculiar twist of Miranda herself being part of the homage.

From the moment of her death, Carmen Miranda's legacy has been interpreted, questioned, and revisited in a myriad of ways by fans, critics, writers, film directors, artists, singers, and performers, whose works constantly renew the magnitude of Miranda's stardom and performativity. National commemorations and institutional, academic, and personal initiatives in music, film, literature, and art continue to legitimize Carmen Miranda's position in Brazil's cultural memory and to remember, celebrate, and draw from the uniqueness of her *Latinidade* in the United States, each nation contributing to the immortalization of Carmen Miranda's legacy.

Remembering: Film, Music, and Revival Shows

In a retrospective appreciation of Carmen Miranda's films, the singer and writer Caetano Veloso comments on the perfection of her art, the definition in the movements, and her talent for the polished finished product as he attempts to pinpoint the reasons for her popularity.[2] The legacy of Carmen Miranda's films is tightly intertwined with that of the Hollywood musical, which occasionally goes through periods of revival with new releases of classic films or certain anniversaries of the Hollywood golden age. All Miranda's movies were of the "feel good" variety, living in and relishing the present, as the musical numbers exploded beyond normal limits, filling the viewers' imaginary sense with a world of dazzling songs, music, and dance. In the United States, Miranda's stardom stemmed from Broadway but was consecrated on the silver screen, and it is this visual image of her magnificent costumes—far more than her explosive screen characters—that has come to represent her star image. As Gledhill writes, "while other entertainment industries may manufacture stars, cinema still provides the ultimate confirmation of stardom" (*Stardom* xiii). In Miranda's case, this was definitely true in the United States: her Broadway songs would long have been forgotten had they not been immortalized through her Twentieth Century-Fox productions. Camp culture has likewise enabled a constant revisiting of Miranda's star persona, providing a means to reread her performativity and endear a new generation to Miranda's excesses. It is not by chance that the film that has been most viewed at special revival screenings, *The Gang's All Here*, is also the film that cemented Miranda's place in the camp hall of fame.

In Brazil, as the media attempted to come to terms with the unexpected death of one of the nation's most beloved singers of the radio days, her voice and musical hits received the most coverage in the Brazilian press.[3] *O globo* predicted, with great lament, that Miranda's death marked the end of Brazilian popular music.[4] Representing the consensus among her composers, Josué de Barros remembered how fabulous and quick she was to learn new music; she knew how to sing and did so with expression and grace.[5] Miranda's talent and stage presence enabled her to mark her niche in an emerging industry of popular music as she brought radio, the art of live performances, and discography to a greater level of popularity than ever before. Both on and off the stage in Rio's 1930s society, where she became a household name in a category apart from all others, Miranda was the epitome of the modern female celebrity: a free spirit who playfully and audaciously pushed the boundaries of conventions and was able to leave her unique imprint on the performance scene with her uninhibited renovation and re-creation of her star status. Her performance style was genuinely "Miranda": her natural talent resonated throughout her shows and recordings, and although she was widely imitated, she was never surpassed as a performing artist.

The world over, undoubtedly any Brazilian Carnival celebration or Brazilian-themed soirée, by metonymy of Miranda's representing Brazil abroad, inevitably takes form in the shadow of Brazil's most famous international performer to this day.[6] As Dunn rightly comments, whenever Brazilian music is mentioned, the suggestion of Miranda is always there; she is "Brazil as viewed by foreigners" ("Tropicalista Rebellion" 133–35). In Brazil, Carmen Miranda as a singer has merited several significant re-enactment shows, with three interpreters unavoidably rising to the forefront of the genre: Marília Pêra, Stella Miranda, and Erick Barreto. These artists *interpret* Carmen Miranda rather than *imitate* her, in that they appropriate songs from Carmen Miranda's repertoire to create their own performances. Marília Pêra (1946–) is a Brazilian actress of renown who for over half a century has been interpreting Carmen Miranda, beginning in 1965 as part of Carlos Machado's dance troupe in Mexico City,[7] and then most notably in 1972 with the show *A pequena notável* (The remarkable young girl) at the "Night and Day" nightclub in Rio,[8] a brief filmed segment in *Mixed Blood* (1985), the one-night show *A Pêra da Carmem* at Rio's Canecão venue in 1986,[9] *A Tribute to Carmen Miranda* at New York's Lincoln Center in 1995, and then a more elaborate rendition in 2005 titled *Marília Pêra canta Carmen Miranda* (Marília Pêra sings Carmen Miranda), this time touring the theaters of Rio and São Paulo through 2006.[10] The way Marília Pêra performs should be understood not as Marília *being* Carmen but rather Carmen *through* Marília, or as one critic writes, "an interpretative performance . . . an actress who evokes a personage, whether in song or in body language."[11] Pêra brings Carmen Miranda's music back to life in shows that, rather surprisingly, remained popular despite Pêra's ill-executed choreography; brightly colored but tasteless costumes that draw from the Miranda motif but do very little for Pêra's physique, along with platform shoes that topple her balance; and her lack of Miranda's youthfulness, grace, style, beauty, and charismatic appeal. One can only suspect that the success of the live show was mostly due to the memory of Carmen Miranda rather than Pêra's kitschy and awkward interpretation.

The singer and actress Stella Miranda (1950–) has interpreted Carmen Miranda as part of several stage shows and guest television appearances with talent, energy, and humor since 2001, when she took the stage as one of the two Carmen Mirandas in Miguel Falabella and Maria Carmen Barbosa's musical extravaganza *South American Way: The Carmen Miranda Musical*, which ran for several months at the Scala Theater in Leblon, Rio de Janeiro. Staging the two Carmen Mirandas was an original approach to the different phases of the star's career, yet it also conflated both periods through scenes shared by the two actresses. Stella Miranda was the older, embittered Carmen at the end of her life, and her costar Soraya Ravenle (1962–), also a seasoned actress and singer of the Carioca scene, was the hopeful, lively young Carmen. While both actresses displayed great talent and syntony on the stage, Stella Miranda stole the show with the perfection of her art, diction, and stage presence, and her performance earned her the prestigious theater award, the Prêmio Shell.[12] As one critic writes, "the script favored Stella who was impeccable in all her good-humored interventions."[13] With luxurious sets, exuberant costumes, grandiose musical numbers, scenes filled with chorines, and beautiful choreography, *South American Way* did not disappoint the theatergoers who came night after night to see this major musical spectacle that, according to one reporter, was certainly "deserving of Broadway."[14] The show mixed light-hearted, moving music with deeper themes of self-representation, Miranda's authenticity and place within Brazilian popular culture, and her role as a token Latin American icon. Being a musical with a tropical twist, the result was a "delirious kitsch" spectacle, according to Miguel Falabella, one of the producers.[15] Fitch characterizes the show as a "two hour commercial . . . an advertisement for Brazilian tourism," tellingly sponsored by Petrobrás and a host of tourism-oriented businesses (61). In this, Miranda continues as Brazil's most famous postcard and its most popular international star.

In a less extravagant but no less moving and entertaining show, Stella Miranda returned to perform Carmen Miranda in 2009 for the centennial of Miranda's birth in the production *Miranda por Miranda* (Miranda by Miranda), which she also wrote and directed. As of this writing, after an extended season in Rio beginning in 2009, then touring Brazil on prestigious stages such as the Palácio Quitandinha in Petrópolis in July 2010, this popular show was taken to Porto, Portugal in May 2013, where it was acclaimed by the public, then staged again for two seasons in São Paulo in 2014 (at the Teatro Augusta) and 2015 (Espaço Promon).[16] *Miranda por Miranda* hinges on the paradoxical aspect of Carmen Miranda's life: her sadness as a counterpoint to the tropical representation of Brazil that she personified. Stella Miranda intersperses spoken thoughts about her own life and how it intersects with Carmen Miranda's, all while singing a repertory of over twenty Carmen Miranda songs set to upbeat, modernized arrangements by the awarded composer and musical director Tim Rescala. The rest of the cast consists of four "Miranda boys," likewise modernized with suits and ties, leaning closer to the harmonizing "Blues Brothers" than the original Bando da Lua, and three musicians: a pianist, bassist, and drummer. Stella Miranda's costumes are also subdued in comparison to the exuberant Miranda originals. Emphasizing Carmen Miranda's musical legacy is at the heart of the show: as Stella Miranda mentions in an interview at *Globo*, the public may not recognize all the tunes, but they pay attention and love this music that is part of Brazil's long-forgotten, rich musical abundance from the 1930s and 1940s.[17]

As a third and final example in this group of professional Carmen Miranda interpreters, Erick Barreto (1962–1996), under the stage name Diana Finsk, performed as Carmen Miranda on such a professional level that his art form is far beyond that of the casual Miranda drag or comic performances. Barreto was a drag-queen artist who brought transformism to a new level of artistic performance in Brazil, and Carmen Miranda was one of his most perfected acts. Originally from Recife, Barreto lived and worked in Rio de Janeiro, where he became well known for his fabulous impersonations of unforgettable personages such as Argentina's iconic first lady Eva Perón, one of the greatest Brazilian singers of popular and jazz music of all time Elis Regina, and most notably Carmen Miranda. Barreto's art helped to rid transformism of its social stigma, making it a more widely respected performative genre. From the early 1980s to his premature death in 1996, Barreto fascinated his audience with the perfection of his art, often incorporating costume changes on stage and provocative stripteases, carried out with dignity and precision. Indeed it was in the details of his impersonations that he most excelled, allegedly studying his personages in great depth to faithfully portray them onstage. Barreto's Carmen Miranda numbers were among his most successful, inevitably fascinating his public with his gracious gestures, the batting of his eyes, and the fluidity of his movements, creating the most beautiful rendition of Miranda down to the minutest detail. Barreto performed on a variety of shows, such as *Hebe*, the *Silvio Santos Program*, *Doris Para Maiores*, *Show de Calouros*, and at Cabaret Casanova, one of Rio's oldest gay bars. The most significant evidence of the outstanding quality of his art is his casting in Helena Solberg's documentary *Bananas Is My Business* (1995), in which Barreto is a beautiful Carmen Miranda, as discussed below. One could argue that Barreto is imitating Carmen Miranda, but his demeanor, personal investment, and the reverence with which he performs his numbers set him apart from the comic, camp imitations. In all these Miranda interpretations, Erick Barreto shines from within, doing what he most enjoyed with all the talent, class, and distinction his muse deserved.

Beyond these performances in Brazil, a few significant revival shows have been staged in the United States. Over the years, performing arts centers in the New York area have presented tributes to Miranda. On at least two occasions, in 1995 and 1996, BrazilFest, hosted by the Lincoln Center for the Performing Arts, showcased Carmen Miranda with the participation of a variety of singers such as Bebel Gilberto, Denise Dumont, Elba Ramalho, Aurora Miranda, and Maria Alcina, with over-the-top costumes, a recurring banana theme, and drag impersonations reiterating Miranda's unique image forty years after her death.[18] Arto Lindsay's *Carmen Miranda* took to the stage of the Brooklyn Academy of Music (BAM) Opera House on October 23, 25, and 26, 1991, as part of their ninth Next Wave Festival. The performers consisted of two of Brazil's most sought-after singers, Bebel Gilberto and Gal Costa, with the participation of Aurora Miranda and musical accompaniment by the Afro-Brazilian percussionist Naná Vasconcelos; the Brazilian comic actress Regina Casé impersonating Carmen Miranda in gesture and speech; and poignant, amusing, and satirical commentary, English translation, and musical accompaniment on a synthesizer by the American experimental performance artist Laurie Anderson. As Lindsay commented to the *New York Post*, he viewed Carmen Miranda "as one of the most cult-worthy people in the world," despite the fact that "Hollywood treated her like a caricature of herself," and the BAM show aimed to set the record straight.[19] Aurora Miranda, at age 76, had "a diva's presence," as one reporter commented.[20] She sang Noel Rosa's playful "Você só . . . mente" (You only . . . lie) and then returned for the grand finale with Rio de Janeiro's ever-popular official anthem, "Cidade maravilhosa" (Marvelous city), the Carnival march that Aurora recorded in 1935. Aurora's costume, consisting of a golden dress with wide off-the-shoulder sleeves, necklaces, and a red headscarf, recalls the one she wore decades earlier in Disney's *The Three Caballeros*, a reference that is not left merely implicit as Anderson probes Aurora to talk about her experience "kissing Donald Duck." Halfway through the show, the first backdrop, resembling a café in Rio looking out over the picturesque Guanabara Bay, gives way to an overflowing headdress of money, reminiscent of Miranda's enormous two-dimensional banana headdress in the "Tutti Frutti Hat" number of *The Gang's All Here*, a Busby Berkeley parody that was not lost on the press.[21] Through the choice of songs, spoken word, music, costumes, and talented voices of Gal Costa and Bebel Gilberto, all linked together by Laurie Anderson's dry commentary peppered with humor, sarcasm, and melodious, interactive music on the keyboard, *Carmen Miranda* recuperated Miranda's essential Brazilianness and, foregoing all Miranda's US repertory, the sounds of Rio, her beloved city.

The Muse of Tropicália

After over a year away from Rio de Janeiro, Carmen Miranda returned home in June 1940, hoping to renew her ties with her fans and reclaim her status as the hottest female singer of popular music. Making the performative faux pas of greeting the well-to-do Urca Casino audience in English and singing some of her American-made numbers left the crowd frigid. While some critics attributed the cold reception to the elite status of the patrons at the casino that evening, who were not her usual audience, most likely it was Miranda's Americanization of her performance that upset her audience. As Marshall indicates, viewing a celebrity antipathetically is not uncommon, leading to ridicule and derision, when "the sign of the celebrity . . . represents the center of false value" (xi). In Carmen Miranda's case, the fact that she had successfully built her stardom on authenticated Brazilian performances and returned changed after a year was cause enough for her to be read as "false value." Ironically, some of her last words reported in the media before she left for Broadway were promises of "not forgetting her homeland" and "not becoming Americanized."[22] The harsh criticism extended from the casino floor to the media, with the local newspapers accusing Miranda of adulterating national music (Garcia 190). Miranda learned the hard way that the meaning of her stardom was something that was not immutable, and its transformative nature was to be continuously renegotiated, even from afar.[23]

The Urca Casino reception casts a dark and far-reaching shadow over Miranda's career path, illustrating the idea that "any reception is part of a historical chain of reception, constantly being transformed by the current text's relation to the past" (Marshall 67). Powerless and dismayed, Miranda thought it wise to cancel all further commitments at the Urca Casino until she had regained her fan base and reacclimated herself to the Carioca music scene. The media's rhetoric had also changed: whereas before Broadway the press had focused on Miranda's stardom and her celebrity road to success, the discourse around the casino incident moved emphatically the focus to the audience's reception, underlining the importance of the popular base for performative acceptance. Miranda only performed in the Urca Casino once more, in September 1940, with several new numbers to narrativize the trauma of an artist who has returned from abroad and seeks to reconcile international fame and fortune with the sincerity of her Brazilian roots and love of samba. Her new songs included "Voltei pro morro" (I returned to the *morro*. This refers to the hills of Rio de Janeiro, which for many is symbolically the birthplace of samba) and "Disseram que voltei americanizada" (They say I returned Americanized). Miranda's stage comeback represented more than a performative feat of courage and audience perceptivity; it showed how talented Miranda was at poking fun at her own Americanization, just as she would continue to parody her depiction of the stylized *baiana* through a performative wink to the audience, whether they were the North American moviegoers or her compatriots in Brazil.

The unfortunate episode of the June casino debacle, despite the September comeback, caused deep-rooted scars for Miranda, who would not return to Rio for the next fourteen years. During this time away from Brazil, Miranda's performances continued to be discussed in the Brazilian media among critics and fans who remained divided over the image of Brazil and Brazilian music that she projected abroad and the fact that she continued to star in Hollywood-made films rather than supporting the national film industry.[24] As Simone Pereira de Sá and other critics have discussed, the Brazilian public was proud that Miranda had become a Hollywood star, but they resented the stereotypical portrayal of Brazilianness and the homogeneous image of Latin Americans that she came to embody (21).

Miranda's complicated relationship with her Brazilian public and her paradoxical portrayal of Brazilian culture abroad—simultaneously embodying a stereotypical image of Brazilianness and the most famous Brazilian performance worldwide—was revisited, refurbished, and reinvented by the Tropicália movement in the late 1960s. In a tense climate of political instability, in which Cold War reactions to threats of budding communism throughout the region were spearheaded from afar by the United States National Security Council, vanguard and counter-culture manifestations emerged as an outlet and expression for a critical stance against political models that banished social and cultural freedoms. In this context, the Tropicália artistic movement emerged, a phenomenon that embraced poetry, cinema, theater, and the plastic arts, while most prominently displaying a hybrid music style that mixed national rhythms with foreign imports such as blues, rock 'n' roll, jazz, and psychedelic music. The Tropicalists' reworking of national symbols and destabilizing of artistic hierarchies was imbued with camp sensitivities and coalesced, with irreverent fervor, many celebratory truisms, self-reflective ambiguities, and self-mockery within a climate of censorship and repression.[25] As Schwarz notes, Tropicália was allegorical in nature, with the Tropicalists drawing from "suggestive and dated materials" to emphasize an "atemporal idea of Brazil" (144), recalling the past in images of the present through absurd, irreverent, and often provocative anachronistic combinations.

Carmen Miranda's link to the movement as a cultural sign was first explicitly articulated by the final words of the song "Tropicália" by Caetano Veloso, the since-then much-quoted "viva a banda-da-da, Carmen Miranda-da-da-da-da" that poetically matched Miranda to Chico Buarque's hit song "A banda" (1966), which many have interpreted as an expression of "bread and circus" politics—i.e., it momentarily distracted people from the hardships of reality. The insistent rhyme of the song's concluding verse emphatically harks back to the anti-art Dada movement post-World War I, an anti-Nationalist expression that sought to negate not only art itself but also the bourgeois materialism and culture it fueled. For Dunn, while Tropicália in general plays with forms of parody to recycle dated cultural styles, discourses, and materials, Veloso's reference to Miranda in "Tropicália" is more akin to the aesthetics of pastiche due to the embedded neutrality that embraces Miranda as an image, a sign, a cultural icon deprived of her musical value (*Brutality Garden* 91). As Dunn explicates, there are no mimetic references to her musical style within the song, but the final notes invoke Miranda and leave her image literally resonating, ripe for interpretation. This is the point of neutrality that Veloso refers to, projecting Miranda uncritically after coming to terms with the complexities of her image. This moment can also be viewed as a tipping point, for Veloso goes on to recall that from this moment on Miranda "was no longer a grotesque thing, unpleasant, but was something that began to fascinate me, something I wanted to play with: it had already become lovable for me in many respects" (qtd. in Dunn, "Tropicalista" 132). This admitted playfulness, paired with Miranda's "vulgar iconography" (Dunn, *Brutality Garden* 36), was ripe for the Tropicalists to engage through both camp and kitsch aesthetics. The conflation of Buarque's song and Miranda's provocative image encapsulates incongruous juxtapositions frequently used for camp purposes,[26] which are at the core of the Tropicalists' agenda. In this case, the internal societal injustice and political oppression, implied in Buarque's song, and the nation's internationally revered tropicalism are inevitably evoked by Miranda's image. It is through a camp gesture that the Tropicalist movement adopted Carmen Miranda as their muse, fitting with their proclivity to recycle cultural materials and free them for redefinition, projecting them anachronistically and toying with the disjunction of appearance and meaning. However, Miranda is not viewed as a camp icon but rather a popular cultural image. It was not until he appeared on stage in Miranda drag for his first show after returning in January 1972 from exile in London that Caetano Veloso, playing off his oft-accused androgyny, engaged in a new interpretation by taking Miranda as a full-on camp icon.[27]

By the late 1960s, both Miranda as a cultural sign and her music were thought of as outmoded and obsolete relics of popular culture, items the Tropicalists prized and refurbished.[28] While the intention with which they embraced Miranda was a tongue-in-cheek, camp practice lost on those who read it at face value, the Tropicalists' Miranda representations veered with ease toward kitsch aesthetics consisting of cheap imitations and lofty pretensions, such as grotesque figurines, caricatures, and stylized reproductions of Miranda as a cultural icon. Through Veloso's "Tropicália" song in 1967, Miranda resurfaced out of oblivion, soon to become a key figure at the core of the Tropicália movement's aesthetic concerns, which "appropriated her as one of its principal signs, capitalizing on the discomfort that her name and the evocation of her gestures could create."[29] As a "cause for both pride and shame," their caricature and their X-ray, Miranda is refurbished and no longer imbued with Veloso's proclaimed neutrality. In his memoirs about the Tropicália movement, Veloso later relates how the mere mention of Miranda was "a bomb that the tropicalista guerrillas would, fatefully, seize," an act that required overcoming their initial shame through their acceptance of American mass culture and Hollywood, as well as acceptance of the stereotypes of a hypersexualized, hypercolorful, and fruit-filled Brazil (*Tropical Truth* 167). Miranda's neutrality was also set off balance by the political message that she inevitably projected, which Veloso was cautious to avoid on occasions.[30] Veloso recounts being accused, as had been the case with Miranda, of being "Americanized" because of his hippie appearance, his personal attitude, and his embracing pop music and rock 'n' roll (Dunn, "Tropicalista" 121–25). Therefore, it is perhaps not surprising that twenty years later, Veloso recorded Miranda's above-mentioned comeback song, "Disseram que voltei americanizada," live in concert, actualizing the multifaceted readings of Miranda and crystalizing this moment of Tropicália cultural self-reflection.[31]

A Literary Legacy and Dramatic Staging

Over the years, Carmen Miranda has appeared as a fictional character in several novels, short stories, and plays, a narrative and dramatic presence that, while individually bringing to the texts certain aspects of her star persona, when taken as a whole emphasizes the extent of her impact on North American and Brazilian high and pop art.

With the publication of publicist Abby Hirsch's 1974 pseudomemoir *The Great Carmen Miranda Look-Alike Contest and Other Bold-faced Lies*, Miranda first crossed over into a narrative genre, although not as a full-fledged fictional character. In witty autobiographical style, the author recounts her experience working as a press agent for a screening of *The Gang's All Here* that required last-minute publicity. Desperate for reporter coverage, she promises an ABC-TV assignment editor a lobby full of Carmen Miranda look-alikes (A. Hirsch 115). She enlists the help of a filmmaker, but only four "hastily-costumed drag queens" come to the so-called contest in the lobby, and the event is a complete flop. The ticket-taker's reaction says it all: "My god. . . . It's gay Guevara" (A. Hirsch 116). While this text does not develop Miranda as a narrative character *per se*, it reiterates her image as a gay icon, here transposed to a pseudofictional account.[32]

From the late 1980s, Carmen Miranda has appeared as a literary figure in several different genres of fiction and drama through a process narratologists have termed *metalepsis*, namely "the passage from one narrative level to another" (Genette 243), a transgression of the boundaries between the fictional world and the real world. Carmen Miranda's stylized persona first appeared as a literary figure in a short-story anthology edited by Don Sakers in 1990 and appropriately titled *Carmen Miranda's Ghost Is Haunting Space Station Three*, in which Miranda is a spectral character transposed to the science-fiction realm, defying all realist logic. The collection drew its inspiration from filk artist Leslie Fish's original song, "Carmen Miranda's Ghost," which was released in 1986 and has since been recorded several times, receiving the Pegasus nomination for "Best Humorous Song" in 1993.[33] The lyrics describe the returning presence of Miranda's ghost to Space Station Three and the sense of mystery that surrounds these visits. Throughout the anthology, the authors rehearse elements from Fish's filk song (Fish included, as she has a story in the anthology) with a prominence for the repeated appearance of fruit baskets that Miranda's ghost leaves, the clacking of her maracas (poor Miranda—she never used maracas!), rhumba music, and several references to tangerines rolling unrealistically along the floor despite antigravity. As early as the late nineteenth century, and then more visibly since the early 1930s, there has been a history of space stations as a literary theme, even before the emergence of science fiction as a recognized genre (Westfahl 29). In the case of the Carmen Miranda stories, the space station locale amplifies the eeriness of her premature passing and, in several cases, provides a reassessment of her stardom (with the culture lag of several decades' hindsight) reduced to her films and the incongruity of her costumes (Scott and Barnett 113; Friesner 228). S. N. Lewitt's story "That Souse American Way" stands out as the piece that most approximates Brazilian culture with mentions of *axe*, Afro-Brazilian deities, Carnival, macumba, Latin American stereotypes, and uncanny references to Brazil's having been "foreclosed, repossessed and sold at auction" (149), and it ends with the Brazilian protagonist's personal reassessment of the star, realizing he "had been wrong about her all along. Carmen Miranda did not sell out to the Yanquis. She conquered them" (161). Drawing from the image of Miranda as the quintessential popular-culture symbol of fruit associated with Mother Earth, her presence in an afterlife where she carries on the trope of abundance challenges the way readers typically view space as an infertile dimension and adds an interesting twist to the dominant metaphor of space as sea with the appearance of Miranda's bounty transforming the space station into a sort of oasis.[34] In all these stories without exception, the presence of Carmen Miranda's ghost is marked by the exotic fruit baskets she brings, and in some instances, the fruit plays a crucial role in the plot's development. Why and how Miranda's ghost appears on the space station are central elements to the stories, and the treatments vary greatly: from Miranda's ghost solving mysteries, to saving protagonists from death, to reuniting loved ones, to being unjustly accused of a crime herself. Through the poetic license of science-fiction writing, Miranda's ghost appears through an array of media that include holography circuits, phase generators, and a computer program, or she is summoned by a member of the space station (on occasion even ardent fans) or, in at least one case, explicitly claims that she stumbled upon the station by chance (Mand 299). Overall, these literary texts project Carmen Miranda's ghost as friendly and helpful, dressed in all her Hollywood glory, with the exception of the menacing Miranda of Amanda Allen's "Rolling Down the Floor," described as a ghost with a gruesome, hollow smile, peeling skin, rotten and flyblown fruit, and a filthy, tattered Bahian dress (168), who at the story's conclusion destroys the space station and observes the bobbing corpses with "a contented smirk" (170). Similar to several of the other stories in the collection, in Don Sakers's "Tarawa Rising," Miranda's ghost appears and disappears throughout the narrative, immediately recognizable with her signature fruit headdress and broken English, occasionally dancing or singing a samba. The ghost is particularly present in the life of the title protagonist, Tarawa, a suicidal drag queen whom Miranda saves from death by radiation on the outside of the airlock, leading a repentant Tarawa to change his act to impersonate Miranda. This short story was retitled "The Ghost of Carmen Miranda" and became the title story of a subsequent anthology, *The Ghost of Carmen Miranda and Other Spooky Gay and Lesbian Tales*, edited by Trevelyan and Brassart (1998), emphasizing the drag-queen storyline and reinforcing Miranda's longstanding connection to gay subculture. Despite the commonalities among all the ghost of Carmen Miranda short stories, their humor and creativity make them great entertainment for Miranda and fantasy-writing fans alike, and they contribute to immortalizing her as a cultural icon whose spirit lives on—in Space Station Three.

Carmen Miranda is one of the main literary characters in Leslie Epstein's 1999 *Ice Fire Water: A Leib Goldkorn Cocktail*, the third book by the author to focus on the (mis)adventures of Leib Goldkorn, a Jewish woodwindist who escaped Dachau and, since 1943, has been a resident of the Upper West Side of Manhattan.[35] Written as the humorous yet wistful memoirs of a ninety-four-year-old Holocaust survivor, the narrative is earthly, picaresque, erotic, and crudely raw, with subtexts of anti-Semitism, social injustice, survivor's guilt, and responsibility that give it a deeply poignant edge. The memoir is funneled through the unreliable narrator Leib Goldkorn, creating a mixture of fantasy, tragicomedy, and bedroom humor, and the delusion of a flutist manqué who imagines fortuitous sensual encounters with no less than three leading ladies of Hollywood's golden age, all while aspiring to bring about world peace, thwart Brazil's alignment with Axis Nazis, and revenge anti-Semitism. D. T. Max pertinently summarizes the style of the novel as "its own genre—at once a travel tale, a historical meditation, a Holocaust revenge fantasy, a comedy of manners and a bedroom farce."[36] Following the title's triptych format, the novel intertwines Leib's present life as a flautist in New York's Upper West Side with three episodes of his past. In his late thirties, he had pursued his passion for music and women in the romantic locales of Hollywood, Rio, and Paris, and these three successive, unsuccessful adventures each occupy a section of the book. The most substantial section is the Carmen Miranda encounter, "Fire," that occupies the central part of the novel. It begins with Leib as a stowaway on a steamship heading for Brazil and then reconstructs Leib's recollections of saving Miranda from her Nazi-sympathizing musicians and orchestra leader and lover, Arturo Toscanini. Miranda's trademark fruit-piled headdress is emphasized throughout the narrative, with comedy, irony, and at times sensuality. Whenever Miranda appears in a scene, her ever-changing headdress remains her most prominent feature, often serving as a synecdoche for Miranda herself. At one climactic moment, as Leib escapes his nemesis, Italian orchestra conductor Arturo Toscanini, "a pile of tangelos" starts to talk, introducing beneath a "heaped-up fruit cup" Miranda, who is prompt to offer her services to "cure all [Leib's] protuberâncias" (Epstein 139). Later, in a paternal, condescending moment, the Brazilian president Getúlio Vargas candidly asks Miranda, "May I take off your hat, Dear? It's covered with dates" (Epstein 174). In a comic moment after a torrid sex scene with Toscanini that is abruptly interrupted by a hiding Leib's sneeze (creating a typical theatrical moment of discovery), Toscanini stands "in his birthday suiting" with Miranda right behind him "wearing only her trademark chapeau" (Epstein 145). Infatuated by Miranda, Leib emphasizes his role as rescuing her from the claws of her Nazi-following band and, by association, saving the destiny of Axis-inclined Brazil. In these moments, the narrative becomes a tale of melodramatic honor, with Leib's reiterating his mission and intertwining his love for Miranda and his political agenda. Miranda becomes the key political player in the outcome of Brazil's involvement in World War II, with Vargas endowing the singer with the power to decide the country's allegiance to either the Axis or the Allied powers. A mixture of the political and the sexual abounds throughout the novel, with sexual innuendos concentrated on Miranda's physique and sexually liberated behavior: taking Toscanini's fingers in her mouth to "perform a vibration" (144); sleeping with Toscanini; letting Getúlio Vargas nibble her wrist, mouth the crook of her arm, and put his tongue in her inner ear;

kneeling before Leib and sucking the lumps on his scalp "the way a child might upon a Popsicle array" (141). Beyond the fruit headdress, Leib's descriptions of Miranda focus on the sensuality of her breasts. In the final scene, as Miranda steps in as the understudy for the lead singing part of Aida in Leib's opera, she drops her gown to the floor and reveals "bare breasts, save for, at each pap, a pasty" with, as Leib recalls, "over the infernal region . . . a black piece of cotton, hardly larger than an eye patch, held in place by what I believe is called a string in the key of G" (Epstein 167), conflating musical vocabulary with the female pleasure zone. One narrative thread throughout the novel is Leib's frustrated sexual experience, and while the novel consistently invokes erection, through references to Leib's constant vertical movements (standing upright, escalating stairs, climbing a volcano, being lifted in crates or movie cranes), the phallic symbol of his flute, and repeated references to the conductor's baton as "fully erect," Leib falls short of full-blown ejaculations at each stage of his life because of impotence. The opening section describes the nonagenarian, in the communal bathroom of the hallway of his apartment, attempting unsuccessfully for over three hours to have a physician-prescribed annual ejaculation on his birthday to keep his prostate healthy. In Miranda's cabin on the steamship, he is excited by her sensual sucking, the proximity of her bosoms, and her humming, but it is Toscanini who gets the singer in a game of "knock hockey" atop the bed beneath which Leib is hiding. As Leib hears the couple's "giggles and grunts . . . cries of victory and groans of defeat," the feathers bursting from the mattress cause him to sneeze: with great irony, this is described as the protagonist's "non-voluntary ejaculation" (Epstein 145). This is the pattern of the manqué Don Juan, and if through the protagonist's imagination he is able to embellish the grandeur of his anti-Nazi mission, the reality of his sexual shortcomings is undeniable, concentrated in the figure of Carmen Miranda.

A last North American example of Carmen Miranda's literary "life" is the nostalgic, reflective, and in parts melodramatic novel *Samba Dreamers* (2006) by Kathleen Azevedo, which recounts the experience of Rosea, a second-generation Brazilian immigrant in the United States, as she attempts to reintegrate herself into society after serving time for arson, and chronicles her relationship with Joe Silva, a recently arrived Brazilian immigrant who was tortured under the Brazilian military dictatorship (1964–1985). The narrative focuses on the immigrant experience in Los Angeles, social marginalization, Latin homogenization, poverty, and hypocrisy in a classist and racist system that revolves around the Hollywood film industry's ephemeral stardom. Rosea lives in the shadow of her deceased mother, Carmen Socorro (modeled closely on Carmen Miranda), and the narrative's dominant tone is of rage toward vivid memories of the past and the movie industry that killed Carmen film by film, intertwined with the nostalgic pull of the Brazilian homeland in the form of Carmen's mythical Amazon, an imagined Brazil Rosea has never known, and, in Joe's case, a Brazil freed from the terror of an authoritarian and violent regime.

The narrative begins in 1975, two decades after Carmen Miranda's death. Transposed to the fictional narrative, episodes of Carmen Socorro's life are recalled through her daughter's memories, comments by adoring fans of the belated star, or

the omniscient narrator. The memories filtered through Rosea are the most prominent in the text, interweaving her own intimate memories of her mother and her
outrage at Hollywood, which she metaphorically views as "nothing but a big fat
lie! It's nothing but a bunch of plastic bananas" (K. Azevedo 139). Fans remember
Carmen for her sex appeal, physical beauty, dark hair, round hips, and tight-fitting
clothes (K. Azevedo 44). Melvinor, an old man who, pertinently, runs a fruit and
vegetable stand, refers to Carmen as "the legend, the greatest star in Hollywood"
and remembers her fruit as symbolically nurturing her public during wartime, her
tutti-frutti hat as "the cornucopia for starving Americans" (K. Azevedo 47). At the
conclusion of the novel, Joe, working as a tour guide of stars' homes, demythicizes
stereotypes of Hollywood and tells of the price Carmen had to pay for her fame,
the torture of her hats, the rejection by her people back in Brazil, and how she
ended up broken and died prematurely. An immigrant himself, he sees Carmen
as a symbol of immigrant heartbreak in a country that is "both beautiful and
cruel, innocent and guilty" (K. Azevedo 289), the paradox of Carmen's stardom
in Hollywood. *Samba Dreamers* brings to the forefront the price of Hollywood
stardom, and the perspective of the fictive daughter of a deceased star develops the
intersection of cultural memory, affectivity, and fandom. The unusual narrative
ploy of using a pseudohomonym for the main character creates a margin for poetic
license yet seems rather inconsequential since the text most frequently uses only her
first name, "Carmen." Furthermore, specific mention of Carmen Miranda's films,
her nickname "Brazilian Bombshell," as well as constant references to her fruit-
laden headdress inevitably reference Carmen Miranda. Carmen Socorro's daughter
wrestles with the impossibility of anyone doing justice to her mother's life through
a film: "who knew enough about Carmen to make a film?" (K. Azevedo 201).
Unable to interpret her mother's memory, Rosea throws herself out to sea, symbolically departing toward the Amazon and the birthplace of her mother.

In Brazil, Carmen Miranda has appeared as a fictional protagonist in several
theatrical plays, some of which were staged for the 2009 centenary of Miranda's
birth. These included the one-night performance *O que é que a Carmen Miranda
tem?* (What does Carmen Miranda have?) by Renata Martelli and the Colibri Sextet
(March 18, 2009), with deliberate wordplay on the title of her signature song
"O que é que a baiana tem?," and the original *Foi Carmen* (Carmen is gone) by
Antunes Filho, performed for several weeks from mid-July to the end of September
2009 in São Paulo.[37] *Foi Carmen* was a postmodern show that, as a theatrical technique, integrated abstraction, silence, and absurdly prolonged stage action with
what Antunes calls "fonemol": abandoning Portuguese for the use of a fabricated,
gibberish language with intensified voice modulations.[38]

These were not the first plays to center on Carmen Miranda as a dramatic
figure. The Brazilian dramatist, actor, and director Ronaldo Ciambrone, who is
well known for his transgender plays and acting, wrote *Uma certa Carmen* (A certain Carmen) in 1980. It has been staged several times since then, with Ciambrone
playing the lead role on occasion, and was once performed as a staged reading set
to live music in June 2000.[39] It was also staged as part of the commemorations
of Carmen Miranda's one-hundredth-year birth anniversary in July 2009 by the

São Paulo theatrical company Companhia Instável do Teatro at the Teatro Ruth Escobar in São Paulo, where it ran for several weeks.[40]

As these examples illustrate, *Uma certa Carmen* has been staged by different theatrical groups and for a variety of audiences, a testament to the play's versatile appeal. Part of its originality lies in the doubling of Carmen Miranda on the stage: the main protagonist, "Carmen," and her alter ego, "Carmen Verdade" (translated as "The True Carmen" or "Carmen of Truth"), who appears through the theatrical staging of a mirror to dialogue with "Carmen." As an explicit matrix of "descending metalepsis" from the real world to the fictional world of the play, Carmen Verdade heightens the illusionist impression.[41] The staging of Carmen (as a performed character) and Carmen Verdade mimics the viewer's double awareness of fiction and reality, projecting simultaneously Carmen-as-an-actress and the "real" Carmen, respectively, through the process of tacit and explicit metalepsis. The dialogue between the two Carmens is "harsh and realistic, densifying the protagonist's personal tragedy" (Herculano 18). Carmen delimitates their differences by telling Carmen Verdade: "This is theatre and I am an actress. . . . You are patrimony." This provokes Carmen Verdade to respond: "While you are alive, there is censorship. Once you die, they invent patrimony" (Ciambrone 41). Unlike the Ciambrone performances, in the Companhia Instável production both Carmen roles were played by female actresses, Lilian Grünwaldt and Priscila Labronici, thus eliminating the transgendered component of the original staging. Yet the gender-play is not altogether eliminated and is still expressed through some of the dialogues, as when one of the band members cautions Carmen not to go out in one of her outfits or they'll call her a *viado* (fag) (Ciambrone 39). The camp nature of Miranda's costumes is inseparable from her representation, as this example projects. A taping of the Companhia Instável performance shows that Carmen's costumes closely resemble those Carmen Miranda wore at different phases of her career.

Ciambrone's creative and poignant text draws on anecdotes from Miranda's biography that have long held common currency and is divided into two acts woven around some of Miranda's greatest radio songs in Brazil (Act 1) and her Hollywood hits in the United States (Act 2). David Sebastian is portrayed as slowly killing Carmen, pushing her to the limit, demanding she take pills to sleep and to wake up, forcing her to come back from Brazil to tape the Jimmy Durante show, arguing with her on the day of her death, and, with tragic irony, yelling at Carmen at one point, "If you die, you'll still have a year of engagements!" (Ciambrone 52). The scene "The Marathon of Carmen Miranda's Life Starts" includes explicit stage directions that "this scene must be absurd but extremely lyrical" (Ciambrone 47). Carmen and the Bando da Lua stand ready at the starting line, and David Sebastian symbolically fires the gun to start the "race," a medley of Carmen's recordings but also an analogy of Carmen's overexerted life.

When Carmen explains she needs to finish the first act, Carmen Verdade retorts that her "whole life was only one act," pointing to the artificiality of the staged play's divisions, and asks that Carmen "talk a little about Getúlio Vargas, or the people will forget what a dictatorship is" (Ciambrone 42). Carmen Verdade's exhortation is immediately implemented as the next scene depicts Getúlio ap-plauding the triumph of the revolutionary movement and the reaffirmation of the country's nationalism while pompously expounding, "Have you ever seen such happiness? You and your *balangandãs*, me and my Steel Plant in Volta Redonda, the United States with their military base in Natal and Brazilians marveled by their American dreams" (Ciambrone 42). The seductive nature of the Carmen/Getúlio relationship is exaggeratedly expressed in the diminutive nicknames she uses, "Gê" or "Gegê," and in Getúlio's offering Carmen no less than a fur coat and a diamond broche as parting gifts (Ciambrone 43). As Herculano comments, along with the exchanges between the two Carmens, "equally successful is the doubling of Miranda singing over Getúlio Vargas's speech, that beyond the historical testi-mony creatively expresses her proximity to the populist president" (18).

In the final scene, Carmen Verdade coronates Carmen with her headdress as a sign of approval of the story that has been told, and then the whole cast sings two of Miranda's most well-known songs, "Adeus, batucada" (Goodbye, batucada) and "Cantoras do rádio" ([Female] radio singers). This grand finale transmits several paradoxical messages: the sealing of the play as an authentic representa-tion of Carmen Verdade/Carmen Miranda's life experiences and the success of Carmen as an actress to mirror this "reality" in the diegetic level of the play. Yet at the same time, the finality of life and the motif of the departure (in "Adeus, batucada") are set against the affirmation of Carmen and Carmen Verdade as "the (female) radio singers" who are no longer. Therefore, the end of Ciambrone's play can be read as a mise-en-abîme of Carmen Miranda's stardom, with the reference to the end of *batucada* through her departure to the United States and then through death, yet remembered and beloved in Brazil first and foremost as a radio singer.

While different in genre, there are several commonalities to these literary re-creations of Carmen Miranda. All inevitably depict Miranda's extravagant fruit-laden headdress, borrow from the fruit motif, and include a sampling of Miranda's signature songs. Among the other characters, it is interesting to note the repeated presence of Getúlio Vargas, long identified as an ardent admirer of Carmen Miranda, although the poetic license of these texts takes this relationship to a far more advanced level than historical evidence has ever proven. Other re-peated themes touch on Miranda's personal tragedy through an unhappy marriage, her sadness and longing for Brazil, her rejection at the Urca Casino, and overall a reevaluation of the Carmen Miranda paradox—Brazil's most visible ambassadress abroad and the country's most debated representative. This reconciliation is at the heart of the Helena Solberg docudrama *Bananas Is My Business*, the first fully devel-oped film on the life and career of Carmen Miranda.

Seeking Reconciliation: Helena Solberg's *Bananas Is My Business*

In the summer of 1995, the documentary *Bananas Is My Business* was released and began the circuit of international film festivals, garnering several awards in the "Best

Documentary" category.[42] Directed and narrated by Helena Solberg, a Brazilian native living and working in the United States,[43] the docudrama was mostly well received by critics as an insightful, engaging, and well-produced film despite its flaws. Critics were unanimous in their praise of the valuable retrospective look at the life and career of Carmen Miranda that consists of a hybrid composition of several different genres. In typical biopic style, *Bananas Is My Business* integrates accepted details and moments in Miranda's life "into the genre's conventional narrative pattern, that of the American 'myth of success'" (Curry 130). The documentary intersperses interviews with contemporaries who knew Miranda well (including costars Alice Faye and Cesar Romero; composers Synval Silva and Laurindo Almeida; her sister, Aurora Miranda; the maid of her Beverly Hills residence, Estela Romero; her first boyfriend, Mário Cunha; and her most loyal friends, Jeanne Allan and Aloísio de Oliveira), clips from both her Brazilian and Hollywood films, images of personal items such as photographs, letters staged as being read by Miranda, home videos, historical footage from Brazilian newsreels and Rio in the 1930s, the inside of the Urca Casino (indelibly associated with Carmen Miranda), and sequences in which the transformist artist Erick Barreto impersonates Carmen Miranda, developing historical reenactments to a crescendo of bizarre fantastical dream segments.

The tone of the film is tragic-dramatic with the reenacted scene of her death (which bookends the film) and the first live shots of Miranda's coffin being greeted in Rio de Janeiro by crowds swarming the streets. These glimpses of the funeral procession and wake are juxtaposed with brightly lit filmed segments of Hollywood boulevards, Miranda's square on the forecourt of the Chinese Theatre, and her star on Hollywood Boulevard, reiterating the image of a fallen star, symbolically both sought after and trampled under the feet of tourists bustling around the footprint gallery. Nostalgia is woven throughout the film, coupled with bitterness and sadness as those closest to Miranda remember her fabulous career, her wonderful singing voice, her charisma, her greatest recorded hits, the impact she made on the Brazilian public, and all in all the joie de vivre that permeated her life. That is, until she married David Sebastian: all those interviewed focused on their dysfunctional marriage and the sadness and abuse Carmen endured during those final years. David Foster's interpretation indicates that the film "would have the spectator understand that Miranda had come to occupy a no man's land: repudiated in Brazil, unloved and abused by a husband whose personal sexual drama may have been the reason for his alienation" (120). Miranda's friends and costars focus on how unique and vivacious Miranda was and how perfect she was for Hollywood's musical golden age, and this stands in stark contrast to the interior suffering of her home life. While Miranda's first boyfriend, Mário Cunha, speaks fondly of Miranda as the woman he most loved in his life, Aloísio de Oliveira's memories are particularly moving as he talks of their closeness, having worked with Carmen from 1934 until her death. One short home movie shows Aloísio and Miranda dancing around and having fun on what appears to be a road trip, accompanied by the Nicholas brothers and Carmen's sister, Aurora. These segments of great happiness are interspersed with images of the sea, a grey and cold-looking ocean that symbolically separated Miranda from her beloved fans in Brazil, embodied by her greatest fan of all time, Aloísio, who gazes out toward the horizon. These insistent images of the sea foreshadow the film's final scene that ends with Synval Silva's composition and one of Miranda's most beautiful songs, "Adeus, batucada" (Farewell, batucada), which laments the separation from something that one loves, a jewel that is lost in the ocean, the samba rhythm or lifestyle.[44]

Miranda's paradoxical relationship with her Brazilian public is developed throughout the film, her meteoric rise to stardom as a radio singer and performer, the fiasco at the Urca Casino that left her with pain she would never overcome, and the importance of bringing her body back to Rio de Janeiro, with the narrator commenting that "Carmen had finally come back home." The documentary includes the live footage of Miranda making her imprints in the forecourt of the Chinese Theatre and her accompanying message to her fans back in Brazil, claiming that she was thinking of them. In this, the film shows Miranda constantly reaching out to her first public, the Brazilian nation, despite the different path her career took. This need to reconcile the Brazilian public with Miranda's memory is symbolically embodied by Helena Solberg's own narration of her quest to reappropriate Carmen Miranda's memory, and by the image of Solberg's mother, in a moment of blatant self-indulgence, posing next to Erick Barreto as Miranda in the film's afterward. In this and in Solberg's constant over-indulgent self-referentiality in the parallels she draws between herself and Miranda, the film takes on the characteristics of a performative documentary as defined by Stella Bruzzi.[45] This narrative ploy results in a documentary style that is "highly personal," as Erik Mink writes for the *Daily News*.[46] The narrator, who identifies herself through photographs and references to her youth, portrays her personal quest as a journey that leads her on a mystified search of the archives "after the secrets of Carmen Miranda" and results in recurring dreams. Solberg's metaleptic "intrusion" (Genette 234) as she forces the comparison between herself and Miranda, including self-portraits from her youth and voiceover narration, problematizes the boundary between the extradiegetic narrator and the realm of the documentary, expected to be objectively portrayed with a certain distance between the film director behind the camera and its filmed subject. Solberg tells of the heartache she felt when unable to identify with the woman on the screen, yet after the electric-shock treatment, acute depression, and anxiety that Miranda suffered, Miranda becomes Solberg's broken "dancing doll," as symbolized by a quick shot of one of Tom Tierney's paper dolls and a broken wooden puppet on strings. It is an eerie segment of lost happiness and destruction. It is also one of collective guilt, as the narrator expresses, "we should have kept [Carmen] with us, and never let her go." The film's conclusion focuses again on the narrator's relationship with Miranda as she attempts to understand Carmen Miranda's legacy in Brazilian cultural memory. In somewhat contradictory terms, the narrator concludes that Miranda could never have lived up to all the different expectations people had for her or be the perfect symbol for the nation, despite her undeniable talent as an artist.

While critics have been divided on Erick Barreto's performance in the documentary, this might be because Barreto performs two different types of reenactments: the historical moments (such as Miranda's arrival at the port of New York) to enable the chronology of Miranda's life events and then the more fantastical sequences that add a new dimension to the film that is playful, make-believe, carnivalesque, and camp. In truth, several of these latter segments are definitely a stretch of the viewer's imagination, such as Miranda's escaping from a display case and out of a museum (with real footage of the Carmen Miranda Museum in Rio de Janeiro), jumping out of a television set into the living room of an ardent British fan (Ivan Jack), dancing around an empty dance floor of the Urca Casino, wearing a costume that resembles a pineapple while singing to the tune "I made my money with bananas," and finally, parading with Carnivalesque crowds on top of a float. The ultimate message of all these fantasy sequences is that Miranda is escaping from an existence of entrapment, whether confined symbolically to a museum to be looked at in a showcase and admired for her outward appearance, or bound by a film or television set. Solberg was aware of the stylized nature of these recreations. In an interview for *Américas*, she states, "We were trying to give a feeling of the overly staged, both as a criticism and a celebration of what is 'fake'" (qtd. in Terrell 53). The "overly staged" is simply the performativity of camp, and it is certainly convincing, especially in the scene toward the end of the documentary in which Barreto is filmed dancing as Miranda "in full, feathered tropical regalia, hovering in the sky like a virgin icon surrounded by flying bananas instead of angels" (Terrell 52). David Foster indicates that staging Barreto as an investment from the drag perspective is unclear in the Miranda portrayal, for the viewer is left wondering if the transvestite choice was motivated by Miranda's exuberance or if there was an underlying agenda about her construction as a Brazilian or Latin American actress for US audiences (123–24). Regardless of the camp nature of these scenes, the dancing segments performed by Erick Barreto are extremely captivating: he is indeed Miranda's greatest interpreter to this day. In contrast, while there is certainly great physical resemblance and the costume and makeup team did an outstanding job, the close-ups of Barreto as Miranda in the biographical moments are less convincing.

In this search to provide new meaning to Carmen Miranda's legacy, always from the Brazilian perspective as embodied through the narrator's voice, the film attributes the blame for Miranda's stylized *baiana* on the US public and the demands placed on a Latina star to constantly perform as a stereotype, over-sexed and vivacious, as Rita Moreno discusses. Immediately upon arrival in New York, Miranda's portrayal as a foreigner with a reduced command of English is summarized by the narrator's disbelief: "something happened, this is not our Carmen." Later in the film, when Miranda returns to Brazil in 1955 following her acute depression only a few months before her death, the narrator remarks with great sadness that she is "another Carmen . . . years alone couldn't account for the change in her face, in her expression." Framing the film with her death adds significant gloom to the narrative and contrasts with images of Carmen, youthful, happy, coquettish, and playful, enjoying the camera and the company of her friends, which is reiterated by the repetition of a saying attributed to Miranda: "All I need to be happy is a bowl of soup and the freedom to sing." The cinematic juxtaposition of composers Synval Silva and Laurindo Almeida singing and playing on the guitar some of her most popular songs along with Miranda's recorded voice is powerful and emotionally charged. This technique brings Miranda into the present, and her voice "materializes" Miranda more successfully than any of the reenactments interspersed throughout the film. The final images return to the opening scenes with the drama of Miranda's death, reiterating the tragedy of an inflexible industry and her physical, mental, and emotional fatigue: there is also no redemption for the fan, the viewer, or the director herself. Through the most brilliant archival recovery of this beloved singer in Brazil and amazingly unique and much-loved performer in Hollywood, Brazil in particular may hope to reconcile the past with the present's memory of the "remarkable young girl," but it is too late.

Immortalized *Baiana*

A few months before her untimely death, Miranda spent a few weeks in Rio de Janeiro. It was her first trip back to Brazil in fourteen years, and her name inundated the press with articles reflecting on her past and present stardom and what she had come to represent for Brazil. One reporter, writing for *O jornal* in January 1955, summarized her star status as the product of her own creativity: "In truth Brazil did not make Carmen, it was Carmen who made Brazil; it was not the *baiana* that made Carmen, but she made the *baiana*; her songs did not make Carmen, she made her songs. An artist at 100%, this is manifest in her gestures and in the smallest of movements, singing, dancing and being photographed."[47] Neither before nor after Carmen Miranda has anyone blended, with such efficiency, music, dance, fashion, cinema, samba, and Carnival: Miranda had and did it all, and as such she lived up to her moniker of the "remarkable young girl." Miranda projected the *baiana* on an international platform, both then and now, and although Hollywood greatly transformed the image, it remained indelible as the national symbol by excellence.

Indicative of the *baiana* as representative of the nation was the trend throughout the 1950s and 1960s of Brazilian competitors in the "Miss Universe" pageant wearing the *baiana* costume.[48] Far from the infelicitous outcome of the *baiana* dolls withdrawn from the Exhibition of the Portuguese World, as discussed in Chapter 1, the prestige of the *baiana* that is at the forefront of the national imaginary grew through its international trajectory. This is also apparent in film where, in the recycling of the Hollywood musical in the form of the Brazilian *chanchadas*, the *baiana* of the 1950s and beyond has been tainted with its international projection.[49]

To materialize the memory of Carmen Miranda, the city of Rio de Janeiro—Miranda's hometown, the heart of the recording industry, and the most prominent locale for her live performances in Brazil—has been a central driving force, although not all the initiatives of Carioca enthusiasts have been successful. In Rio de Janeiro, only three days after the star's passing, a bill was presented in the City Council building to name one of the city's streets after the star to publically consecrate Carmen Miranda's enduring importance for her hometown.[50] The original proposal to rename the short street Travessa do Comércio (where the

actress lived from 1925 to 1932) was rejected, and Rio's Rua Carmen Miranda
(Carmen Miranda Street) went to the Jardim Guanabara neighborhood in the Ilha
do Governador.[51] A few years later, sculptor Mateus Fernandes's bronze bust of
Carmen Miranda, which depicts the star in her *baiana* costume and fruit-laden
headdress, was donated to Rio de Janeiro and inaugurated in one of the main
downtown squares, the Largo da Carioca, on September 20, 1960 (Garcia 239).
With the construction of the metro in that area in 1979, the statue was removed
and reinstalled in the Ilha do Governador on a square off Rua Carmen Miranda.

In the United States, the materiality of Carmen Miranda's legacy dates back
to March 24, 1941, when Miranda immortalized her footprints with her trademark platform shoes, handprints, and signature at Grauman's Chinese Theatre. The
inscription reads: "To Sid Viva! in the south american way" (sic), and Miranda's
lack of capitalization for "South American" follows the rules of the Portuguese
language as Miranda makes her mark as the first Latino/a star to have her prints
in the forecourt of the Chinese Theatre. Over the years, the square has cracked
and deteriorated, and the area that contained her right footprint has been patched
(Endres and Cushman 152), but the square continues to attract scores of Latin
American tourists for whom, collectively, Miranda continues to represent the inscribed "South American Way." Only a few feet from Miranda's grey-toned slab is
an intersection that bears the name Carmen Miranda Square. As reported in the
Los Angeles Times, when the Carmen Miranda Square in Hollywood was named in
September 1998, it was one of a dozen Los Angeles city intersections named after
historic personages, such as Wolze Brothers Square in Lincoln Heights and Dosan
Ahn Chang Ho Square near the University of Southern California.[52] A city traffic
sign marks the intersection, keeping Carmen Miranda's name present and visible
for those who pass by.

Carmen Miranda's legacy continues to emerge and develop, often in unexpected contexts, yet always harking back to her unique stardom and the impact she
left on Brazil's music industry and the greatest musical film period in the history
of Hollywood. A few of these eclectic tokens of Miranda's star image include paper
dolls, stamps, coloring books, and Christmas tree ornaments, a host of imitations
that for Melissa Fitch have commodified the Miranda image to the extreme and
have taken on a life (and a market) of their own (57). Over the years in Brazil,
significant state-endorsed and other privately funded initiatives have aimed to preserve Carmen Miranda's legacy as national patrimony. In the mid-1990s, the secretary of culture and sports of the state of Rio de Janeiro inaugurated what turned
out to be a successful campaign: "Adopt Carmen," whose goal was the restoration
of Carmen Miranda's fabulous wardrobe. In 2005 the Museum of Modern Art
(MAM) in Rio de Janeiro curated an elaborate temporary exhibit, *Carmen Miranda
para sempre*, the largest exhibition on the star ever created, whose purpose was "to
give its visitors the opportunity to follow the path to fame of the greatest interpreter of Brazilian music, celebrating all aspects of her life" (Canosa 2). Designed
in a circular disposition to symbolically indicate neither end nor beginning to
Carmen Miranda's legacy, the exhibition consisted of over seven hundred items
that belonged to the family, private collections, and the Carmen Miranda Museum,

recreating the ambiance of Rio in the 1930s as a backdrop to her early career and then accompanying her trajectory through her Hollywood days.[53] The display of Miranda's original clothes and others designed specifically for the event highlighted her importance as a fashion trendsetter and designer. After six weeks in Rio, the exhibition was transferred to the Memorial of Latin America in São Paulo, and then later that year to Salvador, Bahia.[54] Prior to this initiative, other exhibitions had been organized around the country on several occasions, but *Carmen Miranda para sempre* was the most complete exhibition to date.[55]

Of particular note was the year 2009, the one-hundredth anniversary of the singer's birth, for which innumerable activities, some of great proportions and impressive ambition, were organized to commemorate Carmen Miranda's legacy. While many of these initiatives took place in Rio, other cities also participated in the "Miranda year," creating a large number of creative, eclectic, and wide-ranging events. These events often provided an overview of Miranda's life and career in Brazil and the United States, but for the most part in Brazil the focus was on her music. Live performances of Miranda's songs were performed in tributes by Revista do Samba, Edna Pimenta, Carlos Malta and Pife Muderno, Tio Samba, Band 1E99, Pedro Luís and Roberta Sá, Clara Sandroni and Marcos Sacramento, Janaína Moreno, Diana Dasha, Miramar Mangabeira and the band Bola Preta, Janette Dornellas and Bando do Sol, Maria Alcina, Uli Costa and Bando da Rua (a play-on-words with Bando da Lua, Miranda's "Moon Band"), and many others. Most of these sung tributes were staged for only one or two evenings at a variety of venues, ranging from local nightclubs and bars to concert halls, libraries, museums, and even the Brazilian Academy of Letters. Along with these live presentations, several recordings were released, such as the double CD *100 anos Carmen Miranda, duetos e outras Carmens* (100 years of Carmen Miranda, duets and other Carmens; Song BMG/February 2009), Ná Ozzetti's *Balangandãs* (MCD/June 2009), and Banda 1E99's electronic versions in *Carmen Miranda* (CID/November 2008). Focusing on Carmen Miranda's days as a radio singer and performing artist in Rio, *Carmen, o it brasileiro* (Carmen, the Brazilian *it* girl; dir. Antonio De Bonis) was a musical show that presented songs and spoken text from that earlier period, staged at Rio's Teatro Rival for the month of November 2009 with Andrea Veiga in the leading role.[56] Television was not left out of the circuit of the Carmen Miranda centenary celebrations, with special homages airing throughout the year but particularly around the date of the star's birth, February 9, on all the major daytime programs.

During this year, numerous special exhibitions were prepared to showcase Carmen Miranda's life, stardom, and legacy through displays of her costumes, accessories, platform shoes, personal items, photographs, records, magazine covers, and newspaper clippings. The São Paulo Fashion Week (January 2009) used Carmen Miranda's image as a bold statement for its exhibition, with walls covered floor to ceiling with blown-up photographs of the star, films playing on large screens throughout the space, display cases with show-business and personal items, and several life-size mannequins wearing reproductions mixed with a few originals of some of her stage and film costumes. Many of these items were on loan from the Carmen Miranda Museum. During the centennial year, the role of the Carmen

Miranda Museum as a center for educational events, film screenings, debates, and musical shows was paramount, with particularly intense programing the week of February 9. These events were often fortunate to have the participation of Cesar Balbi, the museum's director and specialist on Carmen Miranda, along with Ruy Castro, Brazil's foremost expert on the star and author of the most thorough and insightful biography, *Carmen—Uma biografia* (Carmen—a biography; 2005), who brought his expertise and years of research to debates, film presentations, and the opening ceremony of the week's commemorative events. For the museum's centennial exhibition, *Carmen, notável para sempre* (Carmen, remarkable forever), the sculptor Ulysses Rabelo created several new busts and life-size statues of Miranda to bring the star more vividly to life in her museum.

Since the Carmen Miranda Museum opened its doors, it has been the main public institution to preserve Miranda's memory. Officially created in 1956 but only inaugurated twenty-one years after her death, on August 5, 1976, the original museum in the Botafogo neighborhood of Rio had a permanent exhibition that showcased a small portion of the over three thousand items it owns, consisting of Miranda's accessories, personal belongings, shoes, purses, eleven complete costumes from her Hollywood films, hundreds of photographs, newspaper clippings, dozens of magazines whose covers she graced, and recordings of her music. The collection did an excellent job of illustrating Carmen Miranda's stardom in attractive displays that changed every few months to rotate the Miranda artifacts in the museum's limited space. Difficult to access in a small, oddly shaped park surrounded by four lanes of traffic, the museum was housed in a concrete, windowless bunker-like building (some have referred to it as a "hat box," "donut," or "flying saucer").[57] A refurbished recreation pavilion whose modernist design was the work of the Brazilian architect Afonso Eduardo Reidy (who had also designed the iconic MAM/Museum of Modern Art), the building was adapted for the museum in 1975 by the architect Ulisses Burlamaqui. In 2016, the Carmen Miranda Museum is being integrated into the new MIS/Museum of Image and Sound on the centrally situated Avenida Atlântica in Copacabana, certainly a more tribute-fitting space.

When Carmen Miranda left Brazil for the United States, she was preoccupied with the distance from her national public as her career embarked in a new direction. When she bid her nation goodbye, she ended her speech by reiterating, "Goodbye, my dear friends. . . . Remember me always. I will never forget you. . . . Goodbye, until we meet again."[58] Generations later, Carmen Miranda continues to be remembered, probably far more than anyone at the time could have ever imagined. Memories of "the remarkable young girl" and the "Brazilian Bombshell" continue vividly in Brazilian and US culture. As we seek to understand her stardom in both countries, it is clearly above and beyond this multiplicity of meanings that Miranda lives on as an easily recognizable image. Carmen Miranda remains present as one of the most beloved voices of Brazilian popular music of all time, a unique film personality in the musicals of Hollywood's golden age, and a lasting camp icon. Undoubtedly, Carmen Miranda's long-enduring legacy constantly renews the uniqueness of her visual impact.

NOTES

INTRODUCTION

1. See, for example, "Carmen Miranda is Dead at 41; Movie Comedienne and Dancer," *New York Times*, Aug. 6, 1955; "Carmen Miranda Dies of Heart Attack at Age 41," *Los Angeles Mirror-News*, Aug. 6, 1955.
2. "Carmen Miranda Paid Final Tribute by 300," *Examiner*, Aug. 9, 1955; "Requiem Mass Celebrated for Carmen Miranda," *Los Angeles Times*, Aug. 9, 1955.
3. See "Ainda em Hollywood o corpo de Carmen Miranda," *Correio da manhã*, Aug. 9, 1955; and "Confirmado: Sexta-feira no Galeão o corpo da Carmen!" *Última hora* [Rio de Janeiro], Aug. 9, 1955.
4. The *baiana*—as will be discussed in detail in Chapter 1, refers to a woman from the Northeastern state of Bahia and who, often in traditional dress, would carry her wares in baskets and on trays balanced on a turban on her head.
5. See Augusto Frederico Schmidt, "Carmen Miranda," *O diário* [Santos—Estado de São Paulo], Aug. 21, 1955.
6. "Carmen Miranda Eulogized in Rio," *Los Angeles Times*, Aug. 13, 1955.
7. *Gazeta do rádio*, Aug. 6, 1955.
8. For excellent summaries of Miranda's films and a close reading of her Hollywood screen performances see Shaw, *Carmen*, 38-82.
9. For a discussion of the concept of an icon, see O'Connor and Niebylski, *Latin American Icons*, 1.
10. Available only in VHS format are *Springtime in the Rockies* (1942) and *Scared Stiff* (1953).
11. Contrary to Kirsten Pullen's erroneous claim that *Alô, alô, carnaval!* is no longer extant (127), it was restored in 2002 and is available for viewing at the filmothèque of the MAM in Rio.
12. For a discussion of this in-betweenness see James Mandrell.
13. The Brazilian expression "taí" is a contraction for "está aí," which can be translated as "here is" or "that's" and is used to introduce someone or something.
14. See, for example, the article and telling title of Tinhorão's "Carmen Miranda levou Bando da Lua aos EUA por inspiração de Getúlio" (Carmen Miranda took Bando da Lua to the United States thanks to Getúlio) that appeared in *Jornal do Brasil* on July 20, 1962.
15. See Eaton, *Politics Beyond the Capital*, 74 and 77–80.
16. See Clark, "Doing the Samba on the Sunset Boulevard," for the Hollywoodization of Carmen Miranda's music.

CHAPTER 1

1. A great number of the films made by the Downey-Cinédia partnership were stored at the Sonofilm location and destroyed in a fire in November 1940. The Cinédia film archive suffered a serious flood at its Jacarepaguá installation in 1996.

2. Macumba is a syncretic Afro-Brazilian religion in which the priestesses play a most important part. Here the term is used pejoratively to refer by association to the women practitioners of macumba.

3. This cultural and racial hierarchy was a widely circulated discourse among certain intellectual circles of the Northeast, deriving, as Matory discusses, not from the ethnographers themselves but from explicit claims by African-Brazilian priests and travelers (61).

4. "Pano da costa" can be literally translated as "cloth from the coast." It featured prominently among a few prize commodities such as pepper, straw, and soap that were imported from the "costa" (the West Coast of Africa) and were still being sold in Brazil during the first decades of the twentieth century (Pierson 239). Matory indicates: "Brazilians have long called western Africa 'the Coast' (a Costa), *pars pro toto*, and identified it as the classical origin of the finest in Afro-Brazilian culture" (50). For a detailed ethno-aesthetic analysis of the *pano da costa*, complete with the symbolism of the colors, the choice of fabric, and the socio-religious connotations, see Lody, *O que é que a baiana tem*. See also the details of the *baiana* outfit that confirm Pierson's description in Lody, *Pencas de balangandãs*, 27.

5. There are many variants of the term: *berenguenden, balançançan, cambaio*, and *penca* (Pierson, *Negroes in Brazil*, 246n11); *barangandá, balangandá*, and *belenguendéns* (Ribeiro, *Folclore baiano*, 26).

6. For a reading of the *balangandãs* and other jewelry that the street vendors ubiquitously wore, see Graham, *Feeding the City*, 43–44.

7. See *Beira-mar*, Mar. 7, 1936, 12; and "Onde estão as baianas?" (Where are the baianas?), *A tarde*, June 23, 1936 (qtd. in Pierson, *Negroes in Brazil*, 248n17).

8. The *filhas de santo* are women who are consecrated to the worship of the orishas or emissaries of the gods of the Yoruba religion. The *mães de terreiro* are the priestesses who officiate during the religious ceremonies.

9. Carvalho indicates that the Bahians comprised only 1.49 per cent of the city's total population according to the 1920 census and that the term may have been used loosely (140).

10. Here I am guided by Foucault's definition of this concept of juxtaposed spaces developed in "Of Other Spaces," 25.

11. For a discussion of the Bahian leadership in this context, see Velloso, *A cultura das ruas*, 26–28 and 36–38.

12. Another commonly used term for these street vendors is *quitandeira*, which derives from the Kimbundu term for market, *kitanda*.

13. The Tenentes do Diabo (who presented for the first time in 1867), the Democráticos (created in 1867), and the Fenianos (1869) were three of the most important Carnival associations or clubs that were well liked by the public and existed until the 1940s, when these types of associations appeared antiquated in comparison to the emergence of samba schools.

14. Heitor dos Prazeres, one of the most influential composers and singers of this period, is featured in *baiana*-drag in Cabral, *As escolas de samba*, 59.

15. See J. Green, *Beyond Carnival*, 1.

16. See Cleto, *Camp*, 32.

17. James Green provides a wonderful overview of the balls of the *falsas baianas* during the 1950s in *Beyond Carnival*, "Carnival Queens and Drag Balls," 211–19.

18. For a thorough discussion of the "Falsa baiana" see McCann, *Hello, Hello Brazil*, 81–82.

19. References to Carnival 1942 can be found in *O cruzeiro*, Feb. 14, 1942 (qtd. in Garcia, *O 'it verde e amarelo' de Carmen Miranda*, 119). Critics have repeated Martha Gil-Montero's comments about the prominence of Miranda's *baiana* in Carnival in the 1940s, but without further documental substance. See Gil-Montero, *Brazilian Bombshell*, 152–53.

20. The title of their parade can be loosely translated as "Hello, hello, here you have it: Carmen Miranda" merging the "Alô, alô" part from the beginning of the titles of two of her Brazilian films, *Alô, alô, Brasil!* and *Alô, alô, carnaval!*, with the title of her first commercial success, "Taí," recorded in 1930. In the case of Império Serrano's title, "Taí" evokes the song itself more than the meaning of the expression. The lyrics of the Império Serrano's song also brought in another of Miranda's most popular hits, "Cai, cai" (Fall, fall), by the composer Roberto Martins, recorded in 1939 and later performed by Miranda in *That Night in Rio* (1941).

21. See DaMatta, *Carnivals, Rogues, and Heroes*, 96 and Pinto, *O negro no Rio de Janeiro*, 248.

22. *Manchete*, Aug. 12, 1978: 46.

23. For a thorough discussion of the street vendors in Salvador, Bahia, see chapter 2, "From Streets and Doorways," in Graham, *Feeding the City*, 33–53. Although Graham does not discuss the socio-economic difference between the street vendors, he provides a detailed analysis of their wares, dress, and what they used to carry their goods on their heads.

24. The original is *bruxa de pano*, also known as *bonecra*, etymologically close to the contemporary Portuguese form of doll, *boneca*. *Bonecra* is still used as a popular form in certain regions such as the Azores.

25. See Barros, *Corações De Chocolat*, 28–29 and Tinhorão, *Música popular*, 64.

26. See Barros 29; Castro, *Carmen*, 171; and Neyde Veneziano, "O sistema vedete," *Revista repertório* Feb. 17, 2011.

27. See Gomes and Seigel, "Sabina's Oranges," 17 and Shaw, "What does the *baiana* have?," 94–95.

28. See Hertzman, *Making Samba*, 124.

29. See *Diário carioca*, Jan. 8, 1939: 9.

30. See Afonso Arinos's statements on the disjunction of the different regions of Brazil delivered in a conference *circa* 1915 in Belo Horizonte then published posthumously as *A unidade da pátria* in 1917.

31. See Lisa Shaw's careful reading of this topic in "*São Coisas Nossas*: Samba and Identity in the Vargas Era (1930-45)."

32. The *marchas* or *marchinhas* were seasonal songs created with the celebrations of Carnival in mind and greatly popular during the 1920s and 1930s. The lyrics are often irreverent, but because of the songs' quick tempo, the suggestion of double meanings, and the

inversion of values during Carnival, the overall effect is merriment and gaiety, where all is permitted and nothing is censored. The melodies are typically simple, catchy tunes, making them favorites for Carnival and the revue theater.

33. For a very insightful reading of the 1930s vogue for live radio programs in Brazil and Miranda's participation on the *Programa Casé*, the pioneering radio showcase for live performances, see McCann, *Hello, Hello Brazil*, 48–49.

34. For a detailed account of the genesis of "Aquarela do Brasil," its rise to the status of unofficial national anthem, and its impact on popular music, see McCann, *Hello, Hello Brazil*, 70–78.

35. In the "News of the Radio" section of *Beira-mar*, the journalist S. G. Levy writes: "Carmen Miranda the queen of samba, has recorded another hit . . . 'O que é que a baiana tem?'" "Radiofónicas," *Beira-mar*, Apr. 1, 1939: 6.

36. For a succinct reading of the *baiana*-themed song lyrics, see Garcia, *O 'it verde e amarelo' de Carmen Miranda*, 123–31.

37. *Manchete* Aug. 12, 1978: 46.

38. See Brício de Abreu, "O 'fenômeno' Carmen Miranda no teatro," *Diário da noite* [Rio de Janeiro], Aug. 1955.

39. See "Chanchada: alegria e dois mitos," *O globo*, Aug. 5, 1973: 7.

40. For specific dates and an exhaustive list of Miranda's performances and public appearances from 1929 to 1939 in Brazil and Argentina, see Cardoso Junior, *Carmen Miranda*, 18–27.

41. Ruy Castro rightly observes that *pequena* in the original nickname was a synonym of *garota* (young girl), rather than a reference to her small stature (*Carmen*, 97).

42. There is no mention of Carmen Miranda in Getúlio Vargas's thirteen diaries compiled in two volumes, even though he does mention meeting female musicians and artists such as Margarida Lopes and Brazilian football players and other professional athletes. In October 1937 Vargas takes a serious mistress, whom he refers to as his "*bem-amada*" (beloved) and who adds adventure and, perhaps more importantly, momentary happiness to Vargas's depressive life until her departure from Rio in June 1938. It is highly unlikely that Miranda is this mysterious lover. Ana Rita Mendonça also makes reference to these unfounded rumors (*Carmen Miranda*, 56).

43. *Pranove*, May 1939: 20.

44. See Marshall's definition of the celebrity as a unique identity (*Celebrity and Power*, 43).

45. Female performers and singers such as Araci Cortes, Dircinha Batista, or Aracy de Almeida seemed to draw from Miranda's style in their own performances, often singing the same songs and performing at similar venues around Rio. For a discussion of the differences and overlap between Cortes and Miranda in particular, see Castro, *Carmen*, 50.

46. This is quoted in Jota Efegê, *Figuras e coisas*, 103, originally published in *Beira-mar*, Nov. 10, 1929: 1.

47. "Carmen Miranda," *Cinearte*, June 1, 1938: 13. Carmen Miranda was one of the first female personalities in Brazil to be associated with having "it," a concept that had been popular in Hollywood since the late 1920s when Clara Bow became "the *It* Girl." The expression "it" was first coined by the British novelist, scriptwriter, and glamor icon Elinor Glyn (1864–1943), who wrote a 1927 novel titled precisely "*It*" in which she defines the concept as "that strange magnetism" that attracts both sexes, and even cats (10).

48. *Beira-mar* of October 26, 1935, featured several photographs of the two sisters, both in the main issue and its supplement. See pages 1, 2, and 8.

49. See "Microphonemas," *Beira-mar*, Feb. 22, 1936: 6.

50. See the media's criticism of Yvone Cabral's efforts to imitate Carmen Miranda in "Microphonemas," *Beira-mar*, Feb. 2, 1935: 6; and the praise of the then upcoming singer and actress Durvalina Duarte as "the Carmen Miranda of 'Casa do Caboclo,'" the famous theater company situated in the central Tiradentes square in Rio in "Teatro," *Beira-mar*, May 4, 1935: 6. Several years later, the same publication praised the performances of actress Deonor Amar, calling her the "Carmen Miranda of Ipanema" as a point of reference, in "Radiofonices," *Beira-mar*, Mar. 15, 1939: 5.

51. There are several different versions of this story. Ruy Castro claims that after the chaos of the prostitution scene, the renowned comic Palitos (and uncle of soon-to-be famous comedian Oscarito) managed to calm the audience, Carmen came on stage to sing "Taí," and the show went on (Castro, *Carmen*, 59–60).

52. Lisa Shaw mentions that Miranda may have appeared in an earlier film, *A esposa do solteiro* (The bachelor's wife), in 1925 but that this is not verifiable (*Carmen*, 11).

53. André Filho is mostly remembered nowadays for the unofficial hymn of Rio, the *marcha* "Cidade maravilhosa" (Marvelous city), composed for Carnival 1935 and sung by Aurora Miranda in the film *Alô, alô, Brasil*.

54. *Cena muda*, Feb. 9, 1935: 5. Qtd. in Garcia, *O 'it verde e amarelo,'* 72.

55. *Beira-mar*, Apr. 6, 1935: 5.

56. See Alfredo Sade, *A batalha* [Rio de Janeiro], Feb. 7, 1935, and "Cartas mineiras de São Paulo," *Gazeta de notícias* [Rio de Janeiro], Mar. 19, 1935. Quoted in Gonzaga, *50 anos*, 44–45. See also "Alô, alô, Brasil!," *Correio da noite* [Rio de Janeiro], Jan. 29, 1935.

57. "Alô, alô, Brasil!," *Correio da noite* [Rio de Janeiro], Jan. 29, 1935 and "Alô, alô, Brasil!," *A plateia* [São Paulo], Feb. 11, 1935.

58. According to Garcia, Wallace Downey was more in tune with the realities of the market and favored releasing the popular carnivalesque films at the beginning of the year, followed in early winter by films with some relation to the June Festival (*O 'it verde e amarelo,'* 74). In *Estudantes*, one of Carmen Miranda's songs, "Sonho de papel" (Paper dream), is homage to the São João Festival.

59. One reviewer qualifies *Estudantes* as a "film full of unpardonable defects" and places the blame on Adhemar Gonzaga. "We are no longer in a position to accept a mediocre film only because it is a national production. We need to end this patriotism, that doesn't get us anywhere or bring any benefits to Brazilian cinema. . . . We no longer have the right to produce poor quality films. . . . We have all the technology at our disposal." "Estudantes, estreado," July 8, 1935. Unmarked newspaper cutting from the Cinédia Archive.

60. There is a strong trend of radio-influenced films in Hollywood, especially during the early 1930s, that included either fictive story lines about radio singers or plots as vehicles for genuine radio singers and broadcasters, along with innumerous mentions of radio broadcasting in general. See Etling, *Radio in the Movies*, 66–67.

61. Walter Rocha, "Filmando," *Beira-mar*, Aug. 1, 1936: 6.

62. For an overview of the success of these films, due in part to the ready-made viewing public accustomed to live radio shows and talent contests, see Shaw, *The Social History*, 54.

63. According to its pressbook, the film grossed almost three times what it cost to make during its first year alone, a record at the time that would only later be surpassed by *Bonequinha de seda* (Oduvaldo Vianna, 1936) and Miranda's last Brazilian film before her departure to Broadway, *Banana da terra* (Ruy Costa, 1939). *Alô, alô, carnaval! Pressbook* (2002): 11. Published for the restored film's screening and generously provided by Alice Gonzaga.

64. Walter Rocha, "Alô, alô, carnaval!," *Beira-mar*, Apr. 4, 1936: 6.

65. In the restored version of the film, "Cantoras do rádio" is the film's last number. However, according to the information included in the pressbook, in the original 1936 film version, the final number was "Manhãs de sol" (Sunny mornings), sung by Francisco Alves. When Adhemar Gonzaga reassembled the frames of the film in 1974, he placed "Cantoras do rádio" last, and this is the order that the restored version follows. *Alô, alô, carnaval! Pressbook* (2002): 11, 13.

66. See *Beira-mar*, Feb. 1, 1936: 5.

67. *Rebolar*, literally to "twist the hips," is a common samba female dance step where the hips sway in a circular motion while the dancer stays in her axis position. See Coelho, "Carmen Miranda," 137.

68. Shaw, drawing from João Luiz Vieira, develops an analysis of Miranda's performative style for this number as one that appears "very aware of the kinetic power of cinema, which she exploits to the maximum, producing a kind of hypnotic effect on the spectator" (*Carmen*, 32).

69. "Carnaval em Copacabana," *Beira-mar*, Mar. 11, 1939: 1.

70. For a discussion of the importance of *Alô, alô, carnaval!* in the development of Brazilian film, see Dennison and Shaw, *Popular Cinema in Brazil*, 38–45.

71. *Banana da terra* was the first of the Sonofilms fruit-themed musical films. It was followed by *Laranja da china* (1939) and *Abacaxi azul* (1944).

72. Tinhorão provides an overview of the plot but erroneously states that Miranda, in a duet with Almirante, sings "Boneca de pixe," which, as I discuss in Chapter 2, is pulled from the film at the last minute (*Música popular*, 257).

73. The *Diário carioca* of February 12, 1939, features a photo spread of Dircinha Batista and Carmen Miranda in their respective costumes (20).

74. "Folia cinematográfica, eis o que define bem Banana da terra," *Diário carioca*, Jan. 28, 1939: 7.

75. *Diário carioca*, Feb. 5, 1939: 20 and Feb. 12, 1939: 3.

76. Ibid., Feb. 12, 1939: 3.

77. Ibid., Feb. 18, 1939: 7.

78. Ibid., Feb. 16, 1939: 5 and *Correio da manhã*, Feb. 16, 1939: 14.

79. *Diário carioca*, Feb. 5, 1939: 20.

80. Ibid., Feb. 8, 1939: 7.

81. Ibid., Feb. 9, 1939: 7 and Feb. 12, 1939: 3.

82. See, respectively, the announcements for "Bailes de Carnaval" at the Alhambra in *Diário carioca*, Feb. 18, 1939: 10 and Feb. 3, 1940: 10; children dressed in *baiana* costumes in *Diário carioca*, Feb. 26, 1939; publicity still of Deo Maia in *Está tudo aí* in *Diário carioca*, Feb. 23, 1939: 7.

83. *Oito dias: Revista carioca*, Feb. 24, 1940: 24–25.

CHAPTER 2

1. As Skidmore discusses, the post Second World War wave of political liberation in Asia and Africa made any ideological conviction based on a whitening ideal unsustainable (*Black into White*, 214).

2. As an example of this racist discourse, see Afrânio Peixoto's *Minha terra, minha gente* (My land, my people), an educational text written in the mid-1910s that predicts within three centuries Brazil would be depleted of "the black blood imposed upon the nation" (220).

3. This model of integration would no longer be followed during the more significant black movement of the 1970s, which emphasized an adamant revalorization of Afro-Brazilianness and a rejection of the assimilative process. See "Notes on Racial and Political Inequality in Brazil" by Carlos Hasenbalg and Nelson do Valle Silva for a discussion of these movements set within the racial discourse of the 1930s and 1970s.

4. See Skidmore, *Black into White*, 180–85.

5. For an insightful discussion of Freyre at the helm of the transformation of attitudes toward miscegenation in Brazil, see Vianna, *The Mystery of Samba*, 53–66.

6. See Hanchard, "Culturalism," 67 and Davis, *Avoiding the Dark*, 79.

7. See L. Reis, "Negro em 'terra de branco,'" 41–42.

8. See Fernandes, *The Negro in Brazilian Society*, 187–88.

9. See Degler, *Neither Black nor White*, 139 and Skidmore, *Black into White*, 212.

10. See also Bastide and Fernandes, *Brancos e negros em São Paulo*, 301–4.

11. Although this body of research was conducted during the early 1950s, we can safely surmise that the racial discrimination was similar, and most likely worse, several decades earlier.

12. See Davis, *White Face*, xix.

13. For a history of Cuban blackface theater, see Robin Moore, chapter 2, "Minstrelsy in Havana. Music and Dance of the Teatro Vernáculo," 41–62.

14. De Chocolat was the more common name of João Cândido Ferreira, who apparently was known by this nickname while in France because of his dark skin color and his namesake Chocolat (1868–1917), a famous black performer of the Parisian circus and theater. De Chocolat continued to go by this name upon returning to Brazil, adding a foreign flare to his stage name.

15. See also Skidmore, *Black into White*, 212.

16. I am influenced here by Serge Gruzinski's discussion of mimicry in the colonial context, in which mimicry is a tool for integration and Westernization through "access to a market" (*The Mestizo Mind*, 59).

17. For a detailed discussion of this samba, see Coelho, "Carmen Miranda," 56. The last part of the samba is as follows:
    > In samba, whites break into pieces / In samba, a good black has a swell time / In samba, whites don't have a chance, my good friend / For samba—blacks are born to do it (qtd. in Davis, "Racial Parity," 194).

18. *Diário da tarde* [Recife], Oct. 31, 1932.

19. Here my reading is guided by hooks, *Black Looks*, 26.

20. On the process of cultural interaction, see Gruzinski, *The Mestizo Mind*, 26.

21. Roach insists on the term "circum-Atlantic" (49), as opposed to trans-Atlantic, to under-score the compelling truth of the cultural exchange built up across imperial networks, as discussed by Paul Gilroy.

22. Miranda and Almirante never recorded "Pirolito," either together or separately, but there is a recording of this carnivalesque *marcha* by Nílton Paz dating from January 1939.

23. Coelho believes that Miranda and Almirante performed the song "Pirolito" with the same costumes prepared for "Boneca de pixe" and in blackface, and although there is no proof this occurred, there is also no proof to the contrary ("Carmen Miranda," 77).

24. According to the *Anuário estatístico do Brasil 1939/1940*, 508,059 visitors came to the show that year, and it was open for forty-two days. If the report in the *Correio da manhã* is accurate, one-third of all visitors would have come to the show the day Miranda and Almirante performed.

25. *Correio popular* [Campinas], Jan. 31, 1939: 3. Qtd. in Cardoso, *Carmen Miranda*, 126.

26. *Diário carioca*, Feb. 25, 1939: 7.

27. "Joujoux and balangandãs" was the title of a song written by the popular composer Lamartine Babo for this revue, and it ended up giving the show its name. The film *Joujoux e balangandãs* included another Ari Barroso hit, "Aquarela do Brasil" (Watercolor of Brazil), and the participation of Dorival Caymmi, no longer the unknown Bahian com-poser, with two other songs. One of the film's recurring themes is the *baiana*, also pro-jected in the songs "Nós temos balangandãs" (We have *balangandãs*) and "Yayá baianinha" (Yayá the young *baiana*), fitting with the widespread *baiana* vogue of late-1930s Brazilian theater and cinema. Here a new twist is added to the theme with the juxtaposition of chic French references evoked in both the title and the inclusion of musical numbers such as "Quartier Latin" (the Latin Quarter), "La Lampe" (The lamp), and "Muguets de Paris" (Lilies of Paris).

28. The December 1938 issue of *Cinearte* features a page of New Year wishes from celebrities. Alongside Almirante, Carlos Galhardo, Dircinha Batista, Cesar Ladeira and many others, Miranda wishes the magazine all the happiness in the world ("um milhão de felicidades") and signs the greeting from "Boneca de pixe, Carmen Miranda" (13).

29. The maracatu choreographed pageant (a black tradition brought from Recife to Fortaleza, the capital of Ceará, in the mid-1930s) faced the problem of representing black person-ages with prominently white and brown-skinned Cearenses, and the solution was to introduce blackface, referred to as *falso negrume* (false blackness). See Ronald Conner, "Brazilian Blackface."

30. For a reading of blackface that takes into account both gender and sexuality, see Lori Harrison-Kahan, *The White Negress*, 23–57.

31. According to Mahar, most of the blackface routines confirm that the real essence of minstrelsy was burlesque (*Behind the Burnt Cork Mask*, 335).

32. This fits with Mahar's claim that "minstrel performers usually avoided intellectually difficult issues, preferring instead more direct approaches to their comic material" (*Behind*, 346).

33. For a discussion of minstrelsy, gender roles, cross-dressing, and misogyny, see Mahar, *Behind*, 283; 307–11.

34. On Broadway, for the most part, it would appear that Miranda wore a light foundation, but nothing very dark. In my archival research, I only found two references to her per-forming with distinctively dark make-up. In an article for the *New York Herald Tribune*,

"Gloom Alternates with Joy in the Broadway Box Office, but Twelve Going Concerns is Really not Bad for July," Herbert Drake refers to Miranda's "dark tan" (July 16, 1939: E1), and in an article in the *Philadelphia Record*, February 14, 1940, "Carmen is Good Neighbor Policy in Person," Helen S. Albertson comments that Miranda "still looked fascinating despite a *heavy copper make-up* and a most fantastic mouth" (my emphasis).

CHAPTER 3

1. "Potatoe's Miranda, Brought from Rio, Takes Broadway with an Exciting Flourish," *Houston Chronicle*, July 2, 1939 and "Up from Rio," *The New Yorker*, Oct. 28, 1939: 15. See also an interview with Claiborne Foster published in "Life in Rio is more Exciting than the Stage to Claiborne Foster," *New York Post*, Oct. 21, 1939.

2. The cost of Miranda's buy-out from her Shubert contract varies between $60,000 and $100,000, depending on the source. Regardless of the exact dollar amount, for the time period it was an astronomical amount of money and corroborates Miranda's status as a megastar. See F. Hirsch, *The Boys from Syracuse*, 189.

3. Carmen Miranda's contract with Select Theatres Corporation, dated March 2, 1939. Shubert Archive, clipping files.

4. Letter from Jay Rice to Lee Shubert, March 27, 1939. My emphasis. Shubert Archive, clipping files.

5. Ibid.

6. "Carmen Miranda Coming Here," *New York Herald Tribune*, Apr. 22, 1939.

7. *Cincinnati Enquirer*, July 2, 1939.

8. Ibid.

9. Joe Flynn, "La Miranda Away from the Footlights," press release, n.d.

10. *Hellzapoppin'* ran from September 22, 1938, to December 17, 1941. See S. Green, *Broadway Musicals*, 103.

11. Two examples of this trend were the very successful Irving Berlin/Moss Hart "newspaper" revue *As Thousands Cheer* (1933) and Harold Rome's *Pins and Needles*—even more socially conscious but equally entertaining. See S. Green, *Broadway Musicals*, 2–3; 77.

12. The revue would be cut down to one hour and fifteen minutes when it was taken on the road to Chicago and later brought to the World's Fair as a tabloid with four performances daily. Several of the original cast left the show at this point, including Miranda, Bobby Clark, and Luella Gear. See Cecil Smith, "The Season in Chicago," 17.

13. Brooks Atkinson, "*The Streets of Paris* Moves to Broadway," *New York Times*, June 20, 1939: 29.

14. In the *New York Herald Tribune*, July 16, 1939, and June 30, 1939, respectively.

15. Herbert Drake, *New York Herald Tribune*, June 30, 1939: 16.

16. "*Streets of Paris* Opens Tonight at Broadhurst—Theatrical Business Shows Upturn," *New York Times*, June 19, 1939: 12; "Who's Who in the Cast," Playbill for *The Streets of Paris*. Shubert Archive, clipping file.

17. See "*The Streets of Paris* Corrected Script," Feb. 10, 1940. Shubert Archive.

18. Jean Sablon, sometimes referred to as the French Bing Crosby, was extremely popular as a singer and actor, second only to Maurice Chevalier; Yvonne Bouvier was relatively unknown.

19. Lyrics from *The Streets of Paris* clipping file, Shubert Archive.

20. Henry F. Pringle, "Rolling up from Rio," *Colliers*, Aug. 12, 1939: 23.

21. *Sunday Mirror*, July 23, 1939; *PIC*, Aug. 22, 1939: 21; "Broadway Likes Miranda's Piquant Portuguese Songs," *LIFE*, July 17, 1939: 32 and 34; and "Broadway got her from Brazil," *Tribune*, June 25, 1939.

22. See, for example, Elliot Norton, "Brazilian Beauty Arrives in Hub," *Boston Post*, May 29, 1939: 11.

23. *New York World-Telegram*, June 10, 1939. My emphasis.

24. See also the *New York Herald Tribune*, June 9, 1939: 18.

25. "The Aging Broadway Season Takes a New Lease on Life," *New York Herald Tribune*, June 18, 1939.

26. "News of the Theater," *New York Herald Tribune*, June 13, 1939: 16.

27. "A New Star in the White Lights on Broadway," *Times*, July 2, 1939: RP8.

28. See *Sunday Mirror* [New York], July 23, 1939; Herbert Drake, *New York Herald Tribune*, June 30, 1939: 16; and "Brazilian Bombshell," *PIC*, Aug. 22, 1939: 21.

29. "The 'Sous'-American Way: Carmen Miranda is Inca Goddess of Good Luck to the Cast of 'The Streets of Paris'—And to Herself," *Brooklyn Daily Eagle*, July 9, 1939.

30. *New York Journal and American*, Dec. 2, 1939. The wording of this article is identical to an undated press release by C. P. Greneker, also in the Shubert Archive clipping files.

31. Herbert Drake, *New York Herald Tribune*, June 30, 1939: 16. My emphasis.

32. *Sunday News*, Nov. 16, 1941: 72.

33. C. P. Greneker, "Carmen Miranda's nickname," undated press release (circa August 1941).

34. Herbert Drake, "Gloom Alternates with Joy in the Broadway Box Office, but Twelve Going Concerns is Really not Bad for July," *New York Herald Tribune*, July 16, 1939: E1.

35. *Sunday News*, Nov. 16, 1941: 72.

36. Robert D. McFadden, "Peter Kihss, Reporter for 49 Years, is Dead at 72," *New York Times*, Dec. 30, 1984: 18.

37. Peter Kihss, "Gestures Put It Over for Miranda. 'Con Movimiento'—That's Her Creation," *World-Telegram*, July 8, 1939.

38. Ibid.

39. Herbert Drake, *New York Herald Tribune*, June 30, 1939: 16. Irene Sharaff had been working on Broadway for over ten years when she designed the costumes for *The Streets of Paris* (Owen, *Costume Design on Broadway*, 143).

40. *Women's Wear Daily*, June 22, 1939: 2.

41. Michel Mok, "Ogling New Yorkers, to Carmen Miranda, are the Best Caballeros in Pan-America," *New York Post*, June 23, 1939.

42. *Newark Evening News*, July 14, 1939.

43. *Where to Go*, Dec. 9, 1939.

44. *New York World Telegram*, May 17, 1939.

45. Letter from Jay Rice to Lee Shubert, March 27, 1939. Shubert Archive, clipping files.

46. *New York World-Telegram*, May 17, 1939.

47. Joe Flynn, "La Miranda Away From the Footlights," undated press release. Shubert Archive.

48. *Boston Evening Transcript*, June 3, 1939.

49. Michel Mok, "Ogling New Yorkers, to Carmen Miranda, are the Best Caballeros in Pan-America," *New York Post*, June 23, 1939.

50. One such word was "air-condeeshioend," which she apparently memorized off a "sign board." *Cincinnati Enquirer*, July 2, 1939.

51. *Cincinnati Enquirer*, July 2, 1939.

52. Brooks Atkinson, "'The Streets of Paris' Moves to Broadway," *New York Times*, June 20, 1939: 29.

53. See, for example, *Cincinnati Enquirer*, July 2, 1939.

54. For instance, on the "Playbill" the song "South American Way" is indicated as sung by a large group of performers along with Carmen Miranda (listed in capital letters). The "Playbill" indicates the number is: "Sung by Ramon Vinay, Margo, Kate and Evelyn Hylton, Della Lind, The Show Girls; and danced by Jo and Jeanne Readinger, Gower and Jeanne, The Dancing Girls and Boys, and CARMEN MIRANDA." See also *Colliers*, Aug. 12, 1939: 23.

55. *St. Louis Post*, Oct. 29, 1939.

56. "Brazilian Songstress Who Can't Speak English Giving Blase Times Square a Thrill," *Newark Evening News*, July 14, 1939.

57. See Joyce Dana, "Carmen, Rio Style. This One Has a Last Name (It's Miranda). And She's the Good Neighbor Policy Itself," *Boston Evening Transcript*, June 3, 1939; and *Newark Evening News*, July 14, 1939.

58. "Carmen Gets Unneeded Vocabulary," *Parade*, Oct. 5, 1941.

59. "Carmen Miranda Loaves America—And Vice Versa," *Sunday News*, Nov. 16, 1941: 72.

60. Harry Evans, "Hollywood Diary," *The Family Circle*, Aug. 8, 1941: 10.

61. *Evening Bulletin*, February 1, 1940.

62. Julian Dibbell, "Notes on Carmen," *Village Voice*, Oct. 29, 1991.

63. This micro-managing by Zanuck, one of Hollywood's towering figures for almost half a century who presided over Twentieth Century-Fox from 1935 to 1956 as vice president in charge of production, was not uncharacteristic. A key person in the creation of the Carmen Miranda film-image, Zanuck was known for his strong input regarding story construction and script detail, reading drafts of the scripts and making his own notations in pencil directly on the pages prior to a story conference. The Zanuck conference notes have been preserved along with the various drafts of the scripts, providing an insightful record of the evolution of a project and the modeling of characters and plot. Zanuck produced four of Miranda's films, namely her first three Twentieth Century-Fox films, *Down Argentine Way* (1940), *That Night in Rio* (1941), *Week-End in Havana* (also 1941), and then *If I'm Lucky* (1946).

64. Conference with Zanuck on First Draft Continuity of September 25, 1940, dated Sept. 26 and 30, 1940. UCLA Fox Files 2088-3.

65. Marian Cooper, "English the Hard Way," *Screen Life*, Dec. 1941.

66. Thomas Nord Riley, "South American Rave," *Screen Life,* Oct. 1941: 35.

67. *Hollywood*, Sept. 1941: 20.

68. For a discussion of these terms, with an expressed preference for the "Brazilian Bombshell," see *Modern Screen*, May 1944: 80.

69. Candide, "Love thy Neighbor," *Daily Mirror*, May 26, 1939.

70. "Bombers of Good Will," *Time*, Nov. 20, 1939: 14.

71. Joe Flynn, "La Miranda Away from the Footlights," undated press release, Shubert Archive.

72. Joyce Dana, "Carmen, Rio Style," *Boston Evening Transcript*, June 3, 1939. The subtitle to this article stresses Miranda's incarnation of the Good Neighbor Policy: "This One Has a Last Name (It's Miranda) and She's the Good Neighbor Policy Itself."

73. "Broadway got her from Brazil," *Tribune*, June 25, 1939.

74. *Newark Evening News*, July 14, 1939.

75. C. P. Greneker, press release, Aug. 19, 1941.

76. Maurice Zolotow, "South of the Border—On Broadway," *New York Times*, Feb. 18, 1940: SM6.

77. For a detailed discussion of Hollywood's portrayal of Latin American music in the Carmen Miranda films, the incongruity of context, and the simplification and stylization of lyrics and music, see Clark, "Doing the Samba," 266–68 and 270–72.

78. Dunn discusses Miranda's music for export in comparison to the "cool sophistication" (7) of bossa nova of the late 1950s, drawing from Oswald de Andrade's call for a "poetry for export," a trope that Dunn sees particularly fit as a synecdoche for all forms of cultural production but especially popular music (*Brutality Garden*, 27).

79. "Don't Wiggle," *FRIDAY*, Mar. 15, 1940: 11. It is highly ironic that several years later, in the 1948 MGM film *A Date with Judy*, Miranda's character (Rosita) teaches Wallace Beery (Melvin Foster) to dance the rhumba and declares how easy it is: "a little wiggle here and a little wiggle there, all you have to do is get the right wiggle at the right time!" a dialogue that translates this perception of Latin dance as nothing more than a "wiggle."

80. *Boston Herald*, May 29, 1939.

81. Nona Baldwin, "The Samba Down in Rio. The Voodoo Dancers of Brazil Created a Rhythm for the Days of Carnival," *New York Times*, Mar. 16, 1941: XX7.

82. *Pranove*, May 1939: 19–20.

83. Here Bianca Freire-Medeiros is drawing, respectively, from Mary Louise Pratt, "Arts of the Contact Zone," 33–40 and Gilles Deleuze, "Mediators."

84. Throughout this discussion I am indebted to Charles Ramírez Berg's theory of stereotyping, especially the concept of homogeneity and stereotypes as uncontextualized and ahistorical creators of facile abbreviations through repetition. In Miranda's case, her stereotype remained at the fantastical, performative level and was less believable at face value, unlike some stereotypes that tend to lead to a determined course of action (*Latino Images in Film*, 16–21).

85. On stereotypes as creators of facile abbreviations through repetition, see Berg, *Latino Images in Film*, 17–18.

86. C. P. Greneker, undated press release [approximate date November–December 1941]; *New York Sun*, Oct. 4, 1939.

87. All guest appearances were announced in the "Today on the Radio" column of the *New York Times*.

88. "Música quente para os 'Yankees'" (Hot music for the "Yankees"), *Correio da manhã*, May 5, 1939: 14.

89. "Brazil pledged to participate in World's Fair," *Long Island Daily Star*, July 2, 1937. NYWF archives, box 1952, folder 4.

90. *Cinearte*, Dec. 1, 1938, and *Cinearte*, Mar. 15, 1939: 14.

91. Coelho claims that the Brazilian government paid for the whole six-member band to travel with Miranda, even though Shubert only guaranteed employment for four ("Carmen Miranda," 111).

92. See the *Official Souvenir Book*, the New York World's Fair 1939.

93. "News of the New York World's Fair," *Beira-mar*, Apr. 1, 1939: 7.

94. Original memo dated April 12, 1939, addressed to Armando Vidal, unsigned (probably from Olin Downes, Director of Music for the New York World's Fair), submitting the first of two programs to be conducted by Burle Marx for the Brazilian Government in the World Fair's Hall of Music, May 4, 1939. NYWF Archives, box 302, folder 3.

95. Original memo dated November 14, 1939, from the secretary of A. K. Morgan, public relations for the Fair, to a certain Miss E. Pearson, who had inquired about the Mardi Gras Queens.

96. Original Western Union Direct Wire from Décio de Moura, Secretary General of the Brazilian delegation at the Fair, to Gerald Cole, Supervisor of Import Clearance (and often serving as liaison between the delegations and the Fair commission). July 13, 1939.

97. "Radiofonices," *Beira-mar*, June 10, 1939: 5.

98. A memo dated August 24, 1939, from the desk of the Special Events organizer for the Fair, Guy Robinson, to the Associated Press (via A. H. Uhl) makes specific mention of "Miss Carmen Miranda—well-known artist" as part of the talent on the Coffee Day program.

99. Original memo from Saul Richman of Select Theatres Corporation (on behalf of the Shuberts) to Mr. Schwartzman, Special Events Department for the Fair. Oct. 24, 1939.

100. Original photograph, NYWF Archives, box 2002, folder 1.

101. *Cena muda*, Feb. 20, 1940.

102. Box 1553, folder 8. Article: "Brazilian restaurant," featured in *Gotham Life, The Official Metropolitan Guide* 32, no. 5, Aug. 25–31, 1940: 15 and 18. On the overlapping dynamic between Miranda and Houston, see Seigel, *Uneven Encounters*, 172–78.

103. Malcolm Johnson, "Café Life in New York. Carmen Miranda, Brazilian Singer Star, Will Entertain at Waldorf's Sert Room," *New York Sun*, Oct. 4, 1939.

104. *New York Herald Tribune*, Oct. 20, 1939: 21.

105. Malcolm Johnson, "Carmen Miranda Still News at the Waldorf—The Paradise Show Revised," *New York Sun*, Oct. 17, 1939.

106. See, for example, Theodore Strauss, "News of Night Clubs," *New York Times*, Oct. 8, 1939: 136, and a column signed RWD, "Dining and Dancing," *New York Herald Tribune*, Oct. 7, 1939: 11A.

107. "To Sing in Sert Room. Carmen Miranda Appearing: Many Make Dinner Reservations," *New York Herald Tribune*, Oct. 11, 1939: 27; "Dining and Dancing," *New York Herald Tribune*, Nov. 4, 1939: 9.

108. "Despite Cold and the Snow it was a Hot Moving Day when Brazilian Singer Packed into Club," *Daily Mirror* [New York], Jan. 19, 1940.

109. RWD, "Dining and Dancing," *New York Herald Tribune*, Feb. 7, 1940.

110. These included events such as the Fresh Air Fund Benefit (August 1939), an aid benefit for refugee Jews in Palestine (November 1939), a benefit for the Alice Chapin Adoption

Nursery (October 1939), the Beaux Arts Diamond Ball (January 1940), and a Help Finland Cabaret (February 1940). See, respectively, "Aid for Fresh Air Fund," *New York Herald Tribune*, Aug. 14, 1939: 10; "'Night of Stars' Nets $90,000 for Palestine," *New York Herald Tribune*, Nov. 16, 1939: 17A; *New York Herald Tribune*, Oct. 27, 1939: 25; "Carats for Carmen," *New York Post*, Jan. 25, 1940; and "Cabaret and Ball Given to Aid Finns," *The New York Times*, Feb. 8, 1940: 29.

111. *New York Herald Tribune*, Oct. 5, 1941. The performance also included Bill Robinson tap dancing on Adolf Hitler's coffin, in a true spirit of celebratory victory.

112. Carlyle Burrows, "Notes and Comments on Events in Art," *New York Herald Tribune*, Feb. 25, 1940: E8.

113. Exactly how much Miranda earned per performance depended on the different venues, averaging around $700 per evening. Some examples include $700 at the Waldorf, $455 at the Versailles, $753 at the Colony Club in Chicago, and $2250 per week at Chez Paris, also in Chicago, which had the reputation as the finest club in Chicago.

114. C. P. Greneker, untitled press release, Aug. 20, 1941. Shubert Archive.

115. Albert W. Wilson, "All Credit To Them For They Get The Cash. More Foreign Gal Adepts (sic) at Prying Open Uncle Sam's Purse," *Evening Bulletin*, Feb. 1, 1940.

116. "Who's who in the Cast," *Sons O' Fun* playbill, 32.

117. The *New York Times* of April 30, 1943, reports that by the end of April 1943 the show had reached its six-hundredth performance, then showing at the Forty-Sixth Street Theatre. Only five musicals had played that number of performances to New York audiences. This record had only been topped by their own *Hellzapoppin'* (1404 performances), *Pins and Needles* (1,108), *Irene* (670), and *Student Prince* (607).

118. A photograph that had wide circulation featured Miranda between Olsen and Johnson with a bird's nest and duck on top of her turban and Johnson in a pose about to crack an egg on her head. In the show, Ella Logan, not Miranda, performs the song "Happy in Love" from this scene.

119. *New York Herald Tribune*, Dec. 2, 1941; *Variety*, Dec. 3, 1941.

120. Richard Watts Jr., "They're in Again," *New York Herald Tribune*, Dec. 2, 1941: 24.

121. Kelcey Allen, *Women's Wear Daily*, Dec. 2, 1941.

122. C. P. Greneker, undated press release for *Sons O' Fun*. Shubert Archive, press files.

123. See John Mason Brown, "Sons O' Fun is Another Hellzapoppin, Only More So," *World-Telegram*, Dec. 2, 1941: 18; Richard Lockridge, "'Sons O' Fun' a New Olsen and Johnson, is Offered at the Winter Garden," *The Sun*, Dec. 2, 1941: 26; and Wilella Waldorf, "Sons O' Fun, a New Olsen and Johnson Show, Reaches Broadway," *New York Post*, Dec. 2, 1941: 12.

124. *New York Herald Tribune*, Dec. 2, 1941: 24.

125. In several of the playbills, the title of the song is changed to "Quiri-Quiri-Quiri. La Pelea de Gallos" (Cock-a-doodle-doo. The cocks' fight), but the lyrics are the same.

126. In the playbill for the Winter Garden of December 2, 1941, "Canguru" is cut.

127. John Anderson, "Sons O' Fun Opens at the Winter Garden," *New York Journal-American*, Dec. 2, 1941: 10.

128. "Plays on Broadway," *Variety*, Dec. 3, 1941.

129. C. P. Greneker, "Costumes of Sons O' Fun," undated press release. Shubert Archive, clipping files.

130. Brooks Atkinson, "Olsen and Johnson Hop in with Carmen Miranda and a Basket of Gags Called 'Sons O' Fun,'" *New York Times*, Dec. 2, 1941: 28.

131. Kelcey Allen, article in *Women's Wear Daily*, Dec. 2, 1941.

132. According to the playbill, Rosario is the daughter of a dealer in bull-fighting trappings, and Antonio is her first cousin. They had appeared previously in the film *Ziegfeld Girl* and had created a sensation among the fashionable set at the Waldorf-Astoria over the previous year. They are referred to as "nimble-footed youngsters, not yet out of their teens" (36).

133. *Sunday News*, Nov. 16, 1941: 76.

134. Brooks Atkinson, "Olsen and Johnson Hop in with Carmen Miranda and a Basket of Gags Called 'Sons O' Fun,'" *New York Times*, Dec. 2, 1941: 28.

135. *Sunday News*, Nov. 16, 1941: 72.

136. "Miranda IS the South American Way," *New York Journal and American*, Dec. 2, 1939. Shubert Archive, clipping files.

CHAPTER 4

1. Escapist allusions are clearly evoked in the following titles: *Down Argentine Way* (1940), *That Night in Rio* (with the working title "Road to Rio") (1941), *Weekend in Havana* (1941), *Springtime in the Rockies* (1942), and later, at the tail end of the "escapist vogue," two non-Twentieth Century-Fox films: *Copacabana* (1947) and *Nancy Goes to Rio* (1950). For discussion of the importance of attractive titles for films, see Handel, *Hollywood Looks at its Audience*, 36.

2. As early as the mid-teens, studios were aware of film's role in shaping consumer habits of home-interior decoration and fashion, and explicit business tie-ins soon followed suit. See J. Allen, "The Film Viewer as Consumer" 487–88.

3. Details of the competition appeared in *Screen Guide*, Aug. 1947: 18, opposite a publicity page for *Copacabana*.

4. See Lipovetsky for a discussion of this attachment to pure images ("The Empire of Fashion," 186).

5. Average movie-going numbers between 1935 and 1945 vary somewhere between eighty and eighty-eight million weekly, according to the source. See Gomery, *The Hollywood Studio System*, 82–85 and Thorp, *America at the Movies*, 1.

6. "Weekend in Havana is Swell Dish," *Los Angeles Herald Express*, Oct. 24, 1941.

7. The pressbook was an elaborate, illustrated trade publication that was sent to exhibitors and newspapers. It was full of suggestions on how to market the film, such as ideas for commercial tie-ins, ready-made newspaper ads, and prefabricated movie reviews. See Rebello and Allen, *Reel Art*, 37; Kobal and Wilson, *Foyer Pleasure*, 9; and Gomery, *The Hollywood Studio System*, 69.

8. Unlike what would happen in later years, at this time the competitions specify female participants, despite the explicit gender-bending of Miranda's portrayal.

9. Pressbook for *Greenwich Village*, 6

10. Eckert discusses the dominant role of women in the economy, the gender bias of film tie-ins, and the prominence of women stars and starlets in the star system ("The Carole Lombard in Macy's Window," 119).

11. See Rebello and Allen, *Reel Art*, 13–14.

12. For a detailed discussion of some of the common practices among media reviewers, see Crafton, "The Jazz Singer's Reception," 460–78.

13. For Ellis the narrative image of a film is "the film's circulation outside its performances in cinemas" ("Visible Fictions," 31).

14. Miranda's deleted "True to the Navy" musical number can be viewed on *Hidden Hollywood II: More Treasures from the 20th Century Fox Vaults* (Image Entertainment, 2002). The lighthouse headdress is still visible in one of the scenes in the character's dressing room in the released version of the film.

15. See Robinson, "Introduction," 3.

16. Handel discusses these challenges due to the necessity of promoting each film individually and the importance of a successful opening for the film's entire reception (*Hollywood Looks at its Audience*, 75–78).

17. *Screenland*, Nov. 1940: 18.

18. The exposed leg was more typical of Miranda's costar Betty Grable and was begun by one of Fox's most prominent illustrators, Alberto Vargas (1896–1982), who began painting the leading stars of the Ziegfeld Follies in 1919 and worked at some point for Paramount, Warner Brothers, MGM, and Fox. His artwork became internationally known through his 1940s *Esquire* magazine covers and yearly calendar. Among his most famed Art Deco designs are the posters for *Moon over Miami* (1941). While it is not clear whether Vargas worked on these pictures of Miranda, the style is certainly inspired by his artwork.

19. See Edwards, *The International Film Poster*, 64.

20. Robert Heide and John Gilman provide examples of Miranda's prominence in the posters for *Serenata Argentina* and *A la Habana me voy*, the Spanish versions of *Down Argentine Way* and *Weekend in Havana* (*Starstruck*, 163).

21. For a discussion of marketing strategies, see Ellis, *Visible Fictions*, 26–34.

22. *Silver Screen*, May 1941: 18.

23. "The Shadow Stage," *Photoplay*, June 1941: 115.

24. Pressbook for *The Gang's All Here*, "Catchlines," n.p.

25. *Screenland*, Oct. 1943: 39.

26. One such poster appeared in *Variety*, Oct. 29, 1943, and others are included in the pressbook for *The Gang's All Here*.

27. The publicity materials for *The Gang's All Here* include a caricature drawing of Miranda with the caption "combustible Carmen Miranda . . . brings her volcanic high jinx to 'The Girls He Left Behind.'" ("The Girls He Left Behind" was the film's working title.)

28. See Edwards, *The International Film Poster*, 68, and Schapiro and Chierichetti, *The Movie Poster Book*, 13–14 for a detailed discussion of the different studios' poster techniques.

29. See, for example, the publicity poster included in *Motion Picture*, May 1941: 11.

30. This is typical of the hierarchy embedded in the design of the Hollywood posters. See Robinson, "Introduction," 6.

31. "Review of *If I'm Lucky*," *Variety*, Aug. 28, 1946.

32. Quoted in a press release from the desk of Dannenbaum at Twentieth Century-Fox. N.d.
33. See Walker for a discussion of the industry's neglect of the black population's value to the box office until the late 1960s (*Stardom*, 347; 352).
34. Cesar Romero (1907–1994) was born in New York to a Cuban mother and Italian father.
35. See Stempel, *American Audiences*, 183.
36. I was able to screen the trailers for all of Miranda's Twentieth Century-Fox films with the exception of *Springtime in the Rockies*, *Four Jills in a Jeep*, and *Greenwich Village*. Handel discusses how a trailer's effectiveness depends not only on its skillful composition, but also on the stars' popularity, the story type, and the title (*Hollywood Looks at its Audience*, 88).
37. I am borrowing this expression "visual shorthand" from Gaines, "Costume," 204.
38. See Munich for a discussion of the term "look" in relation to both fashion and film and the implicit act of deliberate seeing ("Introduction," 2).
39. See Schweitzer, *When Broadway was the Runway*, 226.
40. A review of *Something for the Boys* published in *Screen Guide* in November 1944 suggests that "the spectacular show La Miranda puts on is calculated to please masculine movie-goers of every type, in and out of uniform." "Something for the Boys," *Screen Guide*, Nov. 1944: 29.
41. See Lipovetsky for the importance of communicating a "brand-name personality" (*The Empire of Fashion*, 158).
42. "Brief Reviews," *Photoplay*, Apr. 1944: 24; 119–24.
43. Adele Whitely Fletcher, "Who is Hollywood's Best Dressed Woman?," *Photoplay*, Mar. 1943: 84.
44. "Here's Hollywood," *Screenland*, Mar. 1941.
45. In *Photoplay* of November 1942, Miranda is featured dancing with Cesar Romero at "Mrs. Miniver's" New York dance club, shown in a mink coat and shiny turban; in "Cal York's 'Inside Stuff'" in *Photoplay* of April 1945, she is photographed dancing with Ray Bolger at the Trocadero (15); in *Silver Screen* of August 1945, she is pictured in a turban and star-shaped earrings, dancing with Chandra Kaly, at Ciro's (48). These are some among many other examples that appear throughout her contract years at Twentieth Century-Fox.
46. In the gossip section of *Movie Story Magazine*, November 1944, Miranda is pictured with butterflies on top of her hair and Michael O'Shea adding a basket of flowers, with the following caption: "Posies go nicely with butterflies" (25). See also "Tops in Toppers," *Movie Life*, Feb. 1945: 16–17.
47. Carl A. Schroeder, "Hollywood Life," *Screen Guide*, Mar. 1944: 4.
48. An exception to this very positive response was a letter to the editor of the *Dallas Morning News* who likened her "scarlet slash" of a mouth and bodily undulations to those of a demimondaine and viewed her as immoral. John Rosenfield, "Just Brand New Slant on Carmen Miranda," *Dallas Morning News*, Apr. 30, 1941.
49. Ida Zeitlin also refers to the costume Miranda wears on the stage at Grauman's Chinese Theatre as "the plumage of a bird of paradise" in "Sous American Sizzler," *Motion Picture*, Sept. 1941: 19.
50. Harry Brand, Vital Statistics on *Weekend in Havana*, n.p.
51. Pressbook for *Greenwich Village*. Margaret Herrick Library files.

52. "Greenwich Village. Gay Colorful Musical," *Silver Screen*, Nov. 1944: 97.

53. "Carmen Miranda's Latest Film May Set Double-Exposure Mode," *New York Herald Tribune*, Nov. 26, 1944.

54. *Movies*, Dec. 1944: 41.

55. Pressbook for *Doll Face*. Margaret Herrick Library files.

56. "'Souse' American Carmen Miranda takes to North American Ways," Pressbook for *A Date with Judy*. Margaret Herrick Library files.

57. Memo from Herbert L. Kneeter to William Klein, Sept. 22, 1939. Shubert Archive, legal files.

58. This request was signed, "Ben Kanrich on behalf of J. O. S. Corporation." Shubert Archive, legal files.

59. Helen S. Albertson, "Carmen is Good Neighbor Policy in Person," *Philadelphia Record*, Feb. 14, 1940.

60. This is reported in the pressbook for Miranda's penultimate film, *A Date with Judy*, in a column titled "Souse' American Carmen Miranda takes to North American Ways." Margaret Herrick Library files.

61. Documents from the Fifth Avenue Association during the war period show the involvement of women in the designing of New York's store windows (Whitaker, 126).

62. "Miranda, The New Stage Sensation, Good Reason to Check Brazilian Fashions," *Women's Wear Daily*, June 22, 1939: 2.

63. Undated press release by Reuben Rabinovitch, circa October 1939. Shubert Archive, press files.

64. Elizabeth R. Duval, "New Things in City Shops: Costume Jewelry Runs Riot," *New York Times*, July 23, 1939: D7.

65. *New York Journal and American*, Dec. 2, 1939.

66. Helen S. Albertson, "Carmen is Good Neighbor Policy in Person," *Philadelphia Record*, Feb. 14, 1940.

67. "Fashionable Footsteps," *Photoplay*, June 1939.

68. Darr Smith, *Los Angeles Daily News*, May 22, 1951.

69. Unmarked newspaper clipping from the Shubert Archive.

70. Betty Harris, "The South American Way," *Modern Screen*, Mar. 1941: 41; 90–91.

71. Pressbook for *Greenwich Village*, 16. Margaret Herrick Library files.

72. See Berry, *Screen Style*, 21.

73. See Doane, *The Desire to Desire*, 25 and Ohmer, "Female Spectatorship," 54.

74. "Carmen Miranda Sets Fiesta Fashion Trend," Pressbook for *That Night in Rio*, 16.

75. Undated photograph in the Carmen Miranda museum collection, probably late 1939 or early 1940.

76. Joan Crawford, Lana Turner, and Sally Eilers are all pictured wearing turbans in "Topics for Gossip," *Silver Screen*, Jan. 1940: 21; Ginger Rogers in *Silver Screen*, April 1940: 19; and Claire Trevor in *Silver Screen*, July 1940: 66.

77. Duncan Underhill, "I'm Ter-ree-fic," *Hollywood*, Sept. 1941: 20.

78. Letter to Hugh L. Ducker from Lee Schreiber (Executive Manager at Fox), Sept. 1, 1944. Brastoff was hired as a "designer, stylist, fashion expert and assistant to head of wardrobe department." Twentieth Century-Fox Legal Files, Sascha Brastoff Box #1107, File 6066. UCLA Special Collections.

79. Harry Brand, press release, n.d. When Sascha Brastoff impersonated Miranda in the screen version of "Winged Victory," he was at the time a twenty-four-year-old former GI.

80. Published on the same day, the *Variety* reviewer claims the film provides "a generous showing of Carmen Miranda in characteristic song and dance routine," while *The Hollywood Reporter* claims that "as far as Carmen Miranda is concerned, she is hardly in the picture." "Review of 'If I'm Lucky,'" *Variety*, Aug. 28, 1946; *Hollywood Reporter*, Aug. 28, 1946.

81. *Hollywood*, Sept 1941: 20.

82. Virginia Wood, "Carmen's Strangest Experience," *Motion Picture*, Dec. 1944: 10; 12.

83. Berry, *Screen Style*, 196n40.

84. "Gowns Have Unusual Motif," Pressbook for *Down Argentine Way*, 9. Margaret Herrick Library files.

85. "Carmen Miranda Sets Fiesta Fashion Trend," Pressbook for *That Night in Rio*, 16. Margaret Herrick Library files.

86. Paul C. Mooney, Jr. "That Night in Rio," *Motion Picture Herald*, Mar. 8, 1941.

87. Here Shaw is drawing from Huggan, *The Postcolonial Exotic*, 13.

88. William R. Weaver, "Down Argentine Way, Study in Latin Rhythms," *Morning Herald*, Oct. 5, 1940.

89. On the studio's quest for authenticity, see "That Night in Rio Filmed; Romantic, Glamorous" and "Introduces Cafezinho," Pressbook for *That Night in Rio*, 16, 19; Harry Brand, "Vital Statistics on *Week-End in Havana*," n.p.; and Brian O'Neil, "The Demands of Authenticity."

90. "That Night in Rio Gorgeous Color. All Merit Praise in Lavish Hit Show," *Hollywood Reporter*, Mar. 7, 1941.

91. Bob Fredericks, "Fiery Carmen Adds Fuel to Flaming Film," *Miami Herald*, Mar. 14, 1941.

92. The Hays office banned the phrase "sex appeal" and suggested "oomph" or "it" as preferred alternatives (Thorp, *America at the Movies*, 65).

93. "Review: That Night in Rio," *News*, Nov. 28, 1940.

94. *Photoplay*, Dec. 1941: 103.

95. As an example, see Harry MacArthur, "Torrid Carmen Miranda Brightens New Musical," *Washington DC Evening Star*, Nov. 7, 1941.

96. "Carmen Miranda Loaves America—And Vice Versa," *Sunday News*, Nov. 16, 1941: 72.

97. Harry Brand, "Vital Statistics for *Springtime in the Rockies*," 1. Margaret Herrick Library files.

98. Harry Brand, "Vital Statistics for *Springtime in the Rockies*," 2. Margaret Herrick Library files.

99. Pressbook for *Greenwich Village*, 15. Margaret Herrick Library files.

100. Pressbook for *Something for the Boys*, 7. Margaret Herrick Library files.

101. Sara Hamilton, "20th Century Film Swingy," *Los Angeles Examiner*, Nov. 24, 1944. A similar opinion about the sameness of Miranda's South American tune is voiced in "Shadow Stage," *Photoplay*, Feb. 1945: 117.

102. Helen Parker, "Doll Face," *Liberty*, Jan. 26, 1946.

103. Philip T. Hartung, "Doll Face," *Commonweal*, Jan. 18, 1946. This sentiment is also expressed in *Photoplay*, Sept. 1946: 26.

104. On the rise and fall of the fan magazines, see Slide, *Inside the Hollywood Fan Magazine*, 3–4.

105. The golden age of the fan magazines was a good period for the consumer as fan magazines lowered their prices. A month after *Modern Movies'* decision in April 1939 to lower its price from fifteen cents to ten cents, *Screen Romances* also lowered its cover price from twenty-five cents to ten cents.

106. Finch and Rosenkrantz, *Gone Hollywood*, 113.

107. Featured in the section labeled "Ladies Invited," Gloria Mack, "To take advantage of some free handouts reserved for them and them alone," *Photoplay*, Jan. 1942: 84.

108. On this topic see deCordova, *Picture Personalities*, 107.

109. An afghan that Miranda allegedly crocheted is featured with the caption, "Carmen Miranda, the Brazilian Bombshell who'll appear in 'The South American Way,' is proud of the afghan she has crocheted." On the same spread, Ann Sheridan and Dorothy Lamour are also featured relaxing with their crochet. *Screenland*, Apr. 1940: 78. ("The South American Way" was the working title for *Down Argentine Way*.)

110. As Roland Barthes discusses, the signifier of connotation is not to be found at the level of any one of the fragments (here the photographs) of the sequence but at that of the concatenation, which linguists refer to as the "suprasegmental level" (24).

111. *Screenland*, Aug. 1943: 48.

112. *Movie Show*, Nov. 1947: 44.

113. During the time Miranda filmed for *Down Argentine Way*, news reports referred to her as "inexhaustible," filming, then appearing in *The Streets of Paris*, followed by two numbers in a nightclub (*Richmond News Leader*, Oct. 9, 1940). On the set of *That Night in Rio*, Miranda is said to have "worked like a horse from six in the morning until six at night, clean through a siege of influenza. Evenings she practiced her songs and her dances," as reported in *Screen Life*, Oct. 1941: 87.

114. Ida Zeitlin, "Sous American Sizzler," *Motion Picture*, Sept. 1941: 77. *Motion Picture*, Feb. 1945: 135; *Time*, Nov. 9, 1942.

115. See the above-mentioned article "Carmen Miranda Loaves America—And Vice Versa," *Sunday News*, Nov. 16, 1941: 72.

116. Betty Harris, "The South American Way," *Modern Screen*, Mar. 1941: 41; 90–91.

117. "South American Rave," *Screen Life*, Oct. 3, 1941: 35. A brief note under "Topics for Gossip" in *Silver Screen*, June 1941, had previously mentioned that Carmen "likes to hold hands with reporters (if they're male and blond) when they come to interview her" (67).

118. Dick Mook, "Pictures on the Fire!" *Silver Screen*, Mar. 1941: 67.

119. "Sous American Sizzler," *Motion Picture*, Sept. 1941: 19.

120. For a discussion of this shift in representation to include to a significant degree of domestic problems and the importance of sexuality as the stars' best-kept secret, see deCordova, *Picture Personalities*, 120 and 142, respectively.

121. Vivian Reade, "Fruit ees ze Fashion," *Movie Story*, July 9, 1947: 62.

122. See *Parade*, Oct. 5, 1941, and Sidney Skolsky, "Tintypes," *Citizen News*, Aug. 3, 1944.

123. "Carmen Miranda Loaves America," *Sunday News*, Nov. 16, 1941: 76.

124. "Hedda Hopper's Hollywood," *Los Angeles Times*, July 6, 1943: 66.

125. *Screen Life*, Oct. 1941.

126. *News*, Nov. 28, 1940.

127. "'Rio' Recipes," Pressbook for *That Night in Rio*, 20. Margaret Herrick Library files.
128. Pauline Rawley, "The South American Way," *Motion Picture Magazine*, Oct. 1941: 62–63; 93.
129. Marjorie Deen, "The Food of Our Allies: BRAZIL," *Modern Screen*, May 1944: 80–81. In *Women's Home Companion*, August 1941, Miranda is featured as one of "four charming Latin-American neighbors" and provides recipes for "peixe com bananas" (fish with bananas).
130. Ida Zeitlin, "Sous American Sizzler," *Motion Picture*, Sept. 1941: 77.
131. Ida Zeitlin, "Sous American Sizzler," *Motion Picture*, Sept. 1941: 77.
132. *Hollywood*, Sept. 1941: 20.
133. *Los Angeles Times*, Sept. 23, 1948.
134. *Modern Picture*, Dec. 1942: 15.
135. "Silver Screen. Topics for Gossip," *Silver Screen*, Apr. 1941: 20.
136. *Silver Screen*, Feb. 1948: 89.
137. Harry Brand, *Weekend in Havana* "Vital Statistics," circa September 1941. Margaret Herrick Library files.
138. *Life Magazine*, Feb. 12, 1945.
139. For a discussion on how advertising is based on evoking emotions indirectly by correlating "feelings, moods or attributes to tangible objects," see Williamson, *Decoding Advertisements*, 31–38.
140. For the intersection of the history of film and that of the public and its tastes, see Jurca 4.
141. Here I am drawing from Doane's discussion of the fans' approximation to and appropriation of the stars' bodily image, which bring the things of the screen closer (*The Desire to Desire*, 33).
142. Miranda posed for the Paul Meltsner portrait soon after her sensational Broadway début, joining the small circle of celebrities whose paintings became classics of modern portraiture.
143. *Movie Stars Parade*, Sept. 1946: 74.
144. Darr Smith, *Los Angeles Daily News*, May 22, 1951.
145. Quoted in Richard Sennett, *The Fall of Public Man*, 199.

CHAPTER 5
1. This is very similar to the omnipresence of camp that runs throughout the Judy Garland films. See Dyer, "Judy Garland and Camp," 107–14.
2. See S. Roberts 4.
3. Booth discusses the feminine as a primary type of the marginal in society and that camp parodies in an exhibition of stylized effeminacy (*Camp*, 18). *Latinidade* aligns itself as another marginal type in North American society and culture.
4. This is what David Bergman coins the "Liberace effect" ("Introduction," 14).
5. López uses the term "off-center" ("Are All Latins from Manhattan?," 74).
6. Camp's bending of gender "without genitals" is not gender specific, as Gene Kelly's much-celebrated performance in the "Pirate Ballet" at the climax of the 1948 box office hit *The Pirate* illustrates. The "camp display of hypermasculinity" (Cohan, *Incongruous Entertainment*, 179) bears similarities with the campiness of Miranda's hyperengendering.

7. In *Nancy Goes to Rio* (1950), the unobstructed view of Rio's Sugar Loaf Mountain from the window of the hotel and the full view of Corcovado Mountain from the patio of the Carnival club are prime examples of these artificial backdrops. In this case, they also echo the unrealistic plot, complete with Miranda, back in her native Brazil, at one point jumping out of a drum and singing with a pair of clowns while dressed in a headdress of rainbow-colored parasols.

8. This *samba-choro* by Alcyr Pires Vermelho and Walfrido Silva was part of Miranda's pre-Hollywood repertoire that she recorded in 1935.

9. This characterization of Charlotte Greenwood is very similar to the role she played in *Down Argentine Way* as the sidekick aunt who at one point, for inexplicable reasons, appears at the center of a village gathering and performs, complete with her signature kicks, a solo of "Sing, to your Señorita, Sing!" that ends with the protagonist lamenting, "Why, oh why, won't someone sing to me?"

10. Roen theorizes camp as both fun and funny (*High Camp* 2: 8).

11. At this point of the film, I use the real names for Carmen Miranda and Don Ameche, as no mention of their character roles has been made, and they appear as two performers, one Brazilian and the other American. The number itself is an aggregate with no impact on the storyline.

12. For a discussion of the genesis and lack of authenticity of this song in relation to Miranda's songs in general at Twentieth Century-Fox, see Clark, "Doing the Samba," 271.

13. The name of Danny's show makes reference to the 1925 Broadway production "The Garrick Gaieties," which featured the music of Richard Rodgers and Lorenz Hart and is considered their big break on Broadway.

14. With the limitations imposed by the Production Code in full swing at the time, certain references to well-known aspects of Greenwich Village, such as its gay community, are discretely embedded into the script.

15. See Newton, "Role Models," 100.

16. According to script files, the song "I Like to be Loved by You," written by Harry Warren with lyrics by Mack Gordon, was sliced from the production of *Springtime in the Rockies* and recycled for this musical.

17. Fitting with the norms of the Production Code, under the bodice Miranda wears a skin-colored inlay that is barely discernible to the viewer. In this same scene, Vivian Blaine, wearing what appears from a distance to be an extremely low-cut dress, also has a similar inlay.

18. The phrases are from the following sambas: "Cai por cima de mim" (Fall on top of me), "Quando eu penso na Bahia" (When I think of Bahia), "Me dá, me dá ioio" (Give me, give me ioio), and "Eu ia de novo para lá" (I would return there).

19. Shaw perceives Judy Garland along with Barbara Stanwyck as "subtle visual tributes" (*Carmen*, 99) to Miranda's look; however, in my reading, Garland in *Ziegfeld Girl* is first and foremost pure Busby Berkeley camp, and Stanwyck's bolero outfit in *The Lady Eve* is a signature Edith Head costume design similar to the golden bolero Shirley Ross wears in *The Big Broadcast of 1938* (1938) and Head's exquisite outfits for all of Paramount's leading ladies, which predate Miranda's screen début.

20. See Linda Mizejewski's reading of the Minnie performance with an emphasis on Judy Garland's slightly "off" version of a Ziegfeld girl (*Ziegfeld Girl*, 177).

21. For an insightful discussion of Ziegfeld girls and the representation of race, see Linda Mizejewski, *Ziegfeld Girl*, 167–68. Although in this scene the chorines' costumes are rather toned-down, "collective feminine pulchritude" was a staple of Busby Berkeley's choreographies (Berry, *Screen Style*, 60).

22. I'm borrowing the expression from Sennett, *Hollywood Musicals*, 183.

23. This scene is similar to "By a Waterfall" in *Footlight Parade* (1933), in which identical women swim happily between each other's legs. See Mizejewski, *Ziegfeld Girl*, 198.

24. See, for example, Shohat, "Gender and Culture of Empire," 68–69.

25. For a discussion of the music and its childlike qualities, see Clark, "Doing the Samba," 262.

26. In contrast, the title song of *Down Argentine Way* that Betty Grable performs as she continues on from her "Moonlight" ballad foregrounds gaiety and acquiescence: "You'll be as gay as can be, if you learn to 'sí, sí' like a Latin."

27. The "Dames" number in the film of the same name (1934) includes a sequence of kaleidoscopic designs similar to those in the "Tutti Frutti Hat" number, where the precursor to the oversized strawberries are black beach balls, dropping down and creating a diamond-shaped vortex of swirling chorus girls.

28. See Rubin, *Showstoppers*, 74.

29. The scene is also reminiscent of the spectacular all-chorine black and white number on the roof of the New Amsterdam Theatre in *The Great Ziegfeld* (1936), in which twenty chorus girls jump from their beds, serve themselves champagne, and dance around, before returning to their starting position and flopping down as though overtaken by a drunken stupor.

30. Wanda Hale, *New York Daily News*, Dec. 23, 1943.

31. For a reading of how Berkeley bridges the distance between spectator (in the film and in the live audience) and the spectacle, see Robertson, "Feminist Camp," 130.

32. Caetano Veloso, "Caricature and Conqueror, Pride and Shame," *New York Times*, Oct. 20, 1991.

33. This motif of the rising water fountain as curtain will be widely explored the following year in the aqua-ballet grand finale of MGM's Esther Williams vehicle *Bathing Beauty* (1944).

34. "'Gang's All Here' Sumptuous Musical and Visual Treat. Magnificent Effects with Facile Camera," *Hollywood Reporter*, Nov. 26, 1943.

35. As Rubin points out, the introduction of neonized objects recalls the neon-outlined violins of Berkeley's "The Shadow Waltz" number in *Gold Diggers of 1933* that appear when the lights go down and fill the screen (*Showstoppers*, 169).

36. See Fischer for a discussion of the pure-imagery realm of the Berkeley production numbers ("The Image of Woman as Image," 73).

37. Berkeley integrated similar reverse-motion techniques in the numbers "Dames" (in *Dames*, 1934) and "Lullaby of Broadway" (in *Gold Diggers of 1933*, 1933). It was a means of literally defying gravity and upturning the audience's sense of movement.

38. This is a technique that Berkeley had used previously in at least two different films. In the opening credits of *Gold Diggers of 1933*, prior to Ginger Rogers singing her now famous introductory solo, "We're in the Money," the main cast appears one by one set against a silver coin printed with the date 1933 and with their names and roles superimposed in front of the images. Another example is in the musical number "I Only Have Eyes for

You" in *Dames* (1934), where the head of Ruby Keeler looms disembodied over the stage in abstract spectacularization.

CHAPTER 6

1. Ann Walton Sieber, "The Houston International Festival holds a Carmen Miranda talent show at Rich's," *OutSmart*, Mar. 2000. Web. *www.outsmartmagazine.com*. Accessed May 2007.

2. Dylan Otto Krider, "The Music! The Gaiety! The Samba! The Houston International Festival," *Houston Press*, April 6, 2000. Web. *www.houstonpress.com/calendar/the-music-the-gaiety-the-samba-6573833*. Accessed May 2007.

3. For a discussion of "high drag," see Newton, "Role Models," 34.

4. An in-depth socio-ethnographic approach is beyond for the scope of this study.

5. See Babuscio, "The Cinema of Camp," 117–18

6. See Cohan, "Introduction to Part Three," in *Hollywood Musicals*, 103.

7. For gay male obsessions with classic Hollywood female stars, see Michael Moon, *A Small Boy and Others*, 86.

8. For a discussion of gay men's identification with women on the screen as emotional subjects, see Bronski, *Culture Clash*, 95.

9. Here I am following Linda Hutcheon's understanding of parody as defined in *A Theory of Parody*. See, in particular, 16–26 and 50–63.

10. In 1937, Mae West plays dual roles as blond con artist Peaches O'Day and brunette Parisian sensation Mademoiselle Fifi in *Every Day's a Holiday*, similar to the plot reprised in *Copacabana*. Both scripts have very little in common with Guy de Maupassant's 1882 short story with the eponymous title, "Mademoiselle Fifi," in which the title character is an effeminate and unpleasant German captain in the Franco-Prussian war.

11. This distinction actually belongs to the 1977 "Gay Bob" doll, which caused a controversy at the time. See Garber, *Vested Interests*, 2.

12. These examples include Sailor Billy, Cowboy Billy, San Francisco Billy, and others.

13. See Paul Jackson for a discussion of words such as "fruit" to signify effeminate or queer men during World War II (*One of the Boys*, 5).

14. "The Guys are Dolls," *BBC Online Network*, May 31, 1999. Web. Accessed June 5, 2011.

15. See Halberstam, *Female Masculinity*, 29.

16. *New York Herald Tribune*, Jan. 31, 1940: 19.

17. *New York Herald Tribune*, Oct. 13, 1939.

18. The media fueled great anticipation around Miranda's attendance of the show. "News of the Theater," *New York Herald Tribune*, Oct. 19, 1939: 16.

19. *New York Herald Tribune*, Oct. 13, 1939.

20. "1,300 Cheer Show by Hasty Pudding," *New York Times*, Apr. 7, 1940: 44.

21. Although beyond the scope of this study, the Andrews Sisters recorded several songs with Carmen Miranda and several covers of Miranda's hits. See Sforza, *Swing It!*, 217–66.

22. See, for example, Walt, "Time Out for Rhythm," *Variety*, May 28, 1941: 16.

23. Some of the most memorable Three Stooges cross-dressing scenes include: "Three Little Pigskins" (1934); "Pop Goes the Easel" (1935); "Pardon My Scotch" (1935); "Movie

Maniacs" (1936); "Micro-phonies" (1945); "Rhythm and Weep" (1946); "Self-Made Maids" (1950); and "Knutzy Knights" (1954).

24. The song "Mamãe eu quero," or in its Spanish version "Mamá yo quiero" (Mommy I want), was a successful Carnival song written by Vicente Paiva and Jararaca in 1937 and performed by Miranda in *Down Argentine Way* (1940). *Folha carioca* (Sept. 10, 1941) declared it the most popular *marcha* in the world (2), and through the Miranda imitators its popularity would only grow.

25. "Mickey 'Bombshell' Rooney!," *Silver Screen*, Jan. 1942: 40–41.

26. "Babes on Broadway," *New Yorker*, Jan. 10, 1942.

27. "Babes on Broadway (Musical Extravaganza)," *Variety*, Dec. 3, 1941.

28. "The Shadow Stage," *Photoplay*, Feb. 1942: 110.

29. "Film Reviews," *Variety*, Oct. 22, 1941: 8.

30. "Batuque no morro" was first recorded by Linda Batista in 1941. It is an upbeat, repetitive "samba-batucada" that is wonderfully appropriate for this clown-like performance by Hope and Crosby.

31. See Bell-Metereau, *Hollywood Androgyny*, 21

32. For Edwin Schallert of the Los Angeles Times, "tremendously hilarious is the outlandish dance performed by the pair at the spectacular culmination." In "Bing, Bob, Dottie Doughtily Cruise to Rio," *Los Angeles Times*, Jan. 1, 1948. See also *Screen Guide*, Feb. 1948: 99 and "'Road to Rio,' Another Lively Adventure for Hope, Crosby, Lamour," *Citizen-News*, Jan. 1, 1948.

33. Cohan, "Queering," 25.

34. This quote is from the back cover of *Female Masculinity*, and is an issue that Halberstam discusses throughout the text.

35. Barbara Berch, "Daley—the Dentist's Dilemma," *Motion Picture*, Nov. 1943: 54–56.

36. See Newton, "Role Models," 111.

37. "Diplomatic Courier," *Variety*, June 11, 1952: 6.

38. "Diplomatic Courier Gets Varied Reaction," *Los Angeles Times*, July 4, 1952: A7.

39. "Diplomatic Courier," *Variety*, June 11, 1952: 6.

40. As a visual message concerning the shows the soldiers would prefer to see, an article in *Liberty* features a crossed-out picture of Maurice Evans as Macbeth and a photograph of Olsen, Johnson, and Carmen Miranda in *Sons O' Fun* with an "OK" of approval written over it, with the caption "One guess which the boys in camp would rather see!" George Jean Nathan, "A Critic in Camp," *Liberty*, Feb. 14, 1942: 26–27.

41. See Bérubé, "Coming Out Under Fire," 96–97.

42. See, for example, *America Entertains the Troops*, where Miranda performs one of her signature songs, "Tico tico no fubá," and *Celebrity Propaganda*, where she appears with her headdress covered with glitter and jewelry to give a message of hope along with her famous hand twirls and sparkling smile.

43. See Bérubé, "Coming Out Under Fire," 67 and 92.

44. See the script summary dated March 7, 1944, from the office of George Wasson. *Winged Victory* Legal Box 1136, File 5707: 4. Fox legal files, UCLA.

45. "Winged Victory," *Los Angeles Examiner*, Dec. 28, 1944: 12.

46. Depending on the current sponsor and network, the show's name changed over the years of Berle's television stardom, from *The Texaco Star Theater* (1948–1953) to *The Buick-Berle Show* (1953–1955) to simply *The Milton Berle Show* (1955–1956).

47. It is estimated that the show maintained around five million viewers—unprecedented ratings for any television show. "Television's Top," *Newsweek*, May 16, 1949: 56.

48. Among the many celebrities to appear on one of Milton Berle's shows were Phil Silvers, Elvis Presley, Jerry Lewis, Dean Martin, Bob Hope, and Frank Sinatra.

49. "Television's Top," *Newsweek*, May 16, 1949: 57.

50. *Always Leave Them Laughing* was not released on VHS, perhaps due to a "corking up" scene where Berle imitates Al Jolson in blackface in front of the proscenium curtains and gets hosed off the stage. I was able to view the film at the UCLA Film and Television Archive.

51. "The New Pictures," *Time*, Dec. 5, 1949: 104. A typically harsh review is published in "Berle in *Always Leave Them Laughing*," *New York Times*, Nov. 24, 1949: 48.

52. "Wald turns Berle into Screen Star," *Hollywood Reporter*, Nov. 22, 1949. Apart from the Al Jolson impersonation, among some of the more memorable segments Berle as Kip Cooper has a long skit at the piano with a cow emerging from inside and squirting him with milk; and there is the famous sketch about the "comet pen" that can write under water, and to test it out Berle's character ends up inside a tank full of water.

53. "Boys will be Girls," *Screen Guide*, Jan. 1950: 94. The *Screen Guide* issue from the following month gave the film a two-star rating. *Screen Guide*, Feb. 1950: 88.

54. "'Chu Chu' Chugs off from its Charm," *Los Angeles Times*, Aug. 19, 1981.

55. Twentieth Century-Fox, "Just a Couple of Swells," Press release. N.d.

56. Janet Maslin, "Screen: 'Philly Flash,' a Burnett-Arkin Romp," *New York Times*, Aug. 29, 1981.

57. In the Paramount short *Hollywood Victory Caravan* (1945), Olga San Juan performs "Rhumba Matumba" very much à la Miranda, with accelerated singing and exaggerated hand gestures and facial expressions, while dressed in a Spanish ruffled skirt, opulent jewelry, and a token small sombrero slightly to the side.

58. See, for example, the publicity in *Photoplay*, Aug 1947, that refers to Olga San Juan as the "Lively Latin" because of her "rhythmic Brazilian songs and Cuban sambas."

59. Shaw, quoting Shari Roberts, also mentions Margo at RKO and Acquanetta at Universal Studios as "Carmen wannabes" (*Carmen* 132n111). Although Margo was Xavier Cugat's niece, her portrayal of foreign otherness is limited to a castanet-clacking Spanish dancer in the thriller *The Leopard Man* (1943), a French chanteuse in *Gangway for Tomorrow* (1943), and an American secretary stationed in Japan in *Behind the Rising Sun* (1943). Acquanetta, despite her moniker "the Venezuelan Volcano" and exotic beauty, starred as a glamorous "gorilla girl" in the horror and action movie *Captive Wild Woman* (1943) and its sequel *Jungle Woman* (1944) and appeared as a priestess in leopard skin in *Tarzan and the Leopard Woman* (1946), a native island girl in *Rhythm of the Islands* (1943), and an uncredited harem girl in *Arabian Nights* (1942). In these two last examples, she is more similar to sarong-wearing Dorothy Lamour than any resemblance with Carmen Miranda.

60. *Easy to Wed*'s soundtrack includes "Acércate más" (written by Cuban songwriter Osvaldo Farrés and sung by Colombian singer Carlos Ramírez), "Toca tu samba" (by the

Uruguayan composer Raúl Soler, in extended organ version by Ethel Smith), alongside "Viva México."

61. An example of a more modern version, from 2011, can be found in the British drama series *Land Girls*, which depicts the World War II era and opened one of its third-season episodes with an air-raid that intercepts the distinct voice of Carmen Miranda on the radio singing "I, Yi, Yi, Yi, Yi (I like you very much)," once again drawing from a Miranda song as emblematic of that period.

62. F. Scott Fitzgerald died on December 21, 1940, and *That Night in Rio* was released April 11, 1941.

63. "I'm Just Wild about Harry" was a popular tune of the moment and the following year would be performed by Carmen Miranda in *Greenwich Village* (1944).

64. *Porky's Pooch* (1941) also has a very brief Miranda segment impersonated by a mutt named Rover who, through a quick camp transformation, performs a few lines of the song "Mi caballero" by M. K. Jerome and Jack Scholl, originally performed by Ann Sheridan in the role of a nightclub singer in a previous Warner Brothers production, the 1940 film *Torrid Zone*, appropriately set in a Central American banana plantation.

65. For a discussion of Tex Avery and Bob Clampett as the "two cartoon masters of speed," see Klein, *Seven Minutes*, 18.

66. Bugs's talking straight at the audience and the camera is a typical Clampett parodic strategy inherited from Tex Avery. See Ford, "Warner Brothers," 12.

67. For more on the sudden-reversal technique, see Abel, "The Rabbit in Drag," 195.

68. The name of the nightclub is clearly a parody of the nightclub Mocambo (1941–1958) on Sunset Boulevard, which was one of the main hot spots for leading motion-picture actors and actresses, especially during the late 1940s, and which had, most appropriately for a Miranda performance, a Latin American decor. It was just up the street from its main competitor, Ciro's.

69. The *cuíca* is a Brazilian friction drum with a large pitch range; the *ganzá* is a handheld cylinder that is shaken like a rattle.

70. The Rio-specific Hope and Crosby film *Road to Rio* postdates this Popeye cartoon by three years.

71. See also Freire-Medeiros on the context of Zé Carioca and the international image of Brazil in the United States ("Star in the House of Mirrors," 24).

72. "The First of Walt Disney's Technicolor Musical Cartoon-and-Travelogue Impressions of South America," *Film and Radio Discussion Guide*, Jan. 1942: 149. For an insightful discussion of the mixed critical reception of *Saludos Amigos* and *The Three Caballeros* in Latin America, see Borges, *Latin American Writers*, 159–65.

73. Publicity for *Saludos Amigos* drew from the vogue of the "jitterbug" and featured Joe Carioca as the "Brazilian Jitterbird" or "Jiving Jitterbird." See *Photoplay*, Jan. 1943: 163 and *Photoplay*, Mar. 1945: 71.

74. "The Three Caballeros (Walt Disney–RKO)," *Shadow Stage*, Mar. 1945: 116.

75. Durante and Miranda previously appear in the seven-minute TerryToon cartoon short *A Torrid Toreador* (1942), where the toreador cat talks like Jimmy Durante and wants to marry the vivacious Latin cat, Carmen Miranda.

76. In *Leroy and Stitch*, the brief Miranda extra-terrestrial experiment conflates the Brazil/Hawaii overlap of the 1930s and 1940s that Seigel discusses (*Uneven Encounters*, 70).

77. Other Miranda hat-wearing episodes include Kermit the Frog in *Muppet Treasure Island Sing-Alongs* (1996); Ojo, Pip, and Pop in "Dance Fever," episode 221 of *Bear in the Big Blue House*, in which they dance with the blue mouse Grandma Flutter to the "Grandma Mambo" (1998); Oscar the Grouch's pet worm Slimey getting ready for "Wormy Gras" in *Sesame Street* episode 3856 (2000); and Theresa in episode 203 of *Muppets Tonight* (1997), who in the local coffee emporium is the lead vocalist for "The Coffee Song" (also known as "There's an Awful Lot of Coffee in Brazil"— as performed on the Milton Berle Show in 1953).

78. *Despicable Me 2* (2013) also includes a short Chiquita-Banana "minion" fruit dance in the juice factory, blending the "Chiquita Banana" song with the fruit-laden headdress image.

79. In 1987, Chiquita Banana changed its mascot to a woman with a fruit basket on her head, which bears even more resemblance to the Miranda image.

80. Christy Carlson Romano, at the age of twelve, makes her first feature film appearance in Woody Allen's *Everyone Says I Love You* (1996) as a trick-or-treating child, dressed in an elaborate banana costume with headdress and ruffles, who performs a dynamic version of the "Chiquita Banana" song accompanied by two young maraca-shaking mariachis.

81. See blog post "Duckworth's Thoughts: The Cat in the Hat 2003," *Duckworth*, May 10, 2013, Web. June 12, 2013. *duckworth.deviantart.com*; and untitled text by Daniel Eagon, *Film Journal International Online*, Nov. 2003, Web. June 12, 2013. *filmjournal.com*. The only positive review I have read was posted at *GayToday.com* on December 1, 2003, by John Demetry, who sees *The Cat in the Hat* as Mike Myers's best-yet screen performance.

82. "Interview: Pixar's Rob Gibbs Talks about Cars 2 Air Mater Short," *Liveforfilms.com*, Nov. 14, 2011. Accessed Mar. 2012.

83. The McDonald's trademark Happy Meals came with characters from the film, among which Luiz was depicted with his Miranda headdress.

84. See Newton, "Role Models," 109.

CONCLUSION

1. Aline Mosby, "Durante has her OK. Last Carmen Miranda Show on TV Tonight," *United Press Hollywood*. Undated news-clipping from the Margaret Herrick Library.

2. Caetano Veloso, "Caricature and Conqueror, Pride and Shame," *New York Times*, Oct. 20, 1991.

3. *Diário carioca*, Aug. 6, 1955.

4. *O globo*, Aug. 9, 1955.

5. Qtd. in "A primeira canção," *Manchete*, Aug. 13, 1955: 38. See also Braguinha's testimony in *Folha de São Paulo*, Aug. 5, 1977.

6. See, for example, the Brazilian Carnival held at the Hollywood Palladium in 1998 with Miranda as its main theme and the show *Blame it on Rio* presented at the Hollywood Bowl (September 12, 2009), which featured Bebel Gilberto singing a dynamic rendering of some of Miranda's classic songs. Don Heckman, "Miranda Rites," *Los Angeles Times*,

Feb. 19, 1998: 18–20; Reed Johnson, "Blame It on Rio Concert at Hollywood Bowl," *Los Angeles Times*, Sept. 15, 2009.

7. In 1982 Marília Pêra received the National Society of Film Critics Award for Best Actress and is today the most awarded Brazilian actress ever. She has starred in innumerous films, soap operas, and television miniseries, as well as live performances throughout Brazil. See the interview included as part of the special features on the DVD *Marília Pêra canta Carmen Miranda*.

8. Quoted in Solange Bagdadi, "Mito: A volta da garota do It," *JB Online*, Sept. 18, 2005. Accessed September 19, 2005.

9. *Carmem* is an alternative spelling that was sometimes used in Brazil.

10. This show was filmed and released as a DVD with the same name in 2006.

11. Barbara Heliodora, "Para reencontrar a Pequena Notável," *O globo*, Oct. 28, 2005: 20 Caderno.

12. The theater award "Prêmio Shell," established in 1988, recognizes each year outstanding theatrical performances in Rio de Janeiro and São Paulo with awards in an array of categories (director, actor, actress, costumes, music, lighting, etc.).

13. Maura Ferreira, "South American Way," *ISTOÉ Gente*, July 9, 2001.

14. Ibid.

15. Ibid.

16. I am grateful to Carlos Reis for bringing this show to my attention.

17. "Miranda por Miranda: Stella conta a história de Carmem em espetáculo," *Globo.com*, July 2, 2014. Accessed July 15, 2014.

18. "Carmen Miranda Imitators," *Deseret News*, Aug. 27, 1995; "Mob of Mirandas," *(L. B.) Press-Telegram*, Sept. 27, 1995; Jon Pareles, "For Carmen Miranda, with Fruit, of Course," *New York Times*, Sept. 7, 1996.

19. Erika Milvy, "Multi-Cultists Ride New Wave," *New York Post*, Sept. 27, 1991: 26. Weekend edition.

20. Jon Pareles, "Fruit Piled on Her Head, An Icon of Joyful Excess," *New York Times*, Oct. 26, 1991.

21. Ibid.

22. *A carioca*, May 13, 1939. Qtd. in Mendonça, *Carmen Miranda*, 57.

23. On the transformative nature of stardom, see Marshall, *Celebrity and Power*, 48.

24. See Mendonça, *Carmen Miranda*, 131–52.

25. This juxtaposition is summarized in the succinct phrase "brutality garden" of the Tropicalist song "Geléia geral" (General jelly), from which Christopher Dunn drew the title of his seminal text on the movement. See Dunn, *Brutality Garden*, 3 and 94–97.

26. Newton, "Role Models," 107.

27. See Veloso, *Tropical Truth*, 298. On Veloso's androgynous performativity, see Lorraine Leu's insightful interpretation in *Brazilian Popular Music*, 42–43.

28. See Hamilton, *Queen of Camp*, 218.

29. Caetano Veloso, "Caricature and Conqueror, Pride and Shame," *New York Times*, Oct. 20, 1991.

30. A benefit concert at Carnegie Hall in 1989 is one such example. See Dunn, *Brutality Garden*, 35–36.

31. See Dunn, *Brutality Garden*, 217n39.

32. *Film Fan Monthly* of December 1971 discusses the screening of *The Gang's All Here* at the very same Murray Hill Theater, prepared for over a year by film buff Eric Spilker. Unlike the Hirsch account, the event was highly successful, with the lobby decorated in "1940s' garish." See Leonard Maltin, "Welcome Back," *Film Fan Monthly*, Dec. 1971.

33. Filk music refers to a genre of folk music with a science-fiction or fantasy theme. Considered one of the pioneers of the genre, Leslie Fish contributed to the first commercial recordings of filk music in the mid-1970s.

34. For a thorough discussion of the dominant metaphor of space as sea in literature, see Westfahl, *Islands in the Sky*, 33–35.

35. Leib Goldkorn had previously appeared in *The Steinway Quintet* (1976) and *Goldkorn Tales* (1985).

36. D. T. Max, "The Magic Flutist," *New York Times*, Oct. 31, 1999.

37. Antunes Filho explains in an interview that the idea for the play was to talk about "Carmen Miranda is gone, she is no longer, that Rio is gone, the nostalgia of friends that died. Far from throwing a party, I want people to reflect." See Solange Bagdadi, "Mito: a volta da garota do it," *JB Online*, Sept. 18, 2005. Accessed Sept. 28, 2005.

38. *Fonemol* is a technique that Antunes Filho has used previously in his work. See Britton, "Antunes Filho's Prismatic Theatre," 201n1.

39. This was performed by the theater group Sociedade Litero-Dramática Gastão Tojeiro at the São Paulo theater Maria Della Costa. See Marcella Franco, "'Ciclo de musicais biográficos' começa no teatro Maria Della Costa," *Folha de São Paulo*, May 6, 2000.

40. There is a very elaborate blog about this theatrical production at *umacertacarmen. blogspot.com*.

41. See Karin Kukkonen, "Metalepsis in Popular Culture," 18.

42. *Bananas Is My Business* won "Best Documentary" at the Festival of Brasília (1994), the Havana Film Festival (1995), the Chicago International Film Festival (1995), the International Film Festival of Uruguay (1996), and the Encontro Internacional de Cinema in Portugal (1996).

43. Gary Morris, "Carmen Miranda. Bananas Is My Business," *Bright Lights Film Journal*, April 1996. Web. Accessed May 2005. *www.brightlightsfilm.com/16/carmen.html*.

44. See Félix, "The Migrant," 214.

45. See the pertinent discussion of Bruzzi in Félix, "The Migrant," 213.

46. Erik Mink, "Bittersweet 'Bananas' a Life of Miranda," *Daily News*, Oct. 6, 1995.

47. D'Ezequiel, "Night Clubs," *O jornal* [Rio de Janeiro], Jan. 25, 1955.

48. See Garcia, *O 'it verde e amarelo' de Carmen Miranda*, 119.

49. See Dennison and Shaw, *Popular Cinema in Brazil*, 115.

50. "Carmen Miranda Will Be Paid Tribute in Rio," *Los Angeles Times*, Aug. 10, 1955.

51. This neighborhood is far from the center of Rio de Janeiro and the areas that Carmen Miranda frequented; it is part of the largest island in the Guanabara Bay, where the Rio de Janeiro–Galeão International Airport occupies a third of the island.

52. Hector Tobar, "Some City Squares Bring Lives, and History, Full Circle," *Los Angeles Times*, Sept. 26, 1998.

53. "Exposição no Rio e show em São Paulo celebram a cantora," *Folha de São Paulo*, Nov. 30, 2005.

54. *Carmen Miranda para sempre* was in Rio from December 1, 2005, to January 22, 2006, then in São Paulo from March 8 to April 23, 2006, and finally in Salvador, Bahia, from October 27 to November 26, 2006.

55. As part of the events initiated in Salvador, Bahia, in the mid-1990s to revitalize the Historical Centre and the Pelourinho, in particular with "Carnival in the Pelourinho," in 1998 they curated the exhibition "O que é que a baiana tem?," on display in February and March. See exhibition catalogue "O que é que a baiana tem?" by the Secretary of Culture and Tourism of Bahia.

56. Florença Mazza, "Ex-paquita Andrea Veiga estrela musical em homenagem a Carmen Miranda," *O globo*, Nov. 7, 2009.

57. Warren Hoge, "A Museum in Rio Recalls Days of Carmen Miranda," *New York Times*, Apr. 22, 1979.

58. *Pranove*, May 1939: 20.

BIBLIOGRAPHY

ARCHIVES CONSULTED

Arquivo do Museu da Imagem e do Som, Rio de Janeiro
Arquivo Nacional, Rio de Janeiro
Biblioteca Nacional, Rio de Janeiro
Carmen Miranda Museum, Rio de Janeiro
Cinédia Archive, Rio de Janeiro, Courtesy of Alice Gonzaga
FUNARTE, Rio de Janeiro
Manuscripts and Archives Division of the New York Public Library
Margaret Herrick Library, Los Angeles
MOMA Library and Film Collection, Rio de Janeiro
New York Public Library for the Performing Arts
Schomberg Center for Research in Black Culture, New York Public Library
Shubert Archives, New York
Special Collections, Gladys Marcus Library, Fashion Institute of Technology, New York
Twentieth Century-Fox Archive, Los Angeles
UCLA Film and Television Archive
UCLA Special Collections
University of Southern California, Los Angeles

BOOKS AND ARTICLES

Abel, Sam. "The Rabbit in Drag: Camp and Gender Construction in the American Animated Cartoon." *Journal of Popular Culture* 29, no. 3 (Winter 1995): 183–202.

Abernethy, Michael. "Gay Icons: Judy Who?" *PopMatters*. 16 November 2006. Web. Accessed 3 Jan 2007. *www.popmatters.com/column/gay-icons-judy-who*.

Alberoni, Francesco. "The Powerless 'Elite': Theory and Sociology Research on the Phenomenon of the Stars." In *Stardom and Celebrity: A Reader*, edited by Sean Redmond and Su Holmes, 65–78. Los Angeles: Sage, 2010.

Allen, Amanda. "Rolling down the Floor." In Sakers, *Carmen Miranda's Ghost*, 163–70.

Allen, Jeanne. "The Film Viewer as Consumer." *Quarterly Review of Film Studies* 5, no. 4 (Fall 1980): 481–99.

Anuário estatístico do Brasil 1939/1940. Vol. 5. Rio de Janeiro: IBGE, 1941.

Arinos, Afonso. *A unidade da pátria*. Rio de Janeiro: Livraria F. Alves, 1917.

Azevedo, Kathleen de. *Samba Dreamers*. Tucson: University of Arizona Press, 2006.

Azevedo, Thales de. *Les élites de couleur dans une ville brésilienne.* Paris: UNESCO, 1953.

Babuscio, Jack. "The Cinema of Camp (aka Camp and the Gay Sensibility)." In Cleto, *Camp,* 117–35.

Bakhtin, Mikhail. *Rabelais and His World.* Translated by Hélène Iswolsky. Bloomington: Indiana University Press, 1984.

Barrios, Richard. *A Song in the Dark: The Birth of the Musical Film.* New York: Oxford University Press, 1995.

Barros, Orlando de. *Corações De Chocolat: A história da Companhia Negra de Revistas (1926–1927).* Rio de Janeiro: Livre Expressão, 2005.

Barthes, Roland. *Image, Music, Text.* Translated by Stephen Heath. New York: Hill and Wang, 1977.

Bastide, Roger, and Florestan Fernandes. *Brancos e negros em São Paulo: Ensaio sociológico sobre aspectos da formação, manifestações atuais e efeitos do preconceito de cor na sociedade paulistana.* 2nd ed. São Paulo: Companhia Editora Nacional, 1959.

Bell-Metereau, Rebecca. *Hollywood Androgyny.* 2nd ed. New York: Columbia University Press, 1993.

Belton, John. "The Production Code." In *Movies and Mass Culture,* edited by John Belton, 135–50. New Brunswick, NJ: Rutgers University Press, 1996.

Beltrán, Mary. *Latina/o Stars in U.S. Eyes: The Making and Meanings of Film and TV Stardom.* Urbana: University of Illinois Press, 2009.

Berg, Charles Ramírez. *Latino Images in Film: Stereotypes, Subversion, Resistance.* Austin: University of Texas Press, 2002.

Bergman, David. "Introduction." In *Camp Grounds: Style and Homosexuality,* edited by David Bergman, 3–16. Amherst: University of Massachusetts Press, 1993.

Berry, Sarah. "Hollywood Exoticism." In *Stars: The Film Reader,* edited by Lucy Fischer and Marcia Landy, 181–97. New York: Routledge, 2004.

———. *Screen Style: Fashion and Femininity in 1930s Hollywood.* Minneapolis: University of Minnesota Press, 2000.

Bérubé, Allan. *Coming Out Under Fire: The History of Gay Men and Women in World War Two.* New York: Plume, 1991.

Bhabha, Homi. *The Location of Culture.* New York: Routledge, 2004.

Boomer, Lucius. "The Greatest Household." In *The Unofficial Palace of New York,* edited by Frank Crowninshield, 11–18. New York: Hotel Waldorf-Astoria Corporation, 1939.

Boorstin, Daniel. *The Image: A Guide to Pseudo-Events in America.* New York: Atheneum, 1962.

Booth, Mark. *Camp.* London: Quartet Books, 1983.

Borges, Jason. *Latin American Writers and the Rise of Hollywood Cinema.* New York: Routledge, 2008.

Bourdieu, Pierre. *Distinction: A Social Critique of the Judgment of Taste.* Translated by Richard Nice. Cambridge, Mass.: Harvard University Press, 1984.

Brassard, Gail. "Irene Sharaff." In *Late and Great American Designers 1960–2010,* edited by Bobbi Owen, 178–87. Syracuse: US Institute for Theatre Technology, 2010.

Brito, Dulce Damasceno de. *O ABC de Carmen Miranda.* São Paulo: Editora Companhia Nacional, 1986.

Britton, B. Campbell. "Antunes Filho's Prismatic Theatre: Staging Nelson Rodrigues and Brazilian Identities." PhD diss., UCLA, 2008.

Bronski, Michael. *Culture Clash: The Making of Gay Sensibility.* Boston: South End Press, 1984.

Brown, Diana De G. "Power, Invention, and the Politics of Race: Umbanda Past and Future." In Crook and Johnson, *Black Brazil*, 213–36.

Burton, Julianne. "Don (Juanito) Duck and the Imperial-Patriarchal Unconscious: Disney Studios, the Good Neighbor Policy, and the Packaging of Latin America." In *Nationalisms and Sexualities*, 21–41. New York: Routledge, 1992.

Butler, Judith. *Bodies that Matter: On the Discursive Limits of "Sex."* New York: Routledge, 1993.

Cabral, Sérgio. *As escolas de samba do Rio de Janeiro.* Rio de Janeiro: Lumiar Editora, 1996.

———. *No tempo de Almirante: Uma história do rádio e da MPB.* Rio de Janeiro: Francisco Alves, 1990.

Canosa, Fabiano, curator. Catalogue for the Exhibition *Carmen Miranda para sempre.* Rio de Janeiro: Museu de Arte Moderna, 2005.

Cardoso Junior, Abel. *Carmen Miranda: A cantora do Brasil.* São Paulo: Edição Particular do Autor, 1978.

Carvalho, Bruno. *Porous City: A Cultural History of Rio de Janeiro (from the 1810s Onward).* Liverpool: Liverpool University Press, 2013.

Castro, Ruy. *Carmen: A vida de Carmen Miranda, a brasileira mais famosa do século XX.* São Paulo: Campanhia das Letras, 2005.

Ciambrone, Ronaldo. "Uma certa Carmen: A vida trepidante de Carmen Miranda." *Teatro da Juventude* 7, no. 42 (2002): 31–53.

Clark, Walter Aaron. "Doing the Samba on Sunset Boulevard: Carmen Miranda and the Hollywoodization of Latin American Music." In *From Tejano to Tango. Latin American Popular Music,* edited by Walter Aaron Clark, 252–76. New York: Routledge, 2002.

Cleto, Fabio, ed. *Camp: Queer Aesthetics and the Performing Subject: A Reader.* Ann Arbor: University of Michigan Press, 1999.

Coelho, José Ligiero. "Carmen Miranda: An Afro-Brazilian Paradox." PhD diss., New York University, 1998.

Cohan, Steven, ed. *Hollywood Musicals: The Film Reader.* London: Routledge, 2002.

Cohan, Steven. *Incongruous Entertainment: Camp, Cultural Value and the MGM Musical.* Durham, NC: Duke University Press, 2005.

———. "Queering the Deal: On the Road with Hope and Crosby." In *Out Takes: Essays on Queer Theory and Film,* edited by Ellis Hanson, 23–45. Durham, NC: Duke University Press, 1999.

Conner, Ronald C. "Brazilian Blackface: Maracatu Cearense and the Politics of Participation." Master's thesis, University of California, Riverside, 2009.

Core, Philip. *Camp: The Lie that Tells the Truth.* New York: Delilah Books, Putnam Publishing Group, 1984.

Corrêa, Mariza. *Antropólogas & antropologia.* Belo Horizonte: Editora UFMG, 2003.

Crafton, Donald. "The Jazz Singer's Reception in the Media and at the Box Office." In *Post-Theory: Reconstructing Film Studies,* edited by David Bordwell and Noël Carroll, 460–80. Madison: University of Wisconsin Press, 1996.

Crook, Larry, and Randal Johnson. *Black Brazil: Culture, Identity and Social Mobilization*. Los Angeles: UCLA Latin American Center Publications, 1999.

Curry, Ramona. *Too Much of a Good Thing: Mae West as Cultural Icon*. Minneapolis: University of Minnesota Press, 1996.

DaMatta, Roberto. *Carnivals, Rogues, and Heroes: An Interpretation of the Brazilian Dilemma*. Translated by John Drury. Notre Dame: University of Notre Dame Press, 1991.

Davis, Darién J. *Avoiding the Dark: Race and the Forging of National Culture in Modern Brazil*. Aldershot: Ashgate, 1999.

———. "Racial Parity and National Humor: Exploring Samba from Noel Rosa to Carmen Miranda, 1930–1939." In *Latin American Popular Culture: An Introduction*, edited by William H. Beezley and Linda A. Curcio-Nagy, 183–200. Delaware: Scholarly Resources, 2000.

———. *White Face, Black Mask: Africaneity and the Early Social History of Popular Music in Brazil*. East Lansing: Michigan State University Press, 2009.

deCordova, Richard. *Picture Personalities: The Emergence of the Star System in America*. Urbana: University of Illinois Press, 2001.

Degler, Carl N. *Neither Black nor White: Slavery and Race Relations in Brazil and the United States*. Madison: University of Wisconsin Press, 1986.

Deleuze, Gilles. "Mediators." In *Zone 6: Incorporations*, edited by J. Crary and S. Kwinter, 281–293. New York: Zone, 1992.

Dennison, Stephanie, and Lisa Shaw. *Popular Cinema in Brazil, 1930–2001*. Manchester: Manchester University Press, 2004.

Diniz, André. *Almanaque do Carnaval: A história do carnaval, o que ouvir, o que ler, onde curtir*. Rio de Janeiro: Zahar, 2008.

Doane, Mary Ann. *The Desire to Desire*. Bloomington: Indiana University Press, 1987.

Doty, Alexander. *Making Things Perfectly Queer: Interpreting Mass Culture*. Minneapolis: University of Minnesota Press, 1993.

Dunn, Christopher. *Brutality Garden: Tropicália and the Emergence of a Brazilian Counterculture*. Chapel Hill: University of North Carolina Press, 2001.

———. "The Tropicalista Rebellion: A Conversation with Caetano Veloso." *Transition* 70 (1996): 116–38.

Dyer, Richard. "Judy Garland and Camp." In Cohan, *Hollywood Musicals*, 107–14.

———. *Only Entertainment*. 2nd ed. London: Routledge, 2002.

Eaton, Kent. *Politics Beyond the Capital: The Design of Subnational Institutions in South America*. Stanford, CA: Stanford University Press, 2004.

Eckert, Charles. "The Carole Lombard in Macy's Window." In Gaines and Herzog, *Fabrications*, 100–21.

Edwards, Gregory J. *The International Film Poster*. London: Columbus Books, 1985.

Eells, George. *Hedda and Louella*. New York: G. P. Putnam's Sons, 1972.

Efegê, Jota. *Figuras e coisas da música popular brasileira*. Vol. 2. Rio de Janeiro: Edição FUNARTE, 1980.

Ellis, John. *Visible Fictions: Cinema, Television, Video*. London: Routledge, 1992.

Endres, Stacey, and Robert Cushman. *Hollywood at Your Feet: The Story of the World-Famous Chinese Theatre*. Los Angeles: Pomegranate Press, 1992.

Enloe, Cynthia. *Bananas, Beaches and Bases: Making Feminist Sense of International Politics.* Berkeley: University of California Press, 1989.

Epstein, Leslie. *Ice Fire Water: A Leib Goldkorn Cocktail.* New York: Norton, 1999.

Etling, Laurence. *Radio in the Movies: A History and Filmography, 1926–2010.* Jefferson, NC: McFarland, 2011.

Farmer, Brett. *Spectacular Passions: Cinema, Fantasy, Gay Male Spectatorships.* Durham, NC: Duke University Press, 2000.

Félix, Regina R. "The Migrant in Helena Solberg's *Carmen Miranda: Bananas Is My Business.*" In *Migration in Lusophone Cinema*, edited by Cacilda Rêgo and Marcus Brasileiro, 203–19. New York: Palgrave Macmillan, 2014.

Fenwick, Millicent. "More about Music." In *The Unofficial Palace of New York*, edited by Frank Crowninshield, 103–11. New York: Hotel Waldorf-Astoria Corporation, 1939.

Fernandes, Florestan. *The Negro in Brazilian Society.* Translated by Jacqueline D. Skiles, A. Brunel, and Arthur Rothwell. New York: Atheneum, 1971.

Ferreira, Suzana Cristina de Souza. *Cinema carioca nos anos 30 e 40: Os filmes musicais nas telas da cidade.* São Paulo: PPGH-UFMG, 2003.

Finch, Christopher, and Linda Rosenkrantz. *Gone Hollywood.* Garden City, NY: Doubleday, 1979.

Fischer, Lucy. "The Image of Woman as Image: The Optical Politics of *Dames.*" In *Genre: The Musical: A Reader*, edited by Rick Altman, 70–84. London: Routledge and Kegan Paul, 1981.

Fiske, John. "British Cultural Studies and Television." In *Channels of Discourse. Television and Contemporary Criticism*, edited by Robert C. Allen, 254–89. Chapel Hill: University of North Carolina Press, 1987.

———. *Reading the Popular.* Boston: Unwin Hyman, 1989.

Fitch, Melissa. "Carmen, Kitsch, Camp and my Quest for Coordinated Dinnerware." *Chasqui* 40, no. 2 (November 2011): 55–64.

Fontenot, Chester J. "Introduction: On Being a Problem in America." In *W.E.B. Du Bois and Race: Essays Celebrating the Centennial Publications of* The Soul of Black Folk, edited by Chester J. Fontenot and Mary Alice Morgan, 1–10. Macon, GA: Mercer University Press, 2001.

Ford, Greg. "Warner Brothers." *Film Comment* 11, no. 1 (January–February 1975): 10–16, 93.

Foster, David William. "Carmen Miranda as Cultural Icon." In *Latin American Icons: Fame Across Borders*, edited by Dianna C. Niebylski and Patrick O'Connor, 117–24. Nashville: Vanderbilt University Press, 2014.

Foster, Gwendolyn Audrey. *Performing Whiteness.* Albany: State University of New York Press, 2003.

Foucault, Michel. "Of Other Spaces." Translated by Jay Miskowiec. *Diacritics* 16, no. 1 (Spring 1986): 22–27.

Freire-Medeiros, Bianca. "Star in the House of Mirrors: Contrasting Images of Carmen Miranda in Brazil and the United States." *Limina: A Journal of Historical and Cultural Studies* 12 (2006): 21–29.

Freyre, Gilberto. *The Masters and the Slaves: A Study in the Development of Brazilian Civilization.* Translated by Samuel Putnam. 2nd ed. New York: Alfred A. Knopf, 1956.

Friesner, Esther. "In the Can." In Sakers, *Carmen Miranda's Ghost*, 220–46.

Frost, Jennifer. *Hedda Hopper's Hollywood: Celebrity Gossip and American Conservatism.* New York: New York University Press, 2011.

Gaines, Jane. "Costume and Narrative: How Dress Tells the Woman's Story." In Gaines and Herzog, *Fabrications*, 180–211.

Gaines, Jane M. "Wanting to Wear Seeing: Gilbert Adrian at MGM." In Munich, *Fashion in Film*, 135–59.

Gaines, Jane, and Charlotte Herzog, eds. *Fabrications: Costume and the Female Body.* New York: Routledge, 1990.

Galm, Eric A. "Baianas, Malandros, and Samba: Listening to Brazil through Donald Duck's Ears." In *Global Soundtracks: Worlds of Film Music*, edited by Mark Slobin, 258–80. Middletown: Wesleyan University Press, 2008.

Gamson, Joshua. *Claims to Fame: Celebrity in Contemporary America.* Berkeley: University of California Press, 1994.

Garber, Marjorie. *Vested Interests: Cross-dressing and Cultural Anxiety.* New York: Routledge, Chapman, and Hall, 1993.

Garcia, Tânia da Costa. *O 'it verde e amarelo' de Carmen Miranda (1930–1946).* São Paulo: Annablume; Fapesp, 2004.

Genette, Gérard. *Narrative Discourse: An Essay in Method.* Translated by J. E. Lewin. Ithaca, NY: Cornell University Press, 1980.

Geraghty, Christine. "Re-Examining Stardom: Questions of Texts, Bodies and Performance." In *Reinventing Film Studies*, edited by Christine Gledhill and Linda Williams, 183–201. London: Arnold, 2000.

Gil-Montero, Martha. *Brazilian Bombshell: The Biography of Carmen Miranda.* New York: Donald I. Fine, 1989.

Gilroy, Paul. *The Black Atlantic. Modernity and Double Consciousness.* Cambridge, Massachusetts: Harvard University Press, 1993.

Gledhill, Christine, ed. *Stardom: Industry of Desire.* London: Routledge, 1990.

Glyn, Elinor. *"It."* New York: Macaulay, 1927.

Gomes, Tiago de Melo. *Um espelho no palco: Identidades sociais e massificação da cultura no teatro de revista dos anos 1920.* Campinas, Brasil: Editora UNICAMP, 2004.

Gomes, Tiago de Melo and Micol Seigel. "Sabina's Oranges: The Colours of Cultural Politics in Rio de Janeiro, 1889–1930." *Journal of Latin American Cultural Studies* 11, no. 1 (2002): 5–28.

Gomery, Douglas. *The Hollywood Studio System.* New York: St. Martin's, 1986.

Gonzaga, Alice. *Palácios e poeiras: 100 anos de cinemas no Rio de Janeiro.* Rio de Janeiro: FUNARTE, 1996.

———. *50 anos de Cinédia.* Rio de Janeiro: Editora Record, 1987.

Graham, Richard. *Feeding the City: From Street Market to Liberal Reform in Salvador, Brazil, 1780–1860.* Austin: University of Texas Press, 2010.

Green, James N. *Beyond Carnival: Male Homosexuality in Twentieth-Century Brazil.* Chicago: University of Chicago Press, 1999.

Green, Stanley. *Broadway Musicals: Show by Show.* 6th ed. New York: Applause Theatre and Cinema Books, 2008. First published 1985.

Gruzinski, Serge. *The Mestizo Mind: The Intellectual Dynamics of Colonization and Globalization*. Translated by Deke Dusinberre. New York: Routledge, 2002.

Gubar, Susan. *Racechanges: White Skin, Black Face in American Culture*. New York: Oxford University Press, 1997.

Halberstam, Judith. *Female Masculinity*. Durham, NC: Duke University Press, 1998.

Hamilton, Marybeth. *The Queen of Camp: Mae West, Sex and Popular Culture*. London: Pandora, 1996.

Hanchard, Michael. "Culturalism versus Cultural Politics: Movimento Negro in Rio de Janeiro and São Paulo, Brazil." In *The Violence Within: Cultural and Political Opposition in Divided Nations*, edited by Kay B. Warren, 57–86. Boulder, CO: Westview Press, 1993.

Handel, Leo A. *Hollywood Looks at its Audience: A Report of Film Audience Research*. Urbana: University of Illinois Press, 1950.

Haralovich, Mary Beth. "Advertising Heterosexuality." *Screen* 23, no. 2 (July/Aug. 1982): 50–60.

Harrison-Kahan, Lori. *The White Negress: Literature, Minstrelsy, and the Black-Jewish Imaginary*. New Brunswick, NJ: Rutgers University Press, 2011.

Hasenbalg, Carlos, and Nelson do Valle Silva. "Notes on Racial and Political Inequality in Brazil." In *Racial Politics in Contemporary Brazil*, edited by Michael Hanchard, 154–78. Durham, NC: Duke University Press, 1999.

Haskell, Molly. *From Reverence to Rape: The Treatment of Women in the Movies*. New York: Holt, Rinehart, and Winston, 1974.

Heide, Robert, and John Gilman. *Starstruck: The Wonderful World of Movie Memorabilia*. Garden City, NY: Doubleday, 1986.

Herculano, Paulo. "Musicais brasileiros." *Teatro da Juventude* 7, no. 42 (2002): 17–19.

Hershfield, Joanne. *The Invention of Dolores del Río*. Minneapolis: University of Minnesota Press, 2000.

Hertzman, Marc. *Making Samba: A New History of Race and Music in Brazil*. Durham, NC: Duke University Press, 2013.

Hess, Thomas. "J'accuse Marcel Duchamp." *Art News* 63 (1965): 44–45, 52–54.

Hirsch, Abby. *The Great Carmen Miranda Look-Alike Contest and Other Bold-Faced Lies*. With Dale Burg. New York: St. Martin's Press, 1974.

Hirsch, Foster. *The Boys from Syracuse: The Shuberts' Theatrical Empire*. Carbondale: Southern Illinois University Press, 1998.

Hobsbawm, Eric. "Introduction: Inventing Traditions." In *The Invention of Tradition*, edited by Eric Hobsbawm and Terence O. Ranger, 1–14. Cambridge: Cambridge University Press, 1983.

hooks, bell. *Black Looks: Race and Representation*. Boston: South End Press, 1992.

Huggan, Graham. *The Postcolonial Exotic: Marketing the Margins*. London: Routledge, 2001.

Hutcheon, Linda. *A Theory of Parody: The Teachings of Twentieth Century Art Forms*. New York: Methuen, 1985.

Isfahani-Hammond, Alexandra. *White Negritude: Race, Writing and Brazilian Cultural Identity*. New York: Palgrave Macmillan, 2008.

Jackson, Paul. *One of the Boys: Homosexuality in the Military During World War II*. 2nd ed. Montreal: McGill-Queen's University Press, 2004.

Jurca, Catherine. "What the Public Wanted: Hollywood, 1937–1942." *Cinema Journal* 47, no. 2 (Winter 2008): 3–25.

Kirk, Kris. *Men in Frocks*. London: GMP Publishers, 1984.

Kjellman-Chapin, Monica. "The Politics of Kitsch." *Rethinking Marxism* 22, no. 1 (Jan. 2010): 27–41.

Klein, Norman F. *Seven Minutes: The Life and Death of the American Animated Cartoon*. London: Verso, 1993.

Kobal, John, and V. A. Wilson. *Foyer Pleasure: The Golden Age of Cinema Lobby Cards*. New York: Delilah Communications, 1982.

Kukkonen, Karin. "Metalepsis in Popular Culture: An Introduction." In *Metalepsis in Popular Culture*, edited by Karin Kukkonen and Sonja Klimek, 1–21. Berlin: De Gruyter, 2001.

Landes, Ruth. *The City of Women*. 2nd ed. Introduction by Sally Cole. Albuquerque: University of New Mexico Press, [1947] 1994.

Lane, Jill. *Blackface Cuba, 1840–1895*. Philadelphia: University of Pennsylvania Press, 2005.

Leu, Lorraine. *Brazilian Popular Music: Caetano Veloso and the Regeneration of Tradition*. Hampshire, UK: Ashgate, 2006.

Lewitt, S. N. "That Souse American Way." In Sakers, *Carmen Miranda's Ghost*, 145–62.

Linstead, Stephen. "Organizational Kitsch." *Organization* 9, no. 4 (November 2002): 657–82.

Lipovetsky, Gilles. *The Empire of Fashion: Dressing Modern Democracy*. Translated by Catherine Porter. Foreword by Richard Sennett. Princeton, NJ: Princeton University Press, 1994.

Lody, Raul. *O que é que a bahiana tem: Pano-da-costa e roupa de baiana*. Rio de Janeiro: Funarte, CNFCP, 2003.

———. *Pencas de balangandãs da Bahia: Um estudo etnográfico das jóias-amuletos*. Rio de Janeiro: Instituto Nacional do Folclore / FUNARTE, 1988.

López, Ana M. "Are All Latins from Manhattan? Hollywood, Ethnography and Cultural Colonialism." In *Mediating Two Worlds: Cinematic Encounters in the Americas*, edited by John King, Ana M. López, and Manuel Alvarado, 67–81. London: BFI Institute, 1993.

Lott, Eric. *Love and Theft: Blackface Minstrelsy and the American Working Class*. Twentieth Anniversary Ed. Foreword by Greil Marcus. New York: Oxford University Press, 2013.

Machado, Carlos, and Paulo de Faria Pinho. *Memórias sem maquiagem*. São Paulo: Livraria Cultura Editora, 1978.

Mahar, William J. *Behind the Burnt Cork Mask: Early Blackface Minstrelsy and Antebellum American Popular Culture*. Urbana: University of Illinois Press, 1999.

Mand, Mary L. "The Pigeon Sisters on Space Station Three." In Sakers, *Carmen Miranda's Ghost*, 293–300.

Mandrell, James. "Carmen Miranda Betwixt and Between, or, Neither Here nor There." *Latin American Literary Review* 29, no. 57 (January–June 2001): 26–39.

Marshall, P. David. *Celebrity and Power: Fame and Contemporary Culture*. Minneapolis: University of Minnesota Press, 1997.

Matory, James Lorand. *Black Atlantic Religion: Tradition, Transnationalism, and Matriarchy in the Afro-Brazilian Candomblé*. Princeton: Princeton University Press, 2005.

McCann, Bryan. *Hello, Hello Brazil: Popular Music in the Making of Modern Brazil*. Durham, NC: Duke University Press, 2004.

McLeod, Elizabeth. *The Original Amos 'n' Andy: Freeman Gosden, Charles Correll, and the 1928–1943 Radio Serial*. Jefferson, North Carolina: McFarland and Company, 2005.

McNamara, Brooks. *The Shuberts of Broadway: A History Drawn from the Collections of the Shubert Archive*. New York: Oxford University Press, 1990.

Meireles, Cecília. *Batuque, samba e macumba: Estudos de gesto e de ritmo 1926–1934*. FUNARTE / Instituto Nacional do Folclore: Rio de Janeiro, 1983.

Mellencamp, Patricia. "Spectacle and Spectator: Looking through the American Musical Comedy." In *Explorations in Film Theory*, edited by Ron Burnett, 3–14. Bloomington: Indiana University Press, 1991.

Mendonça, Ana Rita. *Carmen Miranda foi a Washington*. Rio de Janeiro: Editora Record, 1999.

Meyer, Moe. *The Politics and Poetics of Camp*. London: Routledge, 1994.

Meyler, Jason Blake. "Reconstructing the US Latino/a Image in Literature and Performance Art." PhD diss., Stony Brook University, 2006.

Mizejewski, Linda. *Ziegfeld Girl: Image and Icon in Culture and Cinema*. Durham, NC: Duke University Press, 1999.

Moon, Michael. *A Small Boy and Others: Imitation and Initiation in American Culture from Henry James to Andy Warhol*. Durham, NC: Duke University Press, 1998.

Moore, Robin. *Nationalizing Blackness: Afrocubanismo and Artistic Revolution in Havana, 1920–1940*. Pittsburgh, PA: University of Pittsburgh Press, 1997.

Moura, Roberto. *Tia Ciata e a pequena África no Rio de Janeiro*. 2nd ed. Rio de Janeiro: Coleção Biblioteca Carioca, 1995.

Mulvey, Laura. "Visual Pleasure and Narrative Cinema." In *Feminist Film Theory: A Reader*, edited by Sue Thornham, 58–70. Edinburg, UK: Edinburg University Press, 1999.

Munich, Adrienne. "Introduction." In *Fashion in Film*, edited by Adrienne Munich, 1–12. Bloomington: Indiana University Press, 2011.

Newton, Esther. "Role Models." In Cleto, *Camp*, 96–109.

Nimmo, Harry. *The Andrews Sisters: A Biography and Career Record*. Jefferson, NC: McFarland, 2004.

Noriega, Chon A. "Internal Others: Hollywood Narratives about Mexican Americans." In *Mediating Two Worlds: Cinematic Encounters in the Americas*, edited by John King, Ana M. López, and Manuel Alvarado, 52–66. London: British Film Institute, 1993.

Nunes, Mário. *40 anos de teatro*. Vol. 3. Rio de Janeiro: Serviço Nacional de Teatro, 1956.

Ohmer, Susan. "Female Spectatorship and Women's Magazines: Hollywood, Good Housekeeping, and World War II." *The Velvet Light Trap* 25 (Spring 1990): 53–68.

Oliveira, Aloísio de. *De banda pra lua*. Rio de Janeiro: Editora Record, 1982.

Ortiz, Fernando. *Cuban Counterpoint: Tobacco and Sugar*. Translated by Harriet de Onís. Durham: Duke University Press, 1995.

O'Connor, Patrick, and Dianna C. Niebylski, eds. *Latin American Icons: Fame Across Borders*. Nashville: Vanderbilt University Press, 2014.

O'Neil, Brian. "The Demands of Authenticity: Addison Durland and Hollywood's Latin Images during World War II." In *Classic Hollywood, Classic Whiteness*, edited by Daniel Bernardi, 359–385. Minneapolis: University of Minnesota Press, 2001.

Orgeron, Marsha. *Hollywood Ambitions: Celebrity in the Movie Age*. Middletown, CT: Wesleyan University Press, 2008.

Ovalle, Priscilla Peña. *Dance and the Hollywood Latina: Race, Sex, and Stardom*. New Brunswick, NJ: Rutgers University Press, 2011.

Owen, Bobbi. *Costume Design on Broadway: Designers and Their Credits, 1915–1985.* New York: Greenwood Press, 1987.

Paiva, Salvyano Cavalcanti de. *Viva o rebolado! Vida e morte do teatro de revista brasileiro.* Rio de Janeiro: Editora Nova Fronteira, 1991.

Peixoto, Afrânio. *Minha terra e minha gente.* 2nd ed. Rio de Janeiro: Livraria Francisco Alves, 1916.

Pierson, Donald. *Negroes in Brazil: A Study of Race Contact at Bahia.* Chicago: University of Chicago Press, 1942.

Pieterse, Jan Nederveen. *White on Black: Images of Africa and Blacks in Western Popular Culture.* New Haven: Yale University Press, 1992.

Pinto, Luiz de Aguiar Costa. *O negro no Rio de Janeiro: Relações de raça numa sociedade em mudança.* Biblioteca Pedagógica Brasileira. Série V. Brasiliana. Vol. 276. São Paulo: Companhia Editora Nacional: 1953.

Pratt, Mary Louise. "Arts of the Contact Zone." *ADFL Bulletin* 100 (1991): 33–40.

Pullen, Kristen. *Like a Natural Woman: Spectacular Female Performance in Classical Hollywood.* New Brunswick: Rutgers University Press, 2014.

Ramos, Arthur. *The Negro in Brazil.* Translated by Richard Pattee. Washington DC: Associated Publishers, [1939] 1951. Originally published as *O negro brasileiro.* Rio de Janeiro: Civilização Brasileira, 1934. .

Rebello, Stephen, and Richard Allen. *Reel Art: Great Posters from the Golden Age of the Silver Screen.* New York: Abbeville Press, 1988.

Reis, Letícia Vidor de Sousa. "Negro em 'terra de branco': A reinvenção da identidade." In *Negras imagens: Ensaios sobre cultura e escravidão no Brasil,* organized by Lilia Moritz Schwarcz and Letícia Vidor de Sousa Reis, 31–53. São Paulo: Editora da Universidade de São Paulo, 1996.

Reis, Raul. "Brazil: Love It and Hate It: Brazilians' Ambiguous Relationship with Disney." In *Dazzled by Disney? The Global Disney Audiences Project,* edited by Janet Wasko, Mark Phillips, and Eileen R. Meehan, 88–101. London: Leicester University Press, 2001.

Ribeiro, Joaquim. *Folclore baiano.* Rio de Janeiro: Departamento de Imprensa Nacional (Cadernos de cultura), 1956.

Roach, Joseph. "Culture and Performance in the Circum–Atlantic World." In *Performativity and Performance,* edited by Andrew Parker and Eve Kosofsky Sedgwick, 45–63. New York: Routledge, 1995.

Roberts, John Storm. *The Latin Tinge: The Impact of Latin American Music on the United States.* 2nd ed. Oxford: Oxford University Press, 1998.

Roberts, Shari. "'The Lady in the Tutti-Frutti Hat': Carmen Miranda, a Spectacle of Ethnicity." *Cinema Journal* 32, no. 3 (Spring 1993): 3–23.

Robertson, Pamela. "Feminist Camp in Gold Diggers of 1933." In Cohan, *Hollywood Musicals,* 129–42.

Robinson, David. "Introduction." In *Fifty Years of Movie Posters.* New York: Crown Publishers, 1973. 3–8.

Rocha, Fernando de Sousa. "'Carmen Mirandaesqueness': Stylizing Gender/En-Gendering Style." *Cercles* 14 (2005): 59–71.

Roen, Paul. *High Camp: A Gay Guide to Camp and Cult Films.* 2 Vols. 1994. Reprint, San Francisco: Leyland Publications, 1997.

Rubin, Martin. *Showstoppers: Busby Berkeley and the Tradition of Spectacle.* New York: Columbia University Press, 1993.

Ruiz, Roberto. *O teatro de revista no Brasil: Das origens à Primeira Guerra Mundial.* Rio de Janeiro: MC/INACEN, 1988.

Sá, Simone Pereira de. *Baiana internacional: As mediações culturais de Carmen Miranda.* Rio de Janeiro: MIS Editorial, 2002.

Sadlier, Darlene. "Good Neighbor Brazil." *Studies in Honor of Heitor Martins: Luso-Brazilian Literary Studies* 3. Edited by Darlene J. Sadlier. (2006): 171–85.

Sakers, Don. "Tarawa Rising." In Sakers, *Carmen Miranda's Ghost,* 247–65.

Sakers, Don, ed. *Carmen Miranda's Ghost Is Haunting Space Station Three.* New York: Bean Publishing Enterprises, 1990.

Sandoval-Sánchez, Alberto. *José, Can You See? Latinos On and Off Broadway.* Madison: University of Wisconsin Press, 1999.

Santos, Lidia. *Tropical Kitsch: Media in Latin American Literature and Art.* Translated by Elisabeth Enenbach. Princeton: Markus Wiener Publishers, 2006.

Schapiro, Steve, and David Chierichetti. *The Movie Poster Book.* New York: Dutton, 1979.

Schwarz, Roberto. "Cultural Politics in Brazil, 1964–1969." In *Misplaced Ideas: Essays on Brazilian Culture,* edited and introduced by John Gledson, 126–59. London: Verso, 1992.

Schweitzer, Marlis. *When Broadway was the Runaway: Theater, Fashion, and American Culture.* Philadelphia: University of Pennsylvania Press, 2009.

Scott, Melissa, and Lisa A. Barnett. "The Carmen Miranda Gambit." In Sakers, *Carmen Miranda's Ghost,* 104–44.

Sedgwick, Eve Kosofsky. *Between Men: English Literature and Male Homosocial Desire.* New York: Columbia University Press, 1985.

Seigel, Micol. *Uneven Encounters: Making Race and Nation in Brazil and in the United States.* Durham, NC: Duke University Press, 2009.

Sennett, Richard. *The Fall of Public Man.* 1974. Reprint, New York: Norton, 1992.

Sennett, Ted. *Hollywood Musicals.* New York: Harry N. Abrams, 1981.

Sforza, John. *Swing It! The Andrews Sisters Story.* Lexington, KY: University Press of Kentucky, 2000.

Shaw, Lisa. *Carmen Miranda.* New York: Palgrave Macmillan, 2013.

———. "The Celebritisation of Carmen Miranda in New York, 1939–1941." *Celebrity Studies* 1, no. 3 (2010): 286–302.

———. "São Coisas Nossas: Samba and Identity in the Vargas Era (1930–45)." *Portuguese Studies* 14 (1998): 152–69.

———. *The Social History of the Brazilian Samba.* Aldershot: Ashgate, 1999.

———. "'What does the *baiana* have?' Josephine Baker and the Performance of Afro-Brazilian Female Subjectivity on Stage." *English Language Notes* 49, no. 1 (Spring/Summer 2011): 91–106.

Shohat, Ella. "Gender and Culture of Empire: Toward a Feminist Ethnography of the Cinema." *Quarterly Review of Film and Video* 13, no. 1–3 (1991): 45–84.

Skidmore, Thomas E. *Black into White: Race and Modernity in Brazilian Thought.* Durham, NC: Duke University Press, 1993.

Slide, Anthony. *Inside the Hollywood Fan Magazine: A History of Star Makers, Fabricators, and Gossip Mongers.* Jackson: University of Mississippi Press, 2010.

Smith, Cecil. "The Season in Chicago." In *The Best Plays of 1939–1940*, edited by Burns Mantle, 12–17. New York: Dodd, Mean, and Company, 1940.

Sontag, Susan. "Notes on 'Camp.'" 1964. Reprinted in Cleto, *Camp*, 53–65.

Sotiropoulos, Karen. *Staging Race: Black Performers in Turn of the Century America*. London: Harvard University Press, 2006.

Stark, Seymour. *Men in Blackface: True Stories of the Minstrel Show*. Philadelphia: Xlibris, 2000.

Stempel, Tom. *American Audiences on Movies and Moviegoing*. Lexington, KY: University Press of Kentucky, 2001.

Terrell, Nena. "Helena Solberg Unmasks a Brazilian Idol." *Américas* 48, no. 1 (January–February 1996): 48–53.

Tinhorão, José Ramos. *Música popular: Teatro & Cinema*. Petrópolis: Editora Vozes, LTDA, 1972.

Thorp, Margaret Farrand. *America at the Movies*. New Haven: Yale University Press, 1939.

Towne, Charles Hanson. "Dining in the Sert Room." In *The Unofficial Palace of New York*, edited by Frank Crowninshield, 94. New York: Hotel Waldorf-Astoria Corporation, 1939.

Trevelyan, Julie K., and Scott Brassart, eds. *The Ghost of Carmen Miranda and Other Spooky Gay and Lesbian Tales*. Los Angeles: Alyson Book, 1998.

Velloso, Monica Pimenta. *A cultura das ruas no Rio de Janeiro (1900–1930): Mediações, linguagens e espaço*. Rio de Janeiro: Edições Casa de Rui Barbosa, 2004.

Veloso, Caetano. *Tropical Truth: A Story of Music and Revolution in Brazil*. Translated by Isabel de Sena. New York: Da Capo Press, 2003.

Vianna, Hermano. *The Mystery of Samba: Popular Music and National Identity in Brazil*. Translated by John Charles Chasteen. Chapel Hill: University of North Carolina Press, 1999.

Walker, Alexander. *Stardom: The Hollywood Phenomenon*. New York: Stein and Day, 1970.

Walters, Debra Nan. "Hollywood, World War II, and Latin America." PhD diss., University of Southern California, Los Angeles, 1978.

Westfahl, Gary. *Islands in the Sky: The Space Station Theme in Science Fiction Literature*. San Bernadino, CA: Borgo Press, 1996.

Whitaker, Jan. *Service and Style: How the American Department Store Fashioned the Middle Class*. New York: St. Martin's Press, 2006.

Williams, Judith Michelle. "Uma mulata, sim! Araci Cortes, 'The Mulatta' of the Teatro de Revista." *Women and Performance: A Journal of Feminist Theory* 16, no. 1 (March 2006): 7–26.

Williamson, Judith. *Decoding Advertisements: Ideology and Meaning in Advertising*. London: Boyars, 1978.

Woll, Allen L. *The Hollywood Musical Goes to War*. Chicago: Nelson-Hall, 1983.

———. *The Latin Image in American Film*. Los Angeles: UCLA Latin American Center Publications, 1980.

FILMOGRAPHY

CARMEN MIRANDA FILMS (IN CHRONOLOGICAL ORDER)

Brazil

A voz do carnaval. Dir. Adhemar Gonzaga. Cinédia, 1933.

Alô, alô, Brasil! Dir. Wallace Downey, João de Barro, and Alberto Riberio. Waldow-Cinédia, 1935.

Estudantes. Dir. Wallace Downey. Waldow-Cinédia, 1935.

Alô, alô, carnaval! Dir. Adhemar Gonzaga. Waldow-Cinédia, 1936. [Restored 2002]

Banana da terra. Dir. Ruy Costa. Sonofilms, 1939.

Laranja da China. Dir. Ruy Costa. Sonofilms, 1940.

United States

Down Argentine Way. Dir. Irving Cummings. Twentieth Century-Fox, 1940.

That Night in Rio. Dir. Irving Cummings. Twentieth Century-Fox, 1941.

Weekend in Havana. Dir. Walter Lang. Twentieth Century-Fox, 1941.

Springtime in the Rockies. Dir. Irving Cummings. Twentieth Century-Fox, 1942.

The Gang's All Here. Dir. Busby Berkeley. Twentieth Century-Fox, 1943.

Four Jills in a Jeep. Dir. William Seiter. Twentieth Century-Fox, 1944.

Greenwich Village. Dir. Walter Lang. Twentieth Century-Fox, 1944.

Something for the Boys. Dir. Lewis Seiler. Twentieth Century-Fox, 1944.

Doll Face. Dir. Lewis Seiler. Twentieth Century-Fox, 1945.

If I'm Lucky. Dir. Lewis Seiler. Twentieth Century-Fox, 1946.

Copacabana. Dir. Alfred Green. United Artists, 1947.

A Date with Judy. Dir. Richard Thorpe. MGM, 1948.

Nancy Goes to Rio. Dir. Robert Z. Leonard. MGM, 1950.

Scared Stiff. Dir. George Marshall. Paramount, 1953.

The Carmen Miranda Collection. Twentieth Century-Fox Home Entertainment, 2008.

GENERAL FILMS

Abby in Wonderland. Dir. Kevin Clash. Genius Entertainment / Kidtoon Films, 2008.

Always Leave Them Laughing. Dir. Roy Del Ruth. Warner Brothers, 1949.

America Entertains the Troops. Narrated by Bob Hope. Silver Screen Video, 1985.

Argentine Nights. Dir. Albert S. Rogell. Universal Pictures, 1940.

Babes on Broadway. Dir. Busby Berkeley. MGM, 1941.

Bananas Is My Business. Dir. Helena Solberg. International Cinema, 1995.

Bathing Beauty. Dir. George Sidney. MGM, 1944.

Beloved Infidel. Dir. Henry King. Videocassette. Twentieth Century-Fox, 1959.

The Cat in the Hat. Dir. Bo Welch. Universal Pictures, 2003.

Celebrity Propaganda. Dir. Mervyn LeRoy, et al. Videocassette. Hollywood's Attic, 1996.

Chu Chu and the Philly Flash. Dir. David Lowell Rich. Twentieth Century-Fox, 1981.

Class of '44. Dir. Paul Bogart. Warner Brothers, 1973.

Dames. Dir. Ray Enright and Busby Berkeley. Warner Brothers, 1934.

Despicable Me 2. Dir. Pierre Coffin and Chris Renaud. Universal Pictures, 2013.

Diplomatic Courier. Dir. Henry Hathaway. Twentieth Century-Fox, 1952.

Easy to Wed. Dir. Edward Buzzell. MGM, 1946.

Está tudo aí. Dir. Mesquitinha. Cinédia, 1939.

Everyone Says I Love You. Dir. Woody Allen. Miramax, 1996.

Flying Down to Rio. Dir. Thornton Freeland. RKO, 1933.

Futurama. The Beast with a Billion Backs. Dir. Peter Avanzino. Twentieth Century-Fox Home Entertainment, 2008.

Gangster Squad. Dir. Ruben Fleischer. Warner Brothers, 2013.

Gold Diggers of 1933. Dir. Mervyn LeRoy. Warner Brothers, 1933.

Gold Diggers of 1935. Dir. Busby Berkeley. Warner Brothers, 1935.

The Great Ziegfeld. Dir. Robert Z. Leonard. MGM, 1936.

Hidden Hollywood II: More Treasures from the Twentieth Century Fox Vaults. Dir. Kevin Burns and Shelley Lyons. Image Entertainment, 2002.

The House Across the Bay. Dir. Archie Mayo. United Artists, 1940.

Joujoux e balangandãs. Dir. Amadeu Castelaneto. Cinédia, 1939.

Ladies' Man. Dir. William D. Russell. Paramount, 1947.

Leroy and Stitch. Dir. Tony Craig and Roberts Gannaway. Disney Television Animation, 2006.

Madagascar: Escape 2 Africa. Dir. Eric Darnell and Tom McGrath. DreamWorks Animation, 2008.

Marília Pêra canta Carmen Miranda. Dir. Liber Gadelha. Som livre, 2006.

Mildred Pierce. Dir. Michael Curtiz. Warner Brothers, 1945.

Mixed Blood. Dir. Paul Morrissey. Cinevista, 1985.

The Muppets Go Hollywood. Dir. Stan Harris. CBS, 1979.

Muppet Treasure Island Sing-Along. Dir. David Gumpel. Walt Disney Company, 1996.

Myra Breckinridge. Dir. Michael Sarne. Twentieth Century-Fox, 1970.

Radio Days. Dir. Woody Allen. Orion Pictures, 1987.

Rio: The Movie. Dir. Carlos Saldanha. Blue Sky Studios / Twentieth Century-Fox Animation, 2011.

Road to Rio. Dir. Norman Z. McLeod. Paramount, 1947.

Saludos Amigos. Dir. Wilfred Jackson, et al. Walt Disney Productions / RKO, 1943.

Small Town Deb. Dir. Harold D. Schuster. Twentieth Century-Fox, 1941.

This Is the Army. Dir. Michael Curtiz. Warner Brothers, 1943.

The Three Caballeros. Dir. Norman Ferguson, et al. RKO, 1945.

The Three Stooges Collection. Sony Home Entertainment, 2014.

The Thrill of Brazil. Dir. S. Sylvan Simon. Colombia Pictures, 1946.

Time Out for Rhythm. Dir. Sidney Salkow. Columbia Pictures, 1941.

Winged Victory. Dir. George Cukor. Twentieth Century-Fox, 1944.

Ziegfeld Girl. Dir. Robert Z. Leonard and Busby Berkeley. MGM, 1941.

CARTOON SHORTS

Baby Puss. Dir. Joseph Barbera and William Hanna. MGM, 1943.

Daffy's Southern Exposure. Dir. Norm McCabe. Warner Brothers, 1942.

Hollywood Canine Canteen. Dir. Robert McKimson. Warner Brothers, 1946.

Juke Box Jamboree. Dir. Alex Lovy. Universal Pictures, 1942.

Magical Maestro. Dir. Tex Avery. MGM, 1952.

Mater Private Eye. Dir. Rob Gibbs. Walt Disney Company, 2010.

Porky's Pooch. Dir. Robert Clampett. Warner Brothers, 1941.

Slick Hare. Dir. Friz Freleng, Warner Brothers, 1947.

The Ticklefeather Machine. Written by W. Watts Biggers. Underdog Television Series. NBC, 1964.

Tin Pan Alley Cats. Dir. Robert Clampett. Warner Brothers, 1943.

A Torrid Toreador. Dir. Eddie Donnelly. Twentieth Century-Fox, 1942.

We're on Our Way to Rio. Dir. Izzy Sparber. Paramount, 1944.

What's Cookin' Doc. Dir. Robert Clampett. Warner Brothers, 1944.

Yankee Doodle Daffy. Dir. Friz Freleng. Warner Brothers, 1943.

TELEVISION BROADCASTS

"Be a Pal." *I Love Lucy*. Dir. Marc Daniels. CBS. October 22, 1951.

The Buick-Berle Show. NBC. 1953–1955.

The Carol Burnett Show. CBS. 1967–1978.

Carol Channing and Pearl Bailey: On Broadway. Dir. Clark Jones. ABC. March 16, 1969.

"Dance Fever!" *Bear in the Big Blue House*. Episode 221. Dir. Mitchell Kriegman. March 9, 1998.

"Home to Roost." *Land Girls*. Series 3. BBC Worldwide. November 7, 2011.

The Jimmy Durante Show. NBS. 1954–1956.

The Lawrence Welk Show. ABC. 1955–1982.

The Milton Berle Show. NBC. 1955–1956.

The Muppet Show. ATV. 1976–1981.

Muppets Tonight. Episode 203. Dir. Gary Halvorson. The Disney Channel. September 21, 1997.

Sesame Street. PBS. Episode 2040 (March 1, 1985); Episode 2358 (November 18, 1987); Episode 3856 (January 10, 2000).

The Texaco Star Theater. NBC. 1948–1953.

NORTH AMERICAN PLAYS AND REVUES

From Vienna. Prod. The Refugee Artists Group. Music Box Theatre. June 20, 1939–August 26, 1939.

Hellzapoppin'. Prod. Olsen and Johnson. 46th Street Theatre. Winter Garden Theatre. Majestic Theatre. September 22, 1938–December 17, 1941.

Hi Yank! Prod. Army Service Forces, Special Services Division. 1943–1944.

Sons O' Fun. Dir. Edward Duryea Dowling. Prod. Lee and J. J. Shubert. Winter Garden Theatre. 46th Street Theatre. December 1, 1941–August 29, 1943.

The Straw Hat Revue. Prod. Lee and J. J. Shubert. Ambassador Theatre. September 29, 1939–December 2, 1939.

The Streets of Paris. Dir. Edward Duryea Dowling. Prod. Lee and J. J. Shubert. Broadhurst
  Theatre. June 19, 1939–February 10, 1940.
This Is the Army. Dir. Sgt. Ezra Ston. Prod. Uncle Sam. Music Irving Berlin. Broadway Theatre.
  July 4, 1942–September 26, 1942.
Yip, Yip, Yaphank. Music Sgt. Irving Berlin. Prof. Uncle Sam. Century Theatre. Lexington
  Theatre. August 19, 1918–September 14, 1918.
Yokel Boy. Dir. Lew Brown. Majestic Theatre. June 6, 1939–January 6, 1940.

BRAZILIAN PLAYS AND REVUES

Boneca de piche. Dir. Luís Iglésias e Freire Jr. Teatro Recreio. December 30, 1938–March 1,
  1939.
Miss Brasil. Dir. Luiz Peixoto and Marques Porto. Teatro Recreio. December 20, 1928–March
  1929.
O bendegó. Dir. Oscar Pederneiras and Figueiredo Coimbra. Teatro Variedades Dramáticas.
  1889.
Tim-tim por tim-tim. Dir. Sousa Bastos. 1892–1902.
Vai dar o que falar. Dir. Luiz Peixoto and Marques Porto. Teatro João Caetano. September 12–
  21, 1930.

INDEX

Page numbers in **bold** refer to illustrations.